SACRED

SECRETS BEHIND THE REAL PROJECT BLUE BOOK, WRIGHT-PATTERSON AFB, ROSWELL, BATTELLE, MEMORY METAL, DR. J. ALLEN HYNEK & UFO COVER-UPS

By Irena McCammon Scott, PhD

Published by
FLYING DISK PRESS
4 St Michaels Avenue
Pontefract, West Yorkshire
England
WF8 4QX

Copyright © 2019 by Irena Scott PhD. All rights reserved. Without limiting the rights under copyright reserved above, no part of this publication may be reproduced, stored in or introduced into a retrieval system, or transmitted in any form by any means (electronics, mechanical, photocopying, recording or otherwise), without the prior written permission of both the copyright owner and the publisher of this book. Cover design is copyright © Daniel Del Toro.

CONTENTS

Acknowledgments

Introduction

Chapter One: Future Human Evolution or Armageddon

Chapter Two: No Threat–"They Could Destroy Life on our Planet"

Chapter Three: Wright-Patterson AFB–Hanger 18, Blue Room, Vaults, Bodies, and much else

Chapter Four Project Blue Book

Chapter Five: The Pentacle Memo

Chapter Six: *Project Blue Book Special Report #14*

Chapter Seven: Memory Metal, UFO Debris, and Roswell–A Million Views

Chapter Eight: Who did the *SR-14* and Why does no one Know? The "Others List"

Chapter Nine: A Small Ohio Town, Roswell, and Advanced Metal Alloys

Chapter Ten: The Trend Explodes–USAF Research on UFOs is Destroyed Forever, Dark Side and Death

Chapter Eleven: The Most Important Question–Why Kill the Study

Chapter Twelve: The Real Dr. J. Allen Hynek

Chapter Thirteen: Conclusions

References

Appendix I The Pentacle Memo

Appendix II The Pentacle Letter (Unpublished Draft) by Jennie Zeidman, Michael Swords, And Mark Rodeghier

Footnotes

******

ACKNOWLEDGMENTS

I am greatly indebted to many people who made this work possible:

Special thanks to Bill Jones, JD, and Jennie Zeidman. Jones is the former Senior Contracting Officer for Federal Projects at Battelle Memorial Institute (Battelle) and the Ohio director of the Mutual UFO Network (MUFON), who helped me greatly to understand how to investigate UFOs. Jennie Zeidman worked with Dr. Hynek, at Battelle and at the Wright-Patterson Air Force Base (WP) in Project Blue Book (BB), and in many similar positions. She is perhaps the only living person who worked both for Project Stork and for BB. She has very generously allowed me to interview her and allowed me to use some of her collection of documents. These are very valuable in all kinds of UFO studies.

Others include the initial UFOlogists I met: Paul and Becky Burrell, who helped me with editing and understanding the general set up of UFOlogy and Pete Hartinger, director of the Roundtown UFO Society. Additional investigators who originally brought me into UFOlogy include members of the Mid Ohio Research Associates (MORA): Frank Reams, pilot; Joe Stets, Battelle scientist; Rebecca Minshall; and Barbara Spellerberg, as did Warren Nicholson, Battelle scientist; Jean and Richard Siefried; and Paul Althouse.

Many others helped me in numerous ways including: my sister, Sue Postle; Kathleen Marden, niece of Betty Hill and abduction expert; and Phyllis Budinger, MS, former Research Scientist from BP/Amoco, and head of Frontier Analysis, Ltd. Others included writer, publisher, and investigator Rick Hilberg; Budd Hopkins, artist, abduction authority, and author of many seminal UFO books; J. Allen Hynek, PhD, noted astronomer, writer, founder of the Center for UFO Studies, and Father of UFOlogy; Leo Sprinkle, PhD; and Bruce Maccabee, PhD. Many thinks to UFOlogists Chris Parsons, Aaron Clark, Thomas Wertman, Linda Stephen Sodomire, Earl Grey Anderson, Art Kasil, Becky Escamilla, Diana Ramirez, Paula Schurle, Roxana Justiz, and many others from Ohio MUFON, the Cleveland UFOlogy Project, Starlight, and many others.

Other UFOlogists have included Walt Andrus, former head of MUFON, with whom I edited a number of MUFON Symposium Proceedings; and Leonard H. Stringfield, who told me about his intensive investigation of the UFO phenomena including Wright Patterson AFB. Also to Julia Shuster, daughter of Walter Haut, who was the Roswell Air Base public information officer who put out its press release about the UFO.

Additional people who were of immense help included: William Allen, OSU professor emeritus who, when I thought I was finished with UFOlogy and began throwing out papers, told me to write a book instead. Thanks to Robert Dixon, PhD, former director of the OSU Radio Observatory "Big Ear," director of the Argus and SETI projects; and Walt Mitchell, PhD, former Astronomy Department professor at OSU. Also, State of Ohio seismologist Mike Hansen, PhD, and Mr. Reams, William Carlisle, and Rick Shackelford, with whom I worked at the Defense Intelligence Agency (DIA). French UFOlogist Jean Sider and I wrote several articles, and the Cordell Hull family members helped with other stories. Art Sill, PhD; Brian Thompson, PhD; Jan Aldrich; fire chief, Virgil Newell; Barbara Osborne; and many others have provided great help. Curtis Cutler, electrician, helped me with electrical questions. My family including John and Rosa Scott who tolerated and aided this work, were also very helpful.

Harley D. Rutledge, PhD, in his Project Identification study and discussions greatly aided my understanding of the phenomena.

Still others who I have met or corresponded with include: Timothy Good, author and investigator; James Spangler; Jerry Ehman, PhD, discoverer of the "Big Ear" telescope 'WOW' signal; and Stanton Friedman, nuclear physicist. Others include Beverly Trout; Robert Orndoff, PhD; Linda Wallace; John Carpenter; Stan Gordon; Diana DeSimone; John Timmerman; Bruce Widaman; and Terry Hamilton. Bob Collins, who was operative "Condor" of the Aviary; and Donald Schmitt, Tom Carey, and Anthony Bragalia, UFO authors who have spent much time exploring the field. Especial thanks also to the many very helpful and insightful witnesses and experiencers that I interviewed

And many thanks to Bruce Ashcroft, PhD, WP historian and archivist, who invited me to meetings, discussed UFOs with me, showed me around the AFB, and helped me to understand much about UFOlogy.

I wish to extend very special thanks to Philip Mantle, director of Flying Disc Press the publisher of this book, whose effort has very greatly improved all aspects of this work.

I would also like to thank the many excellent interviewers who made very useful comments and through podcasts distributed the information about my previous books. These include: Whitley Strieber in Unknown Country, Shirley MacLaine in Independent Expression (IE), Ben & Paul Eno in "Behind the Paranormal," Timothy Beckley in Exploring the Bizarre, and I have been contacted by Owen Slevin of the History Channel and others listed below.

 Additional interviews include: Alejandro Rojas of Open Minds tv/radio, Jim Harold of jim.harold.media, Kat Kanavos of katkan@comcast.net, Dave Schrader of Beyond The Darkness and Guest Host for Coast to Coast, Martin Willis Host & Producer of Dark Matter, Rebecca Roberts and Becky Escamilla on a radio show called Sci-Fi-Sci-EarthTM Beacon of Light Radio, Kevin D. Randle in "A Different Perspective," Bryan Bowden with Ronald Murphy of "Inside The Goblin Universe," and Janet Russell of Long Island Internet Radio. Still other interviewers from the US include: Gene Steinberg of Paracast, Jeremy Scott and Ken Pfeifer of "Into the Paranormal," Rodney Shortridge of Within the Chaos, Arizona Tramp, Jim Heater of Paranormal Geeks, and Rosanna Schaffer-Shaw and Kate Valentine of Shattered Reality and others.
Interviewers from Hawaii include, Janet Kira and Dr. Sashas Lessin of Sacred Matrix on Revolution Radio KCOR.

Interviews by people in the UK have included: Ben Emyln-Jones of HPANWO, Jonathan Dean of Radio City in the UK, and Kevin Moore of the Kevin Moore Show,
From Scotland, I have been interviewed by Alyson Dunlop of BST/UK, and from the Netherlands by Maarten Horst.

******

INTRODUCTION

UFOs might be the greatest mystery of this millennium. They may be the most talked about, but least understood of any modern phenomena. Almost everyone has heard of Flying Saucers, Hanger 18, Roswell, Wright-Patterson Air Force Base (WP), and many associated accounts and legends. Gallup polls rank UFOs near the top of the list of subjects of widespread recognition.

The media is bursting with UFOs stories, such as a new *History Channel* presentation, "Project Blue Book," and blockbuster movies including: *Close Encounters of the Third Kind, E.T. the Extra-Terrestrial, Independence Day, Contact,* and *The War of the Worlds*. TV shows and books are filled with UFO tales: the Hanger 18 shows, "X-Files" episodes, and the best-selling books include *Communion, Ancient Aliens, Witness to Roswell,* and *Pascagoula*. These include eerie accounts, abductions, contact, and disclosure.

Despite this, little is actually known about UFOs (the acronym for "unidentified flying object"). The subject is often considered legend, a ghost story, a joke, or general flimflam. This view is likely due to a very strong and continuing effort of the government to cover up the entire subject. What this book is about is an investigation of this cover-up, the secret meetings, hidden agendas, overt misrepresentation of facts, and much else.

This high consciousness about the topic likely results from many things, people wonder: is earth being visited by beings from another planet, are they dangerous? But, not to worry, the government assures us that they don't exist.

However much evidence shows that they do exist, and scientific studies have been conducted by the government and even leading scientists. Surveys also show that many people think there is something to the subject, but that the government has covered the real information up.

What this book is about is our direct investigation of much of the government works on the subject. This book is needed because unlike nearly all other investigations, this is from the inside. We have traveled down the sacred corridors and highly secure rooms where UFO study took place, interviewed researchers that did the work, taken photographs, and obtained documents. We may have been the only civilians ever to visit some of these places. We examined leaked information, the leakers, hidden studies showing for sure that UFOs exist, talked to informants, and much else.

Our smoking gun discoveries have already attracted much attention and include a possible new Roswell witness, accounts about possible Memory Metal; the Cordell Hull report ands much else. We have continued to peruse these accounts and found many more smoking guns that we are reporting here; some with even more credibility, such as evidence that an alloy company, which had been working with titanium, had received a debris sample to analyze.

We differ from other investigators because we actually worked in some of the most critical organizations and facilities that conducted government UFO research. I have worked at Battelle; the Defense Intelligence Agency (DIA); and have been stationed at WP, the chief government agency for UFO investigation, and have visited and interviewed people at Roswell. I have been in some of the highest security areas in the country.

Probably the best-known events and people associated with UFO phenomenon are the accounts of: Hanger 18; Roswell; Blue Book; J. Allen Hynek, the "Father of UFOlogy"; and WP, and we explore them all.

The famed official government investigation of UFOs is Project Blue Book (BB), which is by far the most massive undertaking associated with UFO study. By its end, researchers had collected and analyzed around 13,000 reports. I have been in the areas where this study took place, talked to some who worked in it or knew about it, and examined its secret hidden studies.

WP where a portion of BB took place is the nation's UFO Mecca because it has been involved in almost all UFO activities since the beginning including, Hanger 18, receiving the Roswell or other debris, and housing BB.

Very few civilians have been inside WP's secured areas and their visits were a long time ago. There are many tales about WPs having underground vaults, and crypts, where aliens and debris are stored. However, I have not only been there and explored these areas, but have taken photographs. And although WP has published a few selected photographs and these are what others have used, I have actually been on base, viewed, and captured photographs of the base and its most secret areas. These photographs differ from the other photography because it was selected by WP to just show views of which they approve. Thus we have much that has not been disclosed anywhere else, such as areas and buildings never shown before, close-up views, and views from different positions.

I have also made an intensive investigation of Blue Book, which took place at both Wright Patterson and Battelle. I have been in some of the areas where it was located, and discussed it with people who worked in it. Not only that but I will show many of its unpublished internal documents that express the heart of BB. Some of these discuss UFOs monitoring a large international military exercise and the government fears that they might affect the oncoming H-Bomb test.

J. Allen Hynek was the best-known Blue Book spokesperson and I have many of his handwritten documents that also have not been published–very few have. These tell about many investigations he was involved in, from plane crashes, odd metallic debris, instances where he was severely derided, mystery objects photographed by telescope, strange encounters, and much more. These may tell more about the inner Hynek than the large number of his typewritten and edited works. They even contain information about Neil Armstrong.

I have had much training in several scientific fields from some top institutes and this has helped me to conduct this work. My PhD was from the University of Missouri College of Veterinary Medicine in physiology with a specialization in radioisotope techniques. I did post-doctoral research at Cornell University. My MS was from the University of Nevada, and my BS was from OSU with majors in biology and astronomy.

I have had a professorship at St. Bonaventure University, done research and teaching at the University of Nevada, and worked in neurophysiology at The Ohio State University College of Medicine.

I am well trained also in photographic analysis and aircraft identification. I have been employed by the DIA in PhD-level (GS-11) research in satellite photography with some of the highest security clearances (above top secret) in the government. I worked in such divisions as Air Order of Battle, which should have been a government monitoring point for UFO activity. I was employed in MS-level work as a Physical Scientist/Cartographer in the Aerospace Center in St. Louis, Missouri, using satellite photography, and I have been stationed at WP.

I have also worked at Battelle. I was a correspondent for *Popular Mechanics* magazine with byline articles and photography in its "Technology Update" and "Science" sections. I was a volunteer astronomer at the Ohio State University Radio Observatory "Big Ear" (noted for the WOW SETI signal that might be humanity's only signal from ET), and am an amateur astronomer. My published photography has appeared in magazines, on TV, and in newspapers. I have papers to document these positions.

My publications include books, numerous research papers in peer-reviewed scientific journals, and articles in magazines, and newspapers. I have also published UFO material in peer-reviewed scientific journals, including the American Association for the Advancement of Science (AAAS) publications, and the Ohio Journal of Science (OJS) of the Ohio Academy of Science.

My UFO publications include books, such as *UFOs Today 70 Years of Lies, Disinformation, and Government Cover-Up*, and articles in numerous UFO publications including, the *MUFON JOURNAL*, the Center for UFO Studies (CUFOS) *International UFO Reporter* (*IUR*), *FATE* magazine, the *MUFON of Ohio Newsletter*, and "The Black Vault."

My UFO background consists of serving on the Mutual UFO Network (MUFON) Board of Directors, serving as a consultant in physiology and astronomy, and serving as a field investigator for both MUFON and CUFOS.

******

CHAPTER ONE

FUTURE HUMAN EVOLUTION OR ARMAGEDDON

Gallup polls rank UFOs near the top of the list of subjects of widespread recognition. For example, even a 1973 survey found that 95 percent of the public had heard of UFOs. This is despite the idea that the subject is viewed as the purview of kooks, No serious astronomer gives any credence to any of these stories ... I think most astronomers would dismiss these. I dismiss them because if aliens had made the great effort to traverse interstellar distances to come here, they wouldn't just meet a few well-known cranks, make a few circles in cornfields and go away again....the idea that only kooks see UFOs is prevalent.

But, however people view them, they are extremely widely recognized and the subject of great attention, why?

Because behind this general interest in UFO phenomena are burning questions, such as: are UFOs real, are we in communication with non-human entities, can we know the future of humanity, are we alone in the universe, is there life after death, do we have alien visitors, have these visitors made advancements far surpassing ours, and will they share them with us.

Actually the advent of the UFO might be the most important event ever to happen to humanity since it began. Perhaps meeting otherworldly life forms is the next step in humanity's evolution. It is not any accident that there is a high level of consciousness about it.

This concern reaches into all spheres of human existence: the scientific world, the religious–what is the spiritual meaning of the phenomena? And the governmental–is there a cover-up and if so, why? And can such advanced beings attack or take us over?

And these concerns are not old– for example a new *History Channel* show, "Project Blue Book," is coming out in 2019 and this year is the 50-year anniversary of its closing. Roswell is discussed all over the Internet. And UFO events remain strong in the media; including Steven Spielberg's *Close Encounters of the Third Kind* based upon Dr. Hynek's classification of sightings–where he became a movie star–, and others that are widely known today. Hence public interest in this material remains high.

Thus, this subject should be of interest and serious philosophical and scientific debate, instead of the general present day idea that it is the purview of flakes, the mentally disturbed, liars, hoaxers, and TV commentators who give each other side-long glances when the subject arises.

How did this state of affairs come about? What in the early history of UFOs caused the subject to arise out of very serious concern from both scientists and government authorities into the view of ridicule seen today?

This book will dig into the roots of these events from the very beginning of the recognition of the phenomena, through many changes, to today. It details new and old UFO events, many smoking guns discovers about Roswell, Wright Patterson vaults and bodies, cover-ups, and Hanger 18. We have fresh unpublished documents and photographs for confirmation. These documents, photographs, and letters come from all levels of the investigators from ones who just had a small part of the studies, too much about such high-level scientists as J. Allen Hynek, and to some who had security clearances even higher than his.

It builds on and further explores our smoking gun discoveries, including possible new Roswell witnesses and our initial discovery of Elroy John Center, who reported that he examined UFO debris at Battelle. This led to massive Internet discussions about such topics as Roswell debris and memory metal all over the world. We were also the first to report about the Cordell Hull family, with its account of alien bodies and debris under the US Capital. We made a number of other initial, smoking gun discoveries and many other topics that will be further examined in this book.

We also have what appears to be an even better account of debris from a New Mexico, crash than that of John Center. It was from an alloy company in Ohio, and the composition of this debris is known.

The documents used in this examination are from studies such as Blue Book (BB), the best known and largest examination of the UFO field. They include many unsolved cases, top-secret clandestine operations, J. Allen Hynek investigating in disguise, dramatic UFO events, freighting encounters, soul searching, laundered money, and much else. It also points out that there are many remaining mysteries about Blue Book.

Many of our documents are simple handwritten notes from those involved in these studies. But these give a live real-time view of what was really going on, unlike later published documents that have been reviewed and polished. They break into the inside layers of the UFO mystery.

Our new unpublished material about Dr. Hynek is likely the most significant portion of this work because anything that he wrote about UFOs is of interest to those in UFOlogy. Also because some of his files and other materials seem to have disappeared and few have seen his handwritten documents, "he also wrote much in private letters, reports, and notes that have been seen by only a few colleagues and friends."

His and other letters give a view of the inside person. They show the person's spontaneity and hidden nature, whereas typewritten and edited documents show the person's outside veneer. The same is true of the first drafts of documents. Not only do such handwritten versions show thoughts that can later be edited out, the differences between the handwritten and the later published versions also are of interest. They show who really are friends, how they got along, some of their inner thoughts about each other, and their thinking about UFOs. For example they show Hynek's interesting acquaintances, such as Neil Armstrong, and what Hynek thought about being photographed with a hoaxer.

They might even document a confirmation of Neil Armstrong's interest in UFOs.

This research covers the major inflection point where the UFO subject went from more serious government study, to today's climate of ridicule. This material details information about the cover-ups and how they have affected today's view of the phenomena.

This work is unique, because unlike other investigators, my co-investigators and I not only probed, but worked in some of the most crucial organizations and facilities that conducted government UFO research. I have worked at Battelle, the world's largest private scientific research and development organization located in Columbus, Ohio, that made the best-known scientific investigation of UFO phenomena. I have also worked at the Defense Intelligence Agency (DIA), a manager of military intelligence for the US Department of Defense in Washington, D. C, and UFO investigative agency, where I had above top-secret security clearances and worked with satellite photography in an Air Order of Battle section to identify all flying craft over a specific area (this photography is still classified). I have been stationed at WP, a government military installation near Dayton, Ohio, and a chief government agency for UFO investigation. Unlike many who have used faked documents, I have been able to obtain authentic documents from the agencies themselves. I have also been acquainted with some of the leading government researchers, which resulted in a privileged track to understanding the organizations, the scientists, and the research results. In addition, John Scott, my husband, worked at Area 51 and on the Nevada Test Site. I have visited and interviewed people at Roswell, White Sands Missile Range (WSMR), and similar places.

The reason other investigators have been unable to directly inspect WP is because of its extreme security. This is a UFO legend and the subject of many UFO accounts by itself. Stories circulate concerning highly placed persons, even presidential candidates, who have been barred. One such story is about Arizona senator and presidential candidate Barry Goldwater, who once asked General Curtis LeMay, Chief of Staff of the Air Force, if he could see the "Blue Room," said to be the holding room for UFO evidence at WP. Goldwater said he was rebuffed in the strongest terms. Similar stories are told about Laurence Rockefeller and FBI Director J. Edgar Hoover.

However this ultra-secret place has been located and we have been inside it. Carey and Schmitt reported that an FOIA analyst at WP said, "the office of record for BLUE ROOM is NASIC." Leonard Stringfield thought the bodies were stored here, and many other myths and legends about this building tell that it contains alien cadavers and UFO debris. Some have said its inside was a hanger type area for dismantling and studying debris. When I was inside, the part I saw looked like a regular group of offices.

I have not only visited but photographed highly secured areas. This photography is useful because the other way to get this type of information is from the government agencies and since it comes from the agencies, it is possible that it contains inaccuracies. This photography can be used as hard evidence to find and analyze the actual scene of places and events that are considered legends. Our photography covers locations never shown before and different views of other areas.

In addition, I have attended staff meetings about UFOs, and found some proof for many UFO stories that are viewed as legends. I even photographed actual proof at WP that UFOs do exist.
This new research incorporates fresh information about the Roswell event, and the scientific analysis of other material. It includes many first-hand, interviews and correspondence with some

of the key original UFO investigators. Because many of these individuals are deceased and others quite old, it is vital to publish these accounts–for a historical record of the thought-processes of those who have made initial and continuing impact in the field of UFO studies.

Our new smoking guns include positive statements from three presidents of Battelle and their colleagues about UFOs, discoveries that might confirm the accounts of vaults under WP, and inside material about the writing of many important documents such as the Pentacle Memo and BB material.

Much other of even the most basic information about BB is still a mystery, such as who did the analysis for the secret study, Project Blue Book Special Report No. 14: Analysis of Reports of Unidentified Flying Objects (*SR-14*). This work shows an investigation into who leaked the Pentacle Memo, that exposed this secret study, and that is still unknown. And additional investigations are made of the many associated mysteries.

This research goes into much detail about this little known but highly significant study (*SR-14*) showing less than one chance in a billion that UFOs are not a real phenomenon. The statistics are rechecked and are much lower than even that. This shows the amazing disdain of the scientists who knew about it and ignored its findings. It shows that even though done by an important corporation, much about it is unknown.

Unlike many other publications, I have documents and photographs to prove that I was where I say I have been.

And this information provides hard evidence to support statements that have previously simply been presented as legend, or facts or conjectures with no real evidence to back them up.

This material shows in detail the time frame and interactions that occurred when the UFO subject was viewed in a scientific manner and then the turning point when it became a subject of derision. This is likely the most important junction of the history of UFO phenomenon and maybe even of human history. It has a great influence today.

Because of the cover-ups, many of which are revealed here and other reasons, it is quite reasonable to revisit the UFO field–it is still hot news today. And we have made smoking gun discoveries about numerous UFO legends and additional topics.

******

CHAPTER TWO

NO THREAT–THEY "COULD DESTROY LIFE ON OUR PLANET"

Dear Sir:
You have my permission to quote give out or reprint my written account and report of nine strange aircraft I observed on June 24th in the Cascade Mountains in the state of Washington. This report was sent to you at your request some days ago. It is with considerable disappointment you cannot give the explanation of these aircraft as I felt certain they belonged to our government.... used as an instrument of destruction in combination with our atomic bomb the effects could destroy life on our planet. Capt. Smith, co-pilot Stevens of United Air Lines and myself have compared our observations in as much detail as possible and agreed we had observed the same type of aircraft as to size shape and form. We have not taken this lightly. It is to us a very serious concern as we are as interested in the welfare of our country as you are.

The above was not written by a kook, but by a highly experienced and credible pilot. It was at first thought that the craft might be some type of foreign missile, with a much better performance than any of our aircraft.

This message was addressed to the Commanding General at Wright Field (WF) Dayton Ohio.

Report to Wright Field
This pilot wrote to this base because it was the most important US AFB, which later became WP one of the largest, most diverse, and organizationally complex bases in the Air Force with a history of flight tests from the Wright Brothers into the Space Age.

It provided the genesis of not only flight (the Wright brothers built the first powered airplane), but also was the main actor in the UFO field. It is an enormous complex of buildings, labs and airstrips occupying almost 13 square miles in 1992. In 1956 it employed 27,000 military and civilian personnel and was the headquarters for Air Material Command (AMC). In 1990, it employed 35,000, many times more people than the Pentagon or any Air Force (AF) base. Consequently it would be the logical place to contact and also to receive possible UFO debris.

Thus if any organization should know about new US aircraft, this base should. This writer was perplexed because he had informed the AB right after his sighting, but by July 12 still had heard nothing from them. As a logical person, he saw the danger such objects represented, including world destruction, and tried to alert the personell about the danger of ignoring this information.

This person was Kenneth Arnold the pilot whose sighting inaugurated the public's idea of UFOs. Arnold was stunned, as any thinking person would be, because the AF did not seem at all interested in this observation, even though there were other witnesses reporting strange effects and numerous witnesses to similar objects.

Obviously the AF was not doing its job of protecting Americans, because they should have immediately made an investigation.

But unknown to Arnold, the AF continued this baffling behavior. For about a week after his sighting, something crashed at Roswell, New Mexico. At first after consulting among officers, they reported this as one of the mystery flying discs that people had begun to see in the area. One might think that after this determination WF would contact Arnold. But to add to the strangeness, they did not.

Instead those higher-ups then claimed that no crash had happened. This was quite strange behavior for those given the task of identifying threats to the country. Arnold did not hear from WP until the middle of July. After that he began to undergo some very odd experiences, as described in my, *UFOs Today*. Just a few of these include happenings that are known to UFO researchers today, but which were unheard of then and that did not appear until years later in reports that at first seemed very strange. These involved a Men-in-Black (MIB) experience, although the MIB were not heard of until years later. It also involved a possible abduction, and a sighting of a group of small UFOs.

As we investigated further into these cover-ups, we made a number of new, smoking gun discoveries and have continued these investigations in this book:

Memory Metal, Battelle, and our Smoking Gun
We were the first to report the smoking gun of the examination of possible extraterrestrial material at Battelle in the *Ohio UFO Notebook* and in *UFOs Today*. This was the account of Elroy John Center that has already led to millions of Internet posts about Memory Metal, Nitinol, and other studies. We also explored in detail what may have happened to material debris from Roswell or other possible crashes. In addition, we reported on a new Roswell witness. These explorations are continued in this book.

Alien bodies hidden under the Capital Building
We reported also published the first report about aliens and craft in secret chambers below the Capital. Because in some ways it seemed that right at the beginning happenings occurred that were advanced and complex, we wondered whether the government already knew about UFOs and if a cover-up might have been in place before Arnold's sighting and the Roswell events.

We thus began to look for earlier events and made the initial description of a very early Roswell-type observation but this was around 1939 and involved possible preserved aliens stored in vaults under our capital building. This was the Cordell Hull event. It was described in the *IUR* article, "Pre-World War II 'Creature' Retrieval?"

Although I was not an author on this, with Jones, I was the first interviewer of the Holt sisters and mentioned several times in the paper. We interviewed the daughters of Reverend Holt, Hull's cousin.

We attempted to interview as many members of the Holt family as possible. The first interview by Jones and Irena Scott was naturally with Holt's eldest daughter. As we got to know Lucile and her husband who is a retired executive of a large Ashland company this assessment was proven true.

Recognition: The authors would like to recognize the efforts of Dr. Irena Scott of Delaware County Ohio for her assistance in the early stages of the investigation of this story.

I interviewed the sisters and others related in this story such as Linda Wallace and thought all seemed sincere and very interested in the outcome of the investigations.

Conclusion: It is possible the UFO secrecy began before Arnold. Information from other sources differs about when the cover-up began. Concerning government investigation, several sources report that studies started at the beginning of 1947. Dr. Michael Swords reported that in the summer of 1947, UFO accounts were coming from everywhere but investigation, which involved WP, the Pentagon and the FBI, was disorganized. In addition, little interest came from the higher echelons. The Pentagon first involved WP about mid-July. In September 1947, an investigatory setup was ordered. This evolved into Project Sign. At that time (and maybe now) the government agencies did not act in unison–the WP group took a pro–extraterrestrial position, whereas the Pentagon took the opposing side and the Washington DC group eventually won out.

However others noted cover-up activities began much earlier. England's Harold Wilkins wrote that although Arnold's sighting spread like wild fire, soon a afterward censorship began and overnight saucer stories stopped appearing in the newspapers. Edward Ruppelt, a BB head, reported that by the end of July 1947, the UFO security lid was down tight. UFOlogist Donald Keyhoe said that on July 4 the Air Force stated that no further investigation was needed; it was all hallucination. Obviously, the cover-up involved the Roswell events. Although such cover-ups receive the generic label of government cover-up, it appeared likely that most components of the government were not in on what was going on. It is also evident that some of the initial cover-ups were very sophisticated. Even today, it is unknown what agencies were involved.

*****

CHAPTER THREE

WRIGHT-PATTERSON AFB–HANGER 18, BLUE ROOM, VAULTS, BODIES, AND MUCH ELSE

My very first trip to WP could have turned me off WP for the rest of my life. My family with my father driving our old blue Buick, my sister and I as young kids anticipating who knows what, and Mom with the baby, took off for the WP Air Force Museum. We arrived and drove around trying to figure out where we were.

Suddenly we found ourselves sort of caged in by buildings. Then even more suddenly about five military men surrounded us with rifles aimed at us right through the windows.

We were told to leave. My father had a tendency to rebel against any command and seldom did as told. So we stiffened up and waited for the outcome.

But Dad decided not to argue and left even though still lost, so we were saved from the military men who seemed to be threatened by a lost Middle America family, from innocuous Ohio, that had taken a wrong turn somewhere. My sister, who was even younger, also recalls the adventure.

So my ventures here began when I was very young and maybe were some sort of prescience of the future.

Although WP is the Mecca and central focus of UFO studies, very few UFOlogists have been inside this base. Numerous books, articles, movies, and all other media presentations have been made about it, but the UFOlogists who have actually been inside it could about be counted on the fingers of one hand. This is because it is one of the country's most heavily secured areas.

To show WP's incredible security, because the above is the sort of thing that no one believes, it happened again recently. Here a family, including children age eight and five, the mother, and a grandmother, experienced a horrific nightmare when they went to see the museum but were yanked out of their minivan and forced to their knees at gunpoint. They were held at gunpoint for more than an hour when four officers including three in military fatigues drew guns on them in the parking lot. The children began hysterically screaming when they saw the guns and the five-year-old asked if they were going to shoot grandmother. The mother and grandmother were not only handcuffed and kneeling but remained held down by burly officers. Their crime was looking at the out-of-state licenses in the parking lot. [1]

Although most do not experience this extreme example, its security is legendary and the subject of many UFO accounts by itself. As mentioned before, stories circulate concerning highly placed persons, even presidential candidates, who have been barred from some areas.

Several authors, such as Michael Hesemann and Philip Mantle, have told how on November 1,

1995, after futile attempts to end the civil war in Bosnia-Herzegovina, leaders of the opposing factions arrived in the US for a peace conference. The conference was not held in Washington, D.C. or at Camp David, but at WP in part because of its security. By November 21, the participants had crafted the Dayton Agreement, a treaty that was signed three weeks later. Insiders claim the pressure that brought about the agreement was the "alien card": leaders were shown something that made their own civil war look petty by comparison. Indeed, informants from Dayton whom I've interviewed claim that on the night before the leaders agreed to the treaty, residents of Dayton saw substantial UFO activity in the skies above WP.[2]

More recently noted UFOlogists and writers Thomas Carey and Donald Schmitt were denied entrance to WP as they described in *Inside the Real Area 51*, their book about WP. They wrote that they wanted to take a film crew into WP and interview on camera a base representative discussing the base's history and the importance of a number of facilities. They were specifically interested in the Foreign Technology Division (FTD), Buildings 620, 45, and 18, and Hangar 23.

They wanted to do this because for years they had heard stories about a vast portion of the base being underground with bunkers, tunnels large enough for trucks, manmade hills in Area B, and large hangars with no windows. They received reports of clusters of ventilation pipes coming out of the ground with no buildings around them, and large open areas with heavy metal doors going into the side of a hill. They were told that the Propulsion Research and Development building had a walkway/ramp that lead to an underground door, and also heard about underground-refrigerated rooms. With Stan Friedman they heard about a design for a vault under the base's nuclear reactor. For decades, Carl Day, Len Stringfield, Stan Friedman and many others have taken testimonies of the witnesses to such things.

They were able to get the attention of NBC and trimmed down an earlier proposal, which proposed that noted commentator Lester Holt do the interviewing. But all this was turned down. They were not allowed on base.

Another book that described the interior of WP is *Exempt from Disclosure*, by Robert M. Collins and Richard D. Doty. Their book included a large section describing various buildings in the secured area of WP.

What these and other books had in common was that the authors had not been in these secured areas or seen the actual buildings and areas that they described. They had interviewed on-base personal and collected additional information that they used in their books.

The information presented in this book differs from previous books because Bill Jones and I have actually been on base and I have photographed these areas and buildings–such as 620, 18, and 23. This provides some hard, even smoking gun, information about WP that is not available elsewhere. These photographs are compared with descriptions from the above authors, who had interviewed WP employees, to find similarities and differences.

Thus, I am very lucky to have been one of the few that have not only been on base but to have also been inside the base's most secured areas, and to have been there several times. In April 1993, my employer sent me to a conference that was being held there and I have attended other work-related meetings. I was allowed free access and traveled all over the base. Bruce Ashcroft, PhD, WP historian and archivist, has invited Jones and me to meetings, where we entered the most highly secured areas, discussed UFOs, were shown around the AFB, shown the portion of the building complex that had once been BB headquarters, and he helped us to understand much about WP and UFOlogy.

I may be the only person to have photographed much of the secured areas of WP. Thus, these photographs are valuable because WP released the few other photographs in the public domain. Hence this photography gives an independent view of the base and its buildings.

While other authors have interviewed people about the buildings and activities taking place here, I have seen them, taken actual photographs of them, and these might show several smoking guns. The following information has been was put together using these experiences, information about WP, and several "informants."

First is some general information about the base and why it is so secure.

WP in Dayton, Ohio, is one of the country's chief military sites, as mentioned. It may be also the best-known site associated with the UFO phenomena (e.g., artifacts from Roswell and other sites have been reported to have been taken to this AFB and it was the home of the well-known Project Bluebook).

Because of its military and possible UFO importance, it is also one of the most secure areas in the country. Its areas are surrounded by tall chain-link fences with barb wire at the top and posted warnings such as, "It is unlawful to enter this area without permission of the Installation Commander...all personnel and the property under their control are subject to search. This area is patrolled by military working dog teams…" as shown in Figure 1, and the highly secured entrances into the base (Figure 2).

Why does this air base with its family friendly US Air Force museum in the sleepy Dayton, Ohio, have this degree of security? Is it to protect military information or could it also protect UFO material.

The following photographs show today's high security at the air base, which is a place of legend for many reasons.

Roswell
Today the Roswell and WP story are so deeply embedded in our culture that almost everyone has heard of the Roswell UFO crash, secret WP vaults, a "Blue Room," and associated accounts, such as WP's Hangar 18–the unloading point for Roswell debris. As a result, a Roswell television series debuted in 1999. Moreover, Hangar 18 stories have flourished, and many of these are reflected in a film called *Hangar 18*, and many additional TV shows, books, and magazine articles, such as the TV shows *UFO Cover-Up: Live!* and many others. WP became a part of the UFO picture immediately, not only because of Arnold's experience, but also because the first UFO reports stated that some Roswell debris was sent to WP.

The Roswell story began only a few days after Arnold's sighting, when something reportedly crashed near Roswell, New Mexico. The first report from Roswell Army Air Field announced that a flying saucer had been captured. This news was broadcast around the world according to what Julia Shuster told me in an interview. She is daughter of Walter Haut who was the public information officer at Roswell Air Base who put out its press release about the UFO.[3] Under orders from superiors, officials at the air field quickly changed their story, and from then on authorities denied not only that there was a UFO, but that there had been a crash at all

That report, however, is highly significant because if any group in the world were trained to identify a UFO, it would have been the officers and scientists in the vicinity of Roswell. The Roswell base was a highly sensitive area from the standpoint of security: in 1947 it was the home of the elite 509 Operations Group, the only military unit in the world able to drop nuclear weapons. The 509th Composite Group was created by the United States Army Air Forces during World War II and tasked with the deployment of nuclear weapons. In August 1945, it conducted the atomic bombings of Hiroshima and Nagasaki, Japan.

In addition, it was near the Army's White Sands Proving Ground (now WSMR) and the Alamogordo Bombing Range, where new weapons, balloons, and rocket systems were being developed and where the first atomic bomb had been detonated two years earlier.

Much has been written about the well-known Roswell crash. But the heart of even these accounts lies in WP. This is because strong proof actually exists that Roswell debris was sent to WP immediately after the crash.

Although it is often viewed as legend, I discovered hard, smoking gun, evidence that Roswell debris was sent to WP. This is based on a discovery I made in Roswell museum archives. I found the original radio broadcast from the Roswell Army Air Field, which reported that William Brazel, who turned the debris over to the Air Force, found crash artifacts. The broadcast said artifacts were sent to Fort Worth, Texas, and from there, according to Brigadier General Roger Ramey, they were to be flown to the Army Air Force Research Center at WF (today's WP) near Dayton, Ohio.

The initial radio broadcast about the debris provided this smoking gun. During his broadcast, radio announcer Joe Wilson said on-air that a few minutes ago, he had just spoken to the officials at WF and they were expecting a delivery but it had not yet arrived. It was shipped to the Army Air Force (AAF) research center at WF Ohio. Wilson noted that Colonel William Blanchard refused to give details of what the disc (the Roswell UFO) looked like.[4]

The announcer's statement on-air that he had just talked to WP about the delivery provides definite hard evidence that the debris was flown to WP.

The Roswell newspaper then published a headline article about the event stating that after the intelligence office had inspected the instrument it was flown to higher headquarters.

And on July 8, 1947, Walter Haut was ordered by the base commander, Colonel William Blanchard, to draft a press release to the public, that announced that the AAFs had recovered a crashed "flying disc" from a nearby ranch.

These activities and Arnold's report instantly associated WP with UFO phenomena. WP is one of the agencies where the first publicized reports of UFO phenomena were collected and investigated, and it once housed BB, the Air Force's chief investigatory unit for UFO matters. (Walter Andrus and I reviewed additional information about the Roswell event in editing *UFOs in the New Millennium,* the proceedings of the MUFON 2000 International UFO Symposium.)[5]

Wright-Patterson AFB

The Roswell debris would likely have been sent to WP because of the base's central position in both aviation and space exploration. WP is not just mythological because of its UFO activity; it is the country's foremost airbase.

WP's reputation lends high credibility to its research. It is named after the Wright brothers of Dayton, Ohio, and is known throughout the world as the "Birthplace of Aviation," because this is where the brothers changed the course of human history when they made the first powered flight. Indeed, those from this midwestern region have played a crucial role in aviation and space exploration–including John Glenn, the first American to orbit the earth, and Neil Armstrong, the first person to walk on the moon.

WP is the government's chief aeronautical research agency and the largest and most organizationally complex base in the Air Force. Developments of the base's Aeronautical Systems Center include such legendary airplanes as the P-51 Mustang, the B-17 Flying Fortress, and the B-52 Stratofortress, and more recently, the B-2 stealth bomber, and the F-22 Advanced Tactical Fighter. WP was a Strategic Air Command (SAC) base, meaning that nuclear missiles were stored there during the Cold War from the 1950s to the 1970.

It is often compared to Nevada's Area 51, but actually, WP has its own Area 51 inside the base. This is also a reason behind its high security.

WP is composed of WF (named after the Wright brothers) south of Route 444, and of Patterson Field, north of Route 444. It is divided into three areas, A, B, and C, as shown in Figure 3, and has extensive research facilities.

Area A contains what was once called the Air Technical Intelligence Center (ATIC), which housed the official studies done on UFOs, such as BB. It employed J. Allen Hynek, PhD, noted astronomer and chair of the astronomy department at Northwestern University, past BB consultant, and a prominent writer."[6]

Hanger 18

This world-famous building is where the Roswell debris reportedly was taken. My information on this diverges from that discussed in the books mentioned and in others on the subject.

Although Hangar 18 may be mythical, Roswell debris was likely unloaded into an actual hangar. A long time Dayton resident told us that the Roswell hangar is the second from the left in a group of connected hangars near the runway in Area B.[7] These hangars can be seen from the public area of the Air Force Museum (they are the buildings that resemble drums cut in half and laid down in a series.). On current maps, this group of hangars is collectively identified as Building 4 A-E; thus, if what the Dayton informant said were true, the so-called Hangar 18 would be Building 4, B. This informant said that the airplane carrying the Roswell artifacts landed and parked by the northeast end of the runway in front of the Hangars (Building 4 A-E); the Roswell debris was then unloaded into the second, or B, Hangar. This would seem logical, because in 1947, this runway was active and the military did indeed unload aircraft into these hangars. Perhaps the second Hangar from the left, B Hangar, is where authorities initially unloaded the Roswell debris.

When I looked over this secured area from on base, a runway still existed to this area, which I accidently drove onto. There is a large apron in front (or south) of this group of hangers and old pictures from the base show that it once connected to the main WF runway/taxiway.

In addition, these hangers were built and active before Roswell. Old photographs taken in 1945 show them with a large paved area in front of them filled with airplanes on display and many people attending what appears to be an air show (this would be on the old runway attached to the area in front of the hangers). This area is also connected to the downslope runway as mentioned. This portion of WP is the old part that was called WF. It was the portion to which Kenneth Arnold wrote and to which the Roswell debris was transported.

Thus because these buildings are hanger shaped and once connected to the runway, they would be logical buildings for Hanger 18.

The account is that a B-29 took off flew from Roswell, flew to Fort Worth Army Air Field (later Carswell Air Force Base and now Naval Air Station Joint Reserve Base, Fort Worth), and then to WP.

According to many reports, the B-29 bomber with four armed MPs aboard carried one or more crates of debris from Roswell to Fort Worth, Texas, and subsequently to WP. Reports claimed that at least one of those crates was approximately 12 feet long, 5 feet wide, and 4 feet high, and that the loading consumed eight hours prior to takeoff for. Some reports said that the crates were specially made and unmarked, that each crate had to be checked for size, and that the crew had to know how to position the crates in the relatively small aircraft. Because a B-29 is a bomber that does not typically carry cargo, it is possible the crates were built on the spot to fit into the plane.

At the National Museum of the US Air Force at WP, Bill Jones and I measured a modified B-29s on display, which had been cut open so people can walk through it. Our measurements confirmed that a crate of the reported size could fit—albeit snugly—in a B-29. Two crates could fit as well, because the aircraft has two bomb bays, one fore and one aft, which could accommodate them.

The plane reportedly flew at a very low altitude, and this suggests the crates might have carried something other than inanimate debris. However, the plane might have flown at this altitude because the four MPs may have been riding in the unpressurized areas where the crates were stowed. Some reports say additional crates were loaded in larger C-54 transport planes that could easily have carried crates of the reported size.

It landed on the WF runway, taxied to the Hanger, and then was unloaded.

In our photograph (Figure 4), the second building from the left in the upper photo was reported to be "Hanger 18," the hanger where the B-29 from Roswell first parked and unloaded the debris. Figure 5 shows a photo of the backside of this hanger taken from on base. Aircraft are still visible on the paved area to the south of the hangers (Figure 4, bottom photo, and Figure 6).

Our photographs show views of a B-29 on one of the old WF runways (Figure 7). To its right can be seen the group of hangars into which the Roswell debris was said to have first been unloaded. In the 1940s, a paved area extended southward from the hangers and connected to these runways/taxiways. Thus these photographs might give a picture of the view when the B-29 from Roswell landed.

There are additional B-29s at WP. One is the Boeing B-29 Superfortress "Bockscar" on display that dropped the Fat Man atomic bomb on Nagasaki on Aug. 9, 1945, three days after the atomic attack against Hiroshima. Bockscar was one of 15 modified "Silverplate" B-29s that were assigned to the 509th Composite Group. Some have speculated that one of the B-29s at WP might have also been the one that transported the Roswell debris to WP.

Perhaps our photos show the very airplane that carried the Roswell debris to WP and it is parked with Hanger 18 in the background.

When I looked over the secured area around the group of hangars from on base, a runway still exists to this area, in fact, I accidentally drove onto it. It is called the accelerated or downslope runway because it slants downward giving the aircraft taking off from it a boost. Robert Collins described it as the acceleration runway/ramp that exists in the WP Area 51 area. It was used for rocket sled testing. This Area 51 sits next to a reported underground hangar that was built during WWII to allow aircraft to be moved underground in case of an enemy air attack. He added that around 1945 under "Project PAPERCLIP" many German scientists and engineers were brought there to work on various classified projects. Thus, two reports described an underground area near Area 51 and the location of the old WF runway, Collins' description and our Superfund map, (Figure 10) shows "Underground Storage" in that area.

Projects such as Paperclip were very secure. Although it is unknown if this story is related, it is about underground facilities. UFOlogist Earl Grey Anderson, said that when he was young his mother told him about working in an underground city, with cafes, golf carts, even movie theaters, which was entered by a very deep elevator. This was somewhere in the desert. He recalled, "I think she was probably involved with Paperclip, through Hughes. She did talk about Von Braun, she did know him. And I'm pretty sure she mentioned Oberth as well…It was mid to late 50s." He said that she knew Howard Hughes and added, "Hughes made his fortune with drilling equipment originally. So tunneling makes sense." He added, Hughes "worked with RAND Corp (my mom said that). It's said that RAND dug most of our underground stuff, with The Army Corp Of Engineers." Later his mother became "tight lipped about it," and that is all he found out. In his effort to find out more, he said, "About the closest I've gotten is a friend of ours who's grandfather worked at Groom Lake…our friend Kim said that her grandfather had worked there, and told the exact story... So I have a bit of confirmation there, and her grandfather did mention the words Area 51." My husband had worked in Area 51 and he also said that most of it is underground. I never asked him if the cafes, theaters, etc., were underground but expect that they were.

In the WP area by the hangers, Area 51, and the underground areas, there have been bombing practice targets--photo targets, such as tanks and an unflyable F-4 located in the areas in front of and to the side of the hangers. Many types of aircraft can be seen such as airplanes with unusual radomes, helicopters, and others as shown in Figures 4 and 6.

This would be a quite logical place to unload the Roswell debris. A map showing the older areas of the base show that these hangers were right off the main WF runway. The wide area to the south of the buildings expands into the runway. Thus it would be quite easy for an airplane to unload here. The other authors mentioned above have theorized that buildings in the old WF area labeled Building or Hanger 18 are actually Hanger 18. However these buildings do not look like hangers, there is no record that they were ever hangers, and they did not connect to the old WF runway.

The hangers in my photographs would match the accounts of what happened to the Roswell debris better than those described in other sources.

Thus, it appears the most logical from the evidence that these Hangar buildings may have been where the plane from Roswell unloaded its cargo and the informant appears to have given us good information. He knew the layout of the old WF.

Area B: "If the bodies exist, they are in that [Building 18] complex."– Crypts, Vaults, Alien bodies, Building 18, Roswell Debris, Blue Room, Blue Book Headquarters[8]
So where was the Roswell debris taken when it left the hanger? Where was it analyzed and stored? Since at that time WP was actually WF, the Roswell debris most likely went to the WP AREA B. Today this area contains the Air Force Museum, which is not fenced and is open to the public. It also has a secured building complex surrounded by fence, which can be entered only through various gates. Within this secured area is the old area of WF with the hangers and other buildings mentioned above. It also contains the Avionics Laboratory a number of Air Force buildings including materials and manufacturing technology buildings, and an old nuclear reactor. Some of these buildings can be seen by looking up the hill from the Air Force Museum.

Among the buildings in this area is a nondescript brick building, Building 18 that could be the source of the famous Hanger 18 stories. Building 18 on the Air Base map is shown as the Aero Propulsion Lab. It is centrally located in Area B, and is closely surrounded by other buildings. This is the building that other authors have generally identified as Hanger 18.

Collins and Doty said that the folklore says it might be a building called "Hanger 18." Through many years of intensive effort, the only evidence that they found to support these stories were a series of buildings called 18 A, B, C, etc., but no Hanger 18.

Carey and Schmidt said that Building 18 was one of eight buildings 18-18G that comprised the Power Plant Laboratory Complex. The original function of this complex was to conduct aircraft engine research, but during WWII, additional structures were added as its role expanded. Building 18, constructed in 1928, was the main research laboratory in the complex and Building 18A was the laboratory office.

So it appears that these authors are referring to the same building. The one that Carey and Schmitt called Building 18 is the same building that Collins and Doty called Hangar 18.

I was there and able to photograph Building 18 (Figure 8). It is actually a series of buildings called 18 A, B, C, etc.

This famous Building 18 is a long brick building that appears to have two somewhat different sections separated by an indented doorway with a handrail and steps. The doors that I could see were too small to allow a craft of the size described to enter. They looked like and were about the size of normal entrances for people. It has two stories with what appear to be ventilation ducts on top.

Beneath the brick portion is a section made of a white material. The east section has openings in this, which look like windows but are blocked. The west portion has openings that appear to be windows into a basement floor.

None of the old maps seem to show it as a hanger. It would look just like a normal office building except for the windows. Each window appears to have something like a blind in the upper part, but each blind in each window is pulled down exactly the same distance–no variation. Hence all of what appear to be blinds in an office building may not be. Some windows seem to have what appear to be curtains along their sides. Some appear more difficult to see through than others. In general, they appear much more consistent than normal glass windows and they appear to use only half the glass space, which would seem to be a waste of money both for the glass and the insulation costs. Often newer buildings that house intelligence operations are windowless.

The bottom of west portion (right side) of the building appears to be less deep than the east portion and only the upper portion of the windows show on its east side. The area is at an incline going uphill to the east, suggesting that the building had originally been built this way.

The side of the building is four windows wide, thus it is long and comparatively narrow. Another building (Building 23) is quite close to the east section of the building.

WP seems to be unsure of its exact purpose. Building 18 is labeled differently in different information sources from WP. On one map, it is labeled the Aero Propulsion Lab. In other 1991 WP material, it is labeled Building 18A-D and called the Power Plant Laboratory Complex.

The ventilation ducts on the top suggest it might contain laboratories or similar structures, rather than an office building.

It is considered very mysterious. Carey and Schmitt described a WP employee who had the highest security clearance. He was told that he could go anywhere except one place and that the security for it was totally separate from the rest of the base. He said that no one but the most powerful people came and went from it and what went on inside was totally unknown. He whispered that if the bodies exist, they are in the Building 18 complex. However we saw nothing to make us think that the security for Building 18 was any higher than anyplace else. However, this does resemble the security for the NASIC building, the only building I have seen with this type of security, to be described.

The history of the building provided by WP is that Buildings 18 and 18G, were built as some of the earliest WF structures, and initially used for engine research. The other structures in the complex were built during World War II and reflect the expanding scope of aircraft engine research being conducted at WF at that time. There is no information suggesting that this was once a hanger. This building did not abut the old runway and appears nothing like a hanger in either structure or dimensions.

Our photograph (Figure 9) shows the building that is said to be where four alien bodies and UFO debris were taken. It shows the east end of Building 18 (right) and, Building 23 (to the left).

Collins said Building 18 might have had something to do with Little Green Men, but that this story should be associated with the building he called Hangar 23, which sits between buildings 18F and 18A.

Thus the building to the left in my photographs is Building 23 and it is between buildings 18F and 18A. This is likely the building that Collins described as Hanger 23. He wrote that the floor of this Hanger 23 had been removed and the craft(s) lowered into the basement. A concrete floor was then placed over this area. When they did this, an entry was built from a vault in the east basement of building 18A to this new basement in Hangar 23.

He said that hangars normally do not have basements, but this hangar was converted into an office building–now called the AF Research laboratory, Sensor Directorate, Target Signature Branch.

Carey and Schmitt wrote that from the descriptions and testimonies, they were persuaded that most of the Roswell crash wreckage as well at least four alien cadavers from the crash were initially delivered to Hanger 23 at WP (then WF). They stayed there until a suitable underground passage was made connecting it to Building 18 for permanent storage could be constructed. They were taken to the AeroMedical Facility (Building 29) and then returned to building 18F. The wreckage would have remained in storage at Building 18 except for when it was being analyzed and tested in Hanger 23. It had easy access from Building 18 and its historical function was of back-engineering foreign technology of earth origin, which was crucial to trying to figure out the nature of the Roswell wreckage.

Figure 10 shows a second view of Building 23. A first question one might ask is why would it need an underground passage that connected it to Building 18 for permanent storage? Perhaps Building 18 provides some sort of testing.

It is a tall building. The only possible windows on the north side are at the top of the building and in the built-up side corners/pillars. The north side has doorways on the east and west sides, and what looks to be a larger entrance between these doorways–probably for unloading large equipment from trucks. The central doorway appears large enough for a truck to enter. There is a second small doorway to the east of it. There does not appear to be a ramp to the large doorway, but it might be low enough to not need one. Possibly a small UFO might be taken through this doorway.

The east and west sides of the building are light colored, appear reflective, and appear to be windows. They comprise a solid set of windows so that these sides look almost like a sheet of windows with no space between them. There appear to be five rows of then as if the building has five floors. Pipes come out of some of these windows.

This building has a very unusual design and it would be an extremely unusual hanger.

This building does not look like a hanger and no evidence exists that it had been a hanger. In addition is not near the location of the old WF runway. The WP information on it is that it was the site of static structures tests on World War II and earlier aircraft.

There also appear to be a series of longitudinal windows below the large layers of glass windows on the west side.

Both authors indicated that an underground passage went between Building 23 and 18 and that Building 18 provides easy access to the basement vault under Building 23 where the Roswell debris is stored.

Building 23's west end is quite close to the east end of Building 18, with only a narrow driveway between them. I was unable to tell whether this area appeared elevated, but it would have been easy to tunnel between these buildings and or to stick a driveway on top of a dug tunnel.

Building 23 (erected in 1934) was built after Building 18 (constructed in 1928), but has lengthy windows facing this building.

Another suggestion that there might be a vault or vault entrance in the east basement of Building 18A is that the lower windows on the east portion of Building 18 appear blocked out, whereas those on the west half of the building appear transparent. Perhaps this blocks the view of a basement vault or entrance into Building 23. Building 18 is downslope from Building 23.

In some WP literature Building 23 is called the Static test Laboratory, Number 1. Other literature describes its renovation. It says Building 23 is in the WF Historic District. According to the US Army Corps of Engineers, this historic test facility was originally built in 1934 to house structural tests for aircraft carriers and parts. They preserved the exterior of the building and transformed the inside of the massive 52,000-square-foot space into a new state-of-the-art Advanced Power Thermal Research Lab.[9].

This is a very odd-looking building. It is a huge but a lot of its space is vertical. It is unclear what the vertical space would contribute, if it were a hanger.

Also Building 18F on the east side of Building 23 was mentioned as containing possible cold storage areas where bodies might have been kept. Its eastern half was said to contain refrigeration equipment. It might have had cold rooms for testing engines at low temperature. Both Buildings 18 and 23 appear to have some connection to the power plant. A transformer yard is located south of Building 23.

In addition, it is highly probable that WP does have underground areas. It was a Strategic Air Command Base and had a nuclear reactor. Most government areas that I have worked in contain underground facilities for evacuation in the case of emergency. It is common to have them under nuclear reactors. These need to meet high specifications such as a moderate or high-hazard facility, including Design-Basis Earthquake (DBE) specifications as described below.[10]

Further evidence of the existence of such facilities as Collins described was contained in a document I came across when working at the Ohio Department of Health. This document, Tritium Consolidation Comparison Study: Risk Analysis, DOE/DP/00248-H1, December 1992, described the T-Building at the Mound Nuclear Plant at Dayton, Ohio, (near WP) as follows:

> [It is an] underground, massive, reinforced concrete structure containing two functional floors. The exterior, reinforced concrete walls of the building are a minimum of 16 feet 7 inches thick. The 30-foot thick ceiling and 8-foot thick basement also are constructed of reinforced concrete...The interior dimensions are approximately 151 ft. wide, 345 ft. long, and 30 ft. high. Entrances to the building include two large doors in the south wall at each end of the upper operations floor that permit vehicles to enter the building.

This building was constructed according to certain specifications: it was designed to comply with the Uniform Building Code current when it was constructed, and it is a moderate hazard facility as defined in Department of Energy (DOE) Order 6430.1A.UCRL-15910, which requires that it be designed for 0.15 g design basis earthquake (DBE). The DOE order also says that if a facility is to be classified as a high-hazard facility, design for a DBE of 0.23 g is required. This would fit the descriptions of the underground buildings at WP. And if the Mound building is an example of a moderate-hazard facility, imagine what the design for an extreme-hazard facility, such as might be like.

Figure 11 shows the WP Nuclear Engineering Test Facility that was said by Carey, Schmitt, and Friedman to be above a vault. Perhaps this vault is similar to the one described above.

Such information suggests that the stories about huge underground chambers and their location may, in general, be true.

Avionics Building 620
Both authors say that north of the Avionics building is the location of large important vaults at WP. Our photography could provide smoking gun evidence of this.

Building 620 is the Avionics Lab and is distinctive because of its two large twin towers. These twin towers are believed to be functional, rather than decorative. They were reportedly used for dropping objects for materials testing purposes. It is windowless and located uphill from the Hangar complex (Hangar 18).

The location of one such vault area is reportedly near to and connects with buildings 620, the Avionics Labs, and Building 739.

Collins writes that in 1947 and later the film storage vaults began to be used to store the recovered "alien bodies" from Roswell and other crashes. These underground storage vaults were known generally by a few people in the photographic detachment.

Collins tells that one entrance to the underground vault system, according to their sources, was down a set of stairs under the avionics tower. He writes that there were two freight-sized elevators under the avionics tower. One of these went to a second basement area.

The authors showed a picture of the north entry on the west side of the building under the avionics tower. Their photo showed an expansion on the northwest corner of 620, but they said that this new basement avoided the area where the tunnel and vault would be further down. The construction team at the time this was built noted that the walls were uneven or 'rolling'. They suspected it might be caused by underground structures.

Collins and Doty said that double vaulted doors in 620 led to a long hallway with a second set of double vaulted doors to possible freight-sized elevators and stairs, and then a tunnel that led to one of the chief vaults under the north parking lot of 620. Perhaps this is the entrance for the trucks. They showed a photograph of a new addition and the north parking lot that they labeled as the location of the vault.

The photography I took around Building 620 may be a smoking gun to confirm this. It is a view I took of a west entrance to Building 620. I have found no other photographs that show this area.

This photograph (Figure 12) shows the entrance ramp to a west door of 620. This ramp is quite wide (it looks like three-four lanes wide) and gives the impression of being very strong and heavy-duty. It is built up over a considerable length, which might indicate that trucks enter the building here rather than just unloading. It could handle very large weights. It leads to a very large door, through which trucks could easily travel. And the ramp suggests that large, heavy vehicles do use these doors. Beside the door are large tanks, which might contain liquid nitrogen. The "twin towers" are in the background.

Collins showed a photograph of the parking lot and labeled this the location of the vault. I have been fortunate enough to observe digging in the area he described. Our photograph (Figure 13) shows the area of his photograph and description. It shows heavy digging equipment and dirt piles in this parking lot area, with the 620 towers in the background. It also shows the new addition described by Collins.

This digging does not appear to just be a parking lot re-surfacement. The equipment was for heavy, deep digging. It includes large Cat-type excavators with different mass excavation buckets for deep digging. These are traditional excavator equipment that normally have a long bucket arm attached to a pivoting cab that can rotate 360 degrees. Large bulldozers push the excavated dirt around. This dirt does not look like the pavement piles found during road and parking lot renovation.

There were no pavement-type vehicles visible, such as scrapers, crushing and screening machines to process and repurpose material, motor graders, cold planers, vibratory soil compactors, asphalt pavers, compactors and similar equipment.

Numerous large dirt piles were visible all through the area. Our photograph (Figure 14) shows one such dirt pile with the new addition building in the background. These dirt piles were quite high and looked nothing like the type of pile from resurfacing a road or parking lot. It appeared that this digging would be quite deep to get so much dirt and such high piles were found throughout the area north of 620. Some digging was in long narrow strips that appeared to follow tunnels.

For security reasons, I did not leave the car to see how deep the digging was or what it uncovered. Area B is on a hill overlooking the prairie area of the base and would be a good place for vaults because of the drainage and limestone bedrock.

It appeared they were digging deep and this digging may have gone into the vaults. I had heard from others that there are other large, hanger-sized underground areas in this same complex, built during WWII, where UFO wreckage could have been stored. According to some sources, these facilities are very large and deep. A source said that while working at WP for a private contractor, he had seen workers open a large cement man-hole-like cover on the floor of one of the WF buildings. He cannot now remember which one it was. The opening was the entrance to a huge vault or tunnel that was very deep.

He noted that WP had trouble with flooding in its tunnels. Several were reportedly full of water and possibly that is what this digging was about.

Building 739 a small cubical building to the west of 620 and of the parking lot (Figure 15). Collins once told me that the location of one such vault area is near to and connects with Buildings 620 and 739. Building 739 is a two-story building with what appears to be a vent that reportedly contains a vaulted entrance to an underground complex, beneath the parking area for these buildings. Behind thick glass doors is a six-inch-thick bank vault door with a combination lock on the front of it. The power supply to this section is reported to be within the vault.

Carey and Schmitt wrote that they had heard about clusters of ventilation pipes coming out of the ground by themselves. Our photographs (Figure 17) might show some of this sort of thing. One is of a small building sticking out of a hill slope. I think it was unlabeled and did not seem to be a part of anything else. It was between the Area B hill area and the power plant, which was downhill from it. Also large pipes can be seen coming from the power plant area that appear to just go into an open area of the Area B hill area.

There are other small, isolated structures popping up in the open area north of Building 620 that do not appear connected to anything else and are of unknown purpose. Also there are long indentations in this area. They look like something has been dug up and the dirt filled in. Possibly they are traces of some kind of tunnels. Another such object was a large cylinder sticking out of an open area by itself in the Area B hill area (Figure 18). Beside it is a black truck and a driveway goes to it. It is unknown what such structures are.

Building 30 (Figure 16) was built in 1942 as the Technical Data Annex No. 1. It was designed as an audiovisual facility, and has continued to function in that capacity for the last fifty years. It is also called the WP Area B, Building 30, Audio-Visual Laboratory.

Collins also described Building 30. He wrote that Building 450, the Flight Dynamics Lab, has a second basement. There is a reported tunnel going from it in the direction of Building 30, which is close to the Medical Building 29. Also near buildings 29 and 30 is a reported small vault that was used for VIP viewing as far back as the Eisenhower era.

Collins had shown us and shown in the TV show, *UFO Cover-Up: Live!* diagrams of the appearance of aliens and perhaps some of these figures had been created here.

He had showed Jones and I computer drawings of "gray-type" aliens. ("Gray-type" aliens or "grays" are presented as grayish in color, short, with large heads, black "wrap-around" eyes, slits for mouths, and small noses or no noses.) The aliens' eyes had several inner eyelids, and their heads resembled the popular archetype of an alien head. The aliens were about three feet tall, had a small amount of webbing between their fingers, and each one's lungs and heart were composed of one organ, as were their kidneys and bladder.

The drawings we saw had numbers and letters in the upper corners that Collins said did not show up on TV. (Collins may have wished to imply that these marks were classified government identifiers.) At the top left, one drawing had writing that looked like it read "FTD-SYD, Veh Type WHDDD4," and another had what looked like "FTD YP" and "28 8100." He also showed us photos with numbers at the top. We asked several people, including Ashcroft, if they recognized these letters and numbers, but none did. (However, I recall that the WP US Air Force National Air Intelligence Center (NAIC) was formerly the FTD. SYD is the three-letter abbreviation for the office responsible for FTD graphics (the office was reported to be under the Directorate of Systems at the Space Systems Division within FTD).

Perhaps the acronym is an older one, and perhaps the photos actually came from this office— possibly as a theoretic alien model, or maybe a graphic of an actual alien.

Another informant, who grew up in the Dayton, OH, area, says that it was common knowledge that WP-had alien artifacts. He recalls that people in his neighborhood (where many WP personnel lived) openly talked about this. Another informant said that people, who work on the base still talk about this subject, but informally, because it is classified.

Where did the dirt go? WP is actually a very large Superfund Site. If one wonders where all the dirt from the possible underground digging went, the included map shows where. It is laden with landfills. It also shows the location of several underground storage tanks. One of these is located near the old WF runway.

This illustration (Figure 19) is a diagram for the contaminated areas at WP, known as the "Wright-Patt Superfund Site," in Fairborn, Ohio. Although the area is highly contaminated, the map shows only surface contamination, suggesting the deeper areas are secured.

Area A: We were inside the famous Blue Room and Blue Book Headquarters
We have not only been inside the legendary "Blue Room" mentioned above, but even attended a UFO meeting there.

The security of WP is incredible. And the most secure of all places is the famous Blue Room that senators, presidential candidates and many others have been turned away from. As mentioned, this blue room has now been identified. As described by Carey and Schmitt, "The office of record for BLUE ROOM is NASIC–the National Air and Space Intelligence Center."

So Bill Jones and I, who were inside the NASIC building (856), are in a rarefied atmosphere. In fact, we may be the only civilians ever to enter its sacred portals.[11]

It is located in Area A, which is also surrounded by high chain-link and barbed wire. This area once contained the old ATIC, the home of various Air Force UFO projects, including BB. The acronym ATIC is found in all the old UFO books. ATIC was later called the FTD where photo analysis and study of foreign aerodynamics, ballistic missile, and space vehicle systems took place. It became the NAIC, and in 2003, the name was changed to the National Air and Space Intelligence Center (NASIC).

This NASIC building is particularly interesting. Its headquarters, Building 856, appeared to me to be by far the most secured on WP. It is so secure that, although located inside WP's secured areas, it has its own high-security zone (Figure 20). There are cameras located on the roof of the building pointing in all directions. A secondary security system composed of machines that look like traffic lights surrounds the periphery of the building. This system extends out as far as approximately 100 feet from the building and into the parking lot (Figure 21). Warning signs state that the grass and private roads surrounding this building are a controlled area as shown. This system gave the impression that it monitored each blade of grass.

It is unknown what the many monitors on the posts surrounding the building are for, because roof top cameras also monitored the area. Possibly they are also motion/infra red detectors or some kind of very sensitive equipment. As mentioned, several authors have said that vaults lie under or near this building and perhaps these monitors could be some sort of security monitor or have something to do with that. These vaults can be very deep and large, such as the nearby Mound facility as described previously, for the safekeeping of highly secured material.[12] They can have their own security system.[13]

The building is large and entirely windowless. It has a light grey corrugated upper portion and a darker grey lower section with vertical posts, has a complex, branched shape, and gives the impression of two or more buildings connected by passageways. Its entrances are very well guarded. I have seen no other WP building with anything like this security. Because it has been said that government UFO work is the most secure in the government, this building appears to hit that spot. The NASIC building appears to be by far the most secure building in the high security portion of WP.

Some of the WP information gives the impression that the building is a hanger type building where foreign material is analyzed and one function is to monitor other countries' weapons and personnel in the air and in space.[14] There was a MIG-29 outside it when I was there.

To me the part of this mysterious building's inside that I saw simply looked like an office building, probably with laboratories, satellite and other aerial or ground monitors and similar apparatus, and a large auditorium, where we heard a presentation.

Also Ashcroft took me to the WP archives and left me alone. This was a very large room filled with folders. I assume they were from the time before computers. I thought I had better not take photographs and I do not remember whether it was in this building or somewhere else.

Alien bodies are said to have been stored in this area. For example, Carey and Schmitt said that according to Springfield's early books, "he came away convinced that UFO artifacts as well as alien bodies were being stored in the FTD building."

Carey and Schmitt said that Stringfield told that one of his informants described the Blue Room as an "Inner Sanctum," a place that resembled a museum containing the artifacts of crashed saucers and the cadavers retrieved from Roswell. He told that when they visited it, they wore blindfolds. When these were removed, they were inside a converted aircraft hangar with the floor and walls entirely painted blue. They also were led to a small locked room and shown large aquariums each containing a small body with grey skin, oversized cranium, huge eyes, and no hair.

Once I asked Dr. Ashcroft about the reason for its high security and he said that it is where the information from satellites is processed. Because of my experience working on satellite photography in the DIA, I was aware of the high security associated with this work, and I also thought that this type of center might be the one that processes UFO information (which might come under the category of foreign technology). Thus, one of the area's functions along with identifying aircraft might be the identification of unknown objects, such as UFOs, and it might still house a modern agency whose work is similar to its former UFO investigation function. This security is also likely why photographic information may be stored in the vault structures under WP. There reportedly are underground vaults near this building and this is likely, simply for the emergency evacuation of high security material.

This building complex is highly important to the UFO field. It includes the AMC Headquarters. The Technical Intelligence Division of the AMC at WF (later WP), assumed control of Project SIGN and began its work in January 1948. Under the acronym ATIC, it once housed BB and the other UFO studies taking place there. It was later called the FTD, where Stringfield thought the bodies were stored.

The complex's history shows how the UFO project fit into this intelligence agency and how the agency grew into today's NASIC. NASIC provides air and space intelligence for the Department of Defense. It is a global intelligence enterprise and aids in shaping national and defense policy. Headquartered at WP, its organizational lineage dates to 1961, but it traces its heritage back to the Foreign Data Section of the Army Signal Corps' Airplane Engineering Department established at McCook Field in 1917 (WP airfield predecessor). After the war ended in Europe a group of pilots collected German aircraft from the battlefield and sent or flew them back to AMC's T-2 Intelligence Department at WF for study. This Operation Paperclip brought German scientists and technicians to WF to work with the American scientists and some began to work in the WF laboratories. In 1947, the Army delivered a large number of captured documents to WF. This revolutionized American industry. Besides the aviation advances, it provided new designs for vacuum tubes, magnetic tape development, night vision devices and many other advances.

AMC's T-2 at WF was established in 1945. T-2 was responsible for the creation of air intelligence, identifying foreign aircraft and related equipment, foreign language documents–much translation was needed, and much else.

On May 1951 the Air Force established the Air Technical Intelligence Center (ATIC) at WP and throughout the 1950s it pioneered the use of computers and much else. BB, located in Building 263 that has now been demolished, was under its auspices. In 1957 following the Sputnik satellite launches in October, its space analysis increased. In 1959, the Air Force renamed ATIC the Aerospace Technical Intelligence Center. In 1961 the Defense Intelligence Agency (DIA) was established.

The FTD was established under Air Force Systems Command in July 1961. It worked in photo analysis and much else.

In the 1970s, WP building 856 was built. In 1992, FTD became the Foreign Aerospace Science and Technology Center (FASTC), in 1993 FASTC became the National Air and Space Intelligence Center, and in 2003 the National Air and Space Intelligence Center (NASIC).

Zeidman has also mentioned that BB was in Building 263, not Hanger 18, and that the NASIC building was the successor to Building 263 as discussed later.

Jones and I found additional WP smoking gun evidence on base. During one visit, we were privileged to have Dr. Ashcroft invite us to the last of the briefings he had arranged for NAIC (now NASIC) employees on the history of this organization. The subject of this briefing was BB. Ashcroft's presentation included a video, *NAIC Alumni Days Operation Blue Book V-7512*, which showed a reunion of former Blue Book employees, including three former Blue Book directors: Robert Friend, George Gregory, and Hector Quintanilla. About 30 officers, enlisted people, and civilians attended the reunion. This event was even more historic because he held it in the main conference room of the NASIC Center headquarters building 856, the complex that has historically housed the WP UFO research.

Ashcroft also played a tape of an interview between Carl Day (a veteran Dayton broadcaster and Emmy-winning television news anchor who worked with WDTN-TV Channel 2) and Hector Quintanilla (the last BB director). In this interview, Quintanilla said BB was completely separate from the Central Intelligence Agency (CIA) and, later, from the Defense Intelligence Agency (DIA). Quintanilla noted that he lacked the required security clearances for intelligence work. He added that authorities at the time thought UFOs were Soviet in origin; thus, they were taken quite seriously.

During the question-and-answer session following Ashcroft's presentation, we might have gained additional smoking gun information. It appeared that classified UFO information may have existed, and it was clear there was no unanimity of opinion about UFOs among the Air Force members and employees in the audience. One officer doubted Ashcroft's claim that all reports about UFOs in Air Force custody had been declassified, and he mentioned a secret message he'd once seen about the pursuit of a UFO by an Air Force pilot. This officer asked Ashcroft if he thought that message would now be declassified. Ashcroft replied, "Yes," and he reminded everyone that the audience included people (Jones and I) who lacked security clearances. To me this suggested that UFO information had continued to be classified, and the discussion might have been different if the audience had included only those having proper security clearances.

Ashcroft's assertion that all UFO reports were now declassified solidified my belief that UFO information had been covered up by the American military. For example, I would certainly think that some information would be classified because it would show our country's technological expertise. Also, in several interviews with government workers I'd heard of films showing Air Force pilots pursuing UFOs; thus, the officer's remark about the pursuit was in line with my own experience. UFOlogist Donald Schmitt, after a Columbus, Ohio, talk about the Roswell crash (January 13, 1994, at Battelle), told me he'd heard that the American military sometimes showed UFO photographs and films to selected people as part of a US government study of witness reactions to such material.

Thus, I thought it suspicious that Ashcroft answered affirmatively to the officer's question about declassification without requesting specifics.

As we were leaving the building after the presentation, two men in civilian clothing, who recognized Ashcroft, asked him if he'd ever talked to a man named John G. Tiffany who had worked at WP.

I recalled that, according to Kevin Randle and Donald Schmitt's research, Tiffany's father was the man dispatched from WF to retrieve the Roswell materials and possibly the space alien bodies at Fort Worth. Tiffany claimed his father picked up metallic debris and a large cylinder that reminded his father of a huge thermos bottle.

Ashcroft said he had not talked to Tiffany's son, and he later explained to us that the son was undoubtedly tired of answering questions about his father's story and would refuse to be interviewed.

After we left the building, I asked Ashcroft if he'd ever contacted Brigadier General Arthur Exon, the Base Commander of WP in the 1960s, for information about UFO investigations on base. Ashcroft responded that as commander of the base, Exon was responsible only for maintenance of base infrastructure and would not have been privy to activities of various agencies on base.

I asked this because in *Witness to Roswell*, the authors said that Exon had been assigned to AMC Headquarters at WP and this was where the Roswell artifacts were sent after the recovery. He also said that after conducting metallurgical tests on the wreckage, the consensus among the scientists involved in the testing was that the material was from space.

General Exon from 1964-66 was the Commanding Officer of WP, where crash material was taken in 1947. He was the highest-ranking military officer to come out and say directly that Roswell had been the crash of a spacecraft and that alien bodies were recovered. Exon was never interviewed and AF investigators completely ignored him. By the time some the Congressional staffers interviewed him in December 1994 he was extremely guarded in his comments. In 1947 he was a Lt.-Colonel stationed at WF at the time of the Roswell crash and he heard of the incident. He said he also had flown over the area of the crash several months later. He said he observed two distinct crash sites and gouges in the "pivotal areas." He said additional UFO-related field operations were staged at W-P during his tenure. Teams of men would fly in from Washington for an investigation and WP would supply them with planes and crews for their operations

He said that when he was a colonel stationed at the Pentagon, he was aware of a UFO controlling committee made up chiefly of very high-ranking military officers and intelligence people. His nickname for these people was "The Unholy Thirteen".

His knowledge of the Roswell events was chiefly second-hand. He said he never saw the Roswell crash debris, but heard about the result of testing by other personnel involved. The same existed for the recovery and shipment of bodies. He also mentioned knowing some of the photographers who photographed the sites.[15]

Much such secondhand information appears readily available at WP. In wandering through the base, once I met the family of a project BB member and interviewed them on film, but they wouldn't give their names. Just in a restaurant once, I had a UFO book and someone came up to tell me all about how his uncle worked there and knew where the bodies were stored.

The above information gave us the even stronger impression that BB was a public relations endeavor rather than an investigative project. For example, as Quintanilla noted, some authorities at that time thought UFOs were Soviet in origin. However, one would expect that if UFOs were thought to be Soviet, the military would have investigated at a much higher level. It was difficult to think that even Quintanilla thought Blue Book had sufficient security and resources to investigate Soviet technology. One would expect UFO evidence to be sent to an agency that could investigate it scientifically, such as WP's Air Force Materiel Command its chief research and development branch, rather than to BB. Likewise, radar visuals would probably have gone to agencies specializing in radar signatures. In 1947 when UFO investigation began, WP had at its disposal some of the world's best American and German scientists. If materials or valid observations had been collected, these would probably have been sent to WP. But there would be no reason for the Air Force to give its best evidence to BB, which lacked the technical specialists, the equipment, and the secured area to conduct appropriate investigations.

We viewed Ashcroft's response to the question about Exon as ridiculous; the fact that Exon was responsible for maintenance of base infrastructure in no way precluded knowledge of Roswell.

Others with direct knowledge about Blue Book have also been skeptical about it as an investigative project. Hynek reported in his 1998 book, *The UFO Experience: A Scientific Inquiry*, that during a visit to Blue Book headquarters he happened upon some cases by accident when he saw material lying on a desk outside the files. These cases were not included in information shown to him by Blue Book personnel. He had access to BB files only when he requested data about a specific case. According to Jennie Zeidman, Hynek often commented that he knew the best cases were withheld. In fact, she described the desperate emphasis or hush-hush of Blue Book as being in an environment of ludicrously slipshod security.

Its security is so intense that although I had been on base before, once while visiting WP, I stuck a camera lens through the security fence and snapped a photo of a building. Even for that some guards immediately came to admonish me.

The Real Little Green Men of WP

There are "green men" at Ohio's WP and they appear to be alien. We know. We have seen them. However, contrary to our ufological expectations, they are not "little." Figure 22 shows Dr. Ashcroft and myself with the Little Green Men. Figures 23 and 24 show examples of this colorful art.

During World War II from 1943 through 1946, part of WP served as a prisoner of war camp for between 200 to 400 German soldiers. Surprisingly, no records exist on the base about this camp or who the soldiers were. What evidence has been found elsewhere, indicates that the prisoners were Nazi enlisted men captured in North Africa and Italy, and transported to the United States after the POW camps in England became full. Not a single photograph of the prisoners has yet been found. Only recently was the location of the camp determined with any certainty. It was located on a hilltop at WF in what is now Area B. Many of the prisoners worked nearby at what was then Patterson Field, now Areas A and C.

These prisoners worked in supply warehouses loading and unloading rail cars, on the grounds and roads of the base, and served food in the mess halls serving the two Fields. One of the warehouses was converted into a dining hall for use by the prisoners. That warehouse is now Building 280, across the street from the headquarters building (856).

On the walls of the prisoner's mess hall, German POW artists had painted a huge mural depicting gargoyle-like folk figures out of Germanic folklore. One of these painted walls survives in a long narrow hallway of the mess hall, now converted to office use. On this wall, about 20 feet high by 70 feet long, appear large brightly-colored figures with eyelids and lips of red and the skin colored primarily green, with touches of blue and black—the "little green men" of WP.

The wall is now protected as the last surviving significant example of prisoner of war art on U.S. Air Force bases around the country. The wall was dedicated in 1992 by then base commander Col. William B. Orellans. It is hoped that the wall will be listed in the National Register of Historic Places.

Are these colorful figures really the source of the seemingly endless number of stories that have been shared by UFO researchers over the years about alien bodies that have been studied and stored at WP? Ashcroft, of course, isn't sure. However it is possible; he feels that they played some small part in the folklore that seems to have been created over the years concerning the presence of alien bodies on the base. As such, these figures— the colorful mural in Building 280

—deserve at least honorable mention in the comprehensive history of UFOlogy that most assuredly will one day be written by one of our descendants. And lest we and our ancestors forget, not all folklore is fiction.

The existing mural in Building 280, built in the 1943, was restored in the 1980s, he said. Dayton Art Institute experts have cleaned the painting as part of the preservation.

There Really is Proof at WP that UFOs Exist
Actual proof that UFOs exist is at WP. No one can argue.

One more item of interest at WP is a display that once was on the main corridor to the cafeteria. Everyone wants a copy but no can find much about it.

However I did photograph it. It is of interest because it displays various UFO cases and gives prosaic explanations for them. All except for one. This one is labeled unidentified.

Carey and Schmitt wrote that there is a UFO exhibit at the WP museum consisting of a single glass case that displays fake UFO photos, hoaxed artifacts, melted plastic, a cinder block and a contraption with radio tubes and wires, which paints a picture that the subject is a sideshow. It also had documents supporting the supposedly negative findings of the various investigations. The hallmark of the jaded exhibit is the contention that the AF never found any reliable evidence to support the theory that UFOs represent anything beyond our own technology.

The gist of the exhibit is that the result of many years of tax-funded investigation led to nothing.

However in contradiction to this, the exhibit did list one unidentified as shown in our Figure 25.

Thus, WP officially proved here that real UFOs truly exist.

Battelle
Evidence indicates that the Roswell and possibly other debris was sent from WP to Battelle.

Battelle headquartered in Columbus, Ohio, has likewise played a crucial role in UFO research. Respected throughout the world for its scientific expertise and reputation, it is the world's largest non-profit independent research and development organization. Accomplishments by Battelle scientists range from the development of the process of xerography that has revolutionized the entire world, the first optical digital recorder that paved the way for the first compact disc (CD), and the first generation of jet engines using titanium alloys. Additional advances included, Snopake, the first correction fluid; the armor plating for tanks in World War II; the fuel for the first nuclear submarine; development of the Universal Product Code; cruise control for automobiles; and many others.

It includes the fabrication of the uranium fuel rods for the first full-nuclear scale reactor, to the participation in the development of the atomic bomb during the Manhattan Project. It not only operates its own research facilities, it also has managed or co-managed many of the atomic age's top national laboratories on behalf of the US Department of Energy, including the Lawrence

Livermore, Oak Ridge, and Brookhaven National Laboratories. During the Cold War, Battelle personnel were a who's who of expertise in numerous scientific fields, including metallurgy, nuclear physics, and chemical and mechanical engineering. Moreover, the institute is adjacent to the main campus of OSU; one of the nation's largest universities, and this proximity allows its scientists to work closely with their counterparts at OSU.

Battelle also has a West Jefferson, Ohio, location, which operated a large hot cell facility and a research reactor. Reactor operations began in 1956, and ended in 1974. The reactor was defueled and partially dismantled in 1975.

Because of such expertise in metallurgy and other fields, Battelle's association with UFO phenomena has been long-term. Evidence exists that WP sent some of its debris to Battelle and to other Ohio institutions. Battelle had some of the world's best metallurgists and if anyone were an authority on metal it would be found here.

For example, under BB, Battelle conducted an extensive study of UFO phenomena. The results of this massive statistical analysis were presented in a report, *SR-14*. Even today, *SR-14* represents the largest such study ever undertaken and reigns as perhaps the most significant collection of evidence that UFO phenomena represent something real.

Much more detail will be presented about Battelle's role in BB and other UFO affairs that will be described in the following chapters.

I did indeed work at Battelle and documentation to prove this in included in this book (Figure 26). This was part time while working full time at OSU. My work included pharmacodynamic studies of such substances as Mirex, sold as an insecticide that was later banned. I worked on a Mirex Atlas Report and other such reports. My government Standard Form 50 shows that I worked for the DIA is shown in *Inside the Lightning Ball: Scientific Study of Lifelong UFO Experiencers*.

Figure 27 shows windows that may contain devices to prevent laser read-outs of the conversations in a room where BB studies were conducted at Battelle. They are reportedly in the area that housed a portion of BB.

Majestic 12 Robert Collins and Richard Doty
Robert Collins and Richard Doty, whose investigations into WP are discussed here, were also important actors in other well-known UFO investigations. Some of these included the Majestic 12 (MJ-12), Aviary, and similar UFO activities that are related to the material here.

Bill Jones and I had some direct experience with the Aviary, MJ-12, and similar events thrown in our face, when we interviewed a principal member of the Aviary Bob Collins (who was operative "Condor") without knowing it. We also interviewed investigators such as Stanton Friedman and gained insight into organizations related to government cover-ups.

We met Collins because of a visit I made to WP. In April 1993 while stationed on base there, I placed an advertisement in the *Skywriter*, the base newspaper, requesting government informants with UFO information to contact our local UFO organization or myself. Robert M. Collins answered the ad. Jones and I did not know it then, but Collins was the operative code-named "Condor." (Timothy Good has identified Collins as "Condor" and Doty as "Falcon.") Although I don't know who, but several Battelle people must have suspected something, for Jones said that some had warned him not to go.

Many, many years have been put into the MJ-12 investigations. It is known throughout the world and is an icon of UFO study. It is highly popular among some UFO conspiracy theorists and the concept has made frequent appearances in popular culture including television, film and, literature, such as the TV show, "UFO Cover-Up: Live!" MJ-12 is now generally believed to have been a hoax, but it has had a great influence upon the field and is a UFO legend.

MJ-12 is the code name of an alleged secret committee of scientists, military leaders, and government officials, which was formed in 1947 by an executive order by President Harry S. Truman to investigate UFO evidence in the aftermath of the Roswell incident and to facilitate the recovery and study of alien spacecraft. This concept originated in a series of supposedly leaked secret government documents first circulated by UFOlogists in 1984. This group has also been called MJ 12, MJ XII, Majority 12, Majic 12, Majestic Trust, M12, and similar names.

Collins told us that he and Doty are members of "The Aviary," a secret group said to be composed of military intelligence insiders, scientists, and government officials, all of whom were opposed to the government's policy of secrecy about UFOs.

Collins claimed to have inside information about many subjects, including Doty, Bennewitz, Moore, and other key MJ-12 figures. (We don't know why he contacted us, and are unable to judge how much of what he said is information and how much is disinformation; thus, we simply relate his account.)

With his information and additional evidence, we documented a paper trail of government cover-ups–including the Majestic 12, Bennewitz, and related affairs–as we found out first hand. In the first instance, a desire to lay hands on documents related to government UFO projects led to the ostracism of one UFOlogist and the physical and mental deterioration of another in what has come to be called the Bennewitz Affair.

In 1980 UFOlogist William Moore co-authored with Charles Berlitz the first book about Roswell, *The Roswell Incident*. That same year Moore received a call from a mysterious individual who gave his code name as "Falcon" and whom Moore thought was a high-ranking government official. Falcon said he represented "The Aviary." Moore was told that this group not only investigated UFOs, but that its members were actually in contact with extraterrestrials. (Falcon was later shown to be Richard C. Doty, who worked closely with Bob Collins. Although to make matters more complicated, some thought that Doty was a stand in for a real Falcon, who was a high ranking DIA official.)

Falcon brought Moore into contact with other members of the intelligence community, including Richard C. Doty, counterintelligence officer with the Air Force Office of Special Investigations. In return for divulging information, the Aviary wanted Moore to provide them with details about UFO researchers and organizations, and to work with Doty to influence an Albuquerque UFO investigator, Paul Bennewitz. Moore, hungry to gain insight into the government's knowledge of UFOs, obliged.[16]

Paul Bennewitz had nearly completed a PhD in physics and had founded the Thunder Scientific Corporation, a manufacturer of high-altitude testing equipment for New Mexico's Kirtland Air Force Base (Kirtland was associated with the green fireball sightings). Bennewitz had also designed a means of eavesdropping on the base's secure radio system. He later began to scan the entire radio spectrum for extraterrestrial signals, and he pestered government officials with his theories.

As Moore and Doty continued to exchange information, Doty began asking Moore for favors. One favor was that Moore supplies Bennewitz with misinformation about UFOs and extraterrestrials, which Moore agreed to do. The plan was to use the misinformation to distract Bennewitz from his monitoring of activity at Kirtland; in addition, it was hoped that Bennewitz would repeat the fictitious information and be discredited. Moore fed Bennewitz certain false documents. Perhaps because of the contents of the documents, Bennewitz's behavior became increasingly bizarre, and eventually he suffered a nervous breakdown. Moore's actions were later condemned by his colleagues as highly unethical, and having become an outcast, Moore eventually withdrew from the field of UFOlogy. Thus Doty, acting on behalf of the US government, was doubly effective: Bennewitz's credibility was ruined, and Moore (the first to bring Roswell to public attention) became a pariah who withdrew from UFOlogy.

After these events, another UFO researcher and filmmaker, Linda Howe, was contacted by a man named Richard Doty. Doty worked for AFOSI (the Air Force Office of Special Investigations). He told Howe the MJ-12 story was true and promised her film footage of an alien. Doty never delivered on this promise, something not surprising as subsequent events revealed Doty to be a skilled disinformation agent.

Before withdrawing from UFOlogy, however, Moore became a key player in the Majestic 12 affair. The earliest known use of the term "MJ-12" was as part of the Doty-Moore plan to discredit Bennewitz. Doty created a fraudulent Air Force Teletype to be given to Bennewitz by Moore. The Teletype mentioned Project Aquarius—supposedly a government venture related to UFOs—and said access to information about this and similar projects was controlled by "MJ-12." The Teletype was dated November 17, 1980; not long thereafter, the Majestic 12 board and the MJ-12 documents would become the subject of controversy and conspiracy theories.

The initial MJ-12 documents purported to include a classified order from President Harry Truman asking that a board be assembled to study the Roswell crash. Increasing amounts of paperwork emerged related to this board, and eventually the MJ-12 documents seemed to represent a treasure trove of material for UFOlogists. But although the documents are well known today, they have never been verified.[17] Indeed, most UFO researchers now think they are fake. However, the historical accuracy of some of the contents, and the huge volume of MJ-12 material, are evidence of an enormous amount of work that went into this hoax—assuming it is, in fact, a hoax.

According to the MJ-12 documents, in 1947 President Truman issued a classified order to Secretary of Defense James Forrestal. This order authorized Forrestal, after consultation with nuclear scientist Vannevar Bush, PhD, to establish a board of high-ranking experts to investigate the Roswell crash. This board, called Majestic 12, would eventually include researchers from institutions such as Harvard University and the Carnegie Institute; high-ranking military personnel from the Air Force, Army, and Navy, such as the Secretary of the Navy and the Chairman of the Joint Chiefs of Staff; and intelligence and security experts, such as individuals associated with the CIA.

Members of the board are said to have included the following: Vannevar Bush, PhD, president of Washington's Carnegie Institute; Rear Admiral Roscoe H. Hillenkoetter, the first CIA director; James Forrestal, Secretary of the Navy and the first Secretary of Defense; General Nathan Twining, Air Force Chief of Staff, Chairman of the Joint Chiefs of Staff, and head of Air Materiel Command at WP; General Hoyt Vandenberg, Air Force Chief of Staff who directed the Central Intelligence Group; General Robert M. Montague, commander of Fort Bliss who headed the nuclear Armed Forces Special Weapons Center; Rear Admiral Sidney Souers, first director of the Central Intelligence Group and first executive secretary of the National Security Council; Gordon Gray, Secretary of the Army, and intelligence and national security expert; Donald Menzel, PhD, Harvard astronomer and cryptologist; Detlev Bronk, PhD, who chaired the National Academy of Sciences; and Lloyd Berkner, PhD, executive secretary of the Joint Research and Development Board.

Also supposedly involved with this board were such celebrated scientists and leaders as Robert Oppenheimer, Albert Einstein, Karl Compton, Edward Teller, John von Neumann, Werner von Braun, Ronald Reagan, and Dwight Eisenhower. Some MJ-12 documents suggest that certain individuals on or involved with the board led double lives as skeptics while involved with UFO studies.

The first individuals to report the existence of the MJ-12 documents included Moore, UFOlogist and nuclear physicist Stanton Friedman, and television documentary producer Jamie Shandera. Moore had become friends with Shandera, and the two were collaborating on a project in 1984 when the first evidence of MJ-12 emerged: a roll of film that appeared in Shandera's mailbox.[18] Moore subsequently received from Doty some documents that mentioned Majestic 12, and Moore showed these papers to fellow UFO researchers Brad Sparks and Kal Korff.

Friedman later asked Moore and Shandera to examine newly declassified Air Force documents at the National Archives (NARA) repository. In the archives, Shandera and Moore discovered a document, dated July 14, 1954, in which Robert Cutler (National Security Council Executive Secretary and Eisenhower's National Security Advisor) told Nathan Twining (Air Force Chief of Staff) of a change of plans for a scheduled Majestic 12 briefing. However, this document, called the Cutler-Twining memo, lacked a distinctive catalog number, and this fact has led many to suspect it was forged and planted in the archives.

Meanwhile Moore engaged in behaviors that later called his credibility into question, such as the duping of Bennewitz. In 1982 Moore approached UFOlogist and former *National Enquirer* reporter Bob Pratt and asked him to collaborate on a novel to be called *MAJIK-12*. Pratt thought the MJ-12 papers were an outgrowth of this proposed novel. Moore also concocted a plan to create counterfeit government UFO documents as a way to induce former military officers to reveal UFO information; in 1983 Moore sought UFOlogist Brad Sparks' help with this plan, but Sparks refused and advised Moore not to move forward. Moore also approached Friedman about creating bogus Roswell documents, again with the idea of drawing in witnesses.

Moore denied creating the MJ-12 papers, and he came to think the person who had created them had set him up. Like the hoax associated with Arnold that some think it was set up specifically to discredit him because of his importance to the UFO subject, this might have been implemented to discredit Moore for the same reason. Possibly something like this happened to Albert Bender, who started one of the first UFO organizations that became a parent to MUFON and many others.

Pratt always thought the documents were a hoax perpetrated either by Moore himself, or by the Air Force Office of Special Investigations (AFOSI) with Doty using Moore as a conduit. Friedman, however, investigated the historical and technical details in the MJ-12 documents and concluded there were no grounds for dismissing the authenticity of some of them. In addition, copies of some MJ-12 documents were mailed anonymously to British researcher Timothy Good in 1987; Good reproduced them in his 1989 book, *Above Top Secret*, but he later decided the documents were fraudulent.

At the 2007 MUFON Symposium, Brad Sparks presented a paper describing the MJ-12 documents as a part of the disinformation campaign by Moore, Doty, and other AFOSI personnel; he based this theory on files from 1981 that Pratt gave to MUFON.

Various additional references have been made to a secret government investigatory group having an MJ-12 type of function. For example, according to Michael Wolf, PhD, a group calling itself the Majestic 12 Special Studies Group was meeting at Battelle in the 1990s. General Exon referred to a secretive UFO controlling committee of high-ranking officers and civilians called "The Unholy Thirteen," which some think referred to Majestic-12. Canadian radio engineer Wilbert B. Smith had the Canadian embassy arrange contact with US officials and was briefed by Robert Sarbacher, PhD, a physicist working for the Defense Department Research and Development Board. This board may have been the department that cleared Major Donald Keyhoe (a former Marine, a Charles Lindbergh aide, and one of the country's earliest and most respected UFOlogists) to publish some articles. Some of Smith's material indicated that a committee of high-ranking people, headed by Vannevar Bush, existed.

Many UFOlogists now think the MJ-12 documents were part of an intentional disinformation campaign by individuals associated with the US military or government, although it leaves one to wonder why they expended so much research and effort if there was no evidence for UFO phenomena.

Regardless of their authenticity, Majestic 12 and the MJ-12 documents have become a significant part of the popular culture that surrounds UFOs. For example, such authors as Stanton Friedman and Whitley Strieber have written books about Majestic 12, and it has been mentioned in TV shows such as *The X-Files* and *Dark Skies*, as well as in video games.

In summary, Carey and Schmitt wrote that they had heard stories about a large portion of the base being underground with bunkers, tunnels large enough for trucks, manmade hills in Area B, and large Hangers with no windows. They said clusters of ventilation pipes coming out of the ground with no buildings around them, and large open areas with heavy metal doors going into the side of a hill had been observed. They were told that the Propulsion Research and Development building had a walkway/ramp that lead to an underground door, and also heard about underground-refrigerated rooms.

In looking for these things on base, I do not recall seeing any heavy metal doors going into the side of the hill. The largest doors I recall were those going into the Avionics Lab, these were large enough for trucks and had a strong built up ramp. Possibly this is the place where the trucks enter the tunnel system.

They described large Hangers with no windows. We saw hanger-type buildings with no windows.

They also mentioned clusters of ventilation pipes coming out of the ground by themselves and we did see several small buildings or structures by themselves in Area B.

We also found suggestive evidence of underground vaults north of Building 620, such as seeing deep digging in that area, as others had reported that they had heard about.

We also saw the Building 18 and 23 complexes and considered that there might be an underground vault system with a tunnel connecting Buildings 18 and 23.

We also saw and drove around a group of buildings that might have included Hanger 18.

We were in the fabled "Blue Room," saw it's intense security, and attended a UFO meeting there.

We found proof at WP that UFOs exist and photographed it.

******

CHAPTER FOUR

PROJECT BLUE BOOK

Blue Book (BB) was one of a series of studies the United States Air Force made of unidentified flying objects (UFOs). It began in 1952, and a termination order was given for the study in December 1969. All activity under its auspices was reported to have ceased in January 1970.

It was the most massive undertaking associated with UFO study. By its end, it had collected around 13,000 reports.[19]

We've investigated and conducted interviews with WP employees, people who worked for BB, families of former BB personnel, listened to taped interviews with directors and others involved, visited WP, Roswell, and Battelle, and discussed it with many people who were involved with the project.

Its headquarters were in WP. Although BB is well known, very few people have visited its headquarters.

In Walter Webb's time the Blue Book headquarters was located in building 263, as he described in "Inside Building 263: A visit to Blue Book."

> Few UFOlogists ever penetrated the inner walls of Blue book. Jennie Zeidman, former student and research assistant to J. Allen Hynek recalled her visits to the project in the March/April 1991 issue of *IUR*. During the early 1950s, she accompanied Hynek about once a month on his trips to Blue Book. Leonard H. Stringfield was another civilian researcher able to get inside the corridors of the Air Technical Intelligence Center (ATIC) at WP.

Still another visitor was the author, Walter Webb, and Donald Keyhoe has been through its magic portals. Thus only about five UFOlogists have ever entered its sacred gateways.

But Jones and I were lucky enough to have been inside. Although the old building 263 is no longer there, we visited the modern office that replaced it, as mentioned when we discussed the Blue Room. Inquiring about the history of BB, we asked the WP archivist, Dr. Bruce Ashcroft to identify the building BB had been located in. He replied that Project Sign, the earlier UFO study, had been located in Building 287 and later moved to Building 263, possibly in 1953. It was later moved to Building 858 and then 275. All of these buildings except Building 858 have since been torn down. The new building that we visited was what the old BB complex evolved into. The new building which houses the operation that included BB is the NASIC building (856) as discussed previously.

In this investigation, we interviewed many people including Jennie Zeidman, who worked for it, Dr. Bruce Ashcroft Battelle archivist, and numerous people who knew about it. We found out much about not only its outside appearance, but its inner workings.

BB had two chief goals:

To determine whether UFOs were a threat to national security, and to scientifically analyze the collected UFO-related data. Although it has been presented this way, actually it never had the goal of determining whether UFO phenomena were real. However that, of course, would be the most logical study and might be a needed predecessor to determining whether the phenomenon was a threat to national security.

Many thousands of UFO reports were collected, analyzed and filed. But, because the Condon Report concluded there was nothing anomalous about UFOs, BB was ordered shut down in December 1969.

Several people have headed the project:

In March 1952, Captain Edward J. Ruppelt was appointed head of Blue Book. He implemented a number of changes that vastly improved Blue Book over its predecessors. He streamlined the way in which UFOs were reported to try to alleviate the stigma and ridicule associated with UFO witnesses. He effected the development of a standard questionnaire for UFO witnesses, so that the data could be used in statistical analysis. He contracted with the Battelle Memorial Institute to create the questionnaire and computerize the data. Using case reports and the computerized data, Battelle then conducted a massive scientific and statistical study of all Air Force UFO cases, completed in 1954 which became known as *"Project Blue Book Special Report No. 14"* (*SR-14*). Hynek developed the Close Encounter categories. Ruppelt left Blue Book in 1953.

After Ruppelt, the project began to change and its scientific methodology declined.

In March 1954, Captain Charles Hardin became head of Blue Book, but had little interest in investigations. Captain Ruppelt said that Harden thought that anyone who even showed a slight interest in UFOs was crazy.

In 1956, Captain George Gregory took over as Blue Book's director. He took an even firmer anti-UFO stance than Hardin. Under him, little or no investigation of UFO reports occurred. He developed ways to classify UFOs such that they more or less disappeared.

In 1958, Major Robert J. Friend became the head of Blue Book. He made a few attempts to reverse the direction Blue Book had taken since 1954, but these were frustrated by a lack of assistance and funding.

In August 1963, Major Hector Quintanilla took over as Blue Book's head. He continued the debunking efforts. Under his direction, Blue Book lost all credibility.

Predecessors
BB is WP's best-known government agency for UFO investigation, but it has had several predecessors. Historically, these agencies date back to the first sighting reports. And some of the initial investigations were done using scientific methodology.

In the beginning when UFOs first appeared, the Air Force did not even exist yet. General Forrestal set up the initial project, which is referred to simply as Project Saucer. This was followed by Project Sign, which was created in September 1947.

Concerning government investigation, several sources report that studies started at the beginning of 1947 as reviewed in my book, *UFOs Today*. These were scientific studies, done by such people as Col. Howard M. McCoy, who later was heavily involved with Project Sign. Dr. Michael Swords reported that in the summer of 1947, UFO accounts were coming from everywhere but investigation, which involved WP, the Pentagon, and the FBI, was disorganized. In addition, little interest came from the higher echelons. The Pentagon first involved WP about mid-July. About July 28-29, McCoy was ordered to send a top-level assessment to eventually go to the Pentagon. In September 1947 an investigatory setup was ordered. This evolved into Project Sign, which became official in January 1948. At that time (and maybe now) the government agencies did not act in unison–the WP group took a pro–extraterrestrial position, whereas the Pentagon took the opposing side and the Washington DC group eventually won out.

In January 1948, the Air Force officially established its first group, Project Sign, to study the UFO reports that flooded in from around the country in the aftermath of the sightings by Arnold and others. At that time the government considered UFOs to be possibly extraterrestrial. For example, Dr. Ashcroft gave me a copy of Project Sign's "U.S. Air Force. Air Materiel Command. (1949a). Unidentified aerial objects: Project "Sign." Technical Report no. F-TR-2274-IA" Amid many other theories, it discussed the possibility that UFOs were from another planet.

These investigators took a scientific stance, did real investigation, and discussed the possibilities the phenomena could encompass.

A few quotes from "Unidentified Aerial Objects Project 'Sign,'" show its serious investigation:

> A special study has been initiated with the Rand Project in accordance with Air Corps Letter…dtd 21 July 1948 to present information that would serve to evaluate the remote possibility that some of the observed objects may be space ships or satellite vehicles.
> A certain proportion of incidents appear to be real aircraft though of unconventional configuration.
> Consideration has been given to the possibility that these unidentified aircraft represent scientific developments beyond the level of knowledge attained in this country.

The last sentence on page nine says, "Another possibility is that these aerial objects are visitors from another planet. The commentary of this possibility by Dr. James Lipp of the Rand Project in Appendix II, indicates that this solution of the mystery connected with the sighting of unidentified flying." Here the sentence ends. Page ten is blank.

A third classification includes extraterrestrial objects. It first mentions meteors, then it mentions:

> 2. Animals: Although the objects as described act more like animals than anything else, there are few reliable reports on extra-terrestrial animals.

3. Space Ships: the following considerations pertain:

a. If there is an extraterrestrial civilization which can make such objects as are reported then it is most probable that its development is far in advance of ours. This argument can be supported on probability arguments alone without recourse to astronomical hypotheses.

b. Such a civilization might observe that on Earth as we now have atomic bombs and are fast developing rockets…Since the acts of mankind most easily observed from a distance are A-bomb explosions, we should expect some relation … between the time of A-bomb explosions the time at which the space-ships are seen.

The report went into great detail on how to obtain good observations, on the importance of getting other witnesses, and similar information. It also made a very detailed assessment of the standard prosaic explanations.

Many Air Force intelligence officers who investigated the initial saucer reports from the summer of 1947 through 1948 treated all of the sightings, including Arnold's, seriously. Arnold's sighting was included as unexplained in a top-secret intelligence memorandum compiled by Air Force intelligence during the late fall of 1948, "Estimate of the Situation" report.

This "Estimate of the Situation," concluded that "based on the evidence, that UFOs were alien spacecraft, or to put it in the terms of the time, "interplanetary craft."

All traces of this report seem to have disappeared.

Making them disappear was easier in those days, before the electronic media. But this is certainly strong evidence of cover-up.

However, in 1948 General Hoyt Vandenberg rejected the Air Force's conclusion. In so doing, he established an Air Force policy that the "interplanetary hypothesis" was to be rejected. Many knowledgeable investigators hotly contested this rejection. Although people viewed this as a generic government cover-up, there was division among government agencies. There seemed to be a hidden Washington agency in control that possibly acted because it had prior knowledge about UFO phenomena, or that wanted a cover-up for other reasons. In addition, the UFO phenomena became the providence of the military, rather than of the scientific sphere, which resulted in its being given security classifications, such that information was withheld from and false information given to the public.

By February 1949, Project Sign was dissolved and its staff generally replaced. A new project was formed, Project Grudge, so called because high-ranking Air Force officers disagreed with Project Sign's conclusions that extraterrestrials could be behind the UFO sightings. The scientific Sign staff was replaced with those who viewed the phenomena as prosaic.

A new organization that replaced them, Project Grudge, was substantially more skeptical than the Project Sign crew, and Project Grudge was more representative of the government's new UFO-debunking policy.

In his *Report on Unidentified Flying Objects* (1956), Captain Edward Ruppelt, former head of BB, said Project Grudge had a two-fold program of UFO debunking: (1) explaining away every UFO report, and (2) saying the Air Force had solved all UFO sightings. Project Grudge personnel expected this dual policy to end UFO reports.

But because eyewitness testimony often could not easily be explained away, and because Air Force personnel could not answer all questions, the military contracted Battelle. In 1952, the Air Force's UFO study project underwent another reorganization, and the name was changed to BB. This new project typically included supervisors such as Ruppelt, four other officers, two aviators, and two civilians, as well as three scientists who'd worked full-time on the earlier Project Bear, and others who'd worked part-time.

In organization, these projects were under the Technical Intelligence Division of the AMC department at WF (later WP) that took control of Project Sign and began work on 23 January 1948.

Because of continued UFO sightings, USAF Director of Intelligence Maj. Gen. Charles P. Cabell ordered a new UFO project in 1952. Project Blue Book became the chief Air Force effort to examine the UFO phenomenon throughout the 1950s and 1960s. The work of identifying and explaining UFOs continued to fall on AMC. With a small staff, ATIC tried to persuade the public that UFOs were not extraordinary. Projects Sign, Grudge, and Blue Book set the tone for the official US Government position regarding UFOs for the next 30 years.[20]

Although Ruppelt did an excellent job with BB against the odds, the above statement is very telling in itself. If its employees did not have the security clearances, they did not know what was really going on and BB was obviously set up that way.

It appeared that BB was being directed by an agency, probably in the Pentagon. This was where the good reports went, which shows that some agency was investigating these.

In January 14, 1953, the Robertson Panel was convened. This panel was comprised of a group of scientists who were presented as examining the UFO evidence collected by BB. But as described under the Pentacle Memo, they didn't have the full data. This panel expressed negative findings and decided to debunk the UFO phenomena. This marked the end of any semblance of real investigation by BB.

But it appeared that some agency was working behind the scene that was interested in collecting real data, and trying to pass BB off as buffoonery.

In conclusion, although one of the most common ideas about UFOs is that BB was a government agency that investigated UFOs and found nothing to them, after conducting research and talking to WP personnel, Jones and I think that Blue Book and similar projects were public relations ventures designed to thwart popular interest in UFOs. Projects Sign, Grudge, and BB were all likely housed at WP because it had the expertise to analyze UFO data, and had participated in this from the beginning. The best data did not, however, go directly to BB. It more likely went to specialists and scientists in secured areas and who worked in fields related to the specific nature of the information. What this means is that some agency was actually collecting the good accounts, as Hynek reported. Kenneth Arnold's experience, discussed in *UFOs Today*, suggested that such upper echelon agencies were generally housed in Washington DC.

However despite its general direction, some employees tried to make it a truly scientific organization, such as Ruppelt and Hynek. And one of its studies—that done by in secret by Battelle, *SR-14*—is probably the most important scientific UFO study ever made. Its findings indicate that some UFO phenomena are real, but the government massaged these findings.

Figure 29 shows the AMC building. This organization housed such projects as Sign and Blue Book.

One AF activity was to try to back engineer UFOs (Figure 30). This still goes on today, such as by the Robert Bigelow organization. Although much has been said about disclosure and many, many books and Internet postings have been made, it appears that it really has not happened. There is not a Flying Saucer in every garage. No country has taken over the world with Flying Saucers.

******

CHAPTER FIVE

THE PENTACLE MEMO

The Pentacle Memorandum has been said to be the most significant existing documentation of the US government's approach to UFO phenomena (Appendix 1). Its importance is that it uncovered BB's secret study, *SR-14*, to be described in more detail later.

Even today, *SR-14* represents the largest such study ever undertaken, it appears to be the only one publicized that has scientific merit, and it reigns as providing the most significant evidence that UFO phenomena represent something real.

The only way anyone found out about this study is through the Pentacle Memo (January 9, 1953). Its importance can be shown by its list of distributees. These were people in very high positions. One was the director of Battelle. Another may have been the head of project Stork. The others were high-level managers and supervisors. Battelle must have viewed this project as significant to have such highly placed employees listed.

They were concerned about whether the Robertson Panel, a panel of scientists that the government set up to render a verdict on the meaning of the *SR-14* results, was being misled. Thus they presented themselves as against government policy, such as the decision to convene the Robertson Panel before *SR-14* had been completed. They bravely stood up for the principles of science against government higher-ups.

SR-14's significance is not only historic, but even today, it remains the only large and serious scientific study of UFO phenomena. It was classified as top secret. The first evidence for the public notice came through the Pentacle Memorandum, and if there were no Pentacle Memo, it is likely that the study would remain unknown.

What is important about this is that it showed that the government was conducting a secret study within BB that even BB employees, such as Dr. Hynek, did not know about.

It was a crucial point along the paper trail documenting government UFO investigation and was discovered by French UFOlogist Jacques Vallée. The document was dated five days before the CIA-sponsored Robertson Panel about UFOs convened. Vallée thought the American government had substantial UFO information, and he speculated that some of this data was so highly protected that it was not supplied to Blue Book personnel or to the Robertson Panel. For example, he notes a passage in the Pentacle Memorandum about what can and cannot be discussed with Robertson panelists. This, of course, turned out to be true.

This once-classified memo began with a recommendation, based on analyses of several thousand UFO reports, to the ATIC regarding future methods of handling the UFO problem. This opening paragraph clearly established that prior to the 1953 Robertson Panel meeting in Washington, massive numbers of UFO reports had been analyzed on behalf of the US government—and that this information was classified. Howard Cross, who signed the Memo, then recommended that the Air Force should conduct a controlled experiment by which reliable physical data could be obtained (Cross's design is similar to that later used by Dr. Harley Rutledge, and with government funding, in general, it would make an excellent research project).

In it, Cross recommended that test areas be set up, such that scientists could make reasonably certain conclusions concerning the importance of the problem of UFOs. Witness reactions could then be studied as a control–which is a normal experimental design for scientific study.

However the information in this Memo shows that this study went way beyond the official mission described for it–designing a questionnaire for UFO reports and a statistical study of UFO observations. It included large study areas, cameras, possible aerial work to simulate UFO activity to be used as controls, and much else. When this much more than the original set up was called for, it is not unreasonable, that debris might have been studied also.

One of the signers, Cross, spoke for the study. He was also a metallurgist. I discovered a possible reason why Cross held such an important place in both metal and UFO research. A Battelle employee told me from that time that Cross likely headed Battelle's Project Stork under which *SR-14* was done.

The excerpt below shows how massive and complex this intended study was:

> This area, or areas, should have observation posts with complete visual skywatch, with radar and photographic coverage, plus all other instruments necessary or helpful in obtaining positive and reliable data on everything in the air over the area. A very complete record of the weather should also be kept during the time of the experiment. Coverage should be so complete that any object in the air could be tracked, and information as to its altitude, velocity, size, shape, color, time of day, etc. could be recorded. All balloon releases or known balloon paths, aircraft flights, and flights of rockets in the test area should be known to those in charge of the experiment. Many different types of aerial activity should be secretly and purposefully scheduled within the area. . . . This should make possible reasonably certain conclusions concerning the importance of the problem of "flying saucers."

The Pentacle Memorandum was addressed to WP's Miles E. Goll, head of intelligence analysis for the Air Materiel Command. In the memo, Cross asserted that he had the authority to speak in an official capacity on behalf of Battelle about its UFO work for the government. Cross also insisted that WP delay the work of the CIA's UFO study group, the Robertson Panel, until after Battelle completed *SR-14*, the statistical study of UFOs commissioned by the Air Force was completed. Because Battelle wanted to keep secret its authorship of *SR-14*, it requested that the organization's name be withheld.

Even more interesting I also learned that on October 2, 1951, in Columbus, Ohio, a Battelle physicist named Howard Cross reported viewing a UFO. It appeared as a bright oval with a clipped tail, and it flew straight and level before fading into the distance after one minute.[21] After uncovering this information, and after discussions with Battelle employees, I suspect that this

Howard Cross is the H. C. Cross of the Pentacle Memorandum (some told me that this sighting was over Battelle). I further speculated that if Cross made the UFO report, the Pentacle Memorandum could have also represented his individual thinking. Cross's sighting and the fact that he reported it suggest to me that he took the UFO phenomena seriously.

In addition, at a time when many scientists were skeptical about UFOs, in the Pentacle Memorandum Cross seems sincerely concerned about valid analyses of UFO data. I think he may have been torn between his own thinking about UFO phenomena and the government's official stance to ridicule it. Thus, because of his own direct interest, he may have had substantial input into the excellent analysis that eventually was published as *SR-14*.[22]

Because of Cross's importance and because he seems to have made a UFO report himself, I asked Jennie Zeidman, who worked with these people, what she remembered about him. She thought he was the author of the Pentacle Memorandum. She said he was "all business." He was a gruff, physically imposing man who would often bang on tables to make a point. As a young woman, she found him frightening; thus, he was an ideal guardian of secret information.[23]

After these investigations in regard to Cross, I made several inferences. First, the Pentacle Memorandum and my own research indicate that Cross was in a supervisory position in relation to UFO studies. Thus, Cross had "clout." Second, Cross had insisted that WP delay the work of the Robertson Panel until Battelle could complete its Air Force commissioned statistical study of UFOs (*SR-14*). Cross's insistence and probable reporting of a UFO sighting together suggest to me that Cross was a scientist concerned with a true examination of the data. His suggestions for further study in his Pentacle Memorandum showed a concern for scientific truth. The CIA consulted with Cross and concurred with him on the need for delay; ultimately, however, both the CIA and Battelle were overruled by the Air Force.[24]

Hence, I think that Cross had a crucial impact upon UFO study, even though the government covered this up. Thus, evidence exists to suggest Battelle also participated in government-sponsored UFO metallurgical studies. Given the caliber of the Battelle staff (the world's top physicists and metallurgists), its security, its proximity to WP, and its state-of-the-art equipment, it is reasonable to think that if metallic debris from UFOs existed, it would have been studied at Battelle.

Out of all the studies and controversy about the UFO phenomenon, only this one published study by the government has shown scientific merit. In addition, its findings were positive.

Battelle's *SR-14* is probably the most important scientific UFO study ever made, and its findings indicate that UFO phenomena are real, but the government massaged these findings.

Cross signed and likely authored, the January 9, 1953, Pentacle Memorandum, and possibly worked on the missing, mystery *Project Blue Book Report No. 13*.

Who is listed on the Pentacle Memo and what are their backgrounds?
The distributees/authors of the Pentacle Memo were people in high positions. One was the director of Battelle. Another may have been the head of project Stork. Thus Battelle must have viewed this

project as significant to have such highly placed employees listed. Not only that but they were staking their reputations in this protest against government policies. They were concerned about whether the Robertson Panel was being misled or misused.

Although much has been speculated about these people, the list shown in Figure 31 would be the best researched because it was done by Battelle scientists who knew the people and their positions.

Battelle later did a study of the Pentacle Memo authors. Those listed on the Pentacle Memorandum were Bertram Thomas, L. R. Jackson, William Reid, Perry Rieppal, V. W. Ellsey, R. J. Lund, Howard Cross, and Art Westerman. All of these individuals are said to have worked for Project Stork. These people were predominately metallurgists or physical scientists.

Project Blue Book had two main objectives: to determine whether UFOs pose a threat to the security of the US; and, second, to determine whether UFOs show any unique scientific information or advanced technology that could contribute to scientific or technical research. In accomplishing these objectives, Project Blue Book endeavored to identify and explain all UFO sightings reported to the Air Force.[25]

An unpublished draft of the article (Appendix II), that was later published as the "Pentacle Letter and the Battelle UFO Project," listed the following objectives of the Battelle study:

> In December 1951...Ruppelt got the go-ahead to go to "Project Bear" (Battelle) and contract with them for help. Battelle was to help in 3 ways:
>
> 1. Employ a psychologist to assess what one might legitimately be able to expect from an observer's observational abilities and memory accuracy, and design a form to maximize the accuracy and data-richness desired in this research.
>
> 2. Do a statistical study of all available UFO reports; break them down according to about 100 variables which would be extractable from the new questionnaires, and place these on IBM punch cards for rapid sorting and pattern analysis.
>
> 3. Be on call for standing advice, ex.: better ideas about cases or data gathering, plus employment of an astronomer for continuous assessment of astronomical alternatives.

The contract with Battelle was for help in the three areas listed above. This information was left out of the article that was published later.

But strangely, in general the investigators were metallurgists and physical scientists. I found quite a mystery here right away and this was that their specialties did not seem consonant with the Battelle study's objectives. Why did they need metallurgists? Did they examine metal too?

And although the study fulfilled the objectives such as the use of a psychologist and those to do a statistical study, it recommended much else such as planning and setting up a complex, expensive study area.

This is why the backgrounds of these scientists are of interest. It is also an aid to understanding the study. These were also high-level people, scientists with excellent metallurgical and physical science credentials, and who worked at the managerial and supervisory level at Battelle, as shown in the Battelle list of their backgrounds.

The Battelle list in the illustration shows information about these people in the reference book, *American Men of Science*. A listing in this prestigious book showed that they had high credentials, had done significant research, and had publications.

Although it did not sound like it later, Battelle must have thought it to be an important study because, as mentioned, even the president of Battelle was among the distributees.

Bertram David Thomas, the first on the list, was once the president of Battelle. He died on February 15, 2004, at the age of 100. Thomas joined the research staff of Battelle in 1934, established the Institute's Division of Chemical Research in 1939, was named assistant director in 1940, and became acting director in 1942. As president between 1957 until his retirement in 1968, he greatly enlarged the organization and enhanced its scientific stature and international presence. During his tenure, Battelle also opened research centers in Frankfurt, Germany, Geneva, Switzerland, and Beirut, Lebanon, and a marine laboratory at Sequim Bay, Washington, and the Seattle Research Center. In 1965 Battelle was awarded the contract for the management of the Atomic Energy Commission's Hanford, Washington, Laboratory. He was also instrumental in establishing the Korean Institute of Science and Technology. He was self-supporting from the age of twelve, graduated from high school at the age of sixteen, and was hired as a bookkeeper at the Pacific Car and Foundry Company in Renton. He received a B.S. in chemistry from the University of Washington in 1928, with a triple major in chemistry, mathematics, and physics, and a PhD in chemistry in 1933. Thomas's field of specialization involved ways of concentrating chemicals.[26]

Loyd Jackson was a metallurgical engineer, who worked on titanium, ceramics, sheet metals, alloys, and aircraft materials. He was a Battelle Research Supervisor, and who was interested in developing engineering materials and applying physics to industrial research.

William Reid was a supervisor for rocket research and is said by some to have written the Pentacle Memo. He may have been the head of Project Stork. His specialty was fuel engineering. He was a supervising engineer, assistant supervisor for combustion research and studied the utilization of solid fuels, fundamentals of combustion processes, the viscosity of coal-ash slags, low-temperature carbonization of coal, the physical properties of coal ash at high temperatures, the effect of the addition of chemicals to solid fuels on combustion characteristics. He was also a chief technology officer, often worked on power sources and fuel cells, and had worked with Boron.

Perry J. Rieppal, who was in welding engineering, and completed his graduate work at Cornell University and the University of Buffalo. He was employed by Battelle from 1943-1977 as Engineer and Manager of Metals Research. He was a welding specialist and one of his papers was titled "Welding Tantalum For High-Temperature Systems." He had worked in welding technology at Curtiss-Wright Corporation in New York, was an assistant supervisor of welding research and won the Lincoln gold medal award of the American Welding Society.[27]

Arthur Westerman, a metallurgist, was a co-worker with Cross. He worked in alloy steel metallurgy, mechanical metallurgy, metallurgy of all kinds of high-temperature alloys, and metallurgy of new light metals.

Howard C. Cross
I discovered a probable reason why Cross held an important place in both metal and UFO research. A Battelle employee told me from that time that Cross likely headed Battelle's Project Stork under which *SR-14* was done.

Cross was the Battelle point person in metallurgy research and in Battelle's later UFO studies. Evidence also exists that Cross was Battelle's chief titanium metallurgist, who has been referred to as "Research Director."

Moreover, Cross was far more than merely a metallurgist; he had extraordinary "clout" and power for his position. Bragalia wrote that his name appeared in unexpected places. For example, Cross interacted with the heads of the Office of Naval Research, the CIA, and Air Force Intelligence. He had close relationships with those in the uppermost echelons of the American government on UFO matters. For example, Cross had a working relationship with the CIA and was visited by the CIA's Chief of Scientific Intelligence, H. Marshall Chadwell, PhD, on official matters.[28] Cross was closely associated with the National Advisory Committee on Aeronautics (NACA, the predecessor of NASA). Vannevar Bush, PhD, chaired NACA, and Cross may have worked with him. According to another document uncovered, in 1952 Cross investigated debris from a crashed flying object in Virginia.

In the late 1940s, Cross helped direct Battelle's metals alloy research into such materials sciences areas as titanium, stainless steel, and chromium. Yet he was also involved in directing Battelle's government-sponsored UFO research. One would wonder why a materials engineer studying exotic alloys would later help lead Battelle's government-funded studies on UFOs, which involved making a questionnaire and statistical studies.

As the message in Figure 32 shows, Cross retired in 1969 and was listed as Assistant Coordination Director and as Senior Fellow. It appeared that he was brought back as a consultant by Gus Simpson after his retirement.

Many have wondered who headed the study.

Vernon W. Ellsey I was told that one of his duties was to carry information from WP to Battelle. He was an author of, *Environmental considerations for oil shale development*,[29] and is listed as a Project Technical Coordinator in the Battelle technical Memorandum, "Adhesive Bonding of Nickel and Nickel-Base Alloys."[30]

Richard J. Lund was a geologist, mineral economist, and director of the Miscellaneous Minerals Division of the. War Production.

Another document (Figure 33) is from the Battelle's research into *SR-14*. It says that Lund,

Jackson, and Cross were at the same level in the Battelle hierarchy.

Westerman spent about one-fourth of his time on BB work.

Below this it says that someone was Stork. Perhaps this refers to a John, maybe Perry John Rieppal Goll to whom the Memo was sent, was a project manager.

It appears that Westerman thought that Cross was a writer of some report probably the Pentacle Memo and that he was strong on internal communication.

Ruppelt was a decent researcher and didn't get in their way.
Westerman did not like Jackson.

This was from an interview with Westerman by Mark Rodeghier of CUFOS.

It's strange that scientists, who appeared to have been predominantly metallurgists (rather than statisticians or others involved with information processing), were selected for the statistical work that lead to *SR-14*. Similarly designing a questionnaire would seem to be out of the field of expertise for these engineers. This suggests that the metallurgical analysis of artifacts may have been a component of the UFO research conducted at Battelle.

There have been many questions about the ranking of the Pentacle Memo distributees. The list shown in (Figure 34) may provide an official answer to some of these questions. The members are listed on the Battelle Contract 1951-1954 except for Westerman. In this list, it appears that Cross (Associate Coordination Director) worked under Jackson (the Coordination Director) during the time of the *SR-14*. However the earlier document said the Lund, Jackson, and Cross worked at the same level. For example the AMOS gave Cross as Supervisor of the Metal Division. They may have had different positions at different times, or there may have been internal changes at Battelle. Thomas later became President. Rieppal was the Division Chief.

History
The Stork projects were not necessarily tied to Battelle UFO work.[31] UFOs were originally investigated by the organization already studying foreign technology in Battelle, and in the ATIC/FTD divisions of WP. This work was already highly classified, and it is where the best reports would have gone. Blue Book and similar projects were likely set up to collect civilian information and influence public opinion about UFOs, but the main examination was done elsewhere.

Zeidman thought that because the Battelle study. *SR-14,* was top secret, it was organized as objective research. (However, she added that the government ensured that the *SR-14* analyses later presented to the public both met with government standards and showed the negative findings the government wanted.) Zeidman said that if WP did have alien artifacts, they would probably have been analyzed at Battelle.

Zeidman and several others whom I interviewed thought Arthur Westerman, a metallurgist who had published scholarly research papers on alloys, might also have worked with alien artifacts. He co-authored studies with Cross and was listed as "H. C. Cross/A. D. Westerman" on the Pentacle Memorandum. Moreover, some UFOlogists thought Westerman might have been involved with the Robertson Panel. Zeidman told me she made a substantial effort to obtain information from him, but he for the most part "didn't crack" (he divulged nothing formally to her or to other investigators). However, she quoted him as once saying, "We were concerned." She interpreted his comment to mean that the Pentacle Group was open to the possibility that ET might well be involved. This in a way might be a smoking gun, because why would they be concerned if there were nothing to it? [32]

Bill Jones, who worked with Westerman at Battelle, said that he had questioned Westerman, but he had not disclosed anything suggesting that he worked with alien artifacts.[33]

The Pentacle Memo Controversy

The Pentacle Memo is controversial, however and others did not necessarily share Vallée's view of its importance.

One article basically presented an opposing view of the importance that Vallee attributed to the Pentacle Memo: "The Pentacle Letter and the Battelle UFO Project" by Jennie Zeidman and Mark Rodeghier. Zeidman, Michael Swords, and Mark Rodeghier had done research on the Pentacle letter in the 1990s at Battelle.

However the article downplayed the Pentacle Memo's importance. In today's world this idea might be questioned, however.

I received a typed version of this article, which appears to be a first draft of the article, "The Pentacle Letter and the Battelle UFO Project." The draft article I received was titled "The Pentacle Letter" by Jennie Zeidman, Michael Swords, and Mark Rodeghier. There were several differences between this article and the one that was later published.

Even before, "The Pentacle Letter" was written there was first a handwritten draft. Both appeared to be preliminary drafts of "The Pentacle Letter and the Battelle UFO Project," they published in the *IUR*. There were differences among all three drafts and what was said and not said may give some more information about the study.

This article, "The Pentacle Letter and the Battelle UFO Project" by Jennie Zeidman and Mark Rodeghier, provides some background for the Pentacle Memo and the later interpretation of it. Some excerpts are below:

> In his 1992 book, *Forbidden Science* Jacques Vallée devotes much attention, and a great deal of emotion, to a letter he found in J. Allen Hynek's papers on June 18, 1967. Dated January 9, 1953, this letter, written by someone to whom Vallée assigns the code name "Pentacle," is classified SECRET.
> This letter so affected the young Vallée that he writes it "was the main reason for my return to Europe in 1967," In his view the Pentacle document amounts to damning evidence that there probably was in 1953, and still is, a secret government study of UFOs. The letter discusses how Pentacle and his team have analyzed "several thousands of reports" and goes on to suggest that

an "agreement between Project Stork and ATIC, Wright-Patterson should be reached as to what can and cannot be discussed at [the Robertson panel meeting]. . . ." Pentacle also recommends that an experiment be conducted so that "reliable physical data can be obtained" about UFOs, an experiment which would involve "[m]any different types of aerial activity . . . secretly and purposely scheduled within the area."

On first reading, this material sounds potentially sensational, and Vallée and colleagues pressured Hynek to confront the author of the letter to demand an explanation.

In the epilogue to *Forbidden Science*, Vallée calls the Pentacle letter an "intellectual scandal." He believes that science was betrayed when the Robertson panel, meeting in January 1953, was barred from access to the research of Pentacle and his group. That panel's recommendations were responsible for the downgrading of BB and the demise of any serious overt government interest in the UFO phenomenon after 1953.

If Vallée's interpretation of the Pentacle letter is correct, then it is, indeed, a major document in the hidden history of the UFO phenomenon. But are his conclusions correct? If not, what were the likely motivations of Pentacle and his colleagues? Why was the letter written in January 1953 and addressed to BB, not Air Force Intelligence in Washington? Why was a secret experiment proposed?

This article will address these questions and will examine how other researchers, including Hynek, have evaluated the letter in their published work. We will provide a close reading of the letter's text and explain what the author most probably meant or implied. Importantly, we will present information gleaned from interviews with Pentacle's surviving colleagues. Additionally, we will provide historical context for the letter by reviewing key elements in the history of the Air Force investigation of UFOs in the early 1950s.

It also gives several reasons why the authors view Vallée's reaction as overblown and emotional. For one it reports that, "The upshot is that there is nothing sinister about Battelle's concern about what can and cannot be discussed at the Robertson panel. Instead, what we see at work is, in part, Battelle's natural concern that a client's project be safeguarded."

It also mentions:

> This point must be remembered: the only UFO data available, as far as the Battelle team was aware, were the reports it had received from Blue Book. Believing the information was of poor quality, Cross and his colleagues would have naturally been concerned that the Robertson panel might draw faulty and premature conclusions from its too brief review. We believe this was probably the prime motivator for their recommendation that the panel not be held, and it was also the rationale for their proposed experiment.

However some reports were of low quality and some were high. In addition, such a huge number of reports can overcome some of poor quality. It might be more likely that they were concerned because a scientific analysis had not been completed and there was much more that could be done.

Still another reason is that no evidence was found suggesting that Battelle might have had and analyzed metallic debris:

During the 1940s and 1950s Battelle was surely one of the premier metallurgy research facilities in the world. It therefore occurred to CUFOS that Battelle would have participated in the analysis of any UFO artifacts for the government. Battelle was well established as a trusted and respected facility for Top Secret work (including the Manhattan Project). Its staff included top metallurgists, welding technology experts, physical chemists, and fuel application specialists. Battelle's proximity to WP (60 miles) made even daily commuting feasible. The supposition that Battelle analyzed Roswell (or other) UFO artifacts is a simple and obvious theory. William of Occam would have approved.

Accordingly, in the course of our investigation, CUFOS has delved (both subtly and overtly) into this possibility. And come up wanting. Much to our surprise and initial puzzlement, none of our interviews and none of our other research have yet provided any evidence that Battelle has ever been in possession of UFO artifacts, for Roswell or any other UFO case.

However evidence suggesting that Battelle might have had debris surfaced later.

And another reason the study was deemed unimportant is that the researchers found no evidence suggesting that UFOs exist:

> In its summary to Special Report No. 14, Battelle states that "it is considered to be highly improbable that reports of unidentified aerial objects examined in this study represent observations of technological developments outside of the range of present-day scientific knowledge." In the conclusions the authors reiterate this point, stating too that "the probability that any of the UNKNOWNS considered in this study are 'flying saucers' is concluded to be extremely small," then adding the telling comment, "since the most complete and reliable reports from the present data, when isolated and studied, conclusively failed to reveal even a rough model." We return to this point below.

This is definitely questionable when Maccabee's report is considered.

Yet another reason given in "The Pentacle Letter" might be paraphrased as that UFOs can cause traffic tie-ups:

> Go-Round created great excitement and confusion around the government and the Pentagon. [It seems to have been this flap and its consequent clogging of lines of communication that aroused intelligence officials to the security problems inherent in UFOs.] It was Wright-Pat's View that publicity spawned more reports. And so the logic was to reduce publicity and emotionalism on UFOs as a requirement for the protection of communication channels.)

In other words the UFO study should not take place and UFOs should be ignored because they can cause traffic tie-ups or clogged lines of communication,

> It is at this juncture that the CIA's influence became most nefarious and that government UFO investigation was forever altered. The CIA connived to get the UFO problem defined as a security, not a scientific, issue. At a meeting on December 4 in the CIA director's office, other agencies, including the Air Force, were pressed to agree to a "review" of the UFO problem. This review became the Robertson panel. Such a high—level review had actually been "approved" in

one hour by the CIA after it was recommended by a group of high-level scientists visiting Blue Book. In short, the fix was in. At a meeting on December 12 with ATIC and CIA personnel (at Wright-Patterson most probably), Battelle learned of the planned "CIA-sponsored meeting," to be held about a month from then. It appears that Ruppelt generally approved of the proposed Robertson panel's review; Battelle, obviously, did not. And therein lies the story of Howard Cross' letter.

Despite these comments about the importance of the Memo, the article stated:

The article concluded that, "if Cross and colleagues had succeeded, who knows how it would have changed the history of UFO study?"

The earlier draft article I received titled "The Pentacle Letter" by Jennie Zeidman, Michael Swords, and Mark Rodeghier is in Appendix II. This article appeared to be a second draft of the published article above and there are differences between this article and the one that was later published. These both provide information about the study and its history.

Although at the time the article by Zeidman and Rodeghier was written, they viewed the Memo as not as significant as Vallée thought. However, more recent evidence would suggest that it could actually be as important as Vallée viewed it.

For example, immediately following the paragraph saying that there is no evidence that the UFO phenomenon exists, an immediate contradiction follows:

> In two articles in the old series of the *Journal of UFO Studies*, "Scientific Investigation of Unidentified Flying Objects," Bruce Maccabee has exhaustively considered the statistical results of the Battelle study. He notes that the authors did not mention these findings in their concluding remarks, perhaps because they could be seen as contradicting their conclusions. [Actually when the findings contradict the conclusions, the study is big trouble.]
> Maccabee points to these intriguing results: (1) that the sightings labeled "Excellent" in quality are more likely to be classified "Unknown", (2) that the Unknowns were, in general, visible long enough to have been identified but were not; (3) that cases from military observers, who were better witnesses, had a higher percentage of Unknowns; and (4) that the characteristics of the Unknowns did not match the Knowns on such things as color, shape, speed, and duration.

In addition, there now exists suggestive information against the idea that no material debris was analyzed.

Although the *IUR* publication, "The Pentacle Letter and the Battelle UFO Project," said that the Pentacle Memo was nothing to Hynek, it appears that at the time, Hynek was outraged that information was being withheld from the Robertson Panel.

The message in our photograph is titled Pentacle Letter – Theoretical Chronology (Figure 35). It gives a theoretical chronology of the Pentacle Memo. It discusses where Hynek's copy of the Memo came from. No one knew. Hynek had always complained that Project BB was not a true investigative agency and a reason for this was that the best reports and information went elsewhere.

This certainly shows Hynek's outrage. He received a copy of the Memo that did not come through official channels. Perhaps he received it from someone sympathetic at WP, possibly Ruppelt. They thought it wouldn't have come from Battelle because he was disliked.

Hynek at this time went to see Cross and talked to the *SR-14* team at Battelle. A classic story about this meeting is that Hynek had acquired the Pentacle Memorandum. He was outraged to learn that some of Battelle's UFO information was being withheld from the Robertson panel. Hynek, a mild-mannered professor, even took the memo to, and confronted Cross, a man with a reputation for anger. Cross responded by lunging and grabbing back the memo, demanding to know how Hynek had gotten it, and insisting that Hynek was not supposed to have it.

However according to this, what actually happened is that Hynek did not take a copy of the letter, but confronted Cross with notes. It was these notes that Cross confiscated. The document adds that Cross had no right to confiscate the notes–he treated Hynek like a child.

They wondered how Hynek got a second copy of the Memo and how many other people got it. In those days making a copy of something could be much more difficult than today. It involved manual labor and the ability to type. Although Battelle was the corporation that developed the Xerox, this message mentioned a carbon. This was used to make copies before the Xerox. The acronym cc, which are still used, stand for Carbon Copy. In this, a sheet of carbon paper was placed between two or more sheets of paper. The pressure applied by the writing implement (generally a typewriter) to the top sheet caused pigment from the carbon paper to produce the same mark on the copy sheet(s). In this case, the carbon copy was stamped separately and in red. Stamping in red ink was normal for this level of security.

The leaker of the Pentacle Memo must have been an insider who had the necessary clearances, and knew those involved. This is because the questions at the bottom of the document ask, "How did a second copy (the one in CUFOS file in '92) get there. What was its origin? Who typed it? How many other people have the letter? The document adds, "Mark said someone–Dave Jacobs? also has a copy." It obviously took some trouble to make a second copy and the copies that were leaked were not the same. Possibly there was more than one leaker, or the leaker went to a lot of trouble making the copies. Also, in those days males, such as the scientists, normally did not type, secretaries did this. An additional suggestion that there might be more than one leaker is that the leakers spelled the name as Goll in one document, but Coll in another.

Thus the leaker/s could enter the most secure files, leave the documents, and likely be recognized by others, without being noticed.

Also this again shows how compartmentalized the government is with secure material–that a secret UFO study at Battelle's was taking place that even Dr. Hynek, the BB spokesperson, did not know about.

The writers of the *IUR* Pentacle article had preliminary lists of what to and what not to discuss in their article, as shown in Figure 36. As an example of what to mention in the article was that BB had been piggybacked on the Battelle Project Stork to hide it.

Why did they want to hide it A common reason presented is that the study, *SR-14*, was secret and Battelle did not want to be associated with UFO studies. But one also might wonder if some agency wanted an unbiased scientific look at the data and to have a real scientific analysis, rather than the fake investigations such as done by BB and the Robertson Panel, which were not classified.

Clyde Williams thought that they would make a major discovery (they did but the government quickly buried it so deeply that it is still buried today). This is a very positive statement from the head of Battelle.

Topics to not mention included the views of the scientists working on the project on Hynek, "that to a man, all had little respect for Allen and thought he wanted the limelight."

However Hynek had a different position than those working on *SR-14*, who had clearances and could not publically talk about their work. Hynek was the BB spokesperson, thus, he interacted with the public whereas they did not. He also had a lower clearance than they did and may have not known about the work they were doing at that time.

Another thing was that although one might now have the impression that the researchers could have been antagonistic about Hynek because he was more accepting of UFO phenomenon than the rest, this would be untrue. At the time the Hynek was the UFO debunker. So that if there were any philosophical difference associated with the lack of respect for Hynek, it might have been for his stance against the phenomena.

Battelle would get the glory: Figure 37 may show additional smoking gun evidence of the reality of UFO phenomena and Roswell, "Clyde Williams, CEO at that time, was the one who wanted the project, on the grounds that maybe there was something to it, and BMI would get the glory"

This again is a very positive statement; especially considering that he made it in a climate where many thought the subject was hooey. He wanted the project. This could make one wonder if Battelle received the project through any of his actions. He was very openminded about the possibility that it might lead to something more and Battelle would get the glory.

In addition, because Williams had been the Battelle head when the Roswell material arrived, he may have had good reason for making these statements.

This document also tells about a few other things. Zeidman asks why there is no letterhead on either copy of the Pentacle letter. A Battelle document should have one. This was to verify that it came from Battelle and to help track down the leaker.

When I worked at Battelle the final drafts of our reports contained letterheads, but I don't recall whether earlier ones did or not. The copies they had received must have been early copies.

She mentioned that one of the distributees is the same person that she referred to in her article, "I remember BB." This likely is Westerman. *SR-14* was hidden in Stork.

In this article, she also described her laundered money. She said her paychecks said OSU. But she wondered about this because most of her work was for ATIC, so she asked Hynek. He told her that she wasn't working for ATIC but for a contractor and added that the contractor didn't want to be known. But the next time the courier came with the weekly reports, she looked at his license plate; it was a private car and had vanity plates. She then discovered that the owner worked for Battelle. They then negotiated with Stork. But one might still wonder why Ohio State University was sending her the checks. Did it know what was going on? Did it know about Stork?

She also mentioned that the BB facility was in building 263, not Hanger 18. However BB would likely not have been the agency to investigate debris. Thus it appears that the NASIC building was the successor to building 263, not building 18.

Her article empathized several times that Hynek was not in the loop about the real UFO work, although he was the BB spokesperson. He was kept out of the inner circle and, even though he had high security clearances, he did not have a right to know.

The information about the additional research on the Pentacle Memo held great significance for a number of reasons. For example, top people including the head of Battelle signed it. It shows Clyde Williams, who was the head of Battelle during Roswell, making positive statements about the study and taking it on. Someone/ones must have been very concerned about the study, because of the leaked the information, which is generally quite risky to the person doing it and looked like it involved some work. In general many mysteries remain about the Pentacle Memo and *SR-14*.

******

CHAPTER SIX

PROJECT BLUE BOOK SPECIAL REPORT #14–ONE CHANCE IN A BILLION

One chance out of a billion or likely even more than a trillion is explosive.

One chance out of a billion is an outlandishly slim chance and would be very odd to find in any scientific study. The chances of winning the world's largest lotto jackpot range into the low millions. There are only about two trillion galaxies and about a trillion-trillion stars in our universe.

However less than one chance out of a billion is what *SR-14* gave as against the possibility that good UFO sightings represent conventional objects (actually in calculating it out by hand, it might even be much less than one in a trillion). In other words, a very well done, credible study very strongly showed that UFO phenomena exist. These statistics are meaningful as will be explained later.

Thus, it holds a very significant place in UFOlogy–quite likely it is the most significant study ever done on this field. This is because it was done by the book. And it showed that UFO phenomena are real.

It was a secret study and the only reason anyone found out about it, is through the leaked Pentacle Memo. A very detailed investigation of this study including studying interviews of some of those in the know about it was done.

Under BB, Battelle made this massive statistical analysis of UFO phenomena *SR-14*. Even today, *SR-14* represents the largest such study ever undertaken and reigns as perhaps the most significant collection of evidence that UFO phenomena represent something real. Although much evidence suggests that the government UFO study projects such as the unclassified portion of BB, the Robertson Panel, and the Condon Report were simply public-relations (brainwashing) endeavors, some research conducted under BB is highly significant and this was the classified work done at Battelle.

BB *SR-14* was a statistical analysis of Blue Book cases to the time the report was completed in 1954. Some 3200 cases were studied and these were the best cases out of about 13,000.

It began in December 1951, when Captain Ruppelt met with members of the Battelle to find experts to assist them in making the Air Force UFO study more scientific. Battelle was to devise a reporting form that later became the standardized reporting form that is still generally in use today. Beginning in late March 1952, Battelle started analyzing sighting reports and encoding the described characteristics onto IBM punched cards for computer analysis.

ST-14 was their massive statistical analysis of BB cases, about 3200 of the best reports, by the time the report was finished in 1954, and after Ruppelt had left Blue Book. The Battelle scientists divided cases into "Knowns," "Unknowns," and a third category of "insufficient information (as discussed in Maccabee in *Historical Introduction to Project Blue Book Special Report No. 14*, and Project Blue Book Special Report #14 by United States Air Force).[34][35]

The Knowns and Unknowns were broken down into four categories of quality, from excellent to poor. For example, cases deemed excellent might typically involve experienced witnesses such as airline pilots or trained military personnel, multiple witnesses, corroborating evidence such as radar contact or photographs, etc. For a case to be considered a "known," only two analysts had to independently agree on a solution. But, for a case to be called an "unknown," four analysts had to agree. Thus the criterion for an "unknown" was quite stringent.

The sightings were broken down into six different characteristics: color, number, duration of observation, brightness, shape, and speed. These characteristics were compared statistically between Knowns and Unknowns to see if there was a significant difference.

The principal results of the statistical analysis were:

* About 69% of these cases were considered known or identified (38% were considered conclusively identified while 31% were still "doubtfully" explained); and about 9% fell into insufficient information. About 22% were classified as "unknown," down from the earlier 28% value of the Air Force studies.

* About, 86% of the Knowns were aircraft, balloons, or had astronomical explanations. Only about 1.5% of all cases were judged psychological or "crackpot" cases. Also the "miscellaneous" category comprised 8% of all cases and included possible hoaxes.

* A significant finding was that the higher the quality of the case, the more likely it was to be classified unknown. For 35% of the excellent cases were deemed Unknowns, as opposed to only 18% of the poorest cases. This finding was the exact opposite of the result predicted by skeptics, who had argued Unknowns were poorer quality cases involving unreliable witnesses that could be solved if only better information were available.

* A highly significant finding was that, in all six studied sighting characteristics, the Unknowns were different from the Knowns at a highly statistically significant level: in five of the six measures the odds of Knowns differing from Unknowns by chance was only 1% or less.

When all six characteristics were considered together, the probability of a match between Knowns and Unknowns was less than 1 in a billion or even much less than that. One chance in a billion shows that there exist tremendous odds against the idea that UFO phenomena are prosaic. Such a finding is almost unheard of in scientific research. However, the authorities, scientists, government officials, concluded that the report showed nothing.

And worse yet, although very poor studies are well-known, almost no one has heard of this study. BB investigated two of the most prominent theories that have been used to disprove UFO phenomena: (1) UFO reports result from a lack of reliable information and witnesses and (2) UFOs are known but misidentified objects. Blue Book scientists at Battelle tested these two theories by analyzing sighting reports and data using rigorous scientific statistical methods, as described by Bruce Maccabee, PhD, in his 1979 work, Historical Introduction to SR–14.

In more detail, the first theory, that unexplained UFO sightings are caused by a lack of information or by inaccurate perceptions, suggests that when reliable observers and a large amount of information are available, the number of unexplained sightings will decrease. The results of the Blue Book study by Battelle scientists were the opposite of those expected. Based on 3,201 of the most reliable sightings (selected from approximately 7,200), the most reliable report category ("excellent") had a higher percentage (33.3 percent) of Unknowns than the least reliable report category (16.6 percent). In addition, 38 percent of the "excellent" sightings were by military personnel, compared to approximately one-quarter of the sightings in the "poor" category. This large study therefore refuted the idea that UFO sightings result from a lack of reliable information and observers.

The second theory is that UFOs are really known but misidentified objects. If this were true, one would expect characteristics of UFOs generally to match those of conventional objects. For example, a certain percentage of conventional flying objects are aircraft with predictable lighting arrangements and a certain percentage are meteors; therefore, the frequencies of such characteristics among UFOs should correspond to these percentages. In the Battelle study, the frequencies of certain characteristics of UFOs and Identified Flying Objects (IFOs) were evaluated according to a standard statistical procedure (the widely used "chi-square"). In five of six categories, the hypothesis that UFOs are misidentifications of conventional objects was disproved. Battelle scientists determined that by every available criterion, the characteristics of the UFOs differed from those of the IFOs, that better qualified observers reported sightings of longer durations and that when more information was available, it was more likely that a report would defy explanation.

In other words, by the standard statistical methodology used in scientific studies, some UFO phenomena very likely represent something real, despite the government's representation that *SR-14* found nothing.

What did the SR-14 Researchers really think about UFO phenomena?
The following documents look like scratchy comments, but they are filled with information. They show the instant, unpolished thoughts of some of the participants of the SR–14 study.

Most are based on interviews with some of distributees of the Pentacle Memo. These people were at a supervisory level and had clearances higher than Dr. Hynek. Some seemed to look down on him.

This information is useful as a real-time commentary, but also because these people are all dead, so it is the last chance to hear from them. Many were quite old when interviewed.

This information reveals several things. Although it is unknown how much the security may have affected the answers, the opinions in general of those managers of the research were that it was useless and nothing was found.

These seem to be truthful conclusions; however, it is awesomely amazing that none of them noticed the highly significant results of the study. This sort of statistic is the first thing a real scientist should check. Scientists go by "Publish or Perish," and the scientific journals often base their decisions on whether to publish an article or not, on statistical significance.

Such information also shows that the basic data was not fudged, because the results that the researchers and government apparently wanted were to show that UFO phenomena do not exist. Thus if data were faked it would likely show that the phenomena did not exist. In fact, after the original study they did a lot of manipulation of the data to try to show that there was nothing to it.

The fact that the study showed just the opposite of the conclusions seemingly was not recognized by anyone.

Figure 38 shows that although William Reid was one of the scientists working on *SR-14*, he would have agreed with the government analysis of the findings that there was nothing to it. He did not seem to show any interest in the actual results showing the amazing statistical analysis. He said, "UFOs are a of matter belief, like religion. I frankly don't believe in them. I doubt very much whether they exist. A bunch of hooey"

His opinion of Dr. Hynek was, "The OSU professor was sold on the idea. He had screwball ideas. BMI had a dim opinion of Hynek."

The interviewer mentioned that, "one time Reid was at WP with Hynek. Hynek says, 'There's a UFO out there!' They all went out to look –for 20 minutes – and even set up a couple planes (but it wasn't anything)."

Could it be that Reid was just "following orders" and agreed with whatever the government told him that the results were, instead of actually examining the results. Or could it show that he did not understand statistics or even the report's basic write-up such as how the Unknowns were selected. One wonders if the statistician had been in communication with the rest of the researchers.

About Clyde Williams he says, "Clyde Williams wanted the project because he always wanted more work for Battelle – he was optimistic it would bring in more work (= $) for Battelle. 'Maybe we would make some discoveries...'" He might have been insinuating that the only reason for Williams' interest was to get more money for Battelle, but his quote would suggest that Williams may have had a deeper interest. Clyde Williams not only had a high position, it was the highest at Battelle. He was Battelle's Director at the time of the Roswell crash. More information about Williams will follow.

It appeared that some who worked on BB *SR-14* and had higher clearances viewed than Hynek viewed him as a "screwball." Several writings show that he was unpopular. He not only had to fight against this perception by the public, but was looked down upon at work also. But his ideas were actually the correct interpretation of the results.

Figure 39 contains notes on interviews of another of the distributees of the Pentacle Memo, Perry Reippel. He also displayed no curiosity at all about the study or its statistical findings. Statistically, one does not get highly significant results from examining a bunch of trash when used in such a well-executed experimental design as this. The protocol for the Chi Square test uses a standard experimental set up. What one gets is the expected probability of no significance from trash, not what they found. This is especially true of *SR-14* because of the massive amount of data studied.

The name Geo Manning on the note is likely George Manning; He held the opinion that *SR-14* was simply a large project to analyze meteors. It is unknown what he had to do with the study. However Battelle also had done some motion studies on UFOs, for example a BB engineering analysis of UFO motion. George Manning was an expert on motion. He became quite famous in a field involving such studies after he left Battelle.

He left Battelle to become very successful as a mechanical engineer. He was in charge of research, development, and quality control for a sporting goods manufacturer. Prior to this, he had been with the Battelle and the True Temper Corporation, where he served in both research and management capacities. While at Battelle and True Temper, the largest manufacturer of golf shafts in the world, he developed and coordinated tests on the famous "True Temper Swing Machine." Manning's machine also known as "Iron Byron" has become the industry standard for performance evaluation.[36]

When the golf manufacturer True Temper first commissioned engineer George Manning to begin working on the project in 1963, he examined high-speed photography of top professional and amateur golfers in his testing facility, measuring their swings against one another.[37]

Manning became the new chairperson of the SGMA International's Baseball & Softball Council. He has had a 45-year career in engineering and as a business executive. His academic credentials include a BS in Mechanical Engineering obtained from the University of Cincinnati and a Masters in Management from Case-Western Reserve University. His career began with his working with the US Army and Battelle. He served as Project Engineer, Operations Manager, and General Manager at True Temper Sports from 1966 to 1979. In 1979, he joined the Hillerich & Bradsby Company. There, he held titles of Manager Technical Services and VP-Technical Services until his retirement that was in 2000. From 1993 to 2000, Manning was a member of the Baseball & Softball Council. Later, he worked with Hillerich & Bradsby in a consulting role.[38]

While he was at Battelle and True Temper, the largest manufacturer of golf shafts in the world, he developed and coordinated tests on the famous "True Temper Swing Machine," Besides his golf expertise, Manning was heavily involved in baseball and softball. He insists that baseball and softball, like golf, is an example of the result of the interaction between matter and motion–physics.[39]

Figure 40 shows another document of the several Battelle investigations into who leaked the Pentacle Memo about *SR-14*.

It contains theories about how copies of the Memo were obtained and it discusses the differences between those of Vallée, Vicki Cooper (who wrote an article about the Memo), and the Battelle copy. The notes are from Battelle, the organization who did the study. As far as I know, the leaker is still unknown today, and this is among the many mysteries linked with the *SR-14* study. It says:

> Theories:
> Our copy (version) of the P letter was typed by someone who knew the correct name was Goll [others used the incorrect name]
> Our copy actually was a draft that came first – (because if you're copying something as quickly as you can, you probably wouldn't type files. Or maybe not even the Project # (G-1579-4).
> –Our copy was typed by someone in a hurry. Number of typos (frequency) suggests it was not a secretary.
> –Secretary would have had access to a "secret" stamp.
> –…access to a Xerox
> If you assume that Vicki [Cooper who wrote an article about it] got her letter from Jacques, (because of their friendship & because of Coll, vs. Goll); Jacques did not Xerox our copy version does not have the secret stamp.
> Vicki got the letter from other than Jacques
> Allen had 2 versions; we've located one, & Jacques located the other
> He says it was stamped (a red) secret security info.

Not only is the leaker unknown, but more than one copy was leaked. The copy that Vallée had was stamped with a red Secret security classification.[40] Top Secret is often stamped in red. The Battelle investigators thought that their copy was done in a hurry and not by a secretary. Their copy was a draft. Because this did not appear to have been done by a secretary, it may have been leaked by one of the scientists. Vallée's copy (that had gone to Hynek) was likely made later. It is unknown how many leakers were involved.

It is unknown what the G portion of the project number meant. Perhaps a search on other G number projects in the same numerical range might show something.

Such leakers have had a long and powerful position. "Deep Throat" brought down a president. This did a great service to the country and to democracy.

A leaker is basically someone who lets people know secret information. This is very hazardous and leakers very frequently have high motivations. A leaker may feel responsible to certain principles, and an important one is that people find out the true facts.

In the BB study, much chicanery took place, the public was unlikely to find out about it, and would be misled about something of great potential importance.

It appeared that although some of those on the Pentacle Memo list, such as shown in Figure 40, expressed the idea that UFO phenomena are hooey, that others may have thought it was important enough to leak. In other words, not all the scientists involved viewed UFOs as flimflam.

Moreover, one of the signers was the president of Battelle. This would make it more dangerous to the leaker, but also shows the study's importance to Battelle and shows the belief that the study meant something.

I don't know if they ever figured out who leaked the letter. But the leaker obviously had a top security clearance and knowledge of the study. The person must have known Hynek and the Battelle BB employees in order to have left the documents in places where they would find them.

Two people that I might suspect as leakers could be William Reid or Vern Ellsey. This is because both were thought by some to have made the first drafts of the Pentacle Memo. Reid, however, debunked the whole idea of UFOs.

The leaker or leakers certainly gave a window into what the government was really doing, and into what some in the study thought about its importance. It also was leaked by someone who understood not only the importance of the study, but must have had an idea of the meaning of the Robertson Panel that was about to convene. And the leaker also must have viewed the leak as important because of managing to leave several copies. And who knows what hidden work is going on today?[41]

What did the Robertson Panel find and do? – A turning point

Although the Robertson Panel is presented as an actual study with reliable conclusions. It was as fishy as it could be. The CIA convened the meeting before it had the data. The Robertson Panel met on January 14, 1953. The SR–14 staff wrote their report at the end of 1953. The conclusions of *SR-14* were published May 5, 1955.

The CIA planned this to make sure that this Panel did not have the data. Thus, people in the CIA were deliberately lying to the public by setting up a false panel, setting up false results, and lying to the tax paying public. Apparently, those in the panel did not care that they were abrogating any semblance of scientific method or even morality.

The Panel members included scientists and military personnel who were skeptical of UFO reports such as: physicist, radar expert, and later Nobel Prize winner Luis Alvarez, PhD; missile expert Frederick C. Durant, PhD; Brookhaven National Laboratories nuclear physicist Samuel A. Goudsmit, PhD; astrophysicist, radar expert, and deputy director of the Johns Hopkins University's Operations Research Office Thornton Page, PhD; physicist Lloyd Berkner, PhD; and Hynek.

These scientists and officers were superbly qualified in their fields, but knew nothing about UFO phenomenon, except Hynek who was excluded from some of the discussions.

Having worked for the government, I have noticed that this is a normal way to hide something. Put someone who knows nothing about it in charge, or convene a panel of big wigs that do not understand anything about the subject they are addressing. This is how the government can bring about the results they want and convince the public of things that are wrong.

The "Robertson Panel" had been commissioned by the CIA in 1952 to respond to UFO reports, particularly those of sightings in the Washington, D.C. area. Howard Percy Robertson, PhD—a physicist, CIA employee, and director of the Defense Department Weapons Evaluation Group—was instructed by the CIA's Office of Scientific Intelligence to assemble prominent scientists to review the Air Force's UFO files. As preparation, Robertson reviewed Air Force files and procedures, and he found the Air Force had commissioned Battelle to study all UFO reports collected by Projects Sign, Grudge, and Blue Book.

The panel's first formal meeting took place on January 14, 1953, under the direction of Robertson. Panel members were briefed on US military activities and intelligence. Despite the impressive credentials of the members, some of those most knowledgeable about the UFO phenomena were excluded from the panel or from some meetings. For example, Zeidman reports that although Hynek was a member of the panel and despite his considerable background in aerospace studies, he was excluded from the Robertson Panel's inner circle and was even made to leave the room during some meetings. This speaks for itself about the intent of and true investigative purpose of the Panel.

Robertson wanted to access the statistical results Battelle had put together for the Air Force, but Battelle refused access, saying scientists had not yet had sufficient time for a proper study.

The report produced by the panel was at first classified as secret. In it, the panel revealed its conclusions that UFOs were not a direct threat to national security, but it did not say that the phenomena didn't exist. The panel also suggested a public relations campaign be undertaken to debunk UFOs and to reduce public interest in the subject. It further recommended that civilian UFO groups be monitored.

This portion of the Robertson Panel's recommendation—to monitor civilian UFO groups—has been highly significant to investigators of government cover-ups because it is suggestive of counter-evidence to the idea that the government would not infiltrate UFO groups. For example, according to Richard Dolan in *UFOs and the National Security State* (2000), a public relations officer named Al Chop told Edward Ruppelt that the panel planned to work up a debunking campaign to plant outlandish UFO claims in magazines and media broadcasts; the goal would be to make UFO reports sound ridiculous. Dolan also reported that several weeks after the Robertson meeting, the Air Force issued Regulation 200-2. This directive ordered Air Force officers not to publicly discuss UFO incidents unless the cases were considered solved. In addition, it ordered that all unsolved cases be considered classified. The 4602nd Air Intelligence Squadron of the Air Defense Command investigated the most important UFO cases; these cases did not go to Blue Book, as Hynek said. Dolan added that four military studies had concluded the UFOs were interplanetary; these included the 1948 Project Sign "Estimate of the Situation" and a 1952 BB engineering analysis of UFO motion. Possibly Manning had taken part in these studies.

The Robertson Panel's overall conclusions—that UFOs were not a direct threat to national security— reverberated throughout the US government. Agencies seemed to interpret that as meaning that the phenomena didn't exist. The CIA abandoned a major UFO investigation. Pentagon UFO research projects were halted. A scientific advisory board that BB's leaders had hoped to establish never materialized.

However, many observers thought the panel's investigation was not conducted in a scientific manner. For example, Zeidman reported that Hynek said, that they are not going to have a scientific investigation. For some strange motive they voted it down. This panel didn't even take a decent look at the data, but they decided to discredit them. Jacobs commented, that these men, apparently ignorant of the phenomenon, were designated to decide on the future of a subject of grave concern. They would spend less than twelve working hours listening to experts like Ruppelt, Hynek, and Fournet and reviewing reports.

The Robertson Panelists did not investigate UFO phenomena–if they did, they would have been interested in the results of the Battelle study. Instead it was a presentation done by the CIA to close off the UFO study. It did not work and later another such fake study, the Condon committee report did this. The Condon committee used professional civilians and apparently, this appeared less fake to the public than did a panel composed of government officials.

The Condon Report
The next point along the paper trail documenting government cover-ups was as obvious as the Robertson Panel, but this resulted in the actual closure of BB. This "study" came in 1966 when the Air Force turned its UFO problem over to the University of Colorado and nuclear physicist Edward Condon, PhD. In so doing, the Air Force failed to choose the most experienced or knowledgeable UFO experts. Zeidman says the fact that the Air Force turned to Colorado and Condon was an insult to Hynek, an Air Force consultant, chairperson of the Astronomy Department at Northwestern University, and the American scientist with the most extensive UFO background. Hynek characterized the appointment of Condon as analogous to appointing a non-cook as head chef at Maxim's.

Condon directed a study of UFOs for the government, and in 1969, the University of Colorado released his 1465-page report, *Scientific Study of Unidentified Flying Objects*, which has come to be called the *Condon Report*. Condon, along with project coordinator Robert Low, allegedly conducted an independent, objective study. However, the two arrived at the negative conclusions the Air Force wanted.

According to Jacobs, in *UFOs and Abductions: Challenging the Borders of Knowledge,* and Story, in *The Encyclopedia of UFOs,* both Condon and Low were contemptuous of their subject. For example, Condon expressed disdain about UFOs before any research took place, and this attitude casts doubt on the study's objectivity. Moreover, neither Condon nor Low conducted field investigations, but the project's researchers who did investigate the sightings found them worthy of further attention. Condon later ousted those who took a scientific approach.

Approximately thirty percent of the cases used in the study were unsolved. Despite this, the study concluded, that nothing should be done with them in the expectation that they would not contribute to the advancement of science. Even more astonishing was their response to the question of a national defense issue of the reports; they claimed that the history of the past 21 years has repeatedly led Air Force officers to conclude that none of the things seen, or thought to have been seen that pass by the name of UFO reports, constituted any hazard or threat to national security. How would they know that if they couldn't explain nearly one third of their data? They added, that they know of no reason to question the finding of the Air Force that the whole class of UFO reports does not pose any defense problem.

These conclusions are amazing because this was the height of the Cold War. A UFO might be an incoming nuclear missile or other advanced weapon; or manned, but off-course airplanes, such as those used in the September 11 attacks; or a drone; or spy plane. Such UFO's could touch off a nuclear war, or even destroy humanity. They should certainly be brought to government attention, recorded, and studied. The last portion of the Condon Report summary cautioned teachers to discourage any interest of pupils in UFOs, because such study would be harmful to their development. (If UFOs do not exist, how would an interest in them harm pupils and why should pupils be brainwashed?)

Story added that some of the reports had left some of the Condon Report authors very puzzled, and practically admitting the physical reality of unconventional UFOs, contrary to the report's conclusions. Jacobs noted that shortly after the report's release, a minority report in book form argued that Condon was biased and had not really considered the data.

Because of the negative conclusions in the summery, the Air Force and the media presented the *Condon Report* as scientific evidence that alien UFOs were nonexistent. However several scientists gave scathing reviews of the report. In short, the investigations behind the *Condon Report* revealed that UFOs were significant phenomena worthy of study, but the published conclusion was that nothing significant was found.

In addition, the Air Force regulations were still in effect for reporting unidentified flying objects that could affect national security. These reports were to be made in accordance with JANAP 146 or Air Force Manual 55-11. The government might not be too concerned about civilian sightings, because they had already been infiltrating civilian groups, and with today's Internet they can find much of this information on-line.

However if they are still taking reports, then some segment of the government is likely working on the subject.

Stanton Friedman: are there mysteries about him?
Stanton Friedman may be Mr. UFO right behind Dr. Hynek. He constantly lectures; gives talks; writes books, columns, and articles; and does much interaction with everyone.

Could there be any secrets involved with him?

The note in Figure 41 says: "Stanton Friedman told me he had worked for "White Stork."" This small post-it type note was attached to the "Pentacle Letter – Theoretical Chronology," shown previously. It follows with: "I don't understand all the stuff at the bottom of pg. 294" and "What's this about Friedman on pg. 304."

I have not been able to find this information on the Internet, but because it is an internal Battelle document, it is likely correct. The author is unknown.

Thus Friedman may have worked in this secret government project at Battelle that studied foreign intelligence but also UFOs. One wonders what his ties to the government in this capacity were and how long they lasted.

The notes below this with the page numbers most likely refer to Vallée's book, *Forbidden Science*.[42]

It is interesting that Friedman may have worked for White Stork for several reasons, one is because of Friedman's involvement with the MJ-12 documents.

The Majestic Twelve, MJ12 documents are something that UFOlogists spent years and years examining. Some UFOlogists including Friedman thought they were real documents. Today many view them as an elaborate hoax. There was never any actual reason to accept them as authentic, but they were so well done, and had taken so much effort to do, that people thought they might have been used in real investigation.

MJ12 was discussed above in relation to Collins and Doty.

Friedman's role in this affair is described below:

The Majestic Documents[43]

Anyone interested in UFOs and the notion that the United States government has covered up the reality of alien visitation and presence in its own country and around the world has heard of the Majestic Documents. For those less familiar with UFO conspiracy theory:

The term "Majestic documents" refers generally to thousands of pages of purportedly classified government documents that prove the existence of a Top-Secret group of scientists and military personnel—Majestic 12—formed in 1947 under President Harry Truman, and charged with investigating crashed extraterrestrial spacecraft and their occupants. Majestic 12 personnel allegedly included a number of noteworthy political, scientific, and military figures, including: Rear Admiral Roscoe Hillenkoetter, the first CIA Director; Dr. Vannevar Bush, wartime chair of the Office of Scientific Research; James Forrestal, Secretary of the Navy and first Secretary of Defense; General Nathan Twining, head of Air Materiel Command at WP and later Chairman of Joint Chiefs of Staff; and Dr. Donald Menzel, an astronomer at Harvard University. Additional members included: Lloyd Berkner, Detlev Bronk, Gordon Gray, Jerome Clarke Hunsaker, Robert M. Montague, and Sidney Souers. Another was Hoyt Vandenberg an Air Force Chief of Staff, and director the Central Intelligence Group who rejected the "interplanetary hypothesis."

More specifically, the Majestic documents refer to a series of allegedly classified documents leaked from 1981 to the present day by unidentified sources concerning Majestic 12 and the United States government's knowledge of intelligent extraterrestrials and their technology. The documents date from 1942 to 1999.

As described earlier, with respect to the leaking of the documents, the story begins in 1984. UFO believer and film producer Jamie Shandera received an envelope that contained photographs of 8 pages of documents that appeared to be official briefing papers describing "Operation Majestic 12."

Shandera had two colleagues involved in studying the leaked documents: Stanton Friedman and William Moore. Shandera and Moore were later (1985) contacted by anonymous individuals about more information via postcards postmarked "New Zealand" with a return address of "Box 189, Addis Ababa, Ethiopia." The postcards contained cryptic messages referring to "Reeses [sic] Pieces" and "Suitland." These were assumed to be a code, but never solved.

A few months later, in an apparent coincidence, Friedman asked Moore and Shandera to examine newly declassified Air Force documents at the National Archives (NARA) repository in Suitland, Maryland. The head archivist was named Ed Reese, revealing two of the code words (Suitland, Reese's). During their visit to the National Archives, Shandera and Moore discovered the Cutler-Twining memo, dated July 14, 1954. It turned up in box 189 (recall the "Box 189, Addis Ababa, Ethiopia" line in the anonymous postcard).

Circumstances of the discovery have led most UFO researchers to see the Cutler-Twining memo as a deliberately planted document. Another problem was its lack of a distinctive National Archives catalog number. It therefore appeared to be planted. Moore and Shandera were accused by some of a hoax, but Friedman defended them by noting the Cutler-Twining memo was not a picture – it was on original onionskin paper widely used by the government at that time. Subsequent research by skeptic Philip Klass showed that Nathan Twining was out of the country at the time he supposedly wrote the Cutler-Twining memo. Nevertheless, some still defend it.

A variety of concerns have been raised in the course of forensic authentication procedures and publication of these efforts, such as apparent anachronistic statements, possible typewriter impression inconsistencies, grammatical errors, departures from standard styles, printing flaws, and virtually identical signatures on different documents.[44]

One cannot help but to wonder here about the coincidence of Friedman asking Moore and Shandera to examine the documents at the National Archives (NARA) repository in Suitland, Maryland. Thus, Friedman asked the men to examine the very documents that contained what was called the Cutler-Twining memo–that was most likely planted and fake.

Another reason that would make anyone think the documents were planted is that they had no National Archives catalog number. But still another reason is that the planter or an associate had obviously visited the National Archives (NARA) repository in Suitland, Maryland. That is how the planter knew that the head archivist was named Ed Reese, which revealed two of the code words (Suitland, Reese's). In addition during their visit, Shandera and Moore discovered the Cutler-Twining memo, it turned up in box 189 (the Box 189, Addis Ababa, Ethiopia) line in the postcard.

Actually they could have instantly found out whether it was a fake as soon as they discovered the document–just check with the archivist.

It would also seem strange that Friedman would be so accepting of the evidence–which sounds quite fishy. For example, someone could easily obtain onionskin paper to use for this. I checked Amazon.com and can get a ream for around $ 26. Another strange thing is that Friedman accepted as real a signature that was exactly like another one, which thus looked copied.[45] Could there have been any influence from White Stork on Friedman here?

74

It appeared that the author of the Battelle note, Figure 41, had gone to considerable trouble to check this out. The author said, "I don't understand all the stuff at the bottom of pg 294" (of Vallée's book).

I also tried to check it out and did not find much about it in the Internet. So the author must have done some heavy digging to find some obscure information about this.

Excerpts from *Forbidden Science* pages 293-294 give the following information–from page 293:

> Condon didn't give a damn whether or not the phenomenon was real. Bob Low was an opportunist. But none of that excuses botching up the job so badly.
> The last half of page 294 says:
> Hynek told me he understood my eagerness to move faster: "I should have asked more questions over my years with the Air Force," he said. "I suspect there was a turning point in the whole project at the time of the Robertson Panel," I told him without mentioning the Pentacle letter. "You may be right, Jacques. You're forcing me to open my eyes." "Let's go over the early years again." "Well, when UFOs first appeared, the Air Force did not even exist yet, as you know. Forrestal set up the initial project, which is referred to simply as Project Saucer. This was followed by Sign which was created in September 1947. When they realized they needed the assistance of civilian scientists, Project Stork was created under the responsibility of Battelle. I served as consultant." "Did you visit their facilities in Columbus?" "From time to time." "Did you follow what they were doing at the time of the Robertson Panel?" "I didn't go there during that period. To tell you the truth they ran the operation in such a cloak and dagger fashion I thought it was laughable. Perhaps I was quite wrong." He drew on his pipe, watched the smoke rising over us, then he went on: "The Robertson Panel put an end to Project Stork. The Battelle Memorial Institute wrote their famous Report #14 at the end of 1953 but it was only released by BB in 1955. The project was then called White Stork. It is much later, under Colonel Friend, that Blue Book became the responsibility of the Foreign Technology Division. Two years later the consulting project became Golden Eagle and the contract went to McGraw-Hill." "How many other scientists are working for BB within the framework of Golden Eagle?

The beginning of page 295 says:

> Hynek seemed taken aback by the question. "To my knowledge I'm the only one. The other people are civilian experts on plasma, propulsion and aeronautics, who are analyzing material gathered by the Foreign Technology Division, primarily data about Russian aerospace technology." "Then let me ask you this: If we were to discover that a secret study had been done apart from Blue Book, should we reveal it?" "Why the hell not? A real crime would have been committed against science, against everything the Constitution holds sacred."[46]

Thus on page 294 they discussed the various government agencies set up to study UFOs. Little information exists about White Stork–page 294 also tells what White Stork was.

According to Hynek, White Stork was a former Air Force project name encompassing the Blue Book project. It, rather than Project BB, released SR–14 several years after its completion. Vallée indicates that Project Stork was keeping the soon-to-meet Robertson Panel in the dark and would decide what they would be allowed to learn. Vallée writes that the memorandum seemed to dictate "a key determinant in what the panel could discuss – and what not, i.e. what would be kept away from the panel. By preselecting the evidence, the conclusion the scientists would reach could thus be known in advance."

Later BB came under the WP Foreign Technology Division. And after that it became Golden Eagle and then the contract was with McGraw-Hill.

Strangely, it appeared that Hynek was the only scientist working on Golden Eagle within the framework of BB.

White Stork was very, very high security at Battelle. Bill Jones, who did not have a clearance but had heard of White Stork, said that once in the company of other Battelle employees and just for the sake of it, he said the words White Stork. He said that he was strongly hushed.

Thus what the author of the Battelle document said appears true–this is confusing.

Hynek also said that he thought the Robertson Panel had been a turning point in the whole project. Although he might have been the best-known expert on UFOs, he was not a full member of the committee and could not attend all the stations.

It was obvious that the Robertson Panel did not concern itself about the real data. Thus its conclusions were political. The panel's negative opinions were that UFOs presented no threat to national security (they concluded this without examining the evidence). These findings were presented as meaning that there was nothing to the UFO phenomena.

Thus a political device, rather than actual examination of the data, was used by the CIA to end Project Stork and try to turn the subject into one of ridicule.

The writer of the note said that he did not understand what they were talking about at the bottom of page 294. Golden Eagle was mentioned at the bottom.

This is very confusing and will be discussed later.

The document's author then asks another question. That is "what's this about Friedman on pg 304?" Page 304 mentions Friedman:

> How could Robertson, Alvarez, Page and other scientists of that caliber listen to some Air Force officers as if they were hearing the Gospel? They were in control. Their reputation was on the line. Why didn't they demand to be briefed exhaustively about the Battelle work?" "It's very likely they just never knew about it," said Hynek, pensively drawing on his pipe. "The CIA and the Air Force may not have told them."…But if there is a secret study in Washington, what good is it for me to continue all this hard work? I might as well go on with my own life, my own career…."Do you really think there's a secret study?" Fred asked. "Yes," I said, "although it may be nothing more than a bunch of space cadets engaged in a misguided, technocratic effort at duplicating the UFO propulsion system. It may be coupled with an in-depth analysis of traces

and material fragments." I thought of Astropower, and of the McDonnell-Douglas Company, who is rumored to have a secret team, employing a physicist named Stanton Friedman to collect physical data in a hush-hush manner. "All those people are glorified rocket engineers, they can hardly put their arms around the real problem." "Don't underestimate them," says Fred. "It's impossible to suppose that they would study UFOs without thinking about their origin, and about the beings that pilot them—" Fine. But I would like to know the answers to a different set of questions.

This indicates that a secret UFO study had continued in Washington.

It also mentions a physicist named Stanton Friedman. This is most likely the Stanton Friedman, who studied UFOs, because he told elsewhere that he had worked here. Stanton Friedman mentioned that he once had a job offer from McDonnell Douglas Astronautics to try to determine how flying saucers worked, so they may have been examining a variety of topics.[47]

Friedman's positions as a physicist were described as his working for 14 years as a nuclear physicist for companies including General Electric (1956–1959), Aerojet General Nucleonics (1959–1963), General Motors (1963–1966), Westinghouse (1966–1968), TRW Systems (1969–1970), and McDonnell Douglas, where he worked on advanced, classified programs on nuclear aircraft, fission and fusion rockets, and compact nuclear power plants for space applications.[48]

Friedman may have once given a lecture at Battelle.

McDonnell Douglas was an aircraft company, but it did some interesting work that did not seem related to aircraft.

When I worked for the Aerospace Center in St. Louis, I knew a physicist working for the McDonnell-Douglas Company and Washington University, Dr. David Sloop. He had given me a Polaroid film, which I had used in UFO studies. I think they were using that type of photography at that time to capture high-speed particle collisions.

Dr. Sloop, as I recall was studying magnetic resonance and he has a number of publications in the field. It seemed a bit strange that an aircraft company might have been studying this type of physics.

Mysteries of SR–14
Many mysteries about *SR-14* exist to this day.

One mystery of immediate notice is the date. The SR–14 staff wrote their report at the end of 1953. However the conclusions of *SR-14* were not published until May 5, 1955. Why was there a two-year lag time between when it was finished and when it was published? Was this done to further obfuscate its results? Many people would forget about it while waiting for two years. Maybe it took the government that long to make the most confusing report possible.

Another mystery is why does no one know about it. How could anything this important be unrecognized, while fake studies such as Robertson Panel, and the Condon Report became well-known?

This might be because of its extreme secrecy. It was so secret that Dr. Hynek, the public face of BB, didn't know anything about it, although he was working for BB and Battelle at the time. As "The Pentacle Letter and the Battelle UFO Project" mentioned:

> By January 1953…. as we have indicated, the Battelle UFO project was only a small part of Project Stork, but the latter project was so secret that, 14 years later, Hynek would still believe that Project Stork dealt only with UFO research. This secrecy, and Battelle's attitudes toward its clients, are crucial for an understanding of the Cross letter, as we explain below.

Thus its report was classified as secret and hidden from the public. It was so hidden that most of those who worked for. BB didn't know anything about it.

Another mystery as mentioned, is who leaked the Pentacle Memo.

How many people did the research? Although some reported that this was done by four people, the Battelle records show that it was done by around a dozen people.
Another almost unbelievable mystery is who did the study:

> Amazingly enough, all three men said that higher level personnel at Battelle did not do the bulk of the project's work. Though no one could recall who was on the committee of 12 or so mentioned in Special Report No. 14 (which developed the project questionnaire, among other tasks), Westerman thought they were all Battelle employees or direct consultants, not outsiders. This makes sense given the classified nature of Project Stork. (In an amusing aside, Westerman noted that the UFO work at Battelle was worth "one hush" for its secrecy level.) The actual work of the project, then, was done by lower-level engineers and scientists. The names on the Cross letter were all at or near the managerial level, with the possible exception of Ellsey.
>
> We asked all three which staffers had actually written the original drafts of Special Report No. 14. None could recall for sure, but Westerman thought it might have been Ellsey. He quickly added that Cross would have reviewed the report before it was sent to the Air Force. ("The Pentacle Letter and the Battelle UFO Project.")

Thus it appeared that around 12 people did the actual research in the study.

It is strange that no one could recall who was on the committee of 12 or so mentioned as the scientists that worked on Special Report No. 14 (which developed the project questionnaire, among other tasks). It is especially strange because it was important enough that the president of Battelle was listed on the Pentacle Memo.

After the passage of so many years, it was reported that because they didn't find the UFO work particularly interesting and because they didn't work full-time on the project, they remembered little about the day-to-day work of UFO-report evaluation. At one point Reid exclaimed that they had certainly seen "lots of lousy pictures," but none could recall particular cases or investigations clearly. Westerman did say that Ruppelt was a "reasonable" Air Force officer with whom to work."

However, they may have "forgotten" the details because the project was highly classified. This is suggested by a hand-written document of Connie Voldrich, Figure 42: "If I did know, I wouldn't tell. Because it was classified." Voldrich worked with Cross and a number of other participants.

She also knew something about the study because she said that she got another assignment at the beginning of the time of the contract on *SR-14*.

In addition, she comments, "the Blue Book project was kept pretty well under cover." Thus she definitely knew something about it. This is because it was highly classified and if she had no knowledge of it, she would not be able to say that much.

Unlike some of the others, she admitted to having an interest in UFOs.

In addition, it appeared that the possible UFO debris was first presented as Soviet material. Perhaps this is all the supervisors knew about it. Possibly the people who actually worked on it were the ones to figure out that it might be alien material.

Unlike the others who knew about the project, Voldrich admitted that she was interested in UFOs. But she does not explain why the subject kept coming up all the time.

The rest of those interviewed that were on the Pentacle Memo seemed to have not paid attention to the UFO subject and professed to have little interest.

The first two objects for Battelle, as mentioned previously (the draft of the "Pentacle Letter and the Battelle UFO Project"), were to help in employing a psychologist to assess what to expect from an observer's observational abilities and memory accuracy, and to hire people to do a statistical study of all available UFO reports.

A third objective was:
    3. Be on call for standing advice,eg: better ideas about cases or data gathering, plus employment of an astronomer for continuous assessment of astronomical alternatives [**They already had Hynek??**]

As mentioned previously, this information was left out of the article that was published later. The contract with Battelle was for help in the three areas listed above.

Several of these items are quite interesting. For one, number 3 called for the employment of an astronomer. This was strange because Dr. Hynek, an astronomer, was already working for BB. The authors questioned why this was done.

However it would be easy to speculate on reasons they might want someone besides Hynek. Could it be because they planned to keep information from Hynek in this project–keep him out of the loop. Hynek worked for Blue Book, which was set up more for public relations than for serious science.

The project planned here was an actual scientific study and may have included astronomers with a different security clearance or something different than Hynek had.

In addition, at this time Hynek was a debunker. He went along with the Air Force line that UFOs do not exist (at least publicly). Under Blue Book, he was just used to find astronomical explanations for UFO sightings.

The project planned would entail much higher security clearances than BB personal had.

Also, they wanted a continuous assessment of astronomical alternatives, as if they wanted someone on-hand to evaluate the data at all times. This also appears to differ from Hynek's work pattern.

> In October and November 1951, Captain Edward Ruppelt began to take the project lead. Visiting scientists had said that the most crucial missing elements in the investigations were better estimates on size, velocity, and altitude of the objects. The project people began to think about better ways to get this sort of information.
> In December 1951, Colonel Frank Dunn (MCI) and Ruppelt were called to the Pentagon to report on renovation of the project...The Project's upgrade was still "hot".

Then in December 1951, Ruppelt got the go-ahead for the project as mentioned.

But much stranger than this were the actual people who were hired for the project. These in general were metallurgists. This is quite strange because they were in an entirely different field than the expertise called for in the objectives.

This leads to several questions: Hiring some of the country's foremost metallurgists would likely entail much more expense than hiring a psychologist and a statistician. And the documents show that Battelle was very conscious of the expense.

But the main question is: why hire metallurgists when these specialists would have little if any expertise or knowledge of psychology or how to do a statistical study. Their expertise and knowledge would be in the field of metals. This leads back to the question of why would they need metallurgists, when they needed psychologists and statisticians. What metallurgists would be needed for is to study metal, which in no part was even mentioned in any descriptions of the project's objectives.

Meanwhile, the project continued to grow (the draft of the *Pentacle Letter and the Battelle UFO Project*):

> From January through March, 1952, Ruppelt was trying to find better ways to collect UFO data. He established good relations with ADC (Air Defense Command), who were concerned about an increase in the number of radar cases. ADC agreed to help in 3 ways:

1. Use radarscope cameras to take pictures of scope activities whenever there was a UFO target manifesting.

2. Scramble fighters to make close approaches to UFOs if possible.

3. Organize the Ground Observer Corps to act like a UFO-spotting network, something which might also create coincident sightings allowing triangulation.

Ruppelt reported that UFOs tended to concentrate in certain geographical areas:…an "organized" watch for UFOs (with cameras) at Holloman AFB (NM) was reported. Dr. Joseph Kaplan, USAF Scientific Advisory Board…came to Wright-Pat to suggest better data-gathering…cameras equipped with diffraction gratings for spectral analysis.

In Boston, the Air Force Technical Advisory Group (the "Beacon Hill Group") suggested the deployment of various detection devices in locations of concentrated UFO sightings. Devices could include sound detectors, and possibly cameras.

In April and May, 1952, interest in UFO phenomena and obtaining better information and advice was still "hot." Ruppelt visited RAND and UCLA (Kaplan) to talk about cameras and data gathering. Some talk was going on, at least within Wright-Patterson Intelligence, if not between AMC and the Pentagon, about the need to increase Blue Book's abilities to operate.** [Need mention of name change—Grudge to BB].**

This led to a letter by Colonel Dunn (MCI) to General Samford dated (5-23-52) requesting an increase in scope which would include a council of name scientists and government officials to continually advise Blue Book, and stand behind pronouncements to ensure public confidence….Many Pentagon intelligence people believed the extraterrestrial hypothesis (ETU) One Colonel suggested that stripped-down highest speed pursuit jets with cameras be made available.

In June, 1952, Colonel Edward N. Porter, Deputy Director for Estimates, handled the reply to Dunn for General Samford. In his letter dated (6-2-52), he stated that Pentagon thinking saw the Council idea as a very good one, and further recommended an outside contractor to intensively look into "the UFO problem" in hopes of an early resolution. RAND Corp. was suggested. RAND had already been contacted about the possibility.

Blue Book was elevated to Section status at T-2. (The Intelligence division at Wright-Patterson AFB). Ruppelt was now directly under MCIA Colonel Donald Bower. Bower went to the West Coast (RAND and Kaplan) to get their ideas about data gathering. The recommendation was to place extreme long focal-length cameras, double-lensed (one with a diffraction grating) around the United States in UFO hot spots. This project was considered a red-hot A-1 priority.

Ruppelt and Dunn were called to the Pentagon in mid—June due to an increase in east coast sightings. One Colonel on Samford's staff [It could have been Porter] took the lead in broaching the ETH as a serious but neglected theory. A Directive which resulted from this meeting was to take further steps to obtain positive identification of UFOs. (Ruppelt's own low—expense, low—tech hope of getting triangulation data spontaneously from multiple observers-say in cities or by GOC net-wasn't panning out.

The Pentagon, ADC, R & D Board et al were wild about saucers then. All were talking about a Top-Secret project, a Big Push, to solve the problem and reveal it to the public.

It was at this point that General Samford shut the lid down on all this enthusiasm by telling WPAFB to continue the directions they were going in.

[An aside: One wonders if the "excess" enthusiasm about ETH, solving all, revealing all, wasn't getting too uncomfortable for Black Box security—leak watchers].

Back at AMC—T—2. Colonel Jack O'Meara (Dunn's assistant) was preparing some thoughts about an Advisory Council for the project. A Who's Who of science and technology giants (Including Teller, Doolittle, Whipple. van Allen, Langmuir, Zwicky, etc., etc.,) are mentioned....By July, 1952, A giant UFO flap was underway, with UFO flybys over Washington airspace... created great excitement and confusion around the government and the Pentagon.... [This seems to be the point at which the CIA really went on the alert about the UFO problem, recommending that it deserved attention right up to the National Security Council.]

In August 1952, Wright—Pat and the Pentagon were still trying to obtain better data and better advice. Cameras were still a high priority idea, as was the formation of Advisory Council

Thus many more goals for the project were gravely considered and it was taken seriously.

SR-14 Unique and very Significant Statistical Results
And while all this was going on with its promise of large, complex, actual scientific study and even financing, the statistical study *SR-14* was yielding fantastic results.

Although *SR-14* is the best done of all UFO studies and it produced very strong and powerful positive results, it is the one study that almost no one knows about.

Maybe because understanding its significance involves understanding statistics.

I have much experience with the use of statistics. I have published papers in top scientific journals using results that are based upon statistical analysis of the data, several examples of these papers are:

1." Leukocytic pyrogen effects on prostaglandins in hypothalamic tissue slices." *Am. J. Physiol.* 253 (Regulatory Integrative Comp. Physiol. 22):R71-76, 1987. I. M. Scott, R. Fertel, and J. A. Boulant.[49]

2. Effects of programmed diurnal temperature on plasma thyroxin, body temperature, and feed intake of Holstein dairy cows. "*Int. J. Biometeorology,*" 27, 47. I. M. Scott, H. D. Johnson, and G. L. Hahn.[50]

For my PhD thesis, I had a statistician design a new procedure to compare different curved data results for significance.

I have taken a number of statistics courses, enough to have a minor on my PhD work.

Thus, I appreciate the meaning of the statistics that were used in *SR-14*. It would make one's hair stand on end!

One reason for this lack of knowledge of this study might be given by Walter Webb (*Inside Building 263: A visit to Blue book, 1956*) that it is highly scientific and statistical–too statistical:

> As Gregory flipped through the pages of Special Report 14, I told him I had read it, thought it was too statistical…(Even my uncle had been unsuccessful in prying loose the full report from the then Blue Book chief Capt. Hardin. I finally read a rented copy obtained by another researcher through his Congressman.)

And a scientist, Webb, wrote the above passage. Thus, it is little wonder that no one understands it.

Basically *SR-14* is a report that would curl one's toenails–that a person would be unlikely to read even with a gun to the head. It contains statistical analysis; it is filled with graphs, tables, charts, and every statistical analysis anyone could think of. But even worse these graphs and the text also are written in such a way to obscure the meaning of the analysis. They do not give the significance of the statistics, one has to carefully read the few instructions and then figure out that significant results existed. It is very weasel worded to cover up its highly significant findings. Many secondary weasel statistics were used to try to blunt the real results.
And another reason is its complex, mathematical nature:

> Project Bear. By May the standard questionnaire to be used to record all pertinent data had been designed. A panel of 12 engineers and scientists, including a psychologist, had been established to assist Ruppelt and his staff in evaluation. In short order, Battelle began processing sighting reports and placing the information on IBM punch cards.[51]

One of its statistical tests is Chi Square. This is a portion of the meat of what it showed, but most would not understand this at all. However it is something that we use by common sense all the time. The Chi Square test simply refines the common-sense approach by framing it with parameters that allow the results to be calculated and compared with others.

To understand the results of the *SR-14*, one needs to examine how Chi square works, but without the math (which can be easily calculated with various computer programs such as Chi Square).[52]

Chi-Square example 1:
An example here is that of a mystery jar. A person who likes black jellybeans is deciding which jar to choose. The person doesn't know its contents and is examining it through sampling. An example of how Chi square works to find out about its contents is discussed as follows. Consider the following very rough example. Consider that you have 3 jars and you know that each of these is filled with jellybeans, half of these are white and half are black. Jar four is the mystery jar; it is covered so you do not know what is in it. So you take samples to see if it is the roughly the same as or different from the other 3 jars. Category 1 is white jellybeans and Category 2 is black jellybeans. (I used 50 black and 50 white jellybeans for the control, thus the variance is the same whether I sampled the black or the white)

If you take 100 samples from each the three jars, you would likely get about 50 white ones or about 50 black ones (whichever you sampled because they are 50/50) because one half of these would be white and one-half black. The samples, from the three jars are 51, 49, and 52 as shown under Categories 1 and 2. If you take a sample from the fourth one you also get around 50 black ones. Your common sense tells you that jar 4 likely has the same contents as jars one to three. And this is what the Chi Square test (Figure 43) confirms; it shows no significant difference between jar 4 and Jars 1-3.[53] This would certainly agree with one's common sense about the relative percent of jellybeans in jar 4.

Chi-Square example 2:
If you test another mystery jar, Jars 1-3 samples remain roughly the same 50/50, but in this case, 90 of the jellybeans from jar 4 are black. Now you want to know how probable it is that this jar has the same contents as the other 3 jars, as shown in Figure 44.

In this case, the P value (.0.03) is less than 0.05, so there is less than a 5 % chance that that the jars contain the same ratio of black vs. white jellybeans. But the P value is greater than 0.01. Thus there is more than a 1 % chance that all the jars contain the same portion of jellybeans. Hence this test is significant at the P<0.05 level, but is not significant at the P<0.01 level.

Chi-Square example 3:
Now you sample another mystery, jar 4, to see if it is the same or different than jars 1-3. In this case 99 of the jellybeans are black. The Chi Square test shows that there is a less than 1 percent probability that Jar 4 is the same as Jars 1-3. So you conclude that the contents of jar 4 differs by 1 out of 100 probability from jars 1-3.

Thus jar 4 is significantly different than jars 1-3 at the P<0.01 level. It has a higher percentage of jellybeans. So if you like black jellybeans, it would be the jar to choose.

The P in p-value stands for probability. In general what the p-value means is that it reflects the strength of evidence against the null hypothesis (in the case of the jelly beans the null hypothesis means that all jars have the same contents). Thus three situations can show whether the strength is strong enough or not strong enough to reject the null hypothesis.

SR-14 Results
Generally, scientists use 0.05 as a threshold. If p > 0.05, (or p is greater than 0.05) it shows that the evidence against the null hypothesis is not strong enough, and they can't reject the null hypothesis (in other words jar 4 has the same contents as jars 1-3). However if p < 0.05, (that is p is less than .05) the evidence against the null hypothesis is strong enough, so one can reject the null hypothesis and accept the alternative hypothesis (in this case that there is less than a 1 % chance the contents of jar 4 is same as those of jars 1-3).[54]

Just to see what would happen I re-did some of statistics in *SR-14*.

In this example, I used the data on "Knowns versus Unknowns on the basis of number" (that had the data adjusted for size) from *SR-14* and did the statistics using a modern computer calculation (Figure 45):

Just to show what these amazing levels of significance were, shown are their figures for the Knowns vs. Unknowns on the basis of duration of observation":

The actual value is 0.005 as shown. Its significance level is less than 0.01

As another example, I used the data on "Knowns versus Unknowns on the basis of duration (that had the data adjusted for size) from *SR-14* and did the statistics (Figure 46). This gives the value of 0.000.

However this P value can actually be calculated in the table shown in Figure 47. This one test shows a probability of less than one out of one thousand. The *SR-14* statics did not show probabilities that low and simply stopped at P<0.01. Even the standard computer programs do not show what the real odds are, likely because such odds are normally not found in scientific work. These odds would be .0004. Just calculating with this using 0.01 for the other 4 categories and using 0.004 for this one would give P<0.000 000 000 004. This is an amazing statistic.

It is unknown how many of the five characteristics actually turned out like this. Maybe some are P<0.000001. So hand calculations, show that the actual probability against the idea that UFOs are prosaic objects might be one out or one trillion or even less. Someday I might do the rest of these calculations to see what they actually are.[55]

What do the results of SR–14 mean?
It very, very strongly shows that UFOs are not prosaic phenomena.

In *SR-14*, the null hypothesis is that UFO sightings, including what are considered excellent sightings, are what would be expected if all UFO observations were actually of commonplace objects. However, the p-value of less than 0.01 means that there is substantial evidence that the objects are something different than earth's normally observed air traffic (less than 1 chance out of 100).

In other words there is a substantial probability that UFO phenomena represents something real–it is not the normal prosaic objects and events that are in the sky.

And this finding is greatly magnified by the results that this happened in 5 out of 6 categories.
The AF itself said,

> In the six sighting characteristics, the Unknowns were different from the Knowns at a highly statistically significant level: in five of the six measures the odds of Knowns differing from Unknowns by chance was only 1% or less.
> When all six characteristics were considered together, the probability of a match between Knowns and Unknowns was less than 1 in a billion.[56]

This shows that a huge strength of evidence exists, it means that UFOs are real (P< 0.000 000 001. This is just based upon calculating the odds on the basis of (0.01) to the fifth power). The actual results are much lower than this.

There is a generally agreed-upon scale for interpreting such p-values with regard to the strength of evidence that they represent:

The list below shows what these P statistics mean (evidence against null):

0.1 Borderline
0.05 Moderate
0.025 Substantial
0.01 Strong
0.001 Overwhelming

And this result is many times more than overwhelming.[57]

Although some researchers said the data was bad, therefor the study was meaningless; this is not a scientific statement. For one reason with random, bad data you do not get a one in a billion probability.

However, although scientists are viewed as rational and unemotional, they seemed to be quite upset about this. They didn't like these results, so they went about fudging. Maccabee described this, he wrote that the investigators tried to rationalize these results, but with little success, such as by explaining the color and shapes as resulting from anomalous distributions of astronomical objects. For example, they tried removing the astronomical objects from the Known group only. However statistically this analogous to creating a winning football team by removing players from the other side until your side wins.

There are a number of reasons why these statistics actually mean something. They were not just obtained by bad data, accident, or bad statistics;

1.   Sample Size:

One reason behind these significant results is that a very large sample size was used–and these samples were selected as the best, most accurate reports from a much larger sample.

The reason that sample size is important is that the basic aim of statistical testing is to find a significant difference when it actually exists. This involves comparing samples between one regime and another (or a control). Sample size is important because a larger sample increases the chance of finding a significant difference.

Statistical significance is a probability statement that tells how likely it is that the observed difference was due to chance only. A larger sample size increases the chance of finding significance because it will more reliably reflect the population mean.

The sample size used here, 3,201 of the most reliable sightings (selected from approximately 13,000) is enormous and well enough to detect significant differences.

2. Characteristics:

For another reason discrete characteristics were examined by the chi-squared tests.

This test gave significant differences in the characteristics of color, number and duration of sighting, shape, and speed.

These characteristics are generally discrete and not subjective. For example, the majority of people can tell blue from red. And most people can roughly estimate the difference between 31-60 seconds and 61 seconds to five minutes.

3. Categories:

Also although the failure of one chi-squared test to show a match between the Known and Unknown reports might be due to chance. The failure of five tests that are based on independent characteristics strongly suggests that the probability of statistical equivalence between the categories is much less than 1%, which means that the Unknowns are not unidentified Knowns.

The scientists had quite an emotional reaction to this as shown by their attempts to distort the meaning of the data. This reaction is likely caused by their inability to control the phenomena, and then superstitiously viewing it as the supernatural. However, some of the data might also be viewed prosaically. We ourselves are sending spacecraft, such as Voyager, out of our solar system. Other objects are coming in, such as 'Oumuamua, the mystery asteroid that arrived from beyond our solar system. Our craft may leave the solar system and float through space for billions of years. Maybe some might crash into a sun, a black hole, or even an inhabited planet.

Perhaps something like 'Oumuamua was what landed at Roswell, or other possible crash sites. Perhaps it escaped another system billions of years ago, or perhaps an inhabited planet that used metallurgy blew up. These substances could float through space for millions or billions of years. And perhaps one could land here. Perhaps it might even contain preserved aliens. If ideas such as crashes are rejected because scientists cannot conceive of aliens, or beings more advanced than ourselves and view such ideas as supernatural, perhaps such explanations as these could be accepted.

This large, well-done study therefore very, very strongly refuted the idea that UFO sightings result from a lack of reliable information and observers. It supported the view that UFO phenomenon is real.

Three Battelle Presidents were positive in their statements about UFOs, one approved the Battelle UFO project, which provides smoking gun evidence that those in the know, viewed Roswell as reality

Three early presidents of Battelle gave positive statements about UFOs as shown in these documents. This is confirming evidence that they were interested, and suggests that they had knowledge of the subject.

Several lines of evidence exist that Roswell material was sent to Battelle, as mentioned. Another line of evidence is records of what the higher-ups, such as Battelle presidents, have said about this. Were they completely negative as many people were, or did they give any positive mentions of the Roswell debris?

Our documents, such as Figure 36, show smoking gun evidence that Clyde Williams was both interested in the UFO project and interested in where further research might lead: "Clyde Williams (one of the distributees said) wanted anything that would bring in more work. At the time he thought maybe they would make a make a major discovery."

This is an incredibly positive statement. He thought it possible that the work could lead to a major discovery. If he thought that there was nothing to this, it is doubtful that he would even accept the project, let alone view it as a possible path to major discoveries. Other of the researchers (Figure 48) said, "Clyde Williams wanted more work for Battelle. Clyde was optimistic it would lead to more work/$. We may make some discoveries."

Williams was the head of Battelle when the Roswell debris came in, thus, he should have known something about it. People reported several times about Williams' positive statements. Once mentioned that Battelle would get the glory: "Clyde Williams, CEO at that time, was the one who wanted the project, on the grounds that maybe there was something to it, and Battelle would get the glory." Again, this not only shows that he thought that Battelle might make an important discovery, but he even associated it with glory.

Also Carey and Schmitt's investigation and interview showed that General Exon told about UFO debris and even alien bodies at Battelle, but his only first-hand experience consisted of flying over the debris field, as mentioned previously.

Bertram Thomas, a later Battelle head, stood up to the government and even courageously bit the hand that feeds him, when he opposed the timing of the Robertson Panel, because he wanted their decisions to be based on good information.

Thus all three Battelle Presidents knew of UFOs and had comments about the subject. These were positive comments; they are documented, and suggest that there is something to it. It is unlikely they would make these statements, or accept UFO contracts for Battelle, if their knowledge of and experience with UFO material were negative.

Hence these new documents with other evidence show that three heads of Battelle were positive on the subject of UFOs

Another important smoking gun in these documents is that Clyde Williams, president of Battelle, gave the ultimate approval for Battelle's participation in government UFO studies. In addition, Williams' statements would suggest that he had an interest in the project. Thus these documents confirm what others have speculated about.

This material answers that question. Bragalia and others speculated that Williams approved the project and these documents show that he did.

Bragalia has written that in 1952, Battelle was chosen to do all the analysis for BB, and supposedly, it was Air Force Captain Edward J. Ruppelt, who headed BB, that selected Battelle for this job. He said that, however, given Battelle's influence at these high levels, it is extremely unlikely that it would be left to a lowly Air Force captain to make this selection, as described in numerous books.[58] This evidence indicates that Bragalia's speculation may be correct.

Moreover as suggested previously, it is strange that an organization that specialized in metallurgy would receive this project, rather than the many universities that would be much better equipped for such a study.

Figure 48 on legal paper is loaded with additional information. It shows the opinion of the research managers on the UFO subject. William Reid did not think that UFOs exist and thought the subject was a bunch of hooey

Clyde Williams' statement that the work might lead to new discoveries shows an interest, open-mindedness, and positive attitude about the study.

Hynek was sold on the idea of scientific investigation. His ideas were described as screwball. The writer adds that Battelle had a very dim opinion of Hynek. This view appeared to be that of higher-ups, whose clearances were above Hynek's and who knew more about the UFO research at that time. Also in those years Hynek was a debunker, so it would appear that they were not calling him a screwball because of his positive attitude toward UFOs.

This document also mentions Howard Blum and William Moore. There is a thick arrow pointing up to the left of their names and a bracket and some sort of design pointing down. Moore's part in a number of UFO ventures has been described. Further investigation into this document and why a generally positive attitude existed among Battelle heads shows:

Clyde Williams had the highest position at Battelle. He was Battelle's Director from 1934 to 1958, which included the time of the Roswell crash. His field was in the chemical and metallurgical industries. He increased Battelle's annual sales greatly and pioneered the concept of contract research for industrial development. He was one of the original board members and for 15 years served for the RAND Corporation. He holds many patents and authored more than 100 technical publications. He also belonged to several notable societies: During World War II, he served as Chairman of the War Metallurgy Committee and as Chairman of the War Metallurgy Division of the Office of Scientific Research and Development. He was also one of the original Board Members and served 15 years for the RAND Corporation.[59]

Because he was Battelle's Director during the time of the Roswell crash, he should have had inside information. If the whole thing had been a hoax or didn't happen, he should not only know but also have a negative opinion of getting Battelle involved in UFO research. Battelle had a very credible reputation in the scientific world and a UFO study might diminish this, so he was taking a chance with such a study. But he not only took it on, he had positive statements about it.

Anthony Bragalia made a number of other claims about Williams' interest in UFOs, his friendship with Linus Pauling, their working together, and their common interest in UFOs. Several have claimed that there is little to back up these other claims. Some skeptical comments are:[60]

Bragalia implies that Pauling may have been involved in UFO research for the US government. A two-page outline for a scientific study of UFOs, dated July 16, 1966 is the evidence presented. Pauling had typed in "Confidential" on the top. During the summer of 1966, the USAF was looking for a top-level scientist independent of the UFO question and a high-profile University to study the UFO problem. This would eventually fall on Dr. Edward Condon and the Colorado University. Pauling was located in California at the time but not teaching at any University. It is possible he might have been contacted about heading the study by another university or heard about it "through the grapevine". This document is probably his ideas on the subject and how he would approach the problem

Pauling had inserted a letter from 1968 to the NM institute of Mining and Technology president Stirling Colgate in the pages of the UFO book *Flying Saucers: Serious Business* by Frank Edwards. Pauling was asking about the Zamora incident (see page. 16). Bragalia states the letter was found in the pages, which mention the Roswell story. However, we have no evidence if this is true. If it was, we have to wonder if Pauling put it there because of Roswell or just because the page is the first page in the chapter that talks about physical evidence? This is one of the links Bragalia makes to Pauling with Roswell.

The final link is a letter sent to Pauling by Dr. Clyde Williams of the Battelle Memorial Institute. This is Bragalia's centerpiece. According to Bragalia, it implies that Dr. Williams was an old friend and it indicates ties to Battelle and Shape Memory Alloy (SMA) research. Actually, the letter talks about Pauling visiting old friends and not specifically that Williams was an old friend. The reason Pauling went to Battelle was to give a single lecture and nothing more. Pauling spent less than a day at Battelle on February 7, 1951. He rarely had any communications with Williams or anybody at Battelle after that. There are no indications he ever spent any significant time communicating with Center, Craig, Fawn, or Eastwood, who are Bragalia's key scientists for SMAs and Roswell. His research notebooks seem to be blank regarding SMAs as well. There is little to indicate that Pauling was involved with Battelle in any significant way. There are certainly no indications he knew anything about a crashed spaceship. Bragalia told me that Pauling "died UFO/ ET obsessed" but you won't find any evidence of this in his papers and Dr. Paradowski denies this was the case. His involvement with Battelle and UFOs was minimal. Dr. Pauling, who was very opinionated on everything controversial, was not the kind of individual who would keep this secret. Suggesting he was involved in such a conspiracy based on some vague connections is not giving the man the respect he deserves.

I remember attending a lecture that Pauling gave at OSU and think it may have been in the 1980s. I think it chiefly concerned Vitamin C. It was very well attended. I don't know if there was evidence of any connection with Battelle. The only lecture I can find that might have been it is a 1983 lecture at the OSU College of Medicine, Columbus, Ohio, March 17, 1983.[61]

In the whole large list of Pauling's activities (above), Battelle is mentioned only once. Thus it is doubtful if he was an old friend with ties to Battelle and Shape Memory Alloy.

Linus Pauling was one of the world's top scientists. Linus Carl Pauling (1901–1994) was a chemist, biochemist, peace activist, author, educator, and husband of American human rights activist Ava Helen Pauling. He published over 1,200 papers and books. The prestigious scientific journal, *New Scientist*, called him one of the 20 greatest scientists of all time, and by 2000, he was rated the 16th most important scientist in history. He was a founder of the fields of quantum chemistry and molecular biology. He worked on the structures of biological molecules, and showed the importance of the alpha helix and beta sheet in protein secondary structure. Pauling's discoveries inspired the work of James Watson, Francis Crick, and Rosalind Franklin on the structure of DNA, which in turn made it possible for geneticists to crack the DNA code of all organisms. He also promoted nuclear disarmament and additional ideas. He received the Nobel Prize in Chemistry in 1954. He was also awarded the Nobel Peace Prize in 1962. He is one of only four people to have won more than one Nobel Prize (the others being Marie Curie, John Bardeen and Frederick Sanger). He is also the only person to have been awarded two unshared Nobel Prizes and one of two people to be awarded Nobel Prizes in different fields–the other being Marie Curie.[62]

Although he was an extreme heavyweight, there was little evidence of his friendship with Williams or much of an interest in UFOs.

However I did find some documented linkages between Williams and some involved with UFOs. For example *Summary Technical Report of Division 18, NDRC Volume 1 War Metallurgy* (*Summary Technical Report of Division 18*) gives Vannevar Bush, Director of the Office of Scientific Research and Development, James B. Conant, Chairman of the National Defense Research Committee, and Clyde Williams, Chief of Division 18 as authors. It was published in Washington, D. C, in 1946 and shows these people working together before Roswell. It was classified as Confidential at that time.[63]

This is interesting to begin with because Vannevar Bush, James B. Conant, and Clyde Williams have all been linked with the UFO scene. An article, "The FBI Debunked These UFO Documents in the Most Childish Way Possible," shows a photo of Vannevar Bush with President Truman, and atomic scientist James Conant all together.[64,65]

Vannevar Bush is important in this scene because he was an engineer, inventor and science administrator. He headed the U.S. Office of Scientific Research and Development (OSRD), through which nearly all wartime military R&D was carried out, including significant developments in radar and the beginning and early administration of the Manhattan Project. He was chiefly responsible for the movement that led to the creation of the National Science Foundation. He was a known for his research on analog computing, his political role in the development of the atomic bomb as a primary organizer of the Manhattan Project, the founding of Raytheon, and the idea of the memex, an adjustable microfilm viewer that is somewhat analogous to the structure of the World Wide Web. He constructed a differential analyzer, an analog computer with some digital components, which could solve differential equations with as many as 18 independent variables. An offshoot of this work at MIT by Bush and others was the beginning of digital circuit design theory. The Office of Scientific Research and Development was where he coordinated the activities of some six-thousand leading American scientists in the application of science to warfare.[66] [67]

His possible involvement with UFOs is shown in Canadian government documents from 1950 and 1951 that involved the Canadian Defense Research Board, Department of Transport, and Embassy in Washington D.C. They indicate Bush as directing a very secret UFO study group within the U.S. Research and Development Board. His participation in this group is further documented by Stanton Friedman in his book "*Top Secret/Majic.*" [68] In addition, the Wilbert Smith Papers show Dr. Vannevar Bush was named as heading a highly secret UFO study group within the U.S. Research and Development Board (RDB).[69]

Bush has been linked in vast troves of UFO literature with the MJ-12 documents. Much UFO literature lists him as a member of MJ-12, as mentioned before. But these documents are thought by many to be fake.

In still another link, Williams was a trustee for the Rand Corporation.[70] In the list of other Rand Corporation Key Players involved in the formation of this new organization are: Williams, Major General Curtis LeMay; General Lauris Norstad, Assistant Chief of Air Staff, Plans; Edward Bowles of the Massachusetts Institute of Technology, consultant to the Secretary of War; Donald Douglas, president of the Douglas Aircraft Company; Arthur Raymond, chief engineer at Douglas; and Franklin Collbohm, Raymond's assistant.[71]

Major General Curtis E. LeMay (1906 –1990), another member of this group of Rand Corporation trustees, with Williams, is still another link. General Curtis LeMay is famous in UFO literature because he was the Chief of Staff of the Air Force, who strongly rebuffed Goldwater, when he asked if he could see the "Blue Room."

An article by Battelle's Bill Jones "General Curtis E. LeMay Commander, Strategic Air Command,"[72] gives more detail about him. LeMay's published statement about the subject is:

> Naturally I am not quoting any classified information. I am giving the straightest answers I can give... The bulk of the [flying saucer] reports could be run down. Some natural phenomenon might usually account for those sightings which had been seen and reported, and thus explain them. However, we had a number of reports from reputable people (well-educated, serious-minded folks - scientists and flyers) who surely saw something.
>
> "There is no question about it: these were things which we could not tie in with any natural phenomena known to our investigators….All I can say is that no natural phenomena could be found to account for them.

An acquaintance of Bill interviewed LeMay after his retirement from the U.S. Air Force during the General's visit to Columbus for another purpose:

> After the interview was concluded the journalist asked LeMay off the record what his opinions were about the subject of UFOs. LeMay replied that UFOs were real and the subject

of serious interest on the part of the government. There was no equivocation in LeMay's response. UFOs were real.

This is certainly a very positive statement from the person famous in UFOlogy for his rebuff of Goldwater. Jones concluded by asking if LeMay's attitudes might have changed after he retired. Actually, LeMay did not in any way say that UFOs don't exist. What he said was that they were very highly classified. That in a way is saying that they exist, for why would nothing be so highly classified.

LeMay held high offices; he was a general in the United States Air Force and the vice-presidential running mate of American Independent Party candidate George Wallace in the 1968 presidential election. He is credited with designing and then implementing an effective, but controversial, systematic strategic bombing campaign in the Pacific theater of World War II. He served as Chief of Staff of the United States Air Force from 1961 to 1965.

LeMay had joined the United States Army Air Corps while studying civil engineering at OSU. He was later placed in command of strategic bombing operations against Japan. Later, he was assigned to command USAF Europe and coordinated the Berlin airlift. He served as commander of the Strategic Air Command (SAC) from 1948 to 1957, where he presided over the transition to a force that focused on the deployment of nuclear weapons. When Chief of Staff of the Air Force, he called for the bombing of Cuban missile sites during the Cuban Missile Crisis.[73] He was certainly tough enough to defend WP security, but possibly this showed that he might have had an idea of what he was defending.

James Bryant Conant was the other author listed with Williams, and Bush. He was an American chemist and government official. He received his PhD in chemistry from Harvard. He was named the 23rd president of Harvard. He worked on the Manhattan Project and as it neared completion, he was appointed as a member of the Interim Committee to make recommendations about the wartime use of the atomic bomb. He encouraged the creation of the Committee's Scientific Panel, which was made up of Manhattan Project leaders Arthur Compton, Ernest Lawrence, J. Robert Oppenheimer, and Enrico Fermi.[74]

In 1949 when Dr. George Valley of M.I.T. was disturbed about Air Defense Systems, he authored a summation of project SIGN. Dr. James B. Conant conducted this. This project had collected material on reports of unidentified aerial intruders in America's airspace, the so-called "flying saucers." SIGN was surprisingly inconclusive about possible novel Russian aircraft, and even entertained an extraterrestrial solution as mentioned previously. The aerial mystery received intensive official scrutiny when the "green fireballs" were seen over highly sensitive atonic installations in New Mexico during the winter of 1948-49.[75]

Thus these three men, Clyde Williams, Vannevar Bush, and James Conant did have documented connections with UFO phenomenon. And they had associates with some connections also. All had positive statements about the subject. And Battelle is where the Roswell debris was sent.

Bragalia had reported also that Clyde Williams was serving on the government's Research and Development Board, which also included in its membership Dr. Eric Walker and Dr. Robert

Sarbacher, both of whom later acknowledged that they knew about the Roswell crash. He said that this is a strong indication that the entire government R&D Board was deeply involved in the UFO/ET issue. And, as mentioned, he added that this connection could explain why, in 1952, it was Battelle that was chosen to do all the analysis for BB.[76]

I don't know if any documentation exists for Walker, Sarbacher, and the entire government R&D Board's involvement. The term Research and Development Board is rather generic and used in many places. I can't find it in any list of William's memberships, except in Bragalia's writing and references to it. The way to verify whether this is accurate is to look at actual government documents and see whether all three men are there.

I checked a number of government documents on the National Defense Research Committee of Office of Scientific Research and Development War Metallurgy Division to find whether Clyde Williams was serving on the government's Research and Development Board, because this is the government Research and Development Board upon which he served. He indeed was listed in these documents. I also checked whether Dr. Eric Walker and Dr. Robert Sarbacher were included as members and they weren't. The members were listed in these documents.

The documents (with government identification) showed that Clyde Williams was a member. He was listed in all of them. However none listed Dr. Eric Walker no Dr. Robert Sarbacher. I found no verification that Walker and Sarbacher served with Williams. I found no listing of Walker and Sarbacher in any of the documents, but all showed Williams

The documents that I checked included:
The National Defense Research Committee Of Office Of Scientific Research And Development War Metallurgy Division Progress Report On Development Of Armor Welding Electrodes: Relation Of The Composition Of Austeijitic (20 Cr-10 Ni) Electrodes To The Physical And Ballistic Properties-of Armor-Weldments (Od-36-2).[77] It listed Williams and gave his position, "Copy No. 29 - Clyde Williams, Chief, War Metallurgy Division (Div. 16), NDRC and Chairman, War Metallurgy Committee," but did not list Walker and Sarbacher.

As mentioned earlier, the *Summary Technical Report of Division 18* gives Clyde Williams, as Chief of Division 18. It was published in Washington, D. C, in 1946 and shows these people working together before Roswell. It was classified as Confidential at that time.[78] It did not list Walker and Sarbacher.

The same was true for the document, "Organizing scientific research for war; the administrative history of the Office of Scientific Research and Development" shows Clyde Williams but neither Dr. Eric Walker nor Dr. Robert Sarbacher.[79]

The National Defense Research Committee shows Clyde Williams but neither Dr. Eric Walker nor Dr. Robert Sarbacher.[80] The National Defense Research Committee (NDRC) was an organization created "to coordinate, supervise, and conduct scientific research on the problems underlying the development, production, and use of mechanisms and devices of warfare" in the United States from June 27, 1940, until June 28, 1941. Most of its work was done with the strictest secrecy, and it began research of what would become some of the most important technology during World War

II, including radar and the atomic bomb. It was superseded by the Office of Scientific Research and Development in 1941, and reduced it to merely an advisory organization until it was eventually terminated during 1947.

Still another document, "What is the most impressive weapon of World War II, apart from the atomic bomb?" shows Clyde Williams but neither Dr. Eric Walker nor Dr. Robert Sarbacher.[81]

Even the "Smithsonian Institution Archives Records, 1902-1965" shows "Box 389 of 459 Folder 31 Broadcast August 8, 1942. Clyde Williams; War Metallurgical Committee of the National Academy of Sciences," but does not show Walker and Sarbacher.

Thus there appears to be no verification that Walker and Sarbacher served with Williams.

Just to double check the organizations to which Williams belonged, I also examined Rand Corporation documents, such as, *The Rand Corporation The First Fifteen Years*.[82] It indeed lists Clyde E Williams (1948-1963) as a former trustee. There was no mention anywhere of either Dr. Eric Walker or Dr. Robert Sarbacher. This board of trustees does not appear to be deeply involved in the UFO issue.

Likewise, the article, *A Brief History of RAND*,[83] lists Williams as a Trustee, but does not include Walker and Sarbacher.

Neither Walker nor Sarbacher appear to be in any of the government documents nor Rand Corporation lists with Clyde Williams. Thus, I was unable to verify Bragalia's information.

Although Dr. Sarbacher did not appear to have served with Williams as Bragalia claimed, he was involved with UFOs. Possibly this is why Bragalia gave his name For example, in a November 29, 1983, letter he wrote to Mr. William Steinman about Roswell he said that John von Neuman was definitely involved, as was Vannevar Bush, and he thought Dr. Robert Oppenheimer were people he could verify.

He added that about the only thing he remembered at this time is that certain materials reported to have come from flying saucer crashes were extremely light and very tough. He was sure the laboratories had analyzed them carefully. Reports existed that instruments or beings operating these machines were also of very light weight sufficient to withstand the tremendous deceleration and acceleration associated with their machinery. He got the impression from talking with some of the people at the office that the "aliens" were constructed like certain insects on earth. He did not know why the high order of classification was given and why the existence of these devices is denied. This article also said that before Sarbacher died, he gave one more clue to help unravel the mystery. He said that although he had not attended the UFO meetings at WP, he knew of another scientist who had. This was Dr. Eric A. Walker.

In one interview, Walker said he did not know about MJ-12 [84] but, in another he did say he knew about it.

This letter was sent from the Washington Institute of Technology. It is listed in a Majestic Documents site.[85] The Majestic 12 documents are thought by many to be fake.

This also involves Canadian radio Wilbert B. Smith, who had the Canadian embassy arrange contact with US officials and was briefed by Robert Sarbacher. Some of Smith's material indicated that a committee of high-ranking people, headed by Vannevar Bush, existed.

My contact with Smith occurred when I sent him some drawings of a UFO sighted by several witnesses. He identified it and said that if I looked at the drawings long enough, they would look like a photograph that he sent me. They looked nothing like the photograph and I had the impression that he had not even read the report.

It is unclear what the notes Harold Blum and William Moore refer to. In his book, *Out There*, the *New York Times* journalist Howard Blum refers to "a UFO Working Group" within the Defense Intelligence Agency. He said that despite the DIA's repeated denials, the existence of this working group has been confirmed to him by more than one member of the group itself, including an independent source in the Office of Naval Intelligence. The majority of the group's members are senior members of the AVIARY: Dr. Christopher Green (BLUEJAY) from the CIA, Harold Puthoff (OWL), ex-NSA; Dr. Jack Verona (RAVEN), DoD, one of the initiators of the DIA's Sleeping Beauty project which aimed to achieve battlefield superiority using mind-altering electromagnetic weaponry; John Alexander (PENGUIN); and Ron Pandnlphi (PELICAN). [86]

William Moore's part in the Aviary and in MJ-12 was described previously.

Donald Douglas another person in this RAND list may also have had some influence in UFO investigation as mentioned previously. He was president of the Douglas Aircraft Company. This company was an American aerospace manufacturer based in Southern California founded in 1921 by Donald Wills Douglas, Sr. It later merged with McDonnell Aircraft in 1967 to form McDonnell Douglas. But Douglas Aircraft operated as a division of McDonnell Douglas afterwards. McDonnell Douglas merged with Boeing in 1997.[87]

Arthur Raymond, chief engineer at Douglas; and Franklin Collbohm, Raymond's assistant as listed also, worked for Douglas.

Thus these documents provide good evidence that three Battelle directors showed interest, concern, and a positive attitude toward UFO study. They were in a position to know whether there was something to it. Bertram Thomas had a concern about how UFO data was handled by Battelle and stood up against the government's giving inaccurate information to the Robertson Panel. Clyde Williams appeared to have a positive attitude on the subject and welcomed the BB project. General Exon also told about UFO debris and even alien bodies at Battelle, but his only first-hand experience consisted of flying over the debris field. This evidence suggests that they may have known about UFO materials, and demonstrates that they were open minded about the UFO subject.

These people also had some linkages with UFO study as shown above in several verified government documents.

******

CHAPTER SEVEN

MEMORY METAL, UFO DEBRIS, ROSWELL-A MILLION VIEWS

Jones and I found and reported the first smoking gun evidence that UFO material may have been studied at Battelle Our investigation about the possibility that Battelle analyzed Roswell artifacts made the big time in the news.

This is still current. Many, many articles have been written about it in recent years. There were almost a million views (roughly) on the subjects, Battelle, John Center, Irena Scott, in 2017, as shown in Figure 49.

Our article reported the original findings associated with Roswell and its artifacts, such as possible "Memory Metal." We reported that Battelle metallurgist; John Center told that he had worked on alien material at Battelle. We published this original account (1994) that well before Roswell was known, Battelle scientist John Center in the 1950s, reported that he was responsible for a secret project, which involved parts from a UFO. *Witness to Roswell* (2009) mentioned this report.

This information was then written about, by people such as Bragalia, Schmitt, and Carey, in many additional reports about "Memory Metal" or Nitinol. It was reported in the original Roswell accounts that it couldn't be destroyed and remembered its shape.

This research has also resulted in numerous new and smoking gun revelations: Its features new accounts of information about witnesses to the Roswell event. One is a man's unique testimony was published in *UFOs Today* for the first time.

Since then, there have been numerous Internet posts and even books about this discovery. Several have been about Nitinol, memory metal, Roswell artifacts, and similar subjects that were mentioned this report.

This provided "Smoking gun evidence" that Battelle was involved in high-level UFO studies. We reported that a man named Elroy John Center told that he was responsible for a project that required him to study "parts" that were represented as retrieved from a flying saucer. An independent witness reported how some of the metallic substance was taken to a forge in New Mexico where they attempted to break it and melt it. They failed, which is remarkable because the forge is famous for having some of the hottest furnaces in the world.

Jones and I found and reported this smoking gun evidence that possible UFO material and maybe the Roswell debris may have been studied at Battelle ("The Ohio UFO Crash Connection and Other Stories") in 1994. We reported as follows:

> In May of 1992 one of us was approached by an informant who told an intriguing story. For the record, he was not a Battelle employee. He had attended North High School in Columbus, Ohio, graduating in June of 1960. Between January and April of 1958, he dated a classmate

named Cathy Center. One evening while he was visiting her home, Cathy's father, Mr. Elroy John Center, told them that while working at Battelle (he had left their employment in 1957) he was responsible for a project which required him to study "parts" retrieved from a flying saucer. The parts had some sort of writing on them and his job was to "find out what the characters meant." He told them that there was "lots more I can't go into. It's been bothering me since I saw it." Given that some of the material (actually described as small I-beams") retrieved from the pre-crash debris field near Roswell, New Mexico in July, 1947 has been described as having some sort of writing on it, the obvious question is did the "parts" Mr. Center study come from the same crash event? The fact that Mr. Center's story was told long before the details were known publicly, the possible confirmation of his story by the later descriptions of that debris cannot be ignored.

Mr. Center's employment at Battelle can be confirmed through the American Men of Science. It was learned from Mr. Center's wife that he died of cancer on July 15, 1991. She told us that he had been keenly interested in the subject of flying saucers, but she knew nothing about any such work while he was at Battelle. His daughter Cathy was contacted and remembers our informant well but does not remember the conversation. She thought she would have remembered it because of her own interest in the subject, but said it is possible that it has been forgotten. She confirmed her father's interest in the subject of flying saucers and, like us, doubts that our informant would make up a story about the conversation.

For those who might think that they can contact Battelle to request verification of this story will not find it there. First of all, too many years have passed and anyone who might know the truth will have long since retired. Secondly, since the information would have clearly been highly classified, the records would have gone back to the Government. Thirdly, Battelle's business practices do not permit it to discuss a client's work. An unidentified Battelle staff member wrote a letter about this company that was published in the September 1993 issue of Just Cause (Citizens Against UFO Secrecy, P.O. Box 218, Coventry, CT 06238) which states this ethic better than we can. "The research Battelle undertakes is done with integrity and an ethical regard for the confidentiality of its clients, both governmental and industrial (commercial). Battelle will not discuss with others the work it does for its clients. Because of this ethical approach to its work, including due regard to matters of national security, Battelle will not respond to inquiries about Blue Book or any of its other work...This should not be seen as proof of cooperation in any sort of imagined cover up. It is part of the ethical tradition that has been part of the Battelle business philosophy since its founding in 1929."

We have heard other reports of Battelle project work by metallurgists during this time period that is also under investigation. These projects were highly secured with a top-secret classification, so that Center must have had the necessary clearances. He likely was actually working on this type of project, or he would not have known anything about it.

There were several projects going on at that time. One was *SR-14* and this involved metallurgists, which Center was.

Another one was an Air Technical Intelligence Center (ATIC) awarded contract to Battelle for translation and analysis of material from Korean War.[88] Because he was to study them and try to understand what looked like writing on them, he might have been working on this project.

This disclosure is especially credible because Center, who is listed in *American Men of Science*, had excellent credentials – a preeminent materials scientist, chemical engineer, and research chemist. He made major and breakthrough contributions in materials and alloys research. His work had centered on developing new techniques for the microanalysis of new titanium alloys. Surprisingly years after his mention of the material, Bragalia discovered that he co-authored the Battelle reports that were suspected as linking to the Roswell crash.

Center's information is important to ongoing studies of physical UFO evidence. An example of the importance of and interest in Roswell research is the fact that the first edition of Thomas J. Carey and Donald R. Schmitt's *Witness to Roswell: Unmasking the Government's Biggest Cover-Up* was the best-selling UFO book of 2007/2008. In the 2009 edition of *Witness to Roswell: Unmasking the Government's Biggest Cover-Up*, Carey and Schmitt summarized our discussions:

> In 1992, Dr. Irena Scott, herself a former Battelle employee, interviewed a close friend of Elroy Center, who had told him a very intriguing story in 1960. The story related to a science and engineering project involving "unique materials" that Center had worked on at Battelle years before. Center told the friend that he had assisted on a baffling science assignment that involved the evaluation of a very unusual material. He was required to study a "piece of unknown nature" that he understood was resultant from the crash of a UFO that had earlier been retrieved by the US government. Center indicated to the friend that the "piece" had some sort of indecipherable "writing" impressed upon its surface. Center had been asked for his input on the "glyphics" and performed various types of technical analysis on the part. He spoke sparingly to his friend and did not provide any more details.

After this Anthony Bragalia, who wrote the paragraph above, and Carey and Schmitt, and many others also began to investigate this.

They conducted many investigations of Memory Metal and Nitinol:

Bragalia claimed he had additional evidence in his reports about Cross, Center, and the Roswell artifacts.[89] He wrote under a section heading "A Scientist under Stress":

> In 1992, Center's friend "Nick" Nicholson (a holder of several US patents and a former Battelle engineer) confessed to MUFON Ohio State Director and Battelle employee Bill Jones and to former Battelle scientist Dr. Irena Scott that John Center had told him something profoundly disturbing in 1957. Center had told Nicholson that while he was at Battelle, he was directed by his superiors to evaluate pieces of unknown material that had "hieroglyphic like" markings on them. The metal debris was kept in a heavily secured safe at Battelle. Center had learned that the material came from a crashed UFO that was retrieved by military some years prior.[90]

Nicholson had told Jones and me that he had been romantically involved with Cathy Center, daughter of John Center, the Battelle metals tester.

Bragalia said that he contacted Center's family, and said they told him that Center became UFO-obsessed. Center's daughter, Cathy, said that Center was aware of Battelle's UFO studies, brought home draft copies of UFO-related reports, and pored over secret reports written for BB by his bosses at Battelle. Center was visited at home by an FBI investigator she thought was named Jack, and Center and Jack frequently discussed UFOs. Cathy Center distinctly remembered overhearing her mother and father discussing UFOs and her father saying, that he didn't know if they should mention this to Cathy at all. Bragalia said that Center was eventually fired by Battelle and was later diagnosed as an alcoholic.

Bragalia also contacted Nicholson, who then confirmed the details of what he had told us nearly two decades ago. Nicholson said Center told also him UFO crash debris was stored in a secure safe and that some of the material contained the element boron.

Nicholson had decided not to tell Cathy about his conversation with Center because she was very impressionable and excitable, and because Center had told him about it in confidence. Bragalia said that Nicholson knew that Center was an alcoholic; however, he is certain Center was lucid when he spoke of the debris. Nicholson added that he was aware of other indications of Battelle having been contracted to study UFOs even into the 1970s. For example, Nicholson says a Battelle superior told him the CIA was still involved in secret UFO studies at that time, as was Battelle.
Although Nicholson was a young man when Center told him he'd been assigned to analyze UFO debris, he is a very credible witness. He was a Battelle scientist specializing in physics and electronics for nearly 20 years. He had top-secret clearances, and he holds several patents for lasers and other designs. He also holds patents with Battelle and with the Medex medical device company, and he has been recognized for his technical achievements.

He became interested in UFO study in part due to his talks with Center, and he later associated himself as an investigator with the civilian research group NICAP (National Investigations Committee On Aerial Phenomena) . Moreover, Nicholson exposed a well-known UFO hoax—the Zanesville, Ohio, barber UFO photo-and obtained a confession from the barber that he had faked the pictures. Nicholson also reported that Battelle employee Gustavus Simpson, Jr., knew more than he ever divulged about UFO phenomena.

I then investigated additional information tying Center to UFO studies. For example, the researchers found documents showing that Center had an association with Howard C. Cross, PhD; a central figure involved in Battelle's UFO studies that our own investigations suggested headed these studies (as shown in our illustrations).[91]

One pertinent report is "*Second Progress Report Covering the Period September 1 to October 21, 1949 on Research and Development on Titanium Alloys* Contract No. 33 (038)-3736" (*Second Progress Report*). The report lists its authors as follows: "Simmons, C. W., Greenidge, C. T., Craighead, C. M., and others." Battelle completed this report for WP's Air Materiel Command. John Center is one of the scientists responsible for a technical subsection of the report, "Analytical Methods for the Titanium Base-Alloy," which refers among other items to a nickel-titanium phase diagram that is required to make the substance nitinol.

This report is important for several reasons. First, its "and others" portion of the author list included researchers, such as L. W. Eastwood, who were important scientists working on titanium alloys and other metals. This is significant because Eastwood published with key Battelle researcher Howard Cross, a metallurgist and an expert in exotic metallurgy, for example, "Development of Cast Aluminum Alloys for Elevated Temperature Service," by Webster Hodge. L. W. Eastwood. C. H. Lorig, and H. C. Cross.

Given that Cross was the Battelle point person in metallurgy research, that he co-authored research results with the creators of the *Second Progress Report*, and that Center wrote one of the report's technical subsections, it is likely that Cross and Center worked on some of the same projects. And if Center worked with retrieved UFO crash debris at Battelle, it's possible that Cross did, too– actually it is probable because as we discovered Cross was probably the head of Stork and thus Center's supervisor.

More importantly, Cross was the point person in Battelle's later UFO studies for BB in the 1950s. Evidence also exists that Cross was Battelle's chief titanium metallurgist he was the scientist who led Battelle's "memory metal" studies. Cross has been referred to as "Research Director."

Center's technical subsection is revealing. His portion of the report begins on page 97 and describes chemical analysis used to detect and quantify metal impurities. To be used for shape-memory metal applications, titanium must be of ultra-high purity. One challenge researchers faced when creating the memory metal nitinol was the detection of oxygen in titanium, and this was Center's area of concentration.

In addition, the information that Center had actually brought home draft copies of the Battelle UFO studies indicates that he participated in classified UFO research. This is because the UFO work was classified at that time.

I also wondered where I might find information about whether this possible study of Roswell debris might have influenced Battelle research. Several long-term Battelle employees thought that the metals research documents would be proprietary and would belong to the organization that sponsored the research. The Battelle library was not, therefore, likely to have copies of the documents; the paperwork would have been returned to the contracting organization or have gone back to the Air Force. If reports were Air Force documents and now unclassified, they belong to the Air Force or to the area where the Air Force archives such information. However, if they were unclassified, they would be difficult to locate because the Air Force has many branches with numerous libraries and repositories. Nevertheless, I learned that some documentation might be housed at Battelle, but not in an area such as the library where a civilian researcher might find them. My sources thought that unlike WP, where the offices of BB and similar projects are thought to no longer exist, some areas of Battelle associated with these studies might still exist and material might even be found in the same places as during the studies, and I discovered that Battelle is protective of these areas. For example, when I took the photo of the devices on the Battelle windows (Figure 27) a guard immediately approached to reprimand me.

Cross and Center weren't the only employees who fit this metallurgist/UFO profile. My interviewees from Battelle mentioned employees other than Center and Cross, who might have worked on or had knowledge of Battelle's metallurgical studies of possible alien artifacts. These individuals included Arthur Westerman, Gustavus (Gus) Simpson, Jr., Dr. Hynek, Jennie Zeidman, and Mr. Livingston.[92]

Jennie Zeidman Of all living sources, Zeidman may be the one with the broadest and most extensive knowledge of government UFO studies. Zeidman began as Hynek's student in his astronomy class. She impressed him with her research skills when she found an explanation for a sighting he was examining. She then became his research and teaching assistant at OSU's department of physics and astronomy. However, through her own detective work she soon discovered that although her paychecks seemed to be from OSU, Battelle was the organization that was paying her. She is perhaps the only living person who worked both for Project Stork at Battelle and for BB at WP. She told me her work for Hynek involved examining incoming UFO reports before he did. She had security clearances, served with some of the top people in UFOlogy, and knew Cross, Westerman, Reid, Rieppal, and others who may have worked with UFO debris. She was also acquainted with members of the Robertson Panel and the Condon Committee. She was employed in the BB offices, and she knew Captain Edward Ruppelt, former head of BB; his temporary replacement, Lieutenant Robert Olsson, and others. She was aware of the positions, the organizational structures, and some of the politics of the government UFO studies. She was also well acquainted with the data on UFO sightings and with how this information was used by the authorities. She has been the principal investigator of many UFO cases such as the Coyne helicopter event, and she has been on both the MUFON and the CUFOS boards of directors. Zeidman also investigated whether Battelle examined alien artifacts.

She had interviewed many knowledgeable people, such as Clyde Tombaugh (Pluto's discoverer) and Lincoln LaPaz. She knew the inner workings of Project Stork, which she and others said began before Battelle's UFO work. Zeidman told that the original mission of Stork was to ascertain the capability of the Soviet Union to engage in technological warfare.

Clyde Tombaugh and Lincoln LaPaz were very interesting people, who sometimes worked together, and who Hynek took an interest in. They were professional astronomers who investigated UFOs and even reported their own sightings.

Clyde W. Tombaugh (1906-1977) was the astronomer who discovered the planet Pluto. He holds the distinction of being the only man in the twentieth century, to have discovered a planet. Mr. Tombaugh has published many articles and was a professor of Astronomy at New Mexico State University Research Center. (Although Pluto is no longer considered a planet, this was an amazing discovery). Also through his careful observation and reliable reporting, he is probably the preeminent astronomer to have reported seeing UFOs, such as several unidentified objects near Las Cruces, New Mexico.[93]

Lincoln LaPaz (1897 –1985) was an American astronomer and a pioneer in the study of meteors. He received his PhD in 1928 at the University of Chicago, and was assistant professor at OSU. At the University of New Mexico, he founded the Institute of Meteoritics, was the Director, was Head of the Department of Mathematics and Astronomy, and was Director of the Division of Astronomy. His UFO work was linked with Roswell, and the N.M. green fireballs. He also had sightings. One occurred two days after Roswell and 70 miles away.[94]

Gus Simpson, Jr. is another person of interest at Battelle. Several informants told me he was involved in UFO studies. My research showed that he was a manager on the Stork projects when

Battelle researchers were investigating UFOs, and that he told Jones he was the author of the first Battelle *Special Report*, a history of the first five years of Project Stork.[95] Simpson also seems to have been involved in BB. When I saw a video taken of the BB Alumni Day, which was held at WP in 1994 on the 25th anniversary of the project's closure, Simpson and all three living BB directors—Robert Friend, George Gregory, and Hector Quintanilla—attended.

Simpson was considered a founder of the Battelle extracts system. He had an interest in metallurgical engineering. He was employed by the Air Force between 1946 and 1951, and later by Battelle in information research. In June 1947 he published work on the properties of R303 aluminum alloy sheet. Most of Simpson's Battelle publications are from the 1960s, and this later work appears to have focused on information processing (work that perhaps was also associated with the Ohio Chemical Abstracts Service, CS, and the Ohio College Library Center, OCLC). However, several Battelle employees told me that Simpson and two others were supervisors with detailed knowledge of UFO projects.[96] As Bragalia told me, "Battelle employee Gus Simpson knew more than he ever had let on about the phenomena [of UFOs]."[97] Nicholson also had said this and it supports my own findings that Simpson knew about Battelle's UFO research and may have even worked on projects concerned with alien artifacts.

Yet another person of interest is Robert Livingston (not sure how to spell his name). An Internet article discusses research by Jones and me into Elroy John Center and Battelle.[98] This evidence suggests that Livingston also either worked with UFO materials or knew about such work. I found no evidence that he had published with any of the others, but his somewhat common name made it difficult to check.

After investigating Battelle and WP, I found smoking-gun evidence from several sources, including Center's statements and those of Exon, suggesting that Battelle performed research on alien artifacts. Moreover, my findings indicate that Center represented the tip of the iceberg. For as I continued searching for more evidence about who else might have been researching Roswell artifacts at Battelle, I located several people who knew Cross, Simpson, or Livingston. I was told that Cross, Simpson, Westerman, and Livingston were managers. Zeidman said she thought Cross was head of Project Stork and had been Simpson's supervisor. She added that, although she did not work in the same area as he did, Cross made his rounds frequently so that she saw him often. She said Simpson and a man named John Morehead worked directly under Cross. Another Battelle informant also said Cross was Simpson's supervisor.

Thus, I located additional persons, such as Westerman, who had career profiles that were quite similar to Center's. These people appear to have associated with Cross and Center. Several Battelle employees (who I interviewed) suspected them of working with alien debris. Hence, they may also have worked with or had knowledge of Battelle's possible research into crash artifacts.

What is truly interesting here is that long before anyone had heard of Roswell, the idea that material UFO evidence was under examination at Battelle was well known and prominent. Battelle had a very powerful grapevine that even included people knowing who did the research, and questioning some of them about artifacts. This was many years before Roswell became common knowledge and took place in spite of the security classification of the work. Such people as Jones and Zeidman talked about this as if it were just common knowledge, and they didn't seem to pay much attention to the idea that no one would have even thought about such studies before the information about Roswell came out.

Because Battelle and WP are the only two places where verified documentation exists about serious government study of UFO phenomena, the people mentioned above and Battelle itself are of considerable interest as an important part of the UFO story.

Moreover, Roswell witnesses described a lightweight, metallic looking, "morphing" material that returned perfectly to its original state after being crumpled. Bragalia suggested that government-funded studies were done in response to the retrieval of material from the 1947 crash. And although Ashcroft told Jones and me that he found no evidence of new directions in research after Roswell, some information suggests that research related to new materials may have been undertaken. This suggests that either no such studies had taken place as Ashcroft said, or he did not have the technical expertise to search in certain directions, or he lacked security clearances needed to view the material, or he knew about the research and was part of a cover-up, or he was exposing us to some information without making formal statements to let us draw our own conclusions.

Because WP is where early reports of UFO phenomena were collected and investigated, some UFOlogists think that authorities from WP had contacted Battelle and asked its scientists to study Roswell debris and to develop a similar material.

Many have speculated about this and some evidence might exist even in the WP literature:

> Operation Paperclip, a follow-on project, brought over 200 German scientists and technicians to Wright Field to work with their American counterparts. Some of the scientists eventually worked in the Wright Field laboratories.
>
> Under the direction of Colonel Howard McCoy, the Army also delivered a large number of captured documents to Wright Field. By the end of 1947, Wright Field personnel had processed over 1,500 tons of documents, adding over 100,000 new technical terms to the English language. The technical knowledge gained revolutionized American industry. Besides the aviation-related advances, new designs for vacuum tubes, the development of magnetic tapes, night vision devices, improvements in liquid and solid fuels, and advances in textiles, drugs, and food preservation were made available to American manufacturers.[99]

This would make one wonder where the documents came from, and what source appeared to be so much more advanced than the US.

Bragalia thought that scientists did hands-on studies of debris, and that one outcome of these studies might have been a substance called nitinol. Nitinol, an alloy of nickel and titanium, exhibits many properties of the reported Roswell debris. Nitinol is a "memory metal" that "remembers" its original shape, is very lightweight, possesses high fatigue strength, and is able to withstand extreme heat. After 1947 laboratory interest in titanium (a nitinol component) rose dramatically; indeed, abstracts show that published work on titanium spiked after 1946. Moreover, Battelle began its titanium studies around the time of Roswell. Some footnotes cited military-sponsored studies into memory metal.

I interviewed employees, who had knowledge of Battelle's activities during the period of interest, and I searched for documents about nitinol and "memory metal" research at Battelle.[100]

Depression
Several Battelle sources thought that Battelle did conduct materials research on UFOs. Indeed some even said this was common knowledge. This research, done as part of Project Stork (later renamed Project White Stork), was performed at the height of the Cold War, and it was classified–even the project names were classified.[101] It's possible the researchers told family members about their work, and investigations into this possibility are ongoing. One interviewee said it was routine to tease the metallurgists rumored to be working with alien artifacts about their research on UFOs. Sources at Battelle also said those selected to investigate alien artifacts were initially told they'd be working with Soviet materials.[102] This was before anyone had heard of Roswell. After they obtained their clearances, they learned the materials were not Soviet. Several informants said the research seemed to depress or even distress people. All of these accounts are consistent with the stories about Elroy John Center.[103]

I was told that Vernon W. Ellzey delivered the material from WP to Dr. Hynek. I was also told that he later committed suicide. He also is the person who reportedly might have written the first draft of the Pentacle Memo. Perhaps he had a deeper knowledge of what was actually going on than did the rest.

The above information about Battelle's role in UFO research is an example that fits into a paper trail documenting a larger, long-term pattern of government investigation and cover-up of UFO information.

This trail began with the first institutional studies at WP such as BB and its predecessors. The fact that these initial studies were classified and unavailable to the public shows that the cover-up was in place immediately. Eventually, as part of the upgrading of BB, Ruppelt (then head of BB), contracted with Battelle for consultants in fields such as astronomy, physics, mathematics, and psychology. This research at Battelle was also classified. For example, according to Hynek and others, such Projects as Stork and White Stork were top secret. Indeed, the first four status reports on Project Stork were classified as "secret," and the fifth and sixth were marked "Restricted Security Information."

Thus, what may have generally happened is that possibly WP crashed disk project personnel heard of a new test procedure at Battelle possibly to analyze orderly metallic crystal structure that was not possible previously. Some Battelle heavyweights accepted the task, knowing what this was about, but they assigned the actual testing to people, such as their top metallurgists, who could best do the actual technique but did not tell them the truth (told them that it is a Soviet device). But some may have begun to realize that these supervisors lied, and they were not dealing with anything even vaguely normal. Even with such a "leak," the whole thing remained classified because no authority figure ever released any information. But it may have taken a toll on the workers, who found out about it.

John Center a Scientist of Stature

Elroy John Center was a scientist of stature, highly credible work, and impressive credentials. Somehow the previous information makes Center sound as if he was some kind of an also-ran who showed up at Battelle, authored a research paper, and then sunk into an alcoholic stupor. This is not true according to my findings.

When I began to investigate his professional side, I discovered that he had made many important contributions into a number of scientific fields. He was a Battelle supervisor, published books and scientific papers, and developed the methodology for a number of metallurgical studies.

He had an amazing number of publications in a wide range of topics This included work with the Atomic Energy Commission and because of this and his work at Battelle, he likely had high security clearances, which is an indication of his credibility. Such clearances might allow him to work on aspects of the *SR-14* project and when he told that he was working on top-secret material this would be compatible with his position. He had highly responsible and supervisory positions.

He is listed in the prestigious *American Men of Science*, Figure 50. His field was chemical engineering where he was a research engineer. At Battelle he was a Supervisor of the Analytic Division, beginning in 1946. He worked in inorganic and organic chemical analysis and instrumental techniques.

He held responsible positions. He is also listed as a Battelle supervisor or director in several additional places; for example, he directed an "analytical group under the direction of E. J. Center."[104]

Center authored a number of books that can still be purchased, such as, *Topical Report on the Direct Micro Determination of Uranium Using a Modified Fluorophotometer* (by E. J. Center, U. S. Atomic Energy Commission, Technical Information Service, 1951) sold by Google Books.[105][106][107] An additional book he authored is, *Topical report on spectrophotometric determination of small amounts of uranium in phosphate rock, shales and similar materials* (Author: E. J. Center; U.S. Atomic Energy Commission Series: BMI (Series), 97, Edition/Format: eBook).[108]

Center developed the methods involved a number of metallurgical studies: "E. J. Center and associates developed a colorimetric for the determination of cadmium in zirconium metal....Method of Battelle Memorial Institute."[109] He developed methodology for numerous additional studies such as one on Boron and was an author on, *Research on A Method for Determining Boron in Boron Steels*.[110]

Center had been involved in work for both Battelle and for the AEC and it appeared that he sometimes worked for both organizations at the same time. He directed research groups and devised analytical methods. All this evidence shows that he was a scientist of substantial knowledge and ability in not only one, but several fields. A number of his papers were published in conjunction with both the Atomic Energy Commission and Battelle such as, such as: *A modified HC1 volatilization method for determining oxygen in zirconium*.[111]

Yet another publication is *Preparation and Examination of Beryllium Carbide*, (by the Electrochemical Society).[112]

He published other books and papers from the Atomic Energy Commission, by itself, such as the book, *Progress report for the month of April 1947*.[113] Another such book is *A modified HCl volatilization method for determining oxygen in zirconium*.[114] He also authored "*Topical Report on the Direct Micro Determination of Uranium Using a Modified Fluorophotometer.*"[115]

As mentioned, one of his papers is included in Battelle *Second Progress Report*, but his papers were also included in the *First Progress Report Research and Development on Titanium Alloys* (AF 33(038)-3736, August 31, 1949). Center wrote one section titled Analytical Methods for Titanium-base Alloys: "The Determination of Oxygen in Titanium by the Cl2 - CCl4 Method," by E.J. Center and A.C. Eckert, and another titled "Analytical Methods for Titanium-base Alloys: Studies on the Chemical Analysis of Oxygen in Titanium by the Chlorine-Carbon Tetrachloride Method," by E.J. Center and A.C. Eckert.

He would have had high clearances both because he worked for the U.S. Atomic Energy Commission (AEC), and was a Battelle supervisor. His resume was quite good and he contributed very credible research.

Thus he likely had the credentials to look at the secret study, *SR-14*, and he also knew some of those working on it.

In addition, I learned that one secured area at Battelle was reserved for work related to foreign or counter-insurgency technology, and that this area included linguists who were among the world's top translators and cryptologists. If this is true, and if the Roswell debris was inscribed with written symbols as some witnesses reported, these people would likely be the ones the Air Force would call on for translations. Possibly Center had done some work in this department because of his description of some sort of writing on the UFO parts he worked on and that his job was to find out what the characters meant.

Why would a scientist such as Center give this account? There is no evidence that he would be interested in making a UFO hoax or making up such a story. For one thing, he would receive neither recognition nor financial gain for this account. Telling this would likely be bad for his career, not only because it would be a security violation, but also because he might be seen as a liar or hoaxer. Although he did not say anything to the public. Nicholson said that he was of sound mind when he gave this information to him. These reasons suggest that he might be truthful.

Also there was nothing published about Battelle's examination of alien artifacts from which he might have gained this information. Roswell was unknown at this time and he did not appear to indicate that he knew about it.
His detailed account appears to describe what others have speculated about in this Battelle study. All of this would suggest that his account was truthful

Possibly Center saw Nicholson as a potential son-in-law and he may have been exposing him to the real world of what he might encounter if he continued his career, or be forming links or relationships with him, or possibly trying to inspire him to investigate the UFO phenomena, which he succeeded in doing.

In general, the suggestions about this story are that it might be true. And indeed it fits with many known facts about the Battelle UFO project, for it would offer an explanation for the mystery of why Battelle hired metallurgists for a project that in no way required them.

And Center may have had a lot of influence in the UFO world. He might be the progenitor of Ohio's main UFO group. This is because he was able to spark an interest in Nicholson. Nicholson's friend was William Jones, who may have been influenced by Nicholson's interest. Jones went on to first found MidOhio Research Associates, which he later transformed into MUFON of Ohio.

A. C. Ekert:

But there is still another quite interesting facet connected with John Center and that is his co-author. A. C. Eckert was Center's co-author on his *Second Progress Report* paper. As mentioned, these investigators did not match the idea of the goals of the study, instead of hiring psychologists and statisticians, Battelle hired metallurgists.

Most of these metallurgists were involved with titanium, ways to purify it, similar substances, and with making alloys, except for Center's co-author, Eckert. His interests seemed to be involved with the effects of magnetic flux on metals or their surfaces and how to measure this. This differed considerably from the work of the others.

It is not known why Center would be paired with someone in this field, because there seemed to be little relation between their two fields.

However if they were studying a strange new substance, perhaps this difference in their fields would be important. Perhaps since a portion of Center's study may have involved parts retrieved from a flying saucer such differences might lead to new ideas. Also there are a number of theories about what kind of surfaces UFOs could have - such as how they can be soundless, disappear, and produce physical effects.

Eckert's papers include, "Investigation of The Effects of Magnetic Flux on Dislocation Movement and Alignment."[116] Its abstract says,

> Observations from previous work led to the hypothesis that under some conditions, magnetic flux influences the movement of dislocations within the grains of a ferromagnetic material. Based on X-ray diffraction extinction contrast, a technique has been derived from the work on this project that makes it possible to make a direct observation of dislocations in nickel foil samples; the dislocation movements can thereby be followed when the samples are subjected to magnetic flux. An unmistakable change in the imperfection structure was observed.

He authored parts of *The Encyclopedia of X-Rays and Gamma Rays*.[117] Eckert's paper in this was *Dislocation Movement and Alignment as Affected by Magnetic Flux: Observations by X-ray Diffraction Topograph*.[118] Another of his publications was, *Commercial and experimental carbon blacks*.[119] He was an author on, *Quantitative analysis of UO•-U• O• mixtures by x-ray diffraction*.[120][121]

These documents from Battelle contained a wealth of information about some of the people knowledgeable about *SR-14*; what they thought of UFOs and the people involved (even though no one knows who they were, except for the Pentacle Memo distributees). They also show material about a number of people in the UFO field, what those at the top thought, and a study showing overwhelming evidence that UFO phenomenon are real. And they showed evidence that some form of debris material may have been examined.

******

CHAPTER THREE (PHOTOS): WRIGHT-PATTERSON AFB–HANGER 18, BLUE ROOM, VAULTS, BODIES, AND MUCH ELSE

Figure 1: WP is one of the most secure areas in the country. It is surrounded by tall chain-link fences with barb wire at the top and posted warnings telling that is unlawful to enter the area without permission of the Installation Commander and it is patrolled by military dog teams.

Figure 2: WP's entrance points have guard posts with one-way windows to double check one's identity, turnstiles, machines to check IDs, thick bars, and even buttresses in front–probably to protect them from drivers trying to ram their way through. As the family mentioned above and I found through experience, armed guards can appear in an instant.

110

MAP OF WRIGHT-PATTERSON AFB (WPAFB) showing Areas A, B, and C.

WRIGHT-PATTERSON AIR
FORCE BASE (WPAFB)

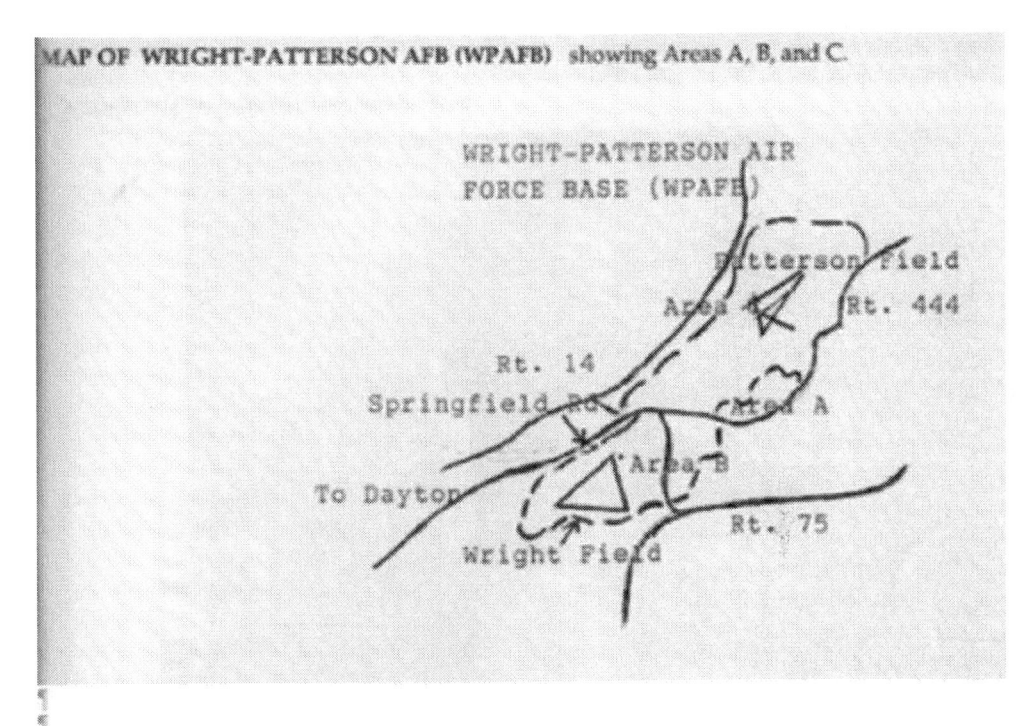

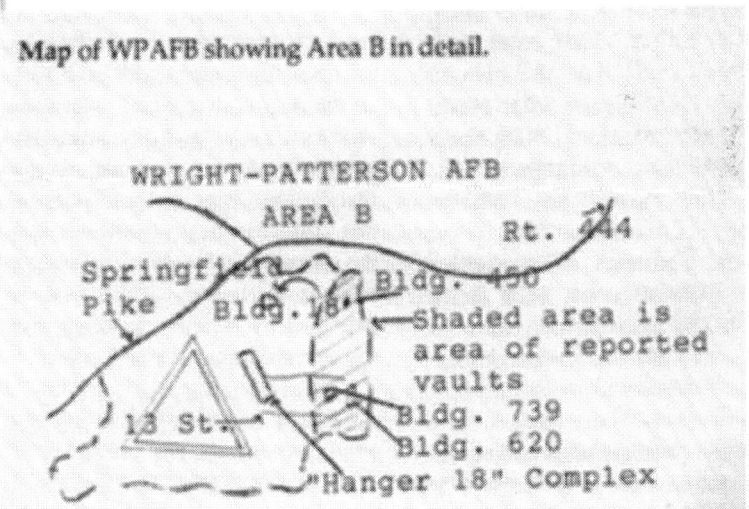

Patterson Field
Area
Rt. 444
Rt. 14
Springfield Rd
Area A
To Dayton
Area B
Rt. 75
Wright Field

Map of WPAFB showing Area B in detail.

WRIGHT-PATTERSON AFB
AREA B
Rt. 444
Springfield Pike
Bldg. 450
Bldg. 18
← Shaded area is area of reported vaults
13 St
Bldg. 739
Bldg. 620
"Hanger 18" Complex

Figure 3: WP consists of Wright Field south of Route 444, and of Patterson Field, north of Route 444. It includes Areas A, B, and C. It has been a Strategic Air Command (SAC) base.

Figure 4: WP Hanger 18. In top photograph, the second building from the left was reported to be "Hanger 18," the hanger where the B-29 from Roswell first parked and unloaded the debris, according to a long-time Dayton resident. In the older photograph at the bottom, aircraft are still visible on the paved area in front of the hangers, the one on the far right may be an unflyable F4, and one on the left is a helicopter. The area in front of the Hangers once was the apron that connected to the old WF runway, and it still contains aircraft.

Figure 5: A view of the backside of the Hanger said to be Hangar 18. This view can be seen from on-base only. These hangars are quite large when viewed up close.

Figure 6: An airplane with what appears to some type of a radome on top parked near the Hanger 18 complex (on the right), and the downslope ramp, and the WP Area 51 (to the left). A radome is the dome-like structure that protects the radar assembly from dangerous things like weather and moving fast. There is still air traffic near these hangers.

Figure 7: Views of a B-29 near one of the old WF runways. To its right on the lower photograph can be seen the "Hanger 18" group of hangars into which the Roswell debris was said to have been unloaded. These photographs might provide a picture of the view when the B-29 from Roswell first landed. It might even be the Roswell airplane.

Figure 8: Building 18, sometimes called Hanger 18 that could be the source of the famous Hanger 18 stories. It is Building 1 of eight buildings 18-18G. Wreckage and at least four alien cadavers from the Roswell crash are said to have once been housed here and some wreckage may remain.

114

Figure 9: Building 18 (on the right or west) and Building 23 (on the left or east). The Roswell crash wreckage and at least four alien cadavers are said to have been initially delivered to Building/Hanger 23. It is said that its floor had been removed and the craft(s) were lowered into the basement. A concrete floor was placed over the area. After they did this, an entry was built from a vault in the east basement of building 18A to this new basement in Building 23. The entry from a Building 18 vault into Building 23, would be beneath the space between the two buildings, which is large enough to drive through.

Figure 10: Building 23 is a tall building with a massive 52,000-square-foot space. Several entrances are visible including one in the center of the north side that appears large enough for trucks. It has a sheet of windows on the east and west sides and at the top of the north side and very strong appearing pillars/posts on its four corners. It has an unusual shape and is said to have housed alien bodies and crash wreckage.

115

Figure 11: The WP Nuclear Engineering Test Facility was said by Carey, Schmitt, and Friedman to be above a vault. It was the result of an Air Force initiative to construct a nuclear-powered aircraft. It was the Air Force's only research reactor and was the seventh largest of its kind in the nation. With a ten-megawatt capacity it could accommodate a full-scale jet engine. Here it is seen in front of the Avionics tower. It is uphill from the "Hanger 18" complex.

Figure 12: The Avionics Laboratory (Building 620) with its distinctive "twin towers." We were able to photograph large entrance doors and a very well built-up, heavy duty ramp leading to them. This entrance should easily handle large trucks that then might travel to the two freight-sized elevators reported to be inside the building. They could then travel to the reported underground vaults and tunnels.

Figure 13: Deep digging and equipment for it can be seen in the parking lot that is said to be built over a large vault north of the Avionics Lab. (shown in the background). This equipment is for deep digging, not for pavement surfacing. This might be a smoking gun to confirm that the reported underground vault, said to be used to store recovered "alien bodies" from Roswell and other crashes, is there. It is said to contain preserved aliens and crash debris.

Figure 14: Large dirt piles from the digging north of Building 620 where the vaults and tunnels are reported to be. These do not appear to contain pavement, and are dug deeper than the parking lot surface.

Figure 15: Building 730 is a small, square, two story, building perhaps with a ventilation duct on top and railing as if the top is used for observation. It is in a completely isolated location but near the Avionics Lab. Collins reported to me that it is the location of one of the entrances to the vaults north of Building 620. It is reported to have a six-inch-thick bank vault door with a combination lock on the front of it on the inside.

Figure 16: Building 30 was reported to have a tunnel going from it to Building 450 the audiovisual facility and a small vault nearby.

Figure 17: A small building that does not appear connected to others in Area B is shown. Behind it is piping from the base power plant that appears to lead to an open area. Ventilation pipes coming out of the ground with no buildings around them, from underground vaults, are reported to be in Area B and perhaps this is one of them.

Figure 18: Another object was a large cylinder sticking out of an open area in the Area B hill area north of Building 620. It is unknown what such structures are or whether they might connect to underground vaults.

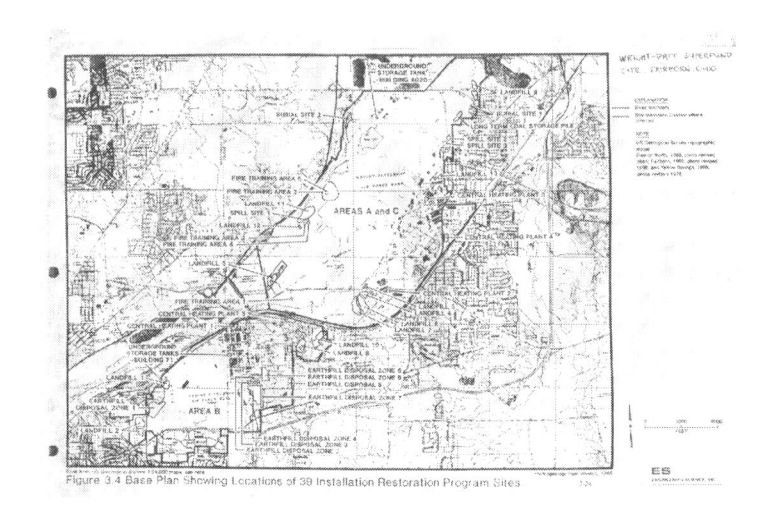

Figure 19: A map showing WP as a Superfund Site. It shows many landfills and underground storage areas.

Figure 20: The NASIC building appears to be by far the most secure building in the high security portion of WP, with rooftop cameras and every inch of surface area around the building's periphery monitored by machines that look like traffic lights. It is the famous "Blue Room;" Carey and Schmitt reported that an FOIA analyst at WP said, "the office of record for BLUE ROOM is NASIC." This organizational complex is of high significance to the UFO field because, under the acronyms ATIC and FTD, it once housed BB and the other UFO studies. Leonard Stringfield thought the bodies were stored here. We have been inside this building.

Figure 21: The NASAC building's security is so intense that it extends even into the Building 865 parking lot.

Figure 22: The photograph above shows the author with Dr. Bruce Ashcroft and the real Little Green Men of WP.

Figure 23: German POW artists had painted murals depicting gargoyle-like folk figures out of Germanic folklore. It makes the entrance passageway appear frightening. Is this one of the real WP Little Green Men?

Figure 24: The photograph above shows a part of the mural that German prisoners of war illustrated (1943) on the walls of what was originally a cafeteria in Building 280. The murals depict large green and devilish goblin-like creatures in a sea of flames against the original cement brick that lines the walls today. The building is set to be demolished in upcoming years but the eerie murals will be preserved to ensure future generations can gawk at the giant green devils.

Figure 25: Proof at WP that UFOs exist. A UFO display case once in the WP corridor leading to the cafeteria showed UFO reports that had been investigated. Out of the rest that they labeled fake, one was labeled Unidentified. This proves that UFOs are real!

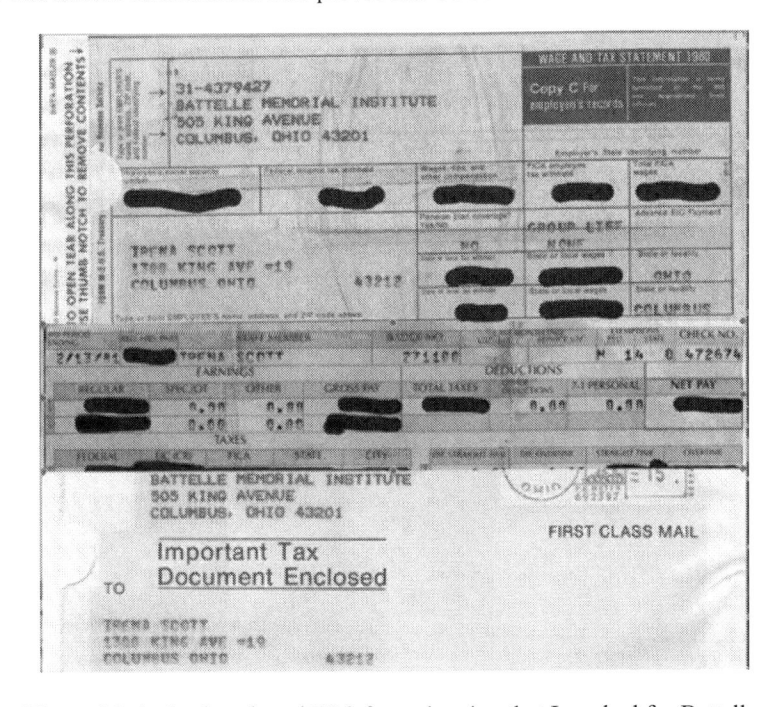

Figure 26: A check stub and W-2 form showing that I worked for Battelle.

123

Figure 27: I was told that a room on an upper floor of a Battelle building was the area where the BB UFO study took place. The Battelle employee told me that attached to the windows of this room are rings allegedly designed to prevent vibrations so spies can't use electronic techniques to listen to conversations going on inside the building, as shown. I was also told that alien material had been in a safe in this room and some might still be there.

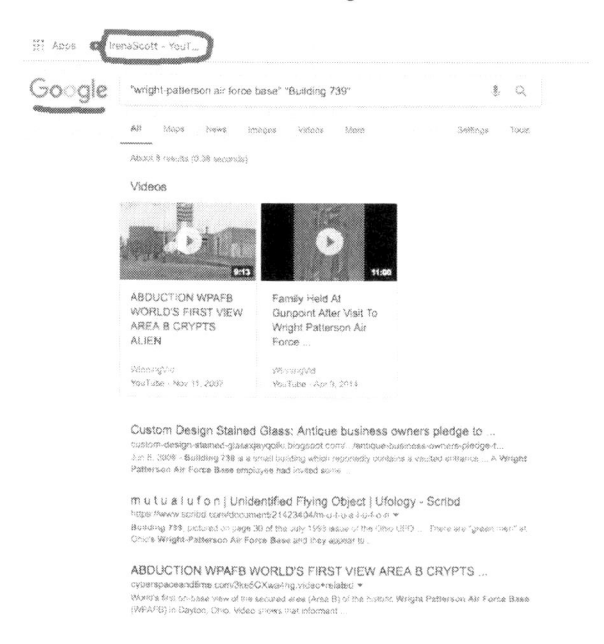

Figure 28: Many of the Google photographs of WP buildings are from videos that I once had on YouTube.

124

CHAPTER FOUR (PHOTOS): PROJECT BLUE BOOK

Figure 29: This photo shows the Air Material Command Headquarters. It is the organization that housed such UFO projects as Sign and Blue Book. The Technical Intelligence Division of the Air Material Command (AMC) at Wright Field (later WP), assumed control of Project SIGN and began its work in January 1948. On the right is one of the aircraft on display by the building.

Figure 30: An example of early government "back engineering" of UFOs.

CHAPTER FIVE (PHOTOS): THE PENTACLE MEMO

Battelle Personnel: "Pentacle" memo.

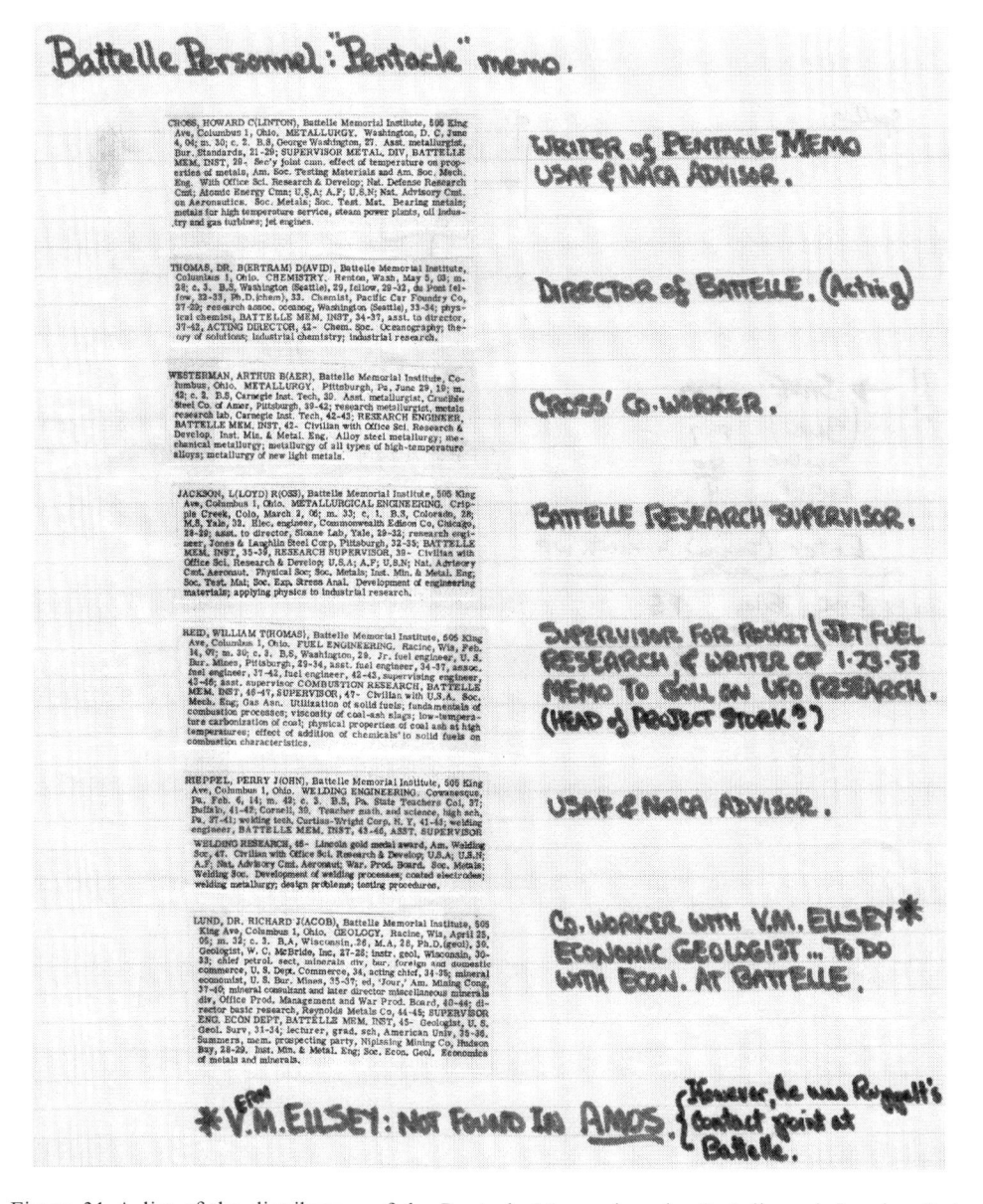

CROSS, HOWARD C(LINTON), Battelle Memorial Institute, 505 King Ave, Columbus 1, Ohio. METALLURGY. Washington, D.C, June 4, 04; m. 30; c. 2. B.S. George Washington, 27. Asst. metallurgist, Bur. Standards, 21-29; SUPERVISOR METAL. DIV, BATTELLE MEM. INST, 29-. Sec'y joint cmn. effect of temperature on properties of metals, Am. Soc. Testing Materials and Am. Soc. Mech. Eng. With Office Sci. Research & Develop; Nat. Defense Research Cncl; Atomic Energy Cmn; U.S.A; A.F; U.S.N; Nat. Advisory Cmt. on Aeronautics. Soc. Metals; Soc. Test. Mat. Bearing metals; metals for high temperature service, steam power plants, oil industry and gas turbines; jet engines.
— **WRITER of PENTACLE MEMO. USAF & NACA ADVISOR.**

THOMAS, DR. B(ERTRAM) D(AVID), Battelle Memorial Institute, Columbus 1, Ohio. CHEMISTRY. Renton, Wash, May 5, 05; m. 26; c. 3. B.S. Washington (Seattle), 29, fellow, 29-32, da Pont fellow, 32-33, Ph.D.(chem), 33. Chemist, Pacific Car Foundry Co, 27-29; research assoc, oceanog, Washington (Seattle), 33-34; physical chemist, BATTELLE MEM. INST, 34-37, asst. to director, 37-42, ACTING DIRECTOR, 42-. Chem. Soc. Oceanography; theory of solutions; industrial chemistry; industrial research.
— **DIRECTOR of BATTELLE. (Acting)**

WESTERMAN, ARTHUR B(AER), Battelle Memorial Institute, Columbus, Ohio. METALLURGY. Pittsburgh, Pa, June 29, 19; m. 42; c. 3. B.S. Carnegie Inst. Tech, 39. Asst. metallurgist, Crucible Steel Co. of Amer, Pittsburgh, 39-42; research metallurgist, metals research lab, Carnegie Inst. Tech, 42-43; RESEARCH ENGINEER, BATTELLE MEM. INST, 43-. Civilian with Office Sci. Research & Develop. Inst. Min. & Metal. Eng. Alloy steel metallurgy; mechanical metallurgy; metallurgy of all types of high-temperature alloys; metallurgy of new light metals.
— **CROSS' CO-WORKER.**

JACKSON, L(LOYD) R(OSS), Battelle Memorial Institute, 505 King Ave, Columbus 1, Ohio. METALLURGICAL ENGINEERING. Cripple Creek, Colo, March 2, 06; m. 33; c. 1. B.S, Colorado, 28; M.S, Yale, 29. Elec, engineer, Commonwealth Edison Co, Chicago, 28-29; asst. to director, Sloane Lab, Yale, 29-32; research engineer, Jones & Laughlin Steel Corp, Pittsburgh, 32-35; BATTELLE MEM. INST, 35-39, RESEARCH SUPERVISOR, 39-. Civilian with Office Sci. Research & Develop. U.S.A; A.F; U.S.N; Nat. Advisory Cncl. Aeronaut. Physical Soc; Soc. Metals; Inst. Min. & Metal. Eng; Soc. Test. Mat; Soc. Exp. Stress Anal. Development of engineering materials; applying physics to industrial research.
— **BATTELLE RESEARCH SUPERVISOR.**

REID, WILLIAM T(HOMAS), Battelle Memorial Institute, 505 King Ave, Columbus 1, Ohio. FUEL ENGINEERING. Racine, Wis, Feb. 14, 07; m. 30; c. 3. B.S, Washington, 29. Jr. fuel engineer, U.S. Bur. Mines, Pittsburgh, 29-34, asst. fuel engineer, 34-37, assoc. fuel engineer, 37-42, fuel engineer, 42-43, supervising engineer, 43-46; asst. supervisor COMBUSTION RESEARCH, BATTELLE MEM. INST, 46-47, SUPERVISOR, 47-. Civilian with U.S.A. Soc. Mech. Eng; Gas Asn. Utilization of solid fuels; fundamentals of combustion processes; viscosity of coal-ash slags; low-temperature carbonization of coal; physical properties of coal ash at high temperatures; effect of addition of chemicals to solid fuels on combustion characteristics.
— **SUPERVISOR FOR ROCKET/JET FUEL RESEARCH & WRITER OF 1-23-53 MEMO TO GOLL on UFO RESEARCH. (HEAD of PROJECT STORK?)**

RIEPPEL, PERRY J(OHN), Battelle Memorial Institute, 505 King Ave, Columbus 1, Ohio. WELDING ENGINEERING. Cowansque, Pa, Feb. 6, 14; m. 42; c. 3. B.S, Pa. State Teachers Col, 37; Bullch, 41-42; Cornell, 39. Teacher math. and science, high sch, 37-41; welding tech, Curtiss-Wright Corp, N. Y, 41-43; welding engineer, BATTELLE MEM. INST, 43-46, ASST. SUPERVISOR WELDING RESEARCH, 46-. Lincoln gold medal award, Am. Welding Soc, 47. Civilian with Office Sci. Research & Develop. U.S.A; U.S.N; A.F; Sn; Advisory Cmt. Aeronaut. War. Prod. Board. Soc. Metals; Welding Soc. Development of welding processes; coated electrodes; welding metallurgy; design problems; testing procedures.
— **USAF & NACA ADVISOR.**

LUND, DR. RICHARD J(ACOB), Battelle Memorial Institute, 505 King Ave, Columbus 1, Ohio. GEOLOGY. Racine, Wis, April 25, 05; m. 34; c. 3. B.A, Wisconsin, 26, M.A, 28, Ph.D.(geol), 30. Geologist, W.C. McBride, Inc, 27-28; instr. geol, Wisconsin, 30-33; chief petrol. sect, minerals div, bur. foreign and domestic commerce, U.S. Dept. Commerce, 34, acting chief, 34-35; mineral economist, U.S. Bur. Mines, 35-37; ed, 'Jour,' Am. Mining Cong, 37-40; mineral consultant and later director miscellaneous minerals div, Office Prod. Management and War Prod. Board, 40-44; director basic research, Reynolds Metals Co, 44-45; SUPERVISOR ENG. ECON DEPT, BATTELLE MEM. INST, 45-. Geologist, U.S. Geol. Surv, 31-34; lecturer, grad. sch, American Univ, 35-36. Summers, mem. prospecting party, Nipissing Mining Co, Hudson Bay, 28-29. Inst. Min. & Metal. Eng; Soc. Econ. Geol. Economics of metals and minerals.
— **CO-WORKER WITH V.M. ELLSEY✱ ECONOMIC GEOLOGIST ... TO DO WITH ECON. AT BATTELLE.**

✱ V.M. ELLSEY: NOT FOUND In AMOS. {However, he was Ruppelt's contact point at Battelle.}

Figure 31 A list of the distributees of the Pentacle Memo done by Battelle and showing their listing in the prestigious American Men of Science.

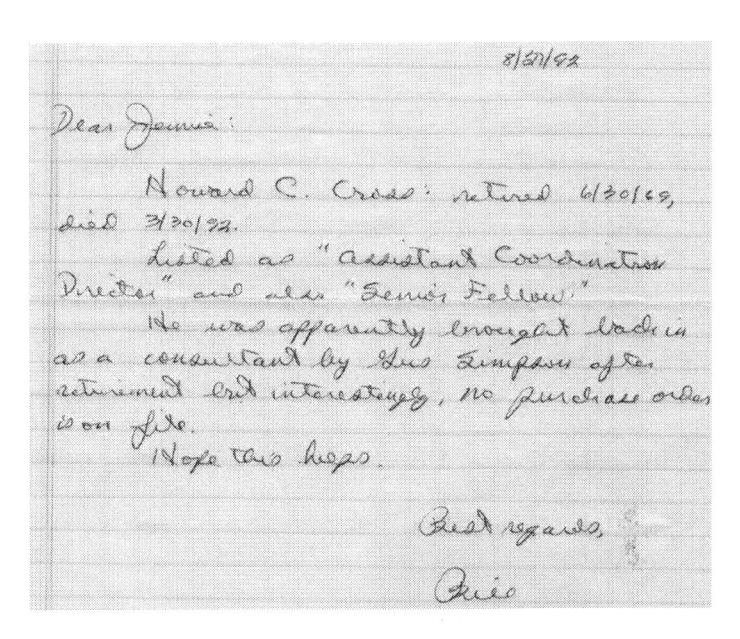

Figure 32: A note from Bill Jones to Jennie Zeidman adding information about Howard Cross.

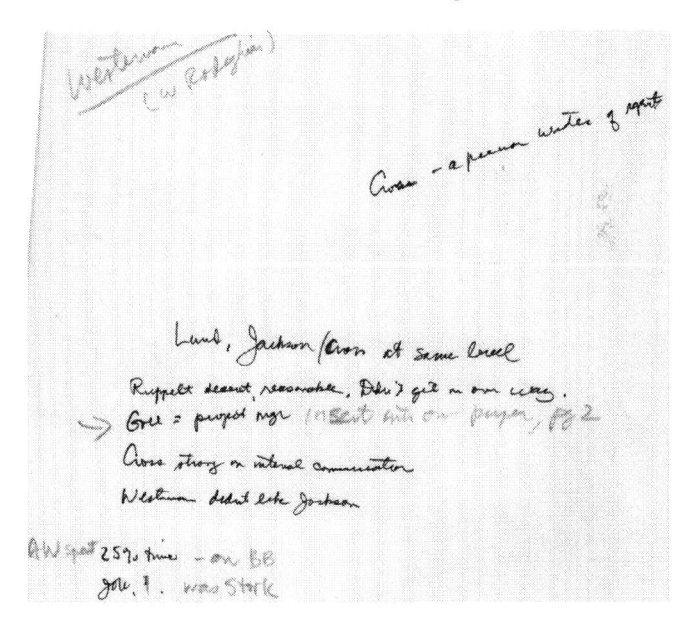

Figure 33: An interview with Art Westerman about the positions of the Pentacle Memo distributees, what they were like, and Westerman's personal opinion about some.

Contract 1951-1954

David Bertram Thomas
1953 - Associate Director and Acting Director
Retired 5/31/68 President
Alive

Howard C. Cross
Associate Coordination Director - 6/24/53
Senior Fellow 1/65, Retired 6/69
Deceased 3/30/92

Lloyd R. Jackson
1953 - Coordination Director
Retired 6/68, same title
Deceased 6/10/76

William T. Reid
1953 - Technical Director
Retired 1/1/78 Principal Research Scientist
Alive

Perry J. Rieppel
1953 - Division Chief
Assistant Director, temination date 10/31/77
Alive

V. W. Ellzey
1953 - Principal Min. (Mineral?) Economist
Retired September 22, 1976 ("Death at 52") Researcher

R. J. Lund
1953 - Manager of Information and Analysis
Retired 4/30/70 as Senior Advisor
Deceased 1/11/87

Figure 34: A Battelle typed copy showing the positions of the Pentacle Memo distributees from 1951 to 1954. All are there but Westerman.

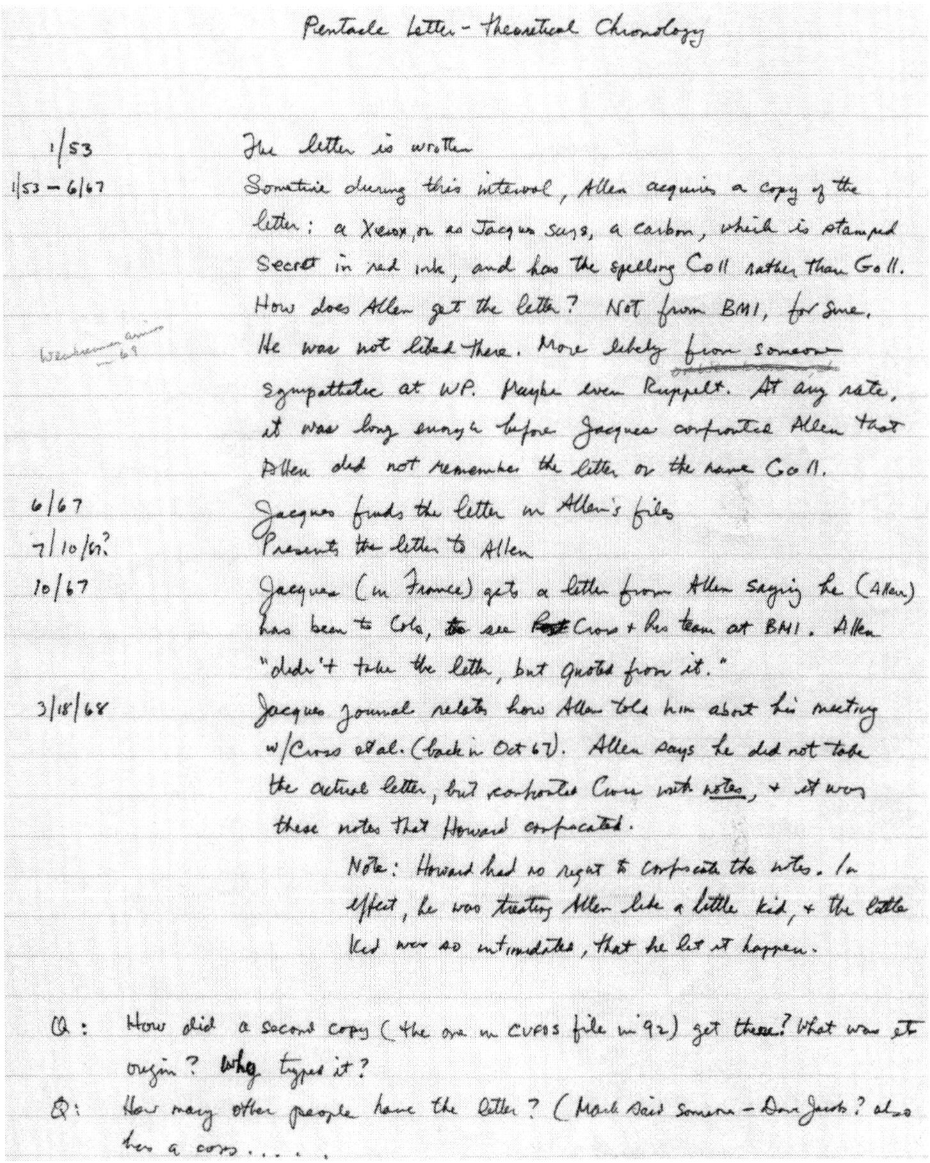

Pentacle Letter - Theoretical Chronology

1/53 — The letter is written

1/53 – 6/67 — Sometime during this interval, Allen acquires a copy of the letter; a Xerox, or as Jacques says, a carbon, which is stamped Secret in red ink, and has the spelling Coll rather than Goll. How does Allen get the letter? Not from BMI, for sure. He was not liked there. More likely from someone sympathetic at WP. Maybe even Ruppelt. At any rate, it was long enough before Jacques confronted Allen that Allen did not remember the letter or the name Coll.

Wednesday aim 69

6/67 — Jacques finds the letter in Allen's files

7/10/67? — Presents the letter to Allen

10/67 — Jacques (in France) gets a letter from Allen saying he (Allen) has been to Col., to see ~~Fort~~ Cross + his team at BMI. Allen "didn't take the letter, but quoted from it."

3/18/68 — Jacques journal relates how Allen told him about his meeting w/ Cross et al. (back in Oct 67). Allen says he did not take the actual letter, but confronted Cross with notes, + it was these notes that Howard confiscated.

Note: Howard had no right to confiscate the notes. In effect, he was treating Allen like a little kid, + the little kid was so intimidated, that he let it happen.

Q: How did a second copy (the one in CUFOS file in 92) get there? What was its origin? Why typed it?

Q: How many other people have the letter? (Mark said someone - Don Jacob? also has a copy....)

Figure 35: A Theoretical Chronology of the Pentacle Memo by the authors of the "The Pentacle Letter and the Battelle UFO Project." They were looking for information about who leaked the Memo. This was important because it was someone with a high security clearance, that knew the people involved, and that also understood what was happening at that time right before the Robertson Panel meeting.

Why are letterhead on either copy of Pentacle?
BMI

What We Want to Tell:
(Not necessarily in chronological order)

1. JZ identified Pentacle "right away" (Glory!!)

2. CUFOS (Rodeghier & Chesney?) located the doc in the files "right away. ("Glory!! Glory!!")

3. Our interpretation differs from Jacques', but we had sense enough to do some research before publishing.

4. We have (JZ first!) interviewed the surviving distributees. (Not giving the # who are alive, or identifying which ones they are).

5. We deplore that the names of the distributees were published. From the beginning we have maintained our respect for Battelle's sensitivity in this matter.

6. One of the distributees is the same man that Zeidman referred to in "I Remember BB". We consider this man to be extremely high-ranking and credible. Also that we know that he did considerable intelligence work through BMI contracts; to the extent of being sent to Viet Nam for 6 months during the last years of the war. *(list of one of what)*

7. One of the men was the person who actually came up with the idea of a "test area."

8. The "test" idea was never implemented.

9. The "G" Number is a BMI internal project #. *— (Is this necessary to tell?)*

10. The mission of Stork was CCCP technical intelligence, NOT UFOs, ~~and that~~ BBSR 14 was hidden within Stork, with no extra money.

11. Pentacle and at least 2 of the others were unhappy with the project because of the extra work load with no extra funds.

12. Clyde Williams, CEO at that time, was the one who wanted the project, on the grounds that maybe there was something to it, and BMI would get the glory. (Obviously not because it was going to bring in more $$.)

13. The document presented by Vicki & the reference in FS both give the wrong name: Coll vs. Goll. Lt. Col. Miles E. Goll was Acting Chief, Analysis Division, T-2.

One of the distributees said only 150k was spent out of Stork funds — not the 600k quoted by Vallée.

Things We Don't Want to Tell:

1. Our Pentacle letter is not the same one that Jacques

Figure 36: This document provides even more detail about the Pentacle Memo and the questions concerning it. (CCCP is a Russian abbreviation for the Soviet Union or Union of Soviet Socialist Republics (USSR).

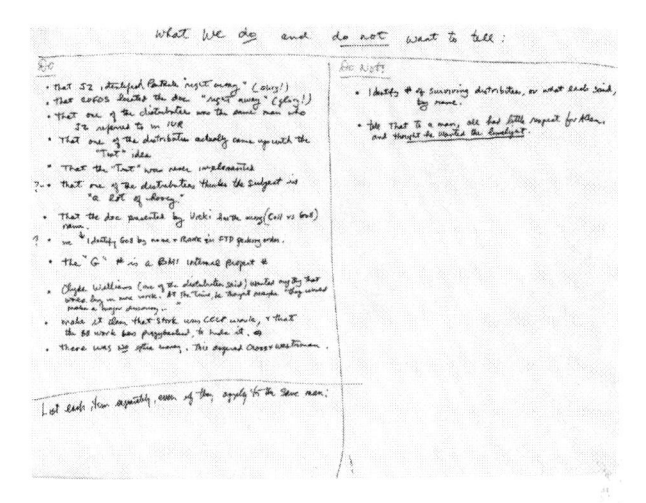

Figure 37: The authors of the "The Pentacle Letter and the Battelle UFO Project" had lists of what topics to mention in this article and what not to mention as this handwritten note shows. This note, as did several others, showed Clyde Williams, the head of Battelle giving positive statements about UFOs.

CHAPTER SIX (PHOTOS): PROJECT BLUE BOOK SPECIAL REPORT #14

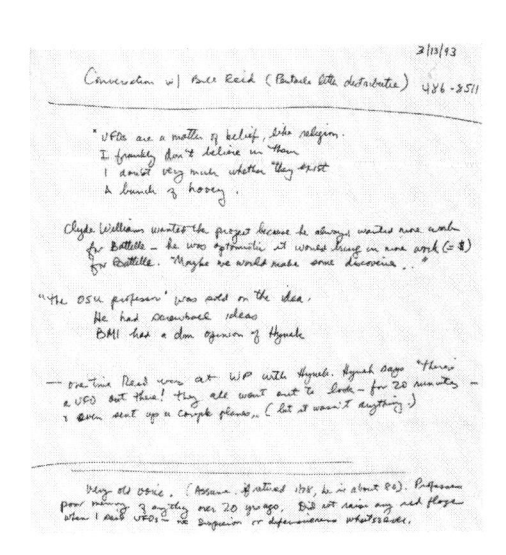

131

Figure 38: This is information from an interview with Bill Reid, one of the Pentacle Memo distributees about the study. He was negative about UFOs and viewed the subject as hooey. He told about Hynek's screwball ideas and activities.

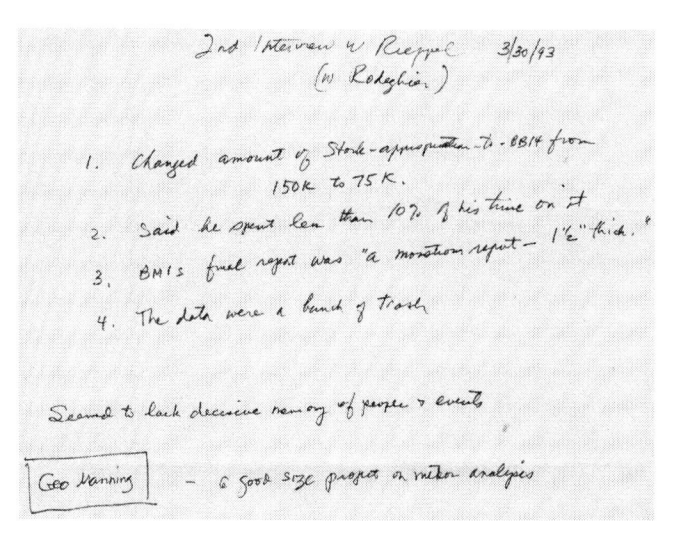

Figure 39: This was information from a second interview with Perry Rieppel about the Battelle study. It told about the time spent on the project and described it as "a monster report." It also mentioned George Manning's opinion of the research.

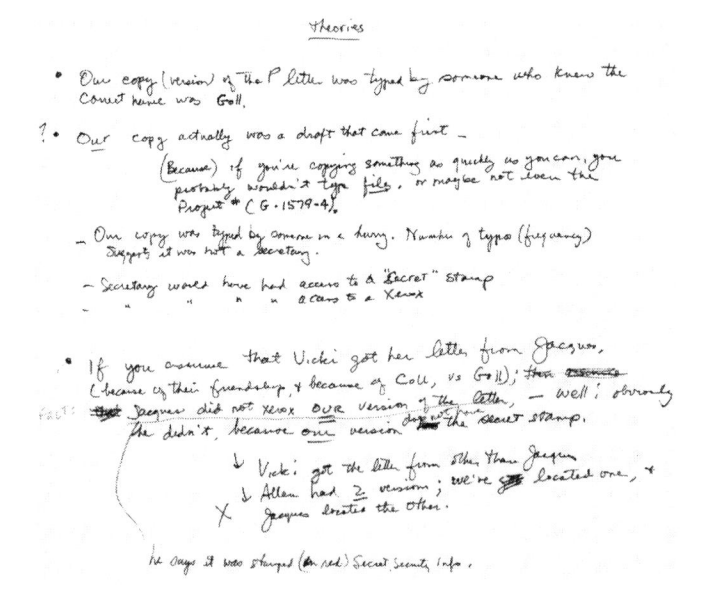

Figure 40: It contains more information and conjecture about who leaked the Pentacle Memo.

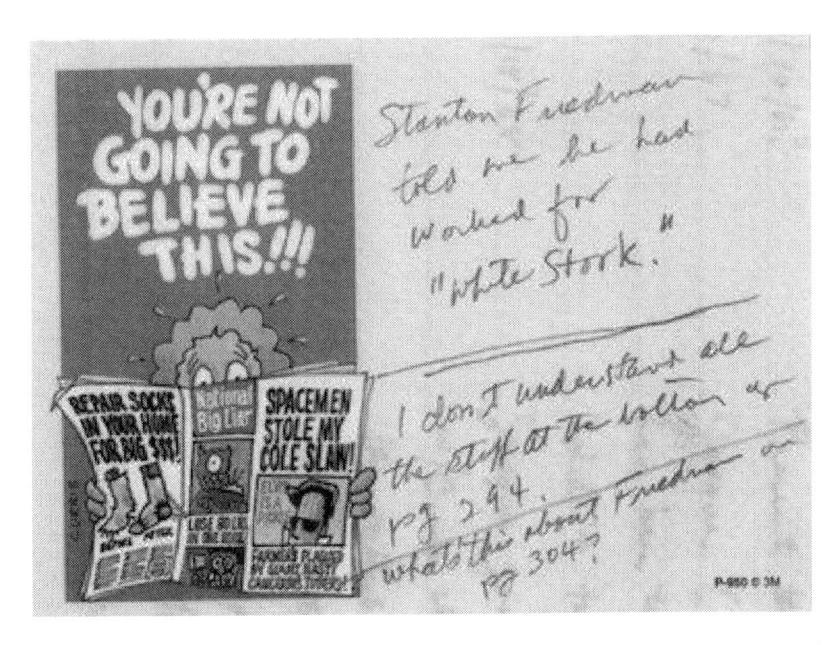

Figure 41: This contains some information on a Post it Note about Stanton Friedman and his relation to Battelle.

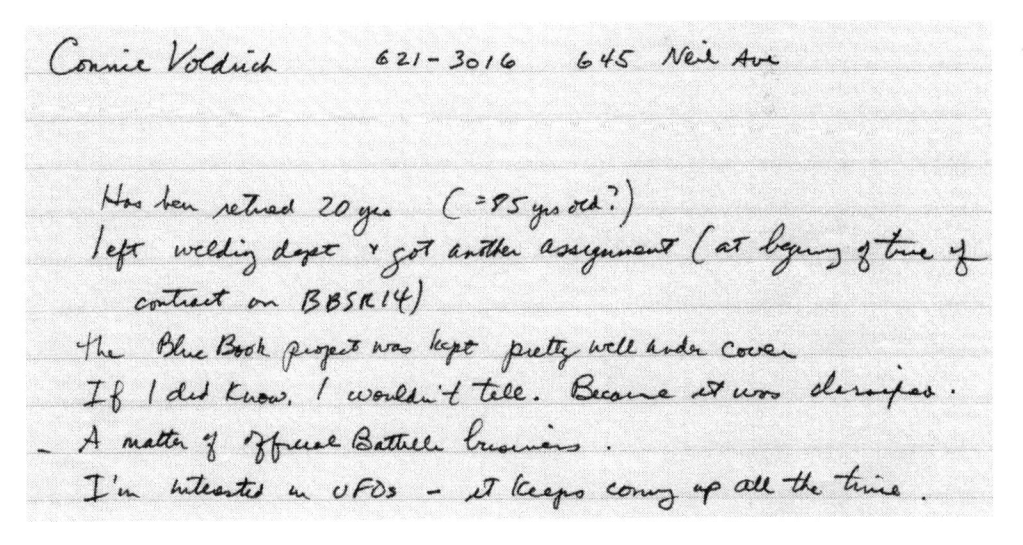

Figure 42: Information from Connie Voldrich. She knew about the study, although she was not a part of it. She was interested in UFOs.

133

Chi-Square Calculator

Success! The contingency table below provides the following information: the observed cell totals, (the expected cell totals) and [the chi-square statistic for each cell].

The chi-square statistic, p-value and statement of significance appear beneath the table. Blue means you're dealing with dependent variables; red, independent.

	Category 1	Category 2	Marginal Row Totals
Group 1	51 (50.99) [0]	52 (52.01) [0]	103
Group 2	49 (49.01) [0]	50 (49.99) [0]	99
Marginal Column Totals	100	102	202 (Grand Total)

The chi-square statistic is 0. The p-value is .997776. This result is not significant at p < .05.

Figure 43: This shows how to use statistics to solve real-world problems, such as determining which jar to choose to find particular contents.

Chi-Square Calculator

Success! The contingency table below provides the following information: the observed cell totals, (the expected cell totals) and [the chi-square statistic for each cell].

The chi-square statistic, p-value and statement of significance appear beneath the table. Blue means you're dealing with dependent variables; red, independent.

	Category 1	Category 2	Marginal Row Totals
Group 1	51 (42.56) [1.67]	52 (60.44) [1.18]	103
Group 2	49 (57.44) [1.24]	90 (81.56) [0.87]	139
Marginal Column Totals	100	142	242 (Grand Total)

The chi-square statistic is 4.9635. The p-value is .025888. This result is not significant at p < .01.

Figure 44: This also shows how to use statistics to solve real world problems.

The results of a contingency table X^2 statistical test

```
data: contingency table

        A       B

1      329     297     626
2       39      37      76
3       46      70     116
4       10      25      35
5       10       5      15

       434     434     868


expected: contingency table

        A               B

1      313.            313.
2       38.0            38.0
3       58.0            58.0
4       17.5            17.5
5        7.50            7.50
```

chi-square = 14.7
degrees of freedom = 4
probability = 0.005

Figure 45: A recalculation of some of the statistics in SR-14.

The results of a contingency table X^2 statistical test

```
data: contingency table

        A       B
1      64      27      91
2      23      21      44
3      38      33      71
4      26      42      68
5      66      99     165
6      75      71     146
7      33      37      70
8     109     104     213

      434     434     868


expected: contingency table

        A              B
1      45.5           45.5
2      22.0           22.0
3      35.5           35.5
4      34.0           34.0
5      82.5           82.5
6      73.0           73.0
7      35.0           35.0
8     106.           106.
```

chi-square = 26.3
degrees of freedom = 7
probability = 0.000

Figure 46: Another recalculation of the SR-14 statistics showing that the results are even more significant than reported earlier.

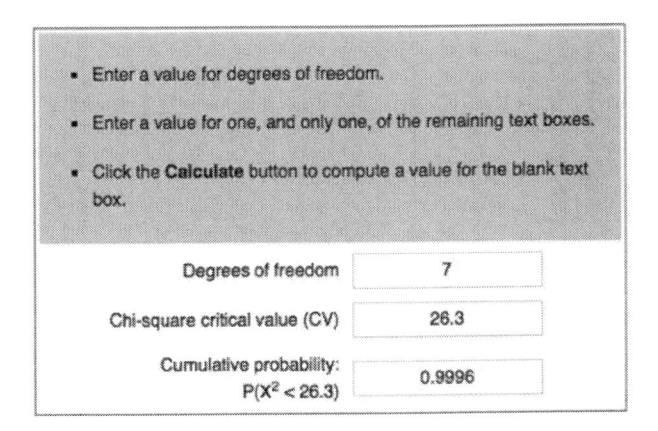

- Enter a value for degrees of freedom.
- Enter a value for one, and only one, of the remaining text boxes.
- Click the **Calculate** button to compute a value for the blank text box.

Degrees of freedom	7
Chi-square critical value (CV)	26.3
Cumulative probability: $P(X^2 < 26.3)$	0.9996

Figure 47: This recalculation shows the extremely significant results showing almost no probability that UFOs represent prosaic objects.

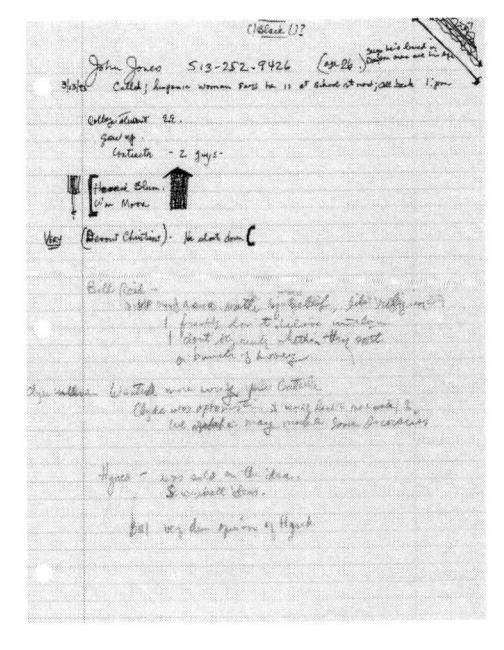

Figure 48: Shows another interview with Bill Reid a distributee of the Pentacle Memo.

CHAPTER SEVEN (PHOTOS): MEMORY METAL, UFO DEBRIS, ROSWELL–A MILLION VIEWS

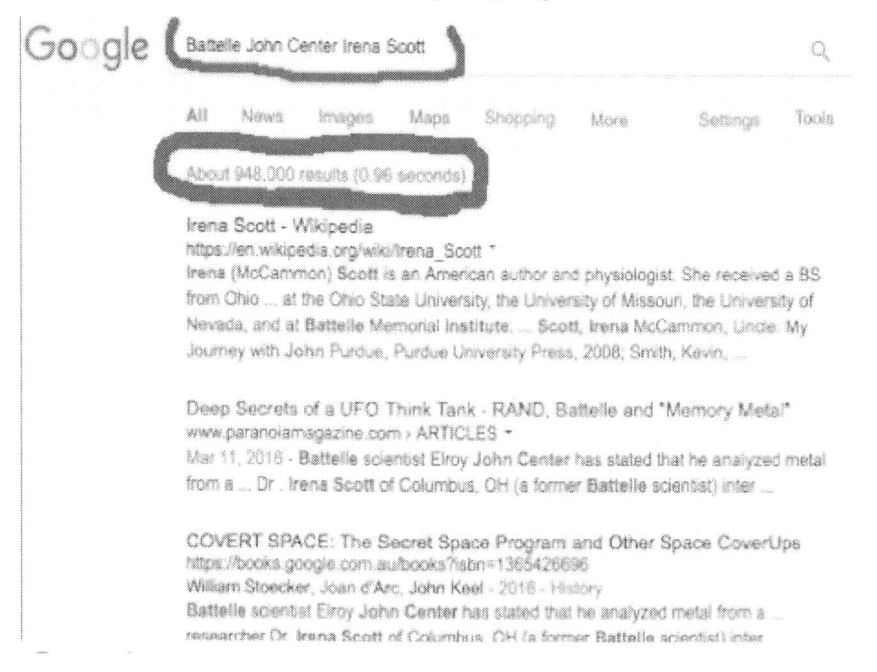

Figure 49: There was much discussion about our smoking gun evidence that UFO material had been studied at Battelle on the Internet. There were almost a million views on the subject on Google.

CENTER, E(LROY) JOHN, Battelle Memorial Institute, Columbus 1, Ohio. CHEMICAL ENGINEERING. Hibbing, Minn, Aug. 17, 17; m. 41; c. 4. B.S, Michigan, 39, 39-40. Chemist, Oliver Iron Min. Co, Minn, 40-41; research engineer, BATTELLE MEM. INST, 41-46, SUPERVISOR ANAL. DIV, 46- Chem. Soc; Soc. Test. Mat; Inst. Chem. Eng. Inorganic and organic analysis; instrumental techniques.

Figure 50: John Center is listed in American Men of Science. He was a highly qualified researcher with numerous publications.

CHAPTER EIGHT (PHOTOS): WHO DID THE SR-14 AND WHY DOES NO ONE KNOW?" THE "OTHERS LIST"

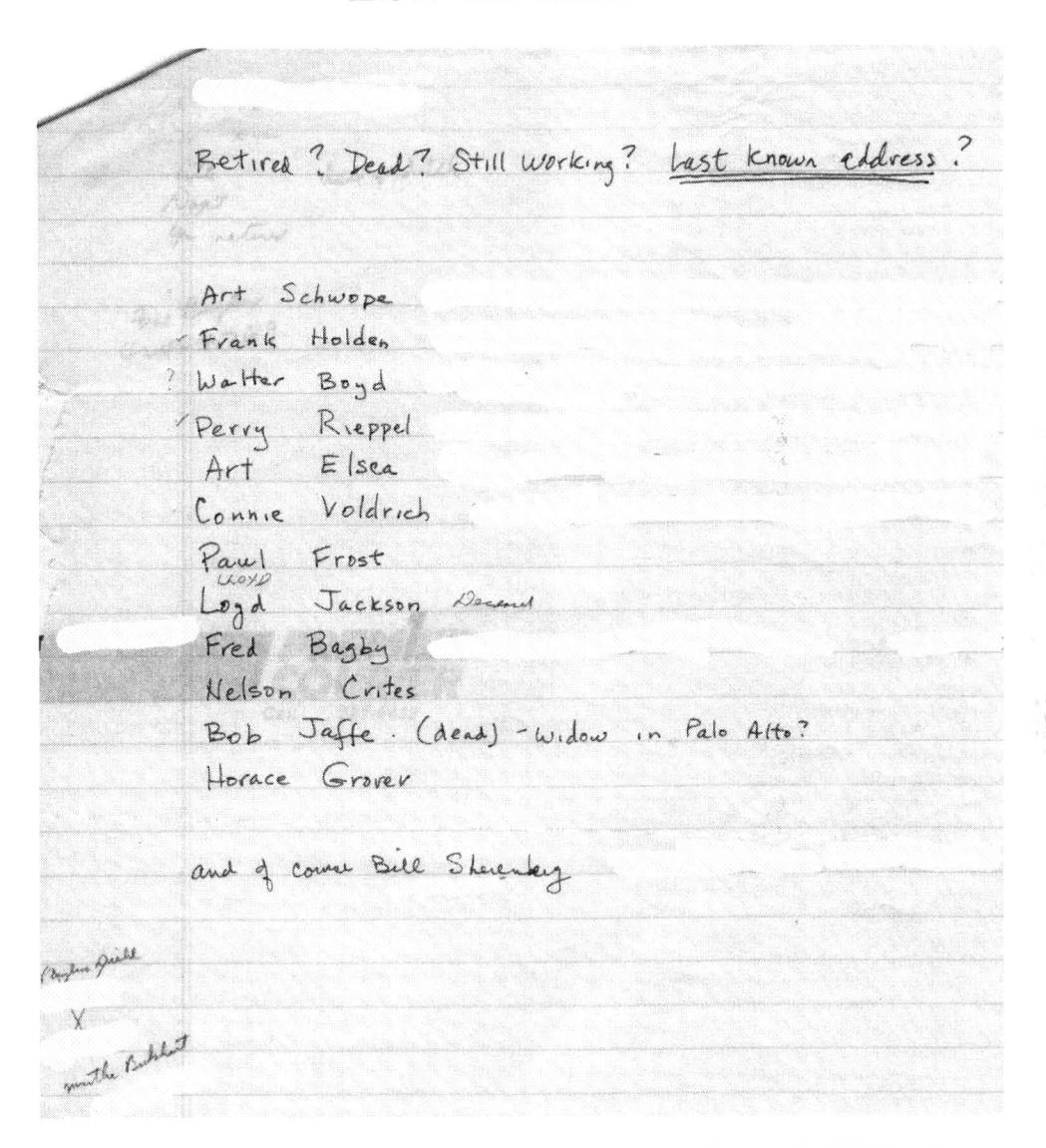

Figure 51: The "Others List," of people who might be knowledgeable about the SR-14 study.

CHAPTER NINE (PHOTOS): A SMALL OHIO TOWN, ROSWELL, AND ADVANCED METAL ALLOYS

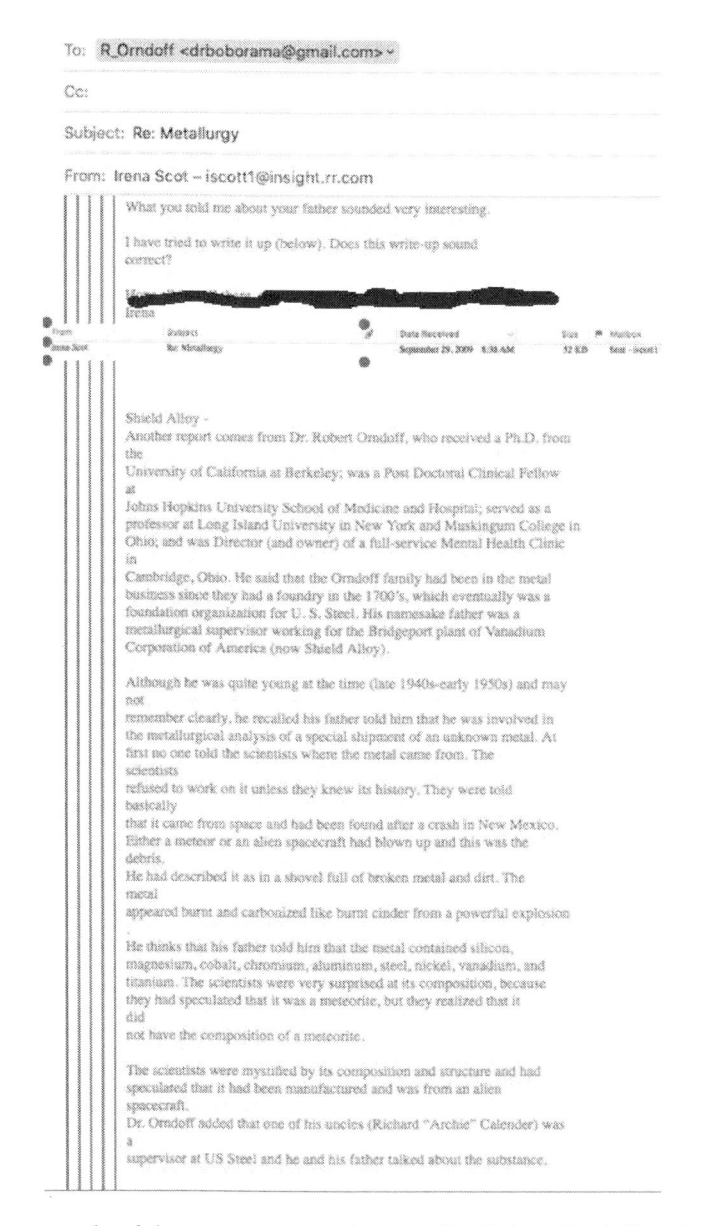

To: R_Orndoff <drboborama@gmail.com>

Cc:

Subject: Re: Metallurgy

From: Irena Scot – iscott1@insight.rr.com

What you told me about your father sounded very interesting.

I have tried to write it up (below). Does this write-up sound correct?

Irena

From	Subject	Date Received	Size	Mailbox
Irena Scot	Re: Metallurgy	September 29, 2009 9:38 AM	12 KB	Sent - iscott1

Shield Alloy –
Another report comes from Dr. Robert Orndoff, who received a Ph.D. from the
University of California at Berkeley; was a Post Doctoral Clinical Fellow at
Johns Hopkins University School of Medicine and Hospital; served as a professor at Long Island University in New York and Muskingum College in Ohio; and was Director (and owner) of a full-service Mental Health Clinic in
Cambridge, Ohio. He said that the Orndoff family had been in the metal business since they had a foundry in the 1700's, which eventually was a foundation organization for U. S. Steel. His namesake father was a metallurgical supervisor working for the Bridgeport plant of Vanadium Corporation of America (now Shield Alloy).

Although he was quite young at the time (late 1940s-early 1950s) and may not
remember clearly, he recalled his father told him that he was involved in the metallurgical analysis of a special shipment of an unknown metal. At first no one told the scientists where the metal came from. The scientists
refused to work on it unless they knew its history. They were told basically
that it came from space and had been found after a crash in New Mexico. Either a meteor or an alien spacecraft had blown up and this was the debris.
He had described it as in a shovel full of broken metal and dirt. The metal
appeared burnt and carbonized like burnt cinder from a powerful explosion

He thinks that his father told him that the metal contained silicon, magnesium, cobalt, chromium, aluminum, steel, nickel, vanadium, and titanium. The scientists were very surprised at its composition, because they had speculated that it was a meteorite, but they realized that it did
not have the composition of a meteorite.

The scientists were mystified by its composition and structure and had speculated that it had been manufactured and was from an alien spacecraft.
Dr. Orndoff added that one of his uncles (Richard "Archie" Calender) was a
supervisor at US Steel and he and his father talked about the substance.

Figure 52: An example of the correspondence between Dr. Robert Orndoff and me. I wrote a piece about what he told me and asked him to check it. He thought it was fine.

CHAPTER TEN (PHOTOS): THE TREND EXPLODES–USAF RESEARCH ON UFOS IS DESTROYED FOREVER, DARK SIDE AND DEATH

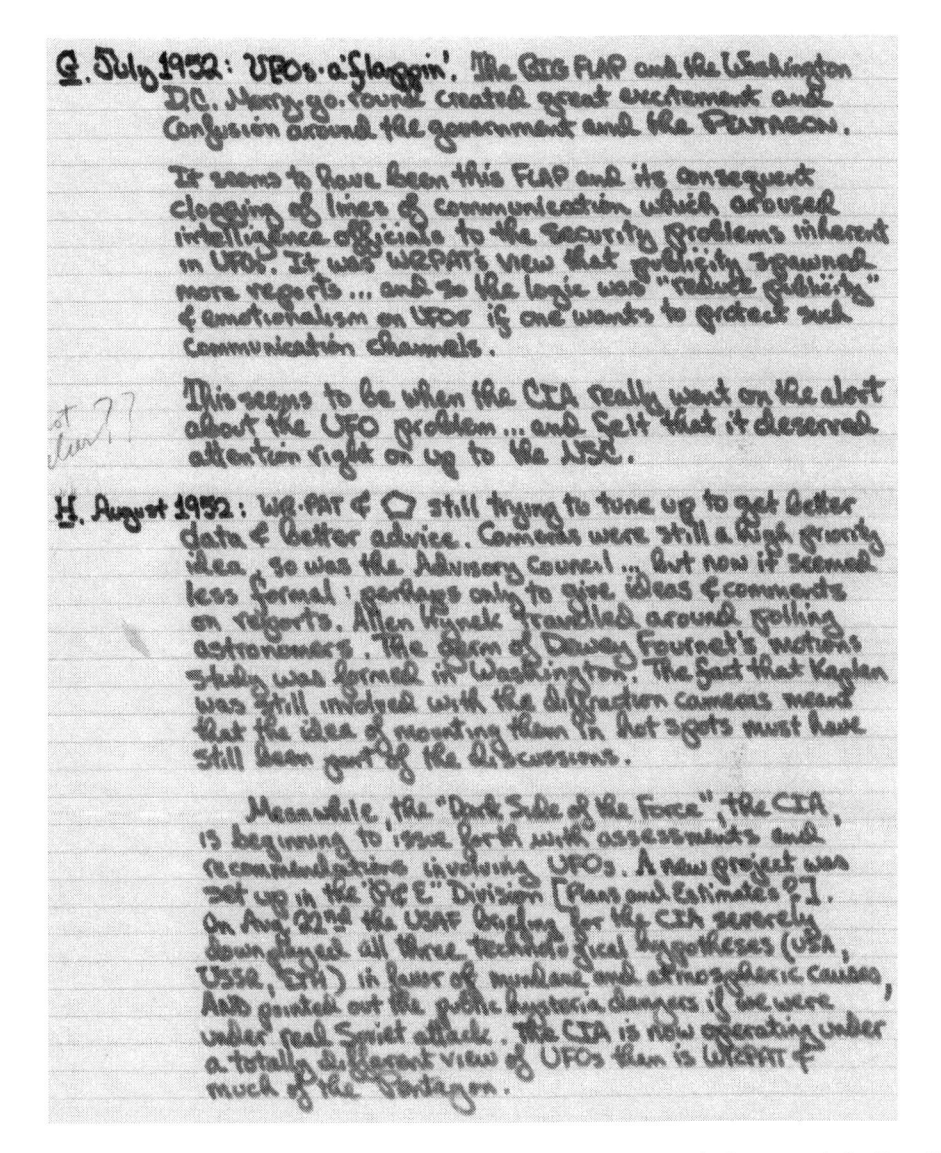

Figure 53: A handwritten early draft of the IUR article "The Pentacle Letter and the Battelle UFO Project." "UFOs a'flappin!," these initial handwritten versions are more colorful, spontaneous, and expressive than the much more edited final version.

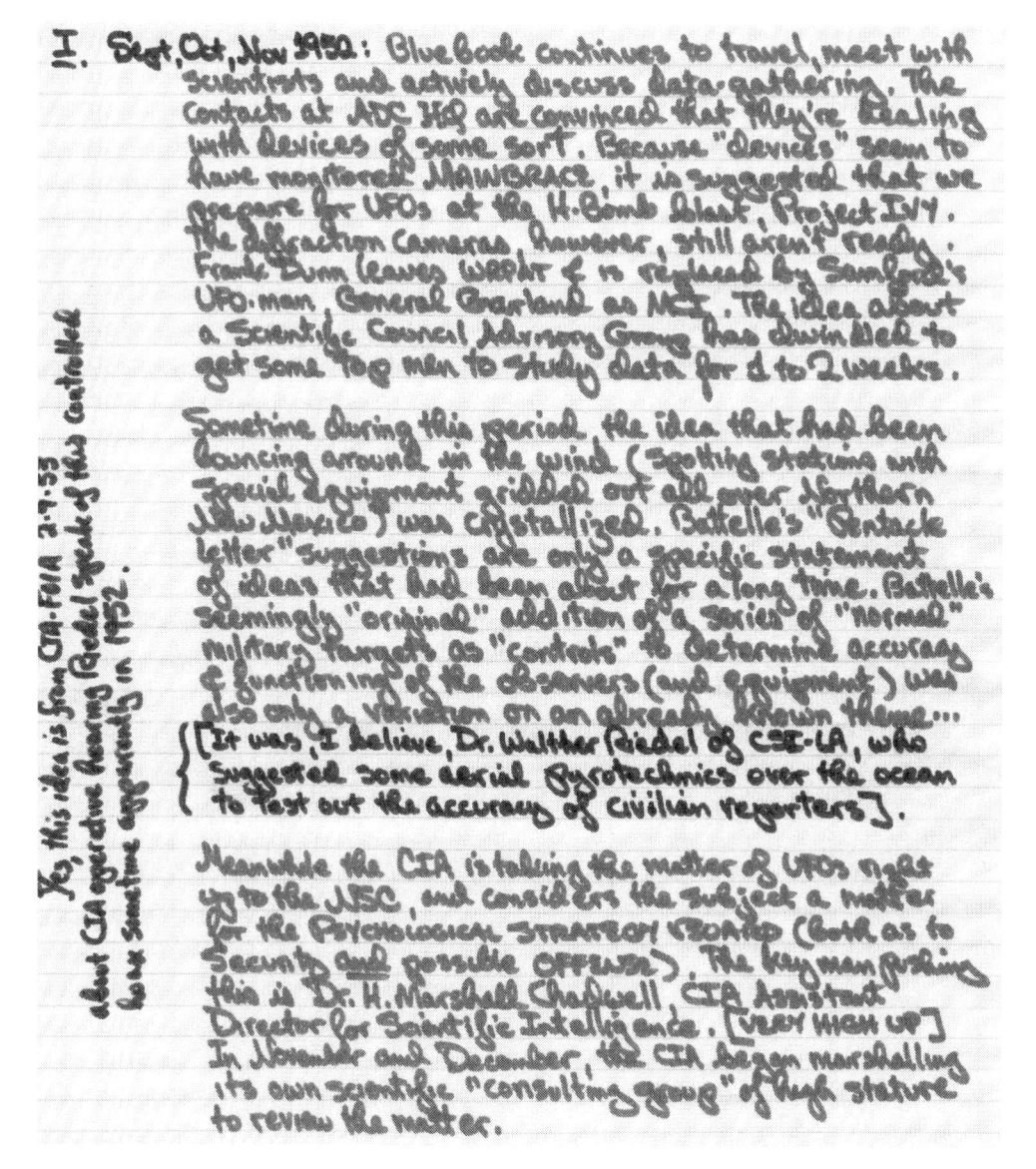

II. Sept, Oct, Nov 1952: Blue Book continues to travel, meet with scientists and actively discuss data-gathering. The contacts at ATIC HQ are convinced that they're dealing with devices of some sort. Because "devices" seem to have monitored MAINBRACE, it is suggested that we prepare for UFOs at the H-Bomb blast, Project IVY. The diffraction cameras, however, still aren't ready. Frank Dunn leaves WPAFB & is replaced by Sanford's UFO man, General Garland as NCE. The idea about a Scientific Council Advisory Group has dwindled to get some top men to study data for 1 to 2 weeks.

Sometime during this period the idea that had been bouncing around in the wind (spotting stations with special equipment gridded out all over Northern New Mexico) was crystallized. Battelle's "Pentacle Letter" suggestions are only a specific statement of ideas that had been about for a long time. Battelle's seemingly "original" addition of a series of "normal" military targets as "controls" to determine accuracy of functioning of the observers (and equipment) was also only a variation on an already known theme...
[It was, I believe, Dr. Walther Riedel of CSI-LA, who suggested some aerial pyrotechnics over the ocean to test out the accuracy of civilian reporters].

Meanwhile the CIA is taking the matter of UFOs right up to the NSC, and considers the subject a matter for the Psychological Strategy Board (both as to security and possible OFFENSE). The key man pushing this is Dr. H. Marshall Chadwell, CIA Assistant Director for Scientific Intelligence. [VERY HIGH UP]
In November and December, the CIA began marshalling its own scientific "consulting group" of high stature to review the matter.

Yes, this idea is from CIA-FOIA 2-9-53 about CIA operative hearing Riedel speak of this controlled hoax sometime apparently in 1952.

Figure 54: Another handwritten early draft of the IUR article "The Pentacle Letter and the Battelle UFO Project." It details some highly significant UFO sightings such as during Project Mainbrace, when they had evidence that UFOs were monitoring this huge multi-country exercise. This made government scientists very concerned/fearful about the upcoming H-Bomb blast. This was the first H bomb test. It was conducted under project Ivy done on November 1, 1952. The government set up procedures for what to do if the UFOs became interactive. Very little was known of this by the public.

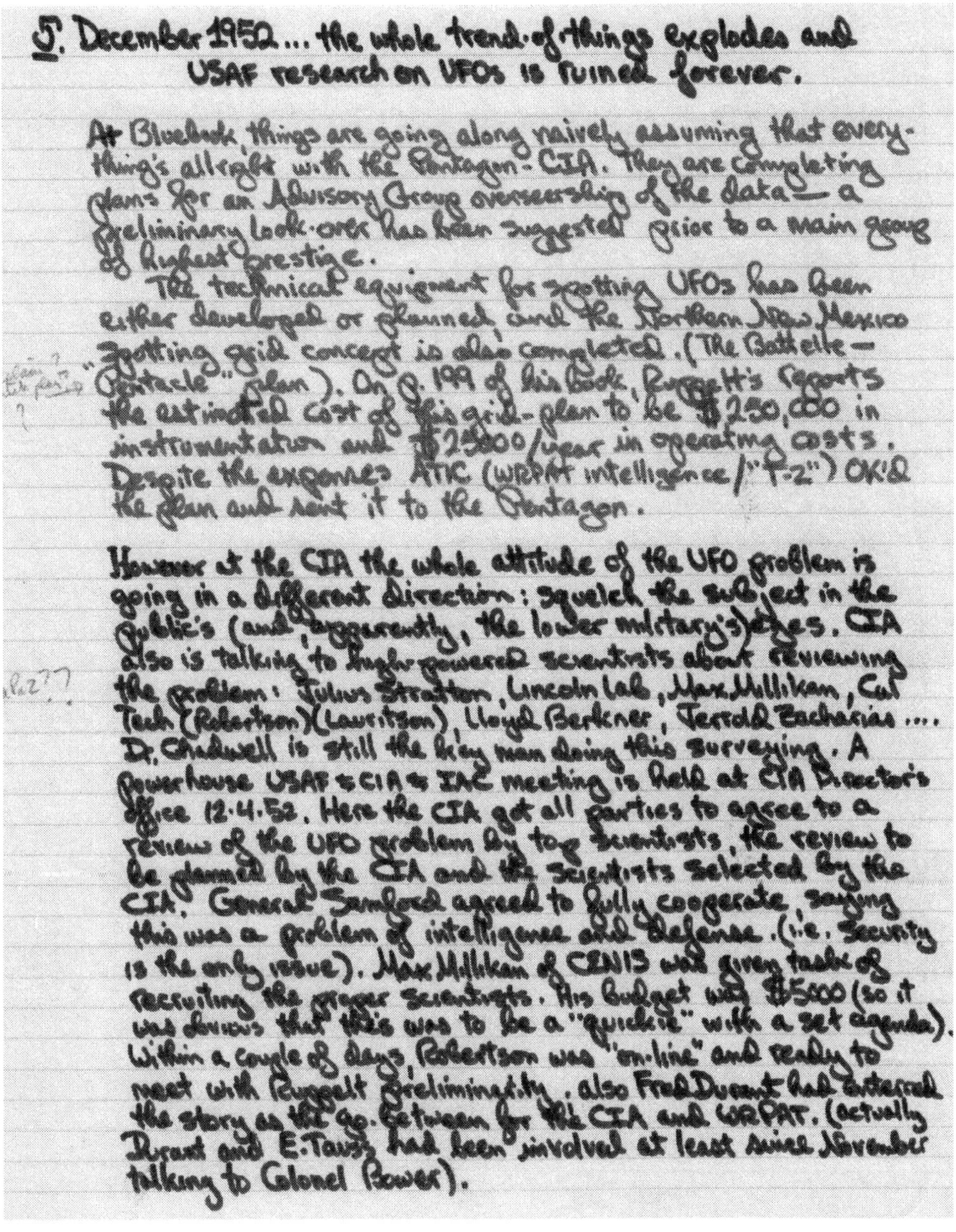

5. December 1952... the whole trend of things explodes and USAF research on UFOs is ruined forever.

At Bluebook, things are going along naively, assuming that everything's all right with the Pentagon - CIA. They are completing plans for an Advisory Group overseership of the data — a preliminary look-over has been suggested prior to a main group of highest prestige.

The technical equipment for spotting UFOs has been either developed or planned, and the Northern New Mexico spotting grid concept is also completed. (The Battelle — "Pentacle" plan). On p. 199 of his book, Ruppelt's reports the estimated cost of this grid plan to be $250,000 in instrumentation and $25,000/year in operating costs. Despite the expenses ATIC (WPAFB intelligence/"T-2") OK'd the plan and sent it to the Pentagon.

However at the CIA the whole attitude of the UFO problem is going in a different direction: squelch the subject in the public's (and, apparently, the lower military's) eyes. CIA also is talking to high-powered scientists about reviewing the problem: Julius Stratton, Lincoln Lab, Max Millikan, Cal Tech (Robertson)(Lauritsen), Lloyd Berkner, Jerrold Zacharias.... Dr. Chadwell is still the key man doing this surveying. A powerhouse USAF + CIA + IAC meeting is held at CIA Director's office 12·4·52. Here the CIA got all parties to agree to a review of the UFO problem by top scientists, the review to be planned by the CIA and the scientists selected by the CIA. General Samford agreed to fully cooperate, saying this was a problem of intelligence and defense (i.e. security is the only issue). Max Millikan of CENIS was given task of recruiting the proper scientists. His budget was $5000 (so it was obvious that this was to be a "quickie" with a set agenda). Within a couple of days Robertson was "on-line" and ready to meet with Ruppelt preliminarily. also Fred Durant had entered the story as the go-between for the CIA and WPAFB. (actually Durant and E. Tauss had been involved at least since November talking to Colonel Bower).

Figure 55: An additional handwritten early draft of the IUR article "The Pentacle Letter and the Battelle UFO Project." The abrupt and unexpected end of the Project, described as "the whole trend of things explodes."

(perhaps late in November) 1952 (Ruppelt doesn't always get dates exact.)

The "preliminary look" at Bluebook data, which occurred in Dayton in December, was in Ruppelt's mind an open-ended "natural" part of a procedure leading toward a serious study by top scientists (naive boy). Actually, it seems to have been the "ritualistic" going-through-the-motions-of legerdemain endemic to CIA covert actions. That this latter seems obvious results from Ruppelt's report that 4 people reviewed the files in (late Nov./December) for 3 days, and recommended that a "High Court" of scientists be approved to look at this. THIS RECOMMENDATION WAS APPROVED BY THE ⬠ IN ONE HOUR. It's obvious that this recommendation was expected/planned for. Also, the recommendation CONTAINED THE NAMES OF THE 6 MEN RECOMMENDED TO SERVE. Only the date (late Dec/early Jan) was still open. I believe that the whole deal was a "done deal" in the CIA/NSC, that the WPAFB meetings were in early December, that Dr. Chadwell (who writes to Hynek telling him how he enjoyed meeting him in Dayton earlier in the month) was the leader of this CIA-science team, & that poor ol' Ed Ruppelt had no idea that the die was already cast. (Robertson and Durant visited WPAFB in the second week of December, also).

__K__. January 1953... "Pentacle" letter.
Robertson panel.
W. Reid of Battelle completes correspondence on filing / IBM project. 1/23/53 -

Ruppelt still didn't clearly hear what was being said. The Bluebook project continues for a little while on momentum. CIA maintained a lot of interest in probing cases and persons (ex. Fred Durant wanted Allen's info on APRO... February '53... Allen seems to have talked to him about them at Robertson Panel ["the meeting"]).

__L__. Later... Bluebook personnel dissipate. Ruppelt takes leave: temp.
⎡ During leave Pentacle Plan rejected, but diffraction cameras
Ruppelt ⎨ on bases OK. Investigations transferred to ADC.
p.229. ⎣

Figure 56: The CIA ends the project, when it was going very well. So well that BB researchers didn't realize that it had ended. Ruppelt is described as "naïve boy."

CHAPTER TWELVE (PHOTOS): THE REAL DR. J. ALLEN HYNEK

Figure 57: Jennie Zeidman and J. Allen Hynek. Biographer Mark O'Connell said that Hynek shared more with Zeidman than he did with anyone else other than his wife (Credit: Jennie Zeidman).

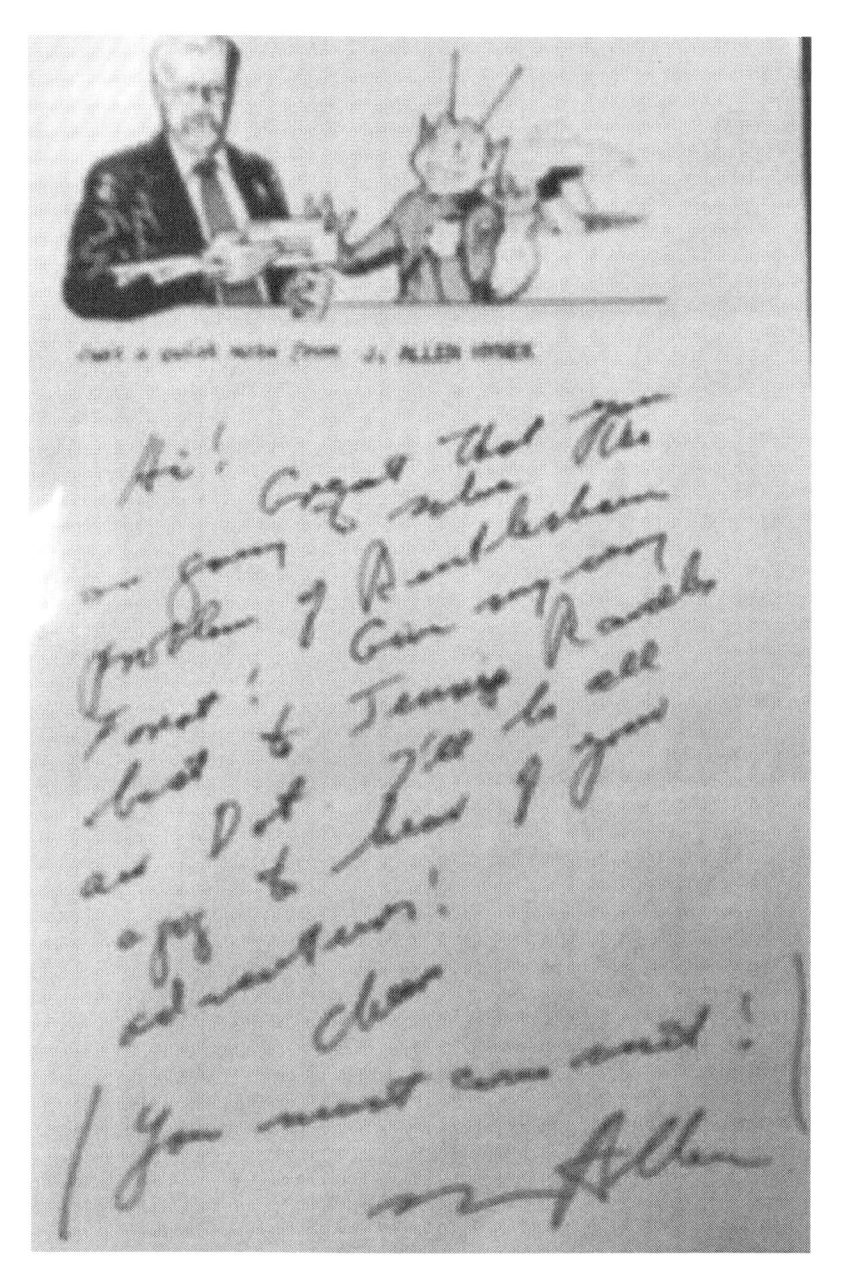

Figure 58: Hynek congratulates Zeidman because she is going to solve the problem of Rendlesham Forest. This is a big problem because it is Britain's Roswell. Hynek is agog.

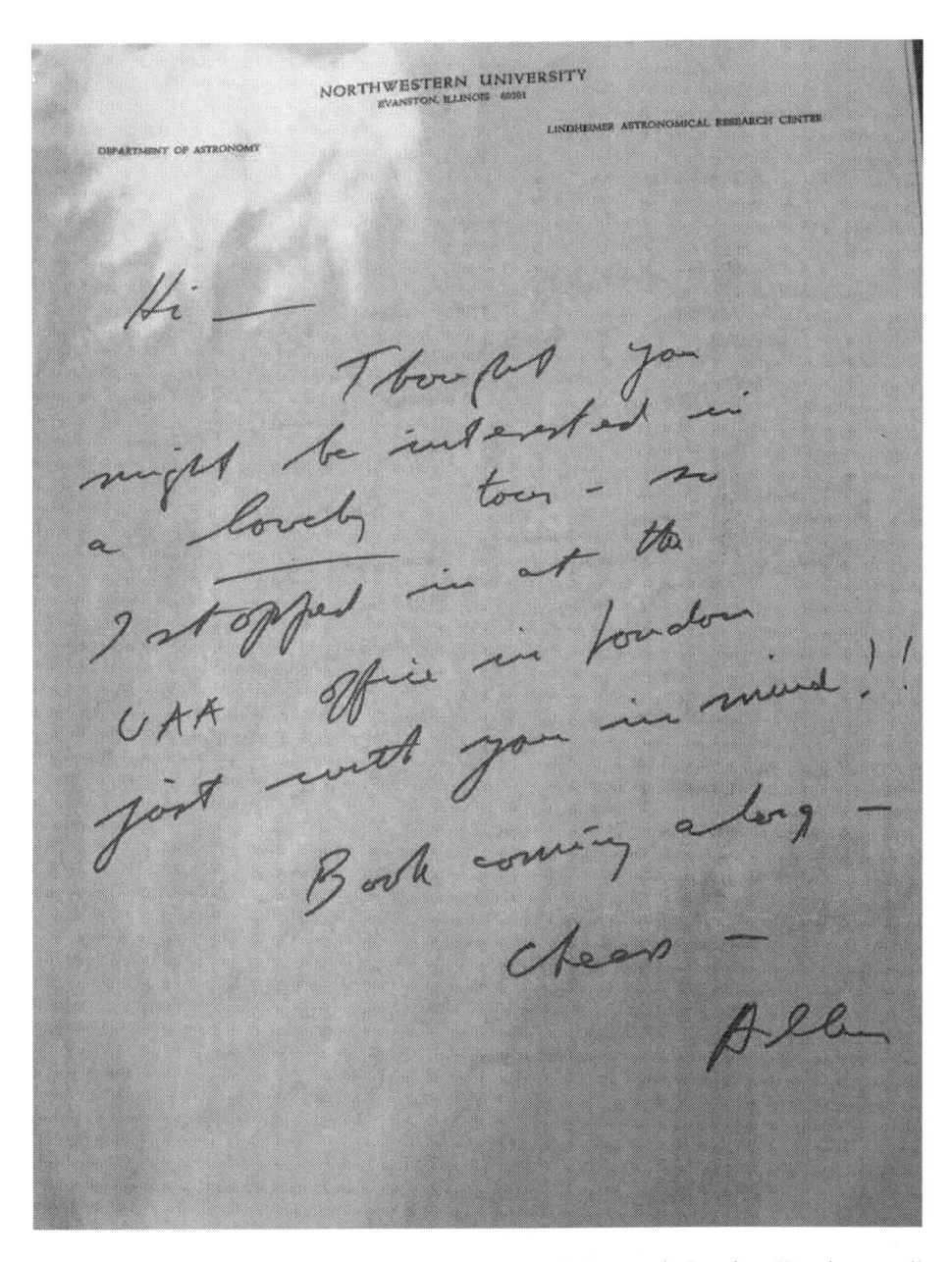

Figure 59: Zeidman wanted a tour, so Hynek stopped while he was in London. Hynek generally writes in a humorous way and usually seems to be in a good mood.

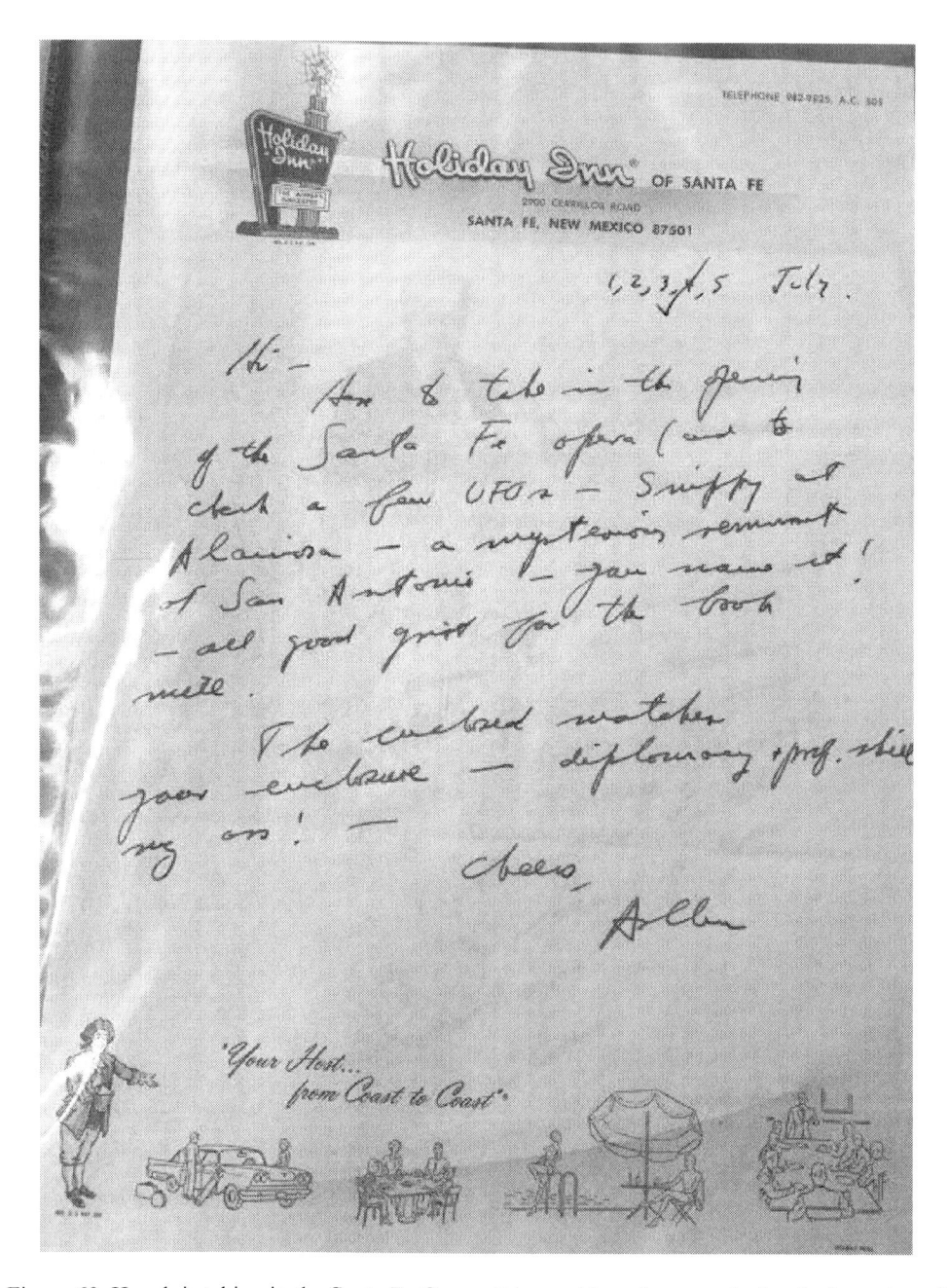

Figure 60: Hynek is taking in the Santa Fe Opera. It has not been known whether he investigated animal mutilations, but this letter shows that he has–he was looking into the Snippy horse event. This may have been the first reported mutilation.

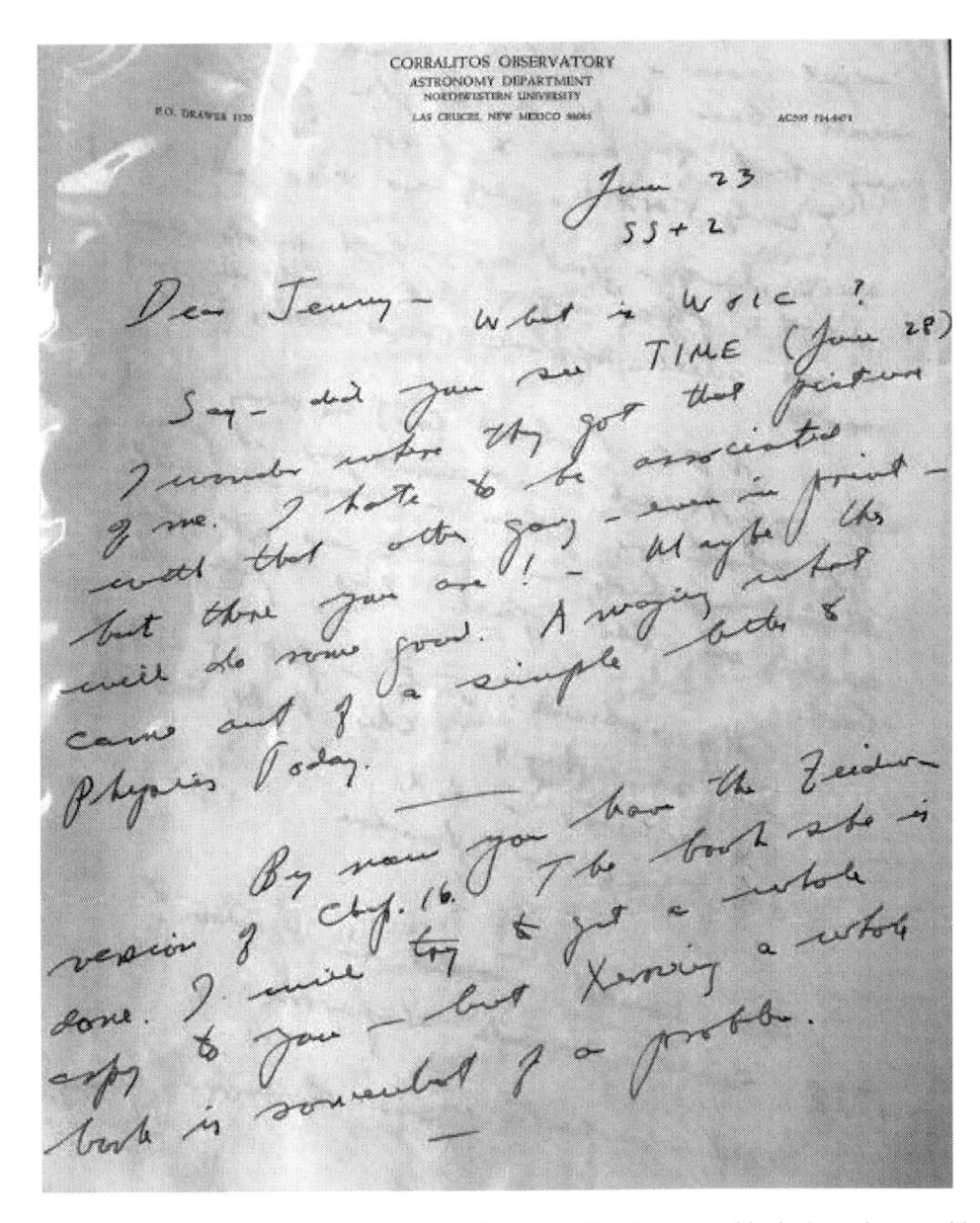

Figure 61: Time magazine had a photograph of Hynek with a hoaxer and he isn't too happy with this. He refers to a letter of his that was published in Physics Today. He was a scientist and his writings were published in a variety of the foremost scientific journals, even though some were about UFOs–a subject normally disdained by such publications.

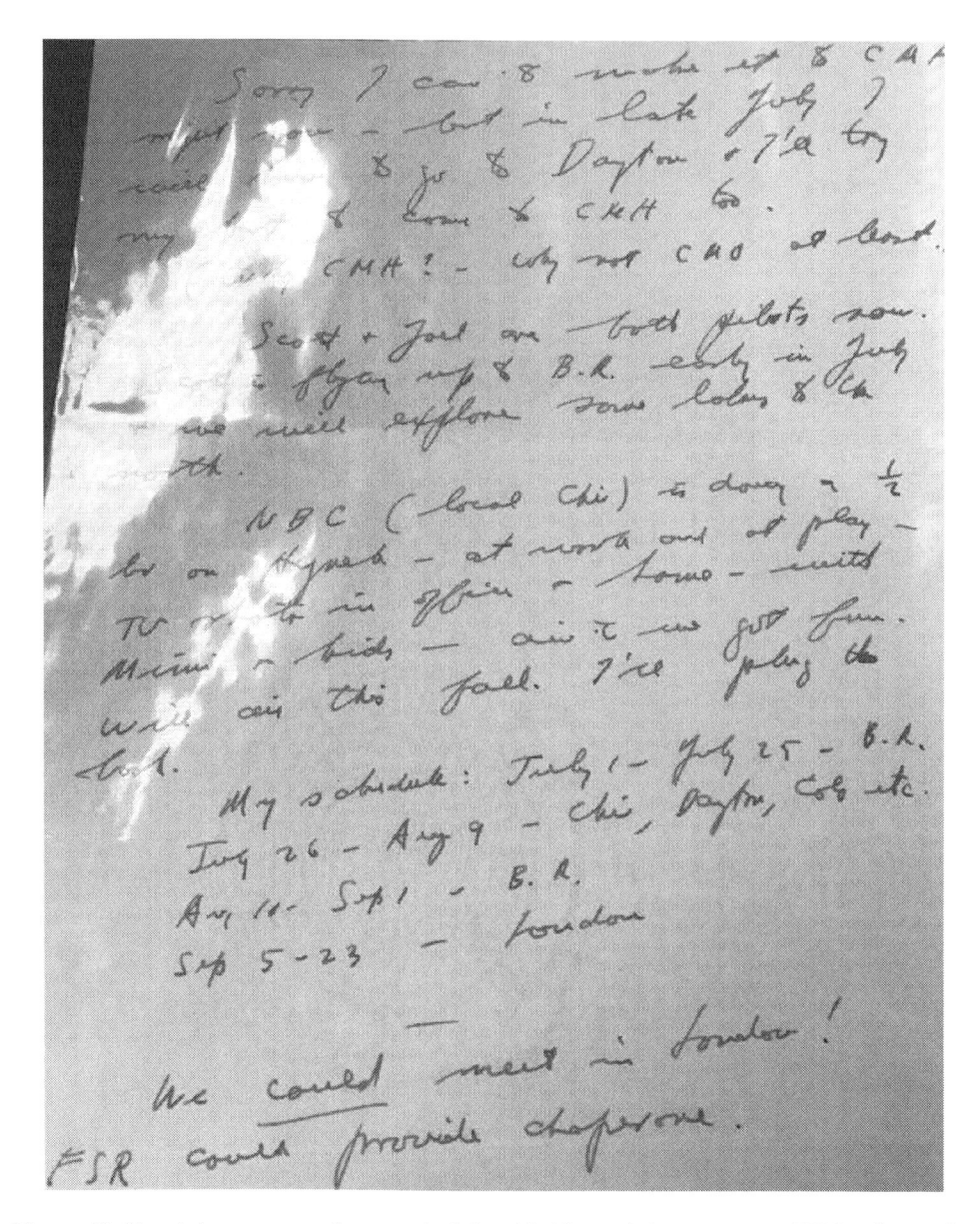

Figure 62: Hynek keeps a very heavy schedule with his work in astronomy, UFOs, the media, writing, and much else. He gives his upcoming schedule which includes travel to locations in the US and England. NBC was going to do a show about him and his family to which he commented, "ain't we got fun." And his comment about using Flying Saucer Review for a chaperone must have made her feel secure.

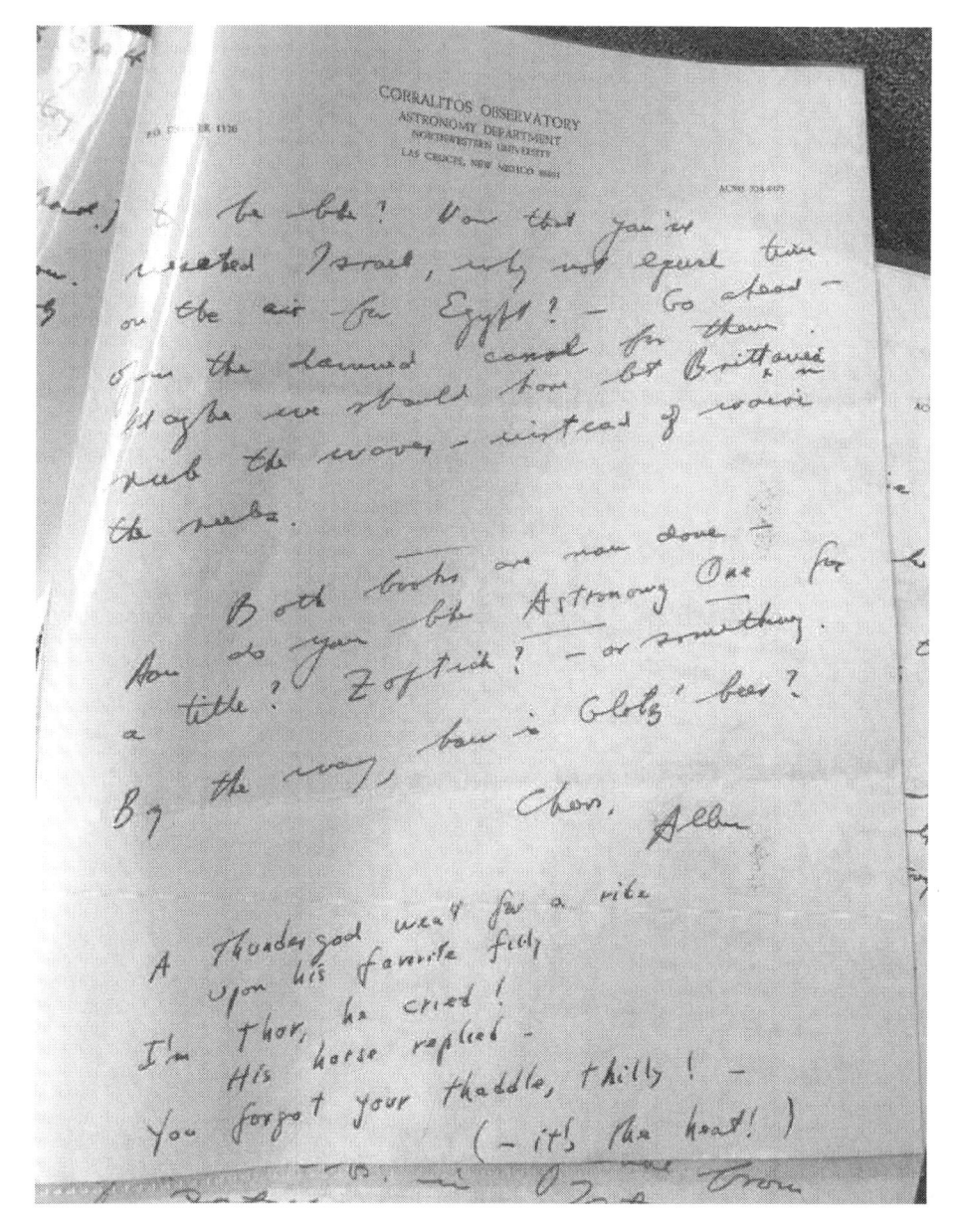

Figure 63: Beneath his scholarly, professor veneer, Hynek was playful, curious, mischievous, liked wordplay, and had much interest in the world news. Here he tells Zeidman to open the Suez Canal, which had been closed for many years. This disrupted both travel and trade over much of the world. He has a large vocabulary of odd words and gets poetic.

CORRALITOS OBSERVATORY
ASTRONOMY DEPARTMENT
NORTHWESTERN UNIVERSITY
P.O. DRAWER 1120   LAS CRUCES, NEW MEXICO 88001   AC505 524-4471

June 28
Acculvan Time

Hi Jennie —

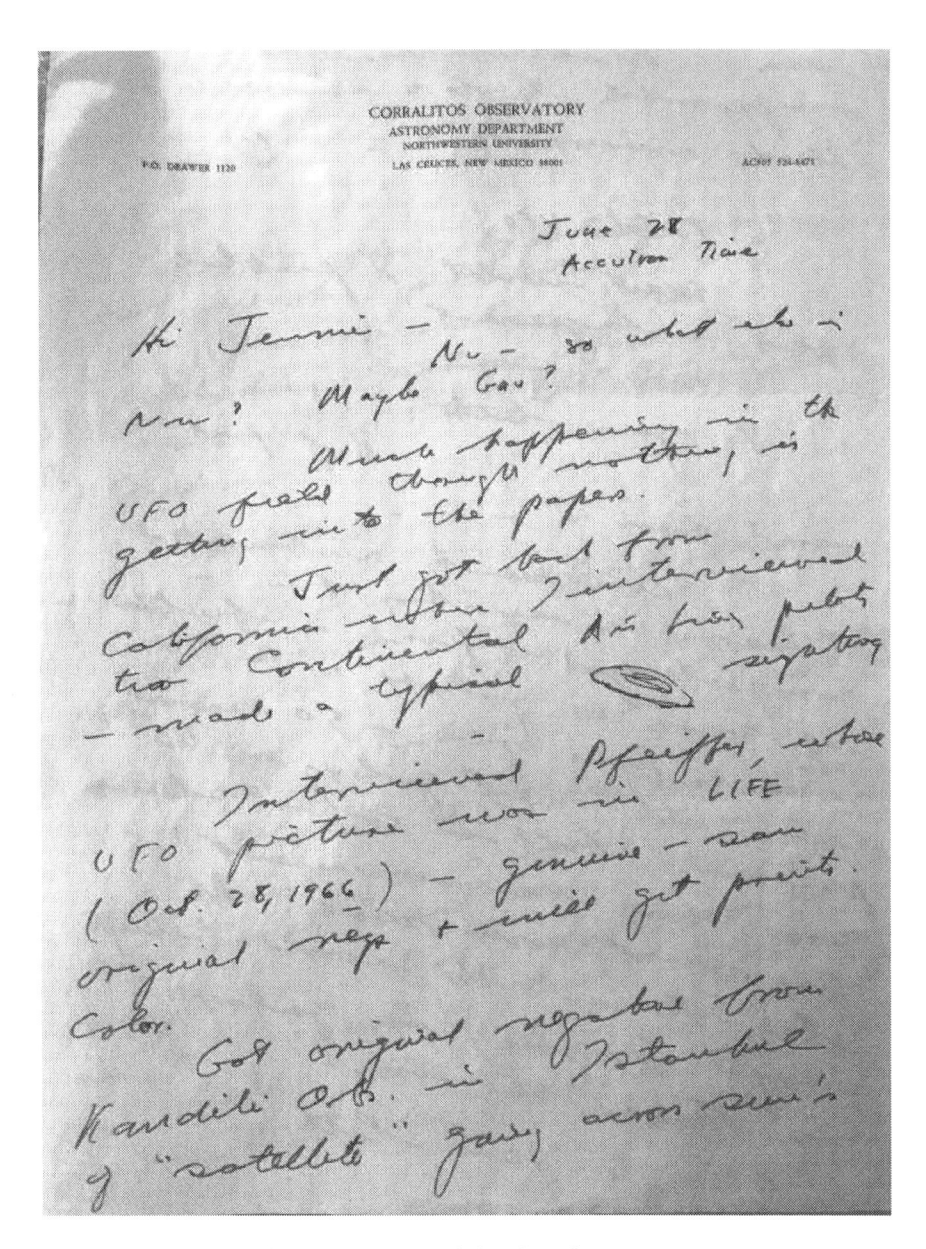

Now? — so what else is new? Maybe Gav?

Much happening in the UFO field though nothing is getting into the papers.

Just got back from California where I interviewed two Continental Air Lines pilots — made a typical sighting.

Interviewed Pfeiffer, whose UFO picture was in LIFE (Oct. 28, 1966) — genuine — saw original neg + will get prints. Color.

Got original negative from Kandili Obs. in Istanbul of "satellite" going across sun's

Figure 64: As usual there is much UFO activity, but the newspapers don't report it. This censorship always irritates him because the public doesn't know what is going on. He is very hands-on in his UFO investigation and goes after cases whether he gets them officially or not. In this letter he mentions two investigations that he is doing, the Pfeiffer report and one in Istanbul. He is interested in and understands the scientific methodology needed to study such reports.

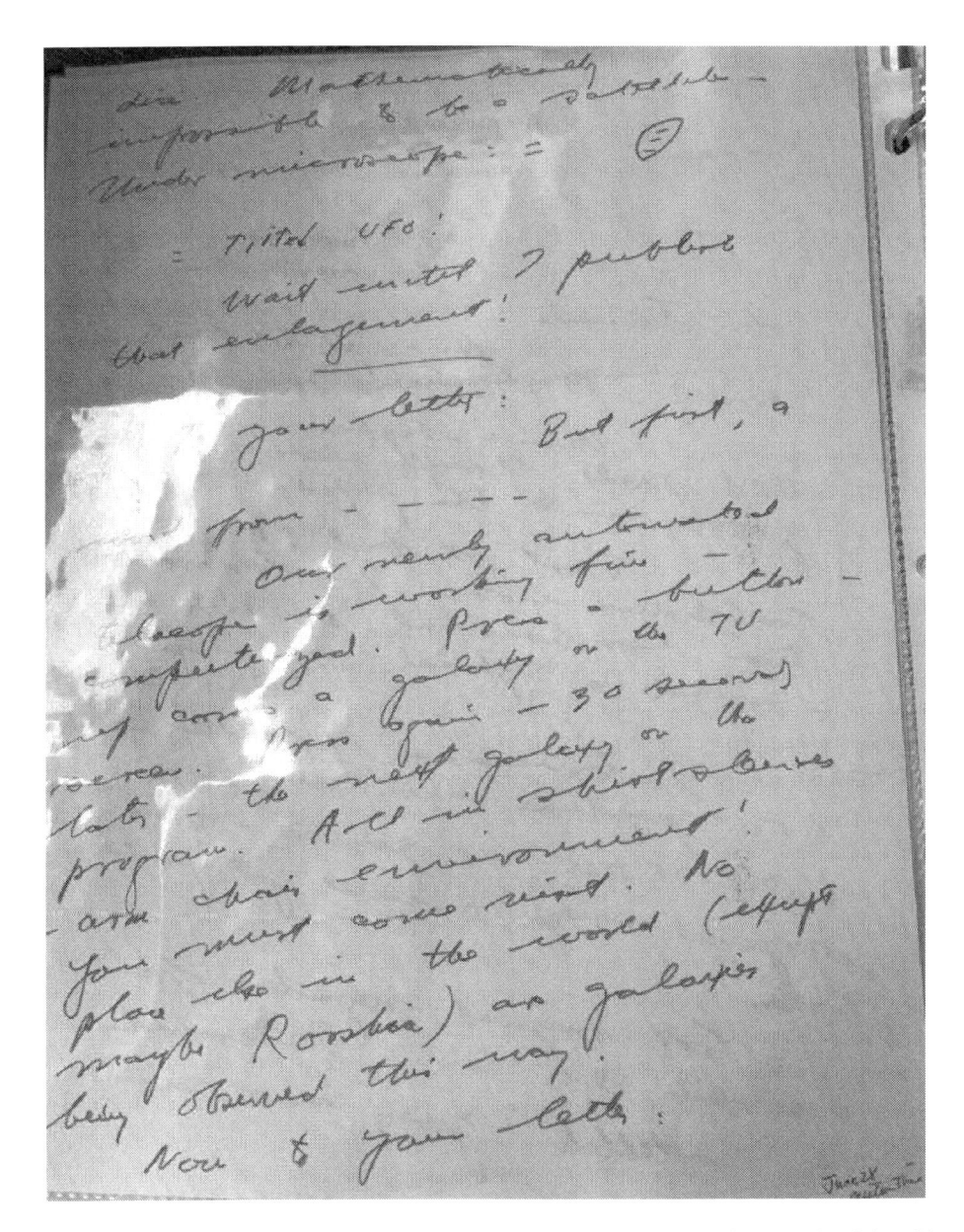

Figure 65: This letter is a continuation of his last letter. He obtained a photograph of the object passing the sun, made an enlargement of it, and is happy with the results. He is also very pleased with the way an automated telescope is working.

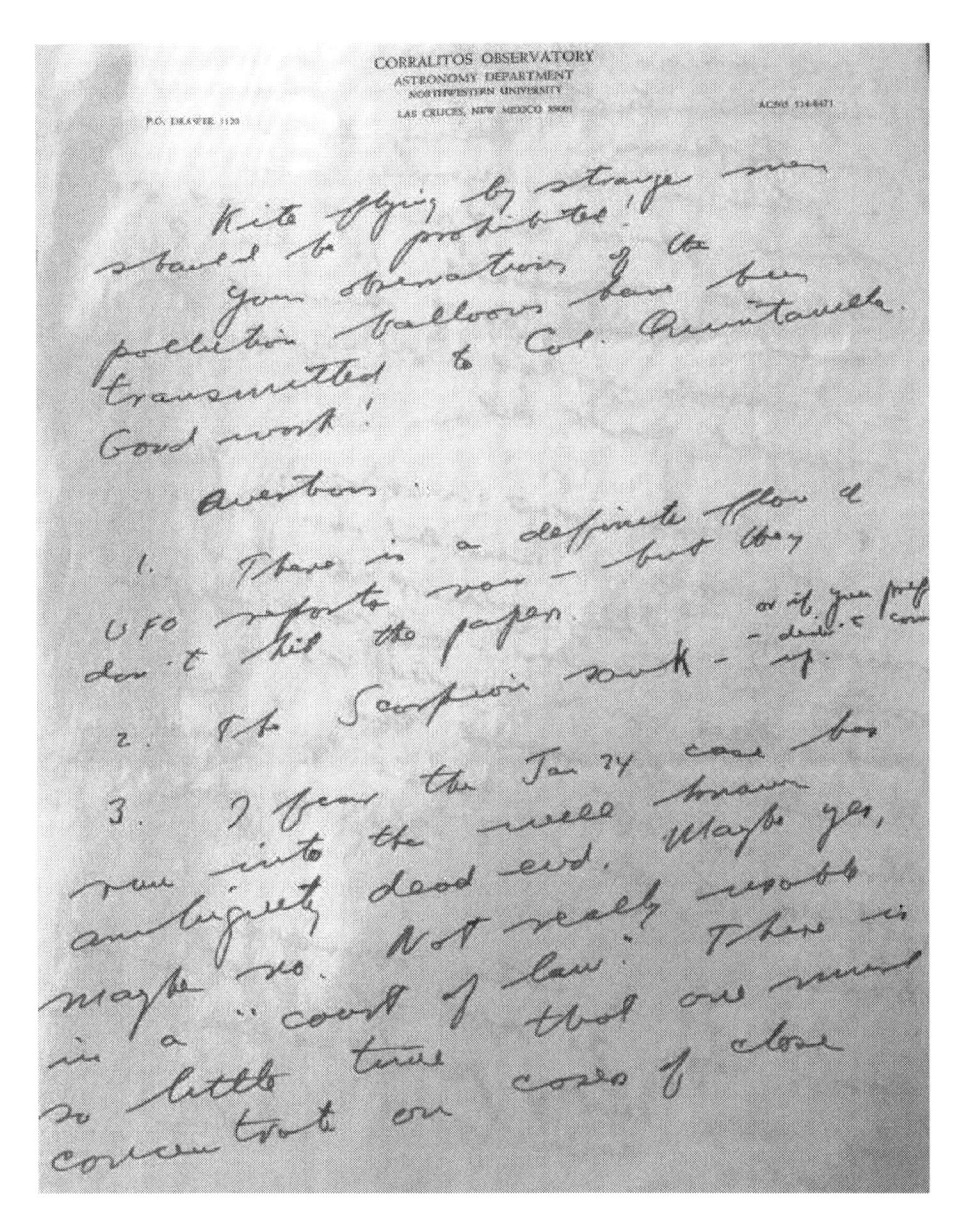

> **CORRALITOS OBSERVATORY**
> ASTRONOMY DEPARTMENT
> NORTHWESTERN UNIVERSITY
> LAS CRUCES, NEW MEXICO 88001
>
> Kite flying by strange men
> should be prohibited!
> Your observations of the
> pollution balloons have been
> transmitted to Col. Quintanilla.
> Good work!
>
> Questions:
> 1. There is a definite slow of
>   UFO reports now — but they
>   don't hit the paper... or if you prefer
>   the Scorpion sank — up.
> 2.
> 3. I fear the Jan 74 case has
>   run into the well known
>   ambiguity dead end. Maybe yes,
>   maybe no. Not really resolved.
>   in a "court of law". There is
>   so little time that one must
>   concentrate on cases of close...

Figure 66: He mentions several UFO cases here. One is the case of an aircraft that disappeared after it seemed to merge with a flying object on radar. Two cases must have been identified–a kite and a pollution balloon. He always wrestles with the fact that UFO activity isn't reported in the media and appears to wish he could do something about that. That would be the scientific thing to do.

154

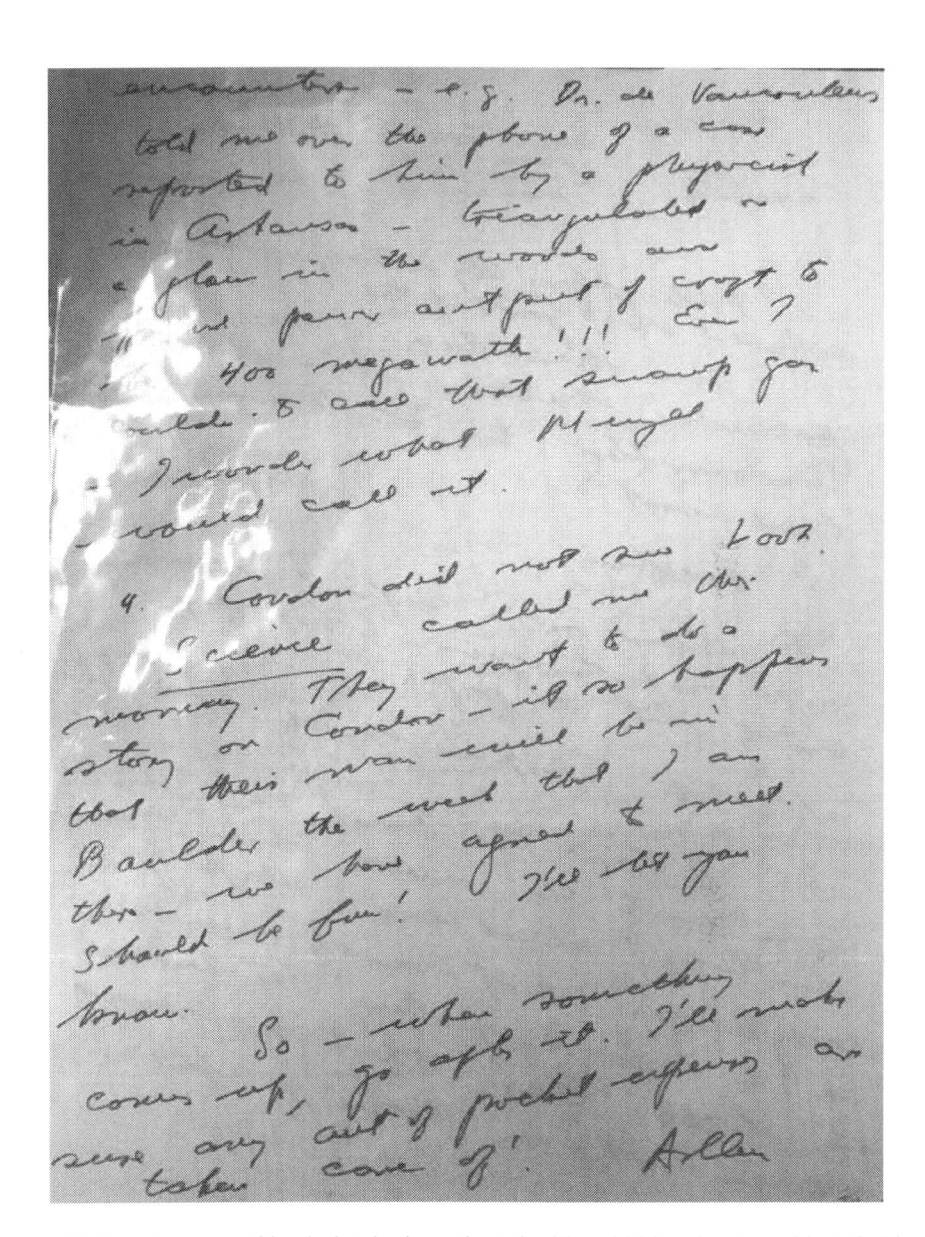

Figure 67: An astronomer friend, that he investigated with, told him about an object that had a massive power output. Science magazine wanted him to do a story about Dr. Condon. He was very critical of Condon's UFO research. He remarks, "Should be fun," but maybe not for Condon. He also mentioned Dr. Menzel, a debunker, who he thought also was unprofessional in his UFO work.

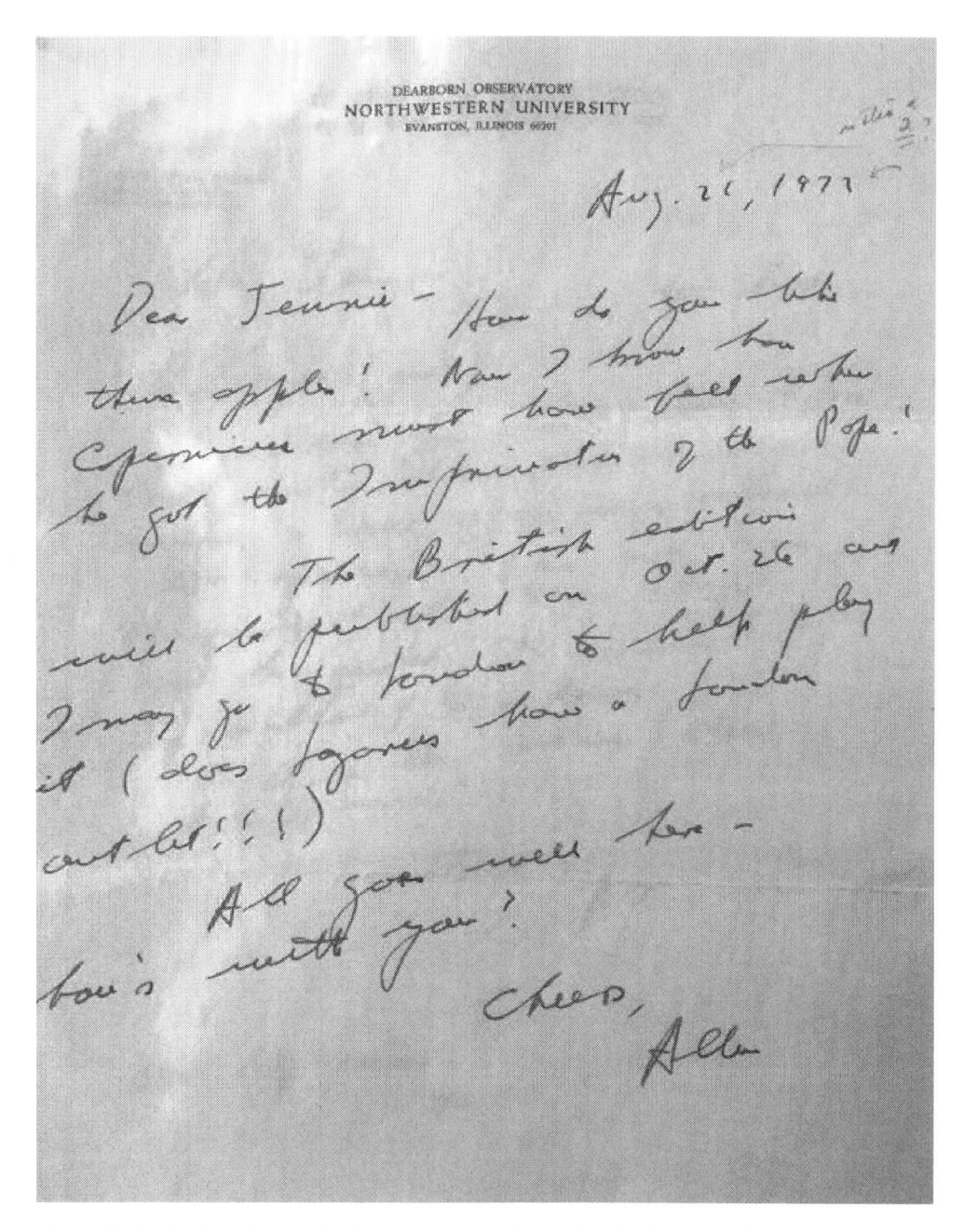

Figure 68: In this letter he is referring to a review of one of his books that had just come out in Science magazine. The author gave a good review.

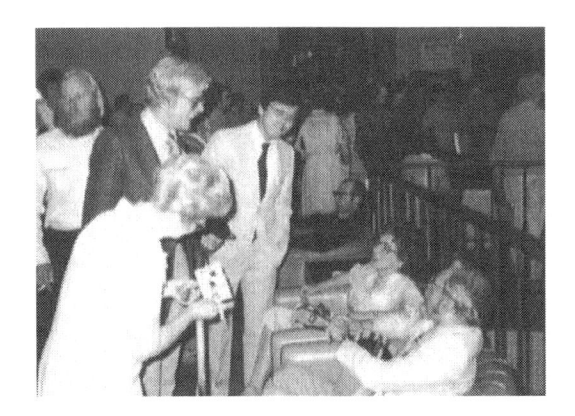

Figure 69: In the previous letter, Hynek had referred to a book signing. He met the public frequently when he did this and gave lectures. He and Zeidman are shown here talking to people.

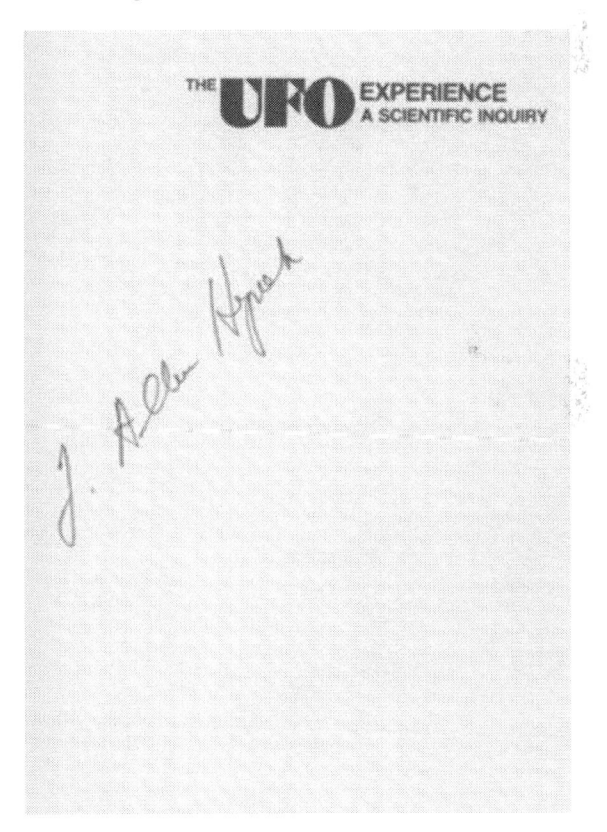

Figure 70: My first collected signature of Hynek's. It was at a book signing.

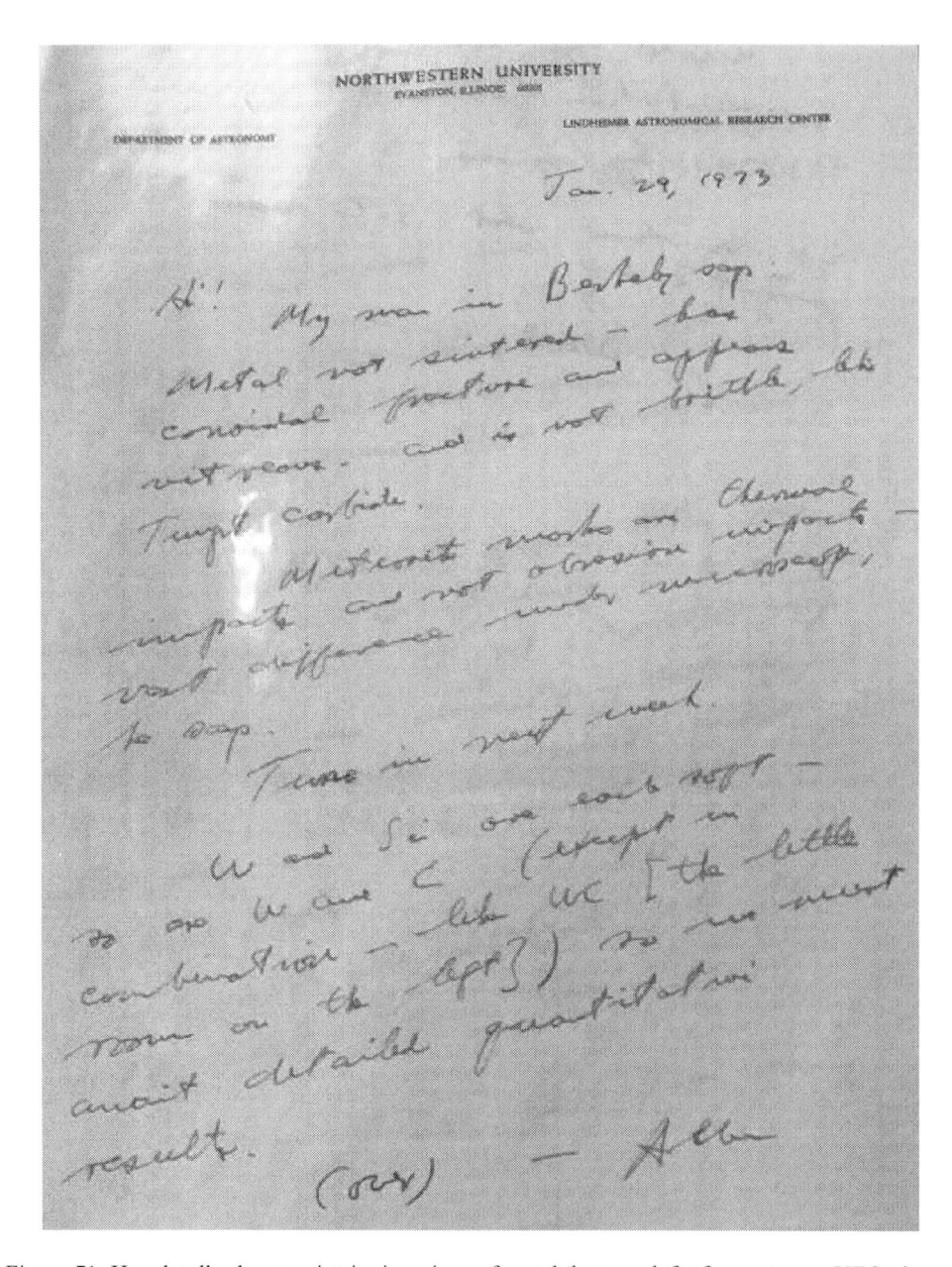

Figure 71: Hynek tells about an intriguing piece of metal that was left after a strange UFO close encounter that took place in Sweden. It was being analyzed and had some very unique properties.

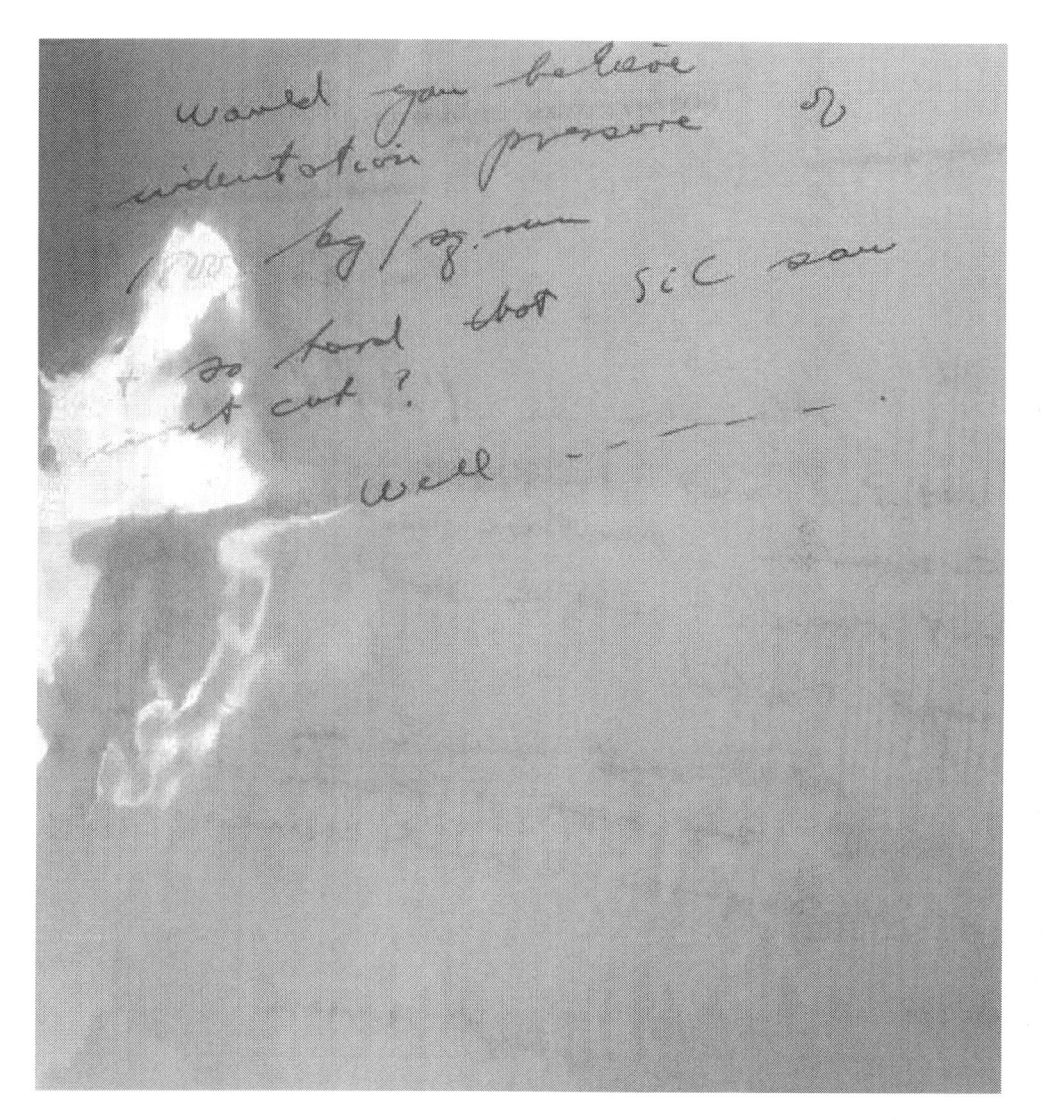

Figure 72: This is a continuation of the previous letter and tells about more of the material's amazing properties.

Valentine's Day —

Hi!
The Dutch have the good sense to recognize me as an authority on the subject — (note the big print on the dust jacket). I wonder if my publisher will ever learn!
Cute letter from there too, isn't it!
Carry on!
No late news on the Swedish incident.

— Allen

(OVER)

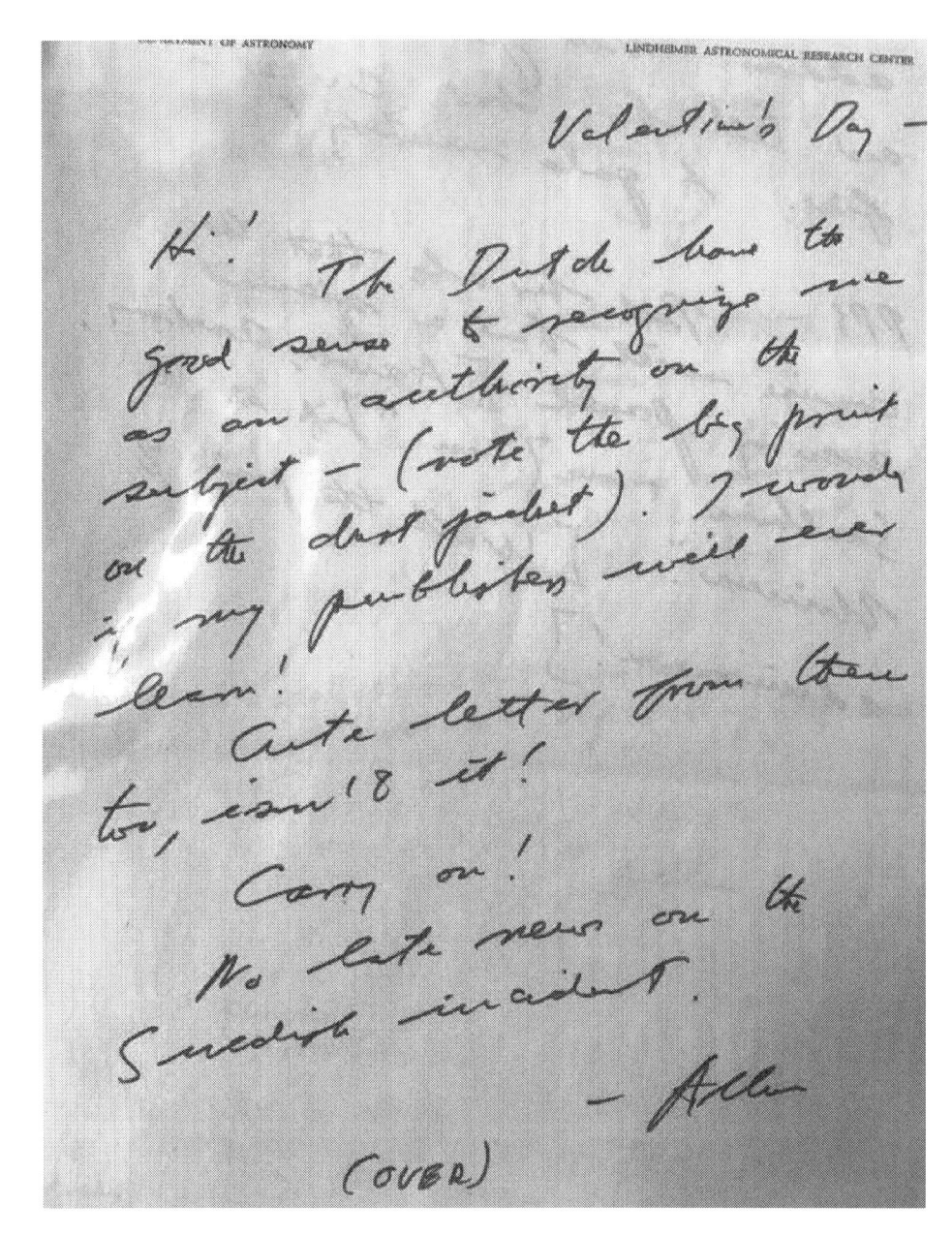

Figure 73: Here he jokes about how to be recognized as an authority. He is waiting for more news about the Swedish event with the odd material, mentioned previously.

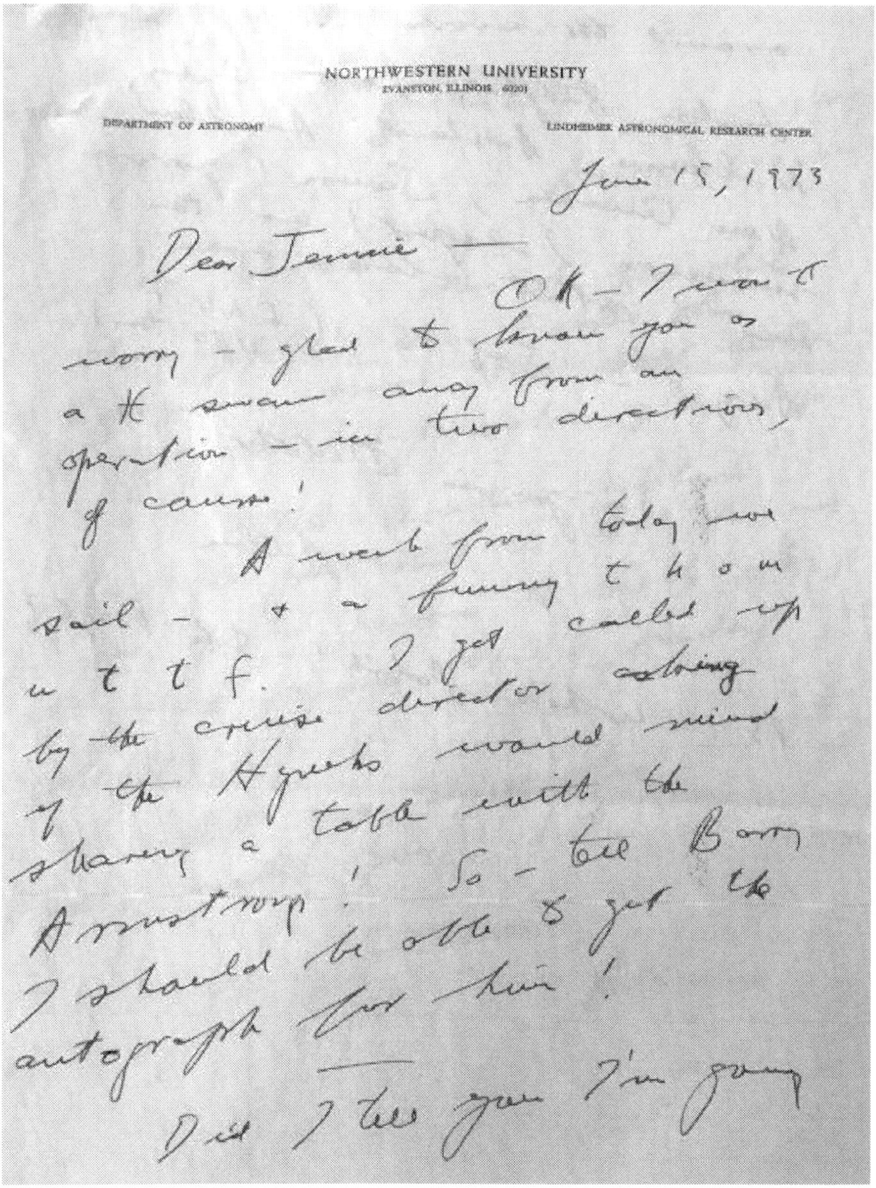

Figure 74: Hynek was asked if his family would like to share a table with the Neil Armstrong family on a cruise. This might tell something about Armstrong, because many have speculated about his views on UFOs and this suggests that he might have had an interest.

around the world in 80½ days?
London, Bangkok, Perth, Sydney, Melbourne, Adelaide, Auckland, New Guinea, Savoa (governor's mansion I expect) and then — to start classes again.

Aug 8 — Sep 16   (I.A.U. + UFO tour)

See you in October

Allen

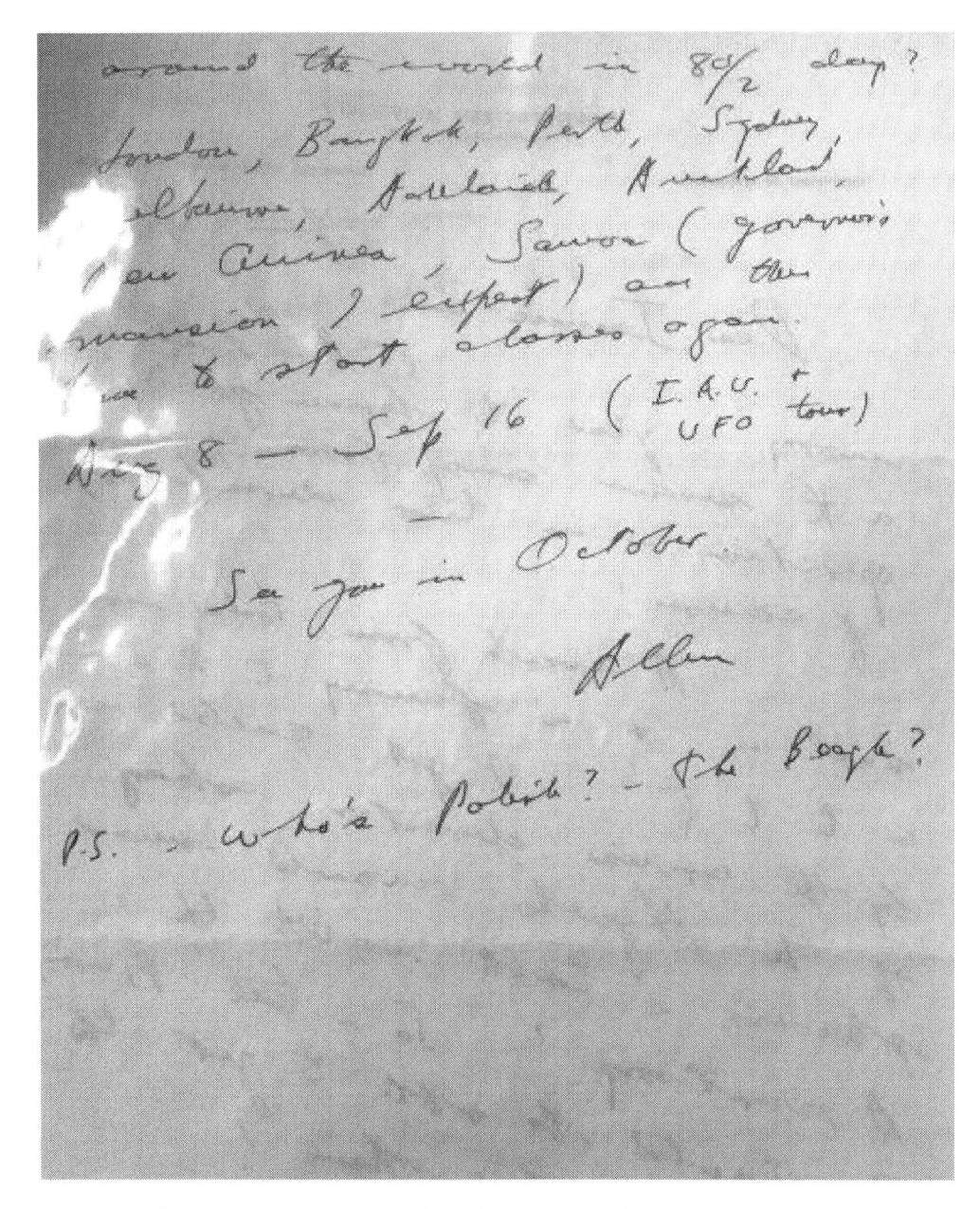

P.S. — Who's Polish? — & the Beagle?

Figure 75: The next letter is a continuation of the last one. He is going on the African Eclipse Cruise July 1973. This was a big event, they will visit countries around the world, and he sounds quite thrilled about it.

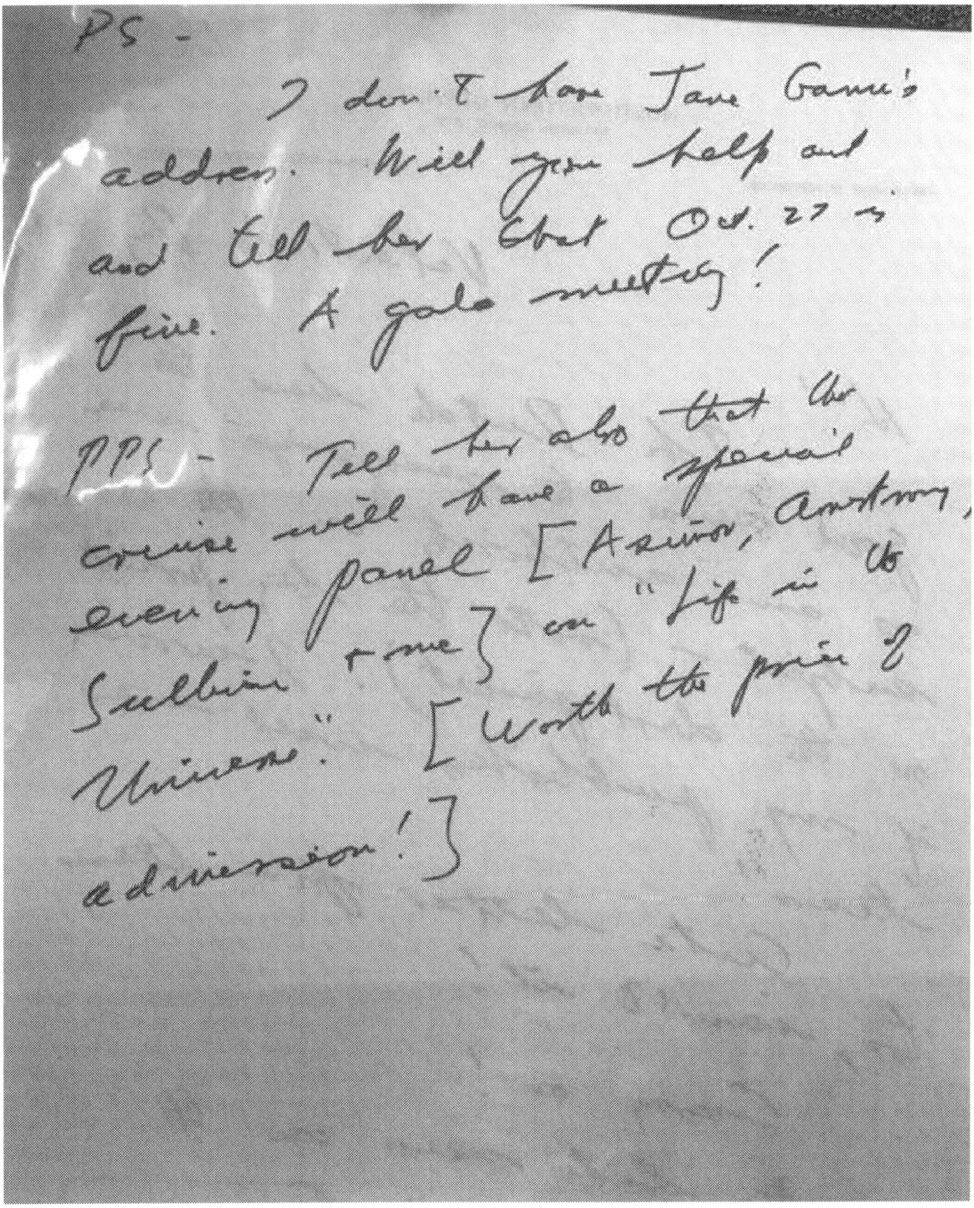

PS –

I don't have Jane Game's address. Will you help out and tell her that Oct. 27 is fine. A gala meeting!

PPS – Tell her also that the cruise will have a special evening panel [Asimov, Armstrong, Sullivan + me] on "Life in the Universe." [Worth the price of admission!]

Figure 76: He sounds elated in this second portion of the letter also. Things were going very well. He will give a lecture with some top scientists on the cruise. He is also going to receive the Ohioana Award in October for his book.

163

Figure 77: J. Allen Hynek at the Northwestern University Lindheimer Observatory with Lake Michigan in the background: (Credit: Jennie Zeidman).

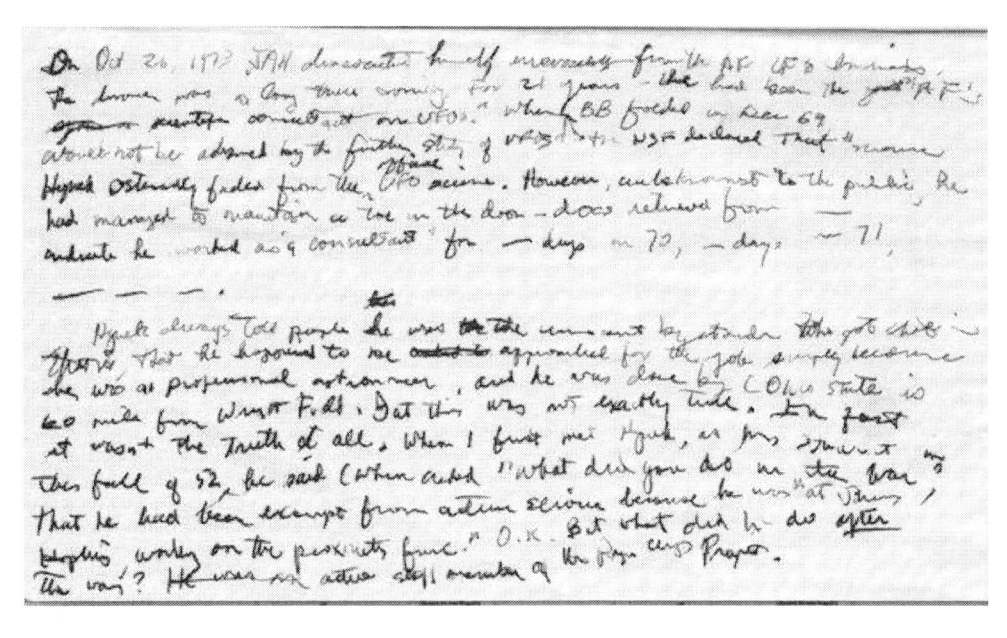

Figure 78: Something had changed when he arrived for his Ohioana award. He had been in quite a good mood about the award and the trip to Columbus, but when he arrived, he was in a bad mood. Zeidman, who spent about as much time researching Hynek as she did UFOs, was stymied and did not understand why. This was at the time he dissociated from his Blue Book work and he took up some other positions, but it was unclear what he was actually doing. In this piece, Zeidman is trying to figure out what was happening.

164

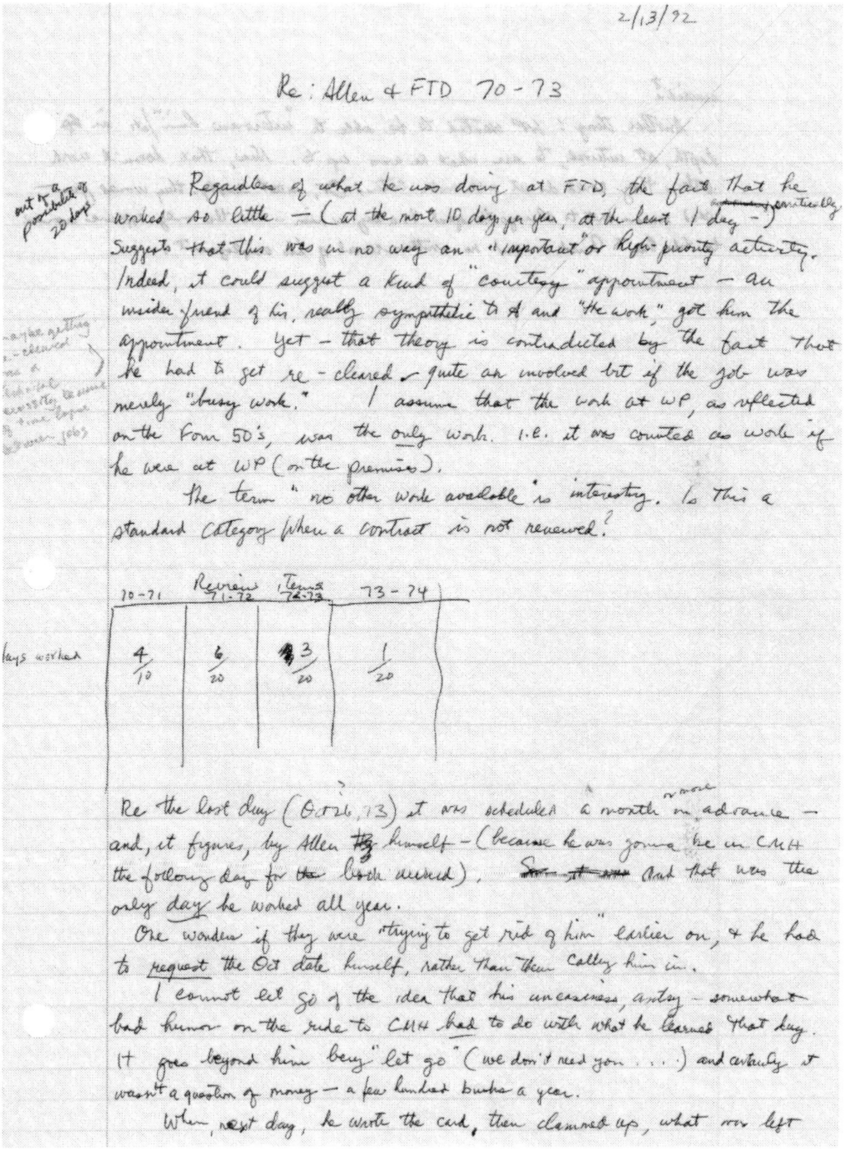

2/13/92

Re: Allen & FTD 70-73

Regardless of what he was doing at FTD, the fact that he worked so little — (at the most 10 days per year, at the least 1 day —) genuinely suggests that this was in no way an "important" or high-priority activity. Indeed, it could suggest a kind of "courtesy" appointment — an insider friend of his, really sympathetic to A and "the work," got him the appointment. Yet — that theory is contradicted by the fact that he had to get re-cleared — quite an involved bit if the job was merely "busy work." I assume that the work at WP, as reflected on the Form 50's, was the only work. i.e. it was counted as work if he were at WP (on the premises).

The term "no other work available" is interesting. Is this a standard category when a contract is not renewed?

(margin: not to be possible of 20 days)
(margin: maybe getting cleaned up a bit — esp with Pres. began winter jobs)

	Review 71-72	Term 72-73	73-74
70-71			
4/10	6/20	3/20	1/20

(margin: days worked)

Re the last day (Oct 26, '73) it was scheduled a month or more in advance — and, it figures, by Allen himself — (because he was gonna be in CMH the following day for the book award). And that was the only day he worked all year.

One wonders if they were "trying to get rid of him" earlier on, & he had to request the Oct date himself, rather than them calling him in.

I cannot let go of the idea that his uneasiness, antsy — somewhat bad humor on the ride to CMH had to do with what he learned that day. It goes beyond him being "let go" (we don't need you ...) and actually it wasn't a question of money — a few hundred bucks a year.

When, next day, he wrote the card, then clammed up, what was left

Figure 79: Zeidman was examining Hynek's relationship to the Air Force and trying to figure out exactly what happened but was unable to.

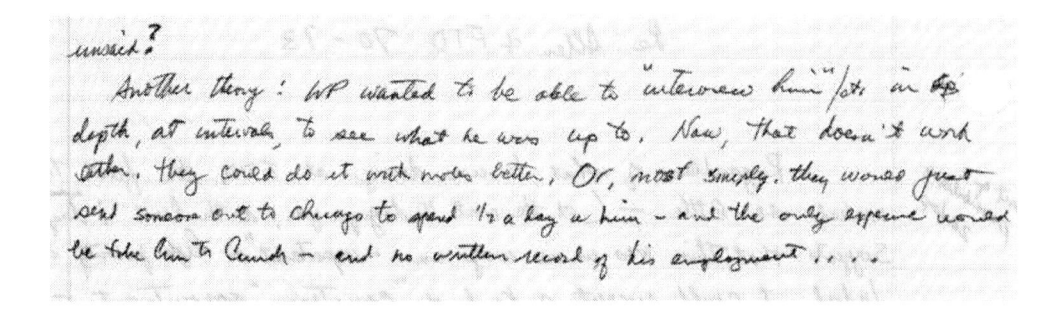

[handwritten note at top of page, partially legible:]

unsaid?

Another theory: WP wanted to be able to "interview him"/etc in depth, at intervals, to see what he was up to. Now, that doesn't work either. They could do it with notes better. Or, most simply, they would just send someone out to Chicago to spend 1/2 a day w him — and the only expense would be the line to Chicago — and no written record of his employment....

Figure 80: Zeidman continues her investigation of Hynek's relationship with the Air Force and continues to not understand it.

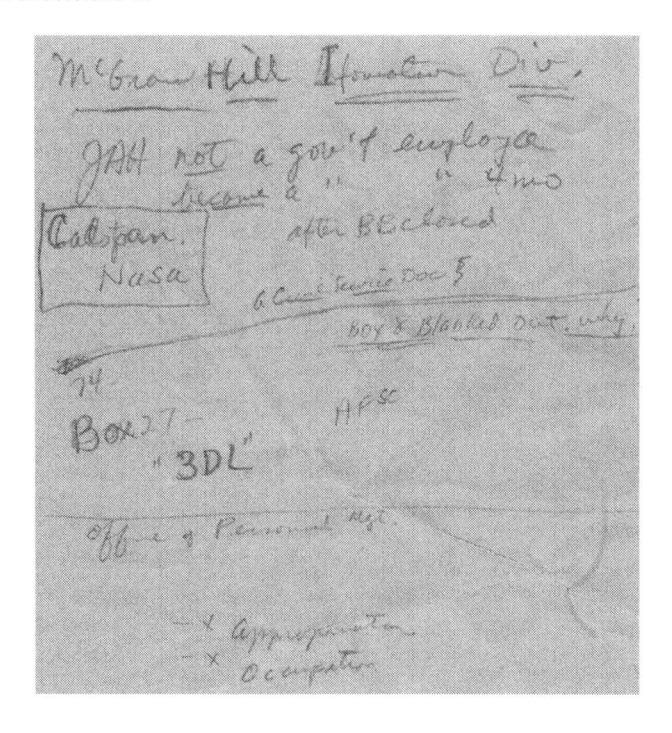

Figure 81: Immediately after Hynek stopped working for the Air Force, he began working for the publishing company, McGraw Hill. He began working for government again a few months later even though BB was closed. It is completely unclear what he was doing and whether his work at McGraw Hill concerned the government or was some sort of continuation of his BB work. He appeared to be the only person doing it. Also a box of his material appeared to be blanked out and Zeidman didn't know why. A Calstpan Corp. exists and one named Calspan, a science and technology company that was part of the Research Laboratory of the Curtiss-Wright Airplane Division, sometimes worked with NASA.

166

CENTER FOR UFO STUDIES
2623 RIDGE AVE. – EVANSTON, ILLINOIS 60201

J. ALLEN HYNEK, Director
Professor of Astronomy
Northwestern University

Hi Jen —

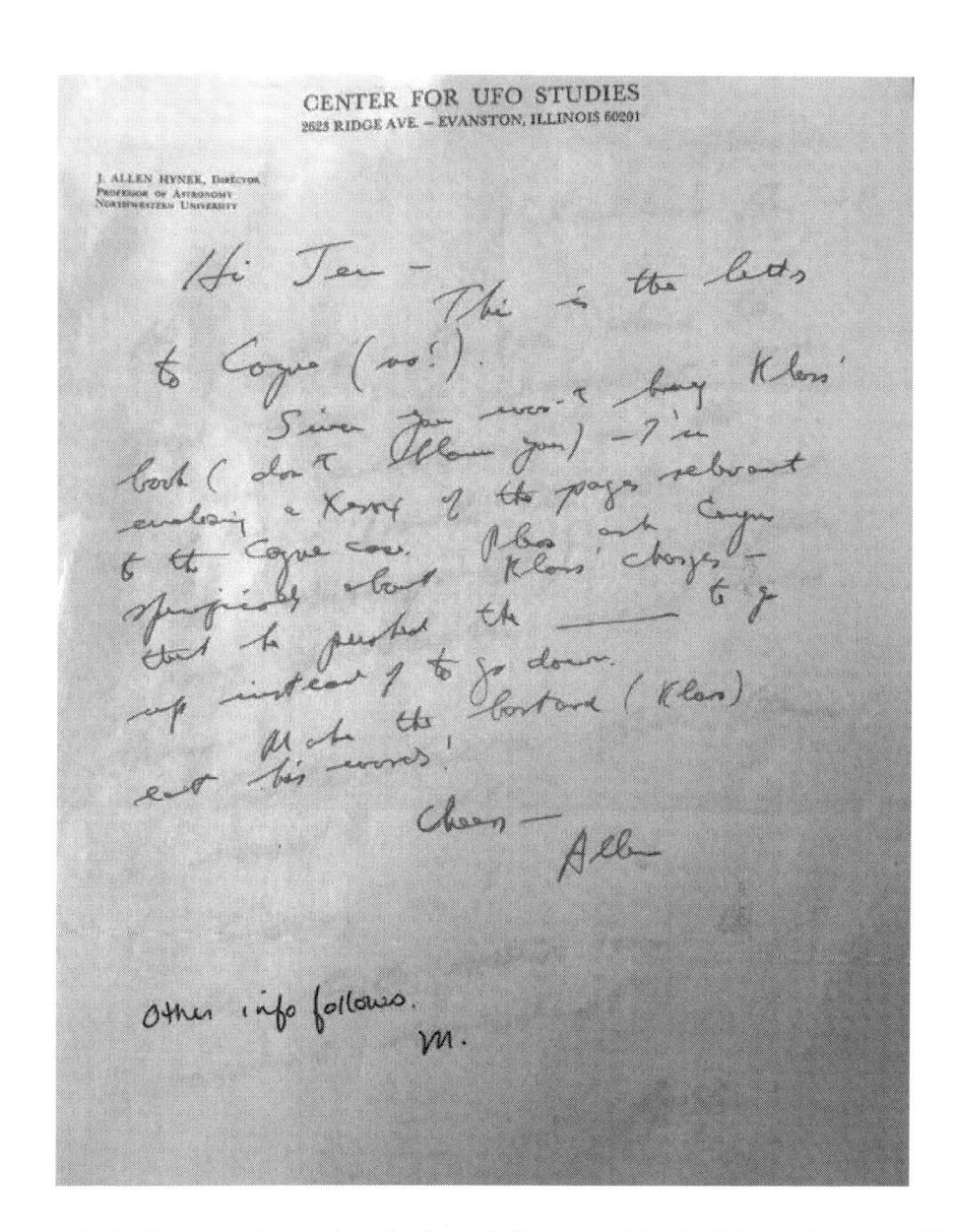

This is the letter to Coyne (oo!). Since you won't buy Klass' book (don't blame you) – I'm enclosing a Xerox of the pages relevant to the Coyne case. Also, ask Coyne suspicions about Klass' charges — that he pushed the ___ to go up instead of to go down.

Make the bastard (Klass) eat his words!

Cheers —
Allen

other info follows.
m.

Figure 82: In this letter, he mentions the Coyne helicopter incident in Ohio, another remarkable event that both investigated. It had been heavily debunked and a chief debunker was the well-known skeptic, Philip Klass. Hynek gave her some good advice about how to address his attacks and make him, "eat his words."

CUFOS

(312) 491-1870

CENTER FOR UFO STUDIES 1609 SHERMAN AVE., SUITE 207 EVANSTON, IL 60201

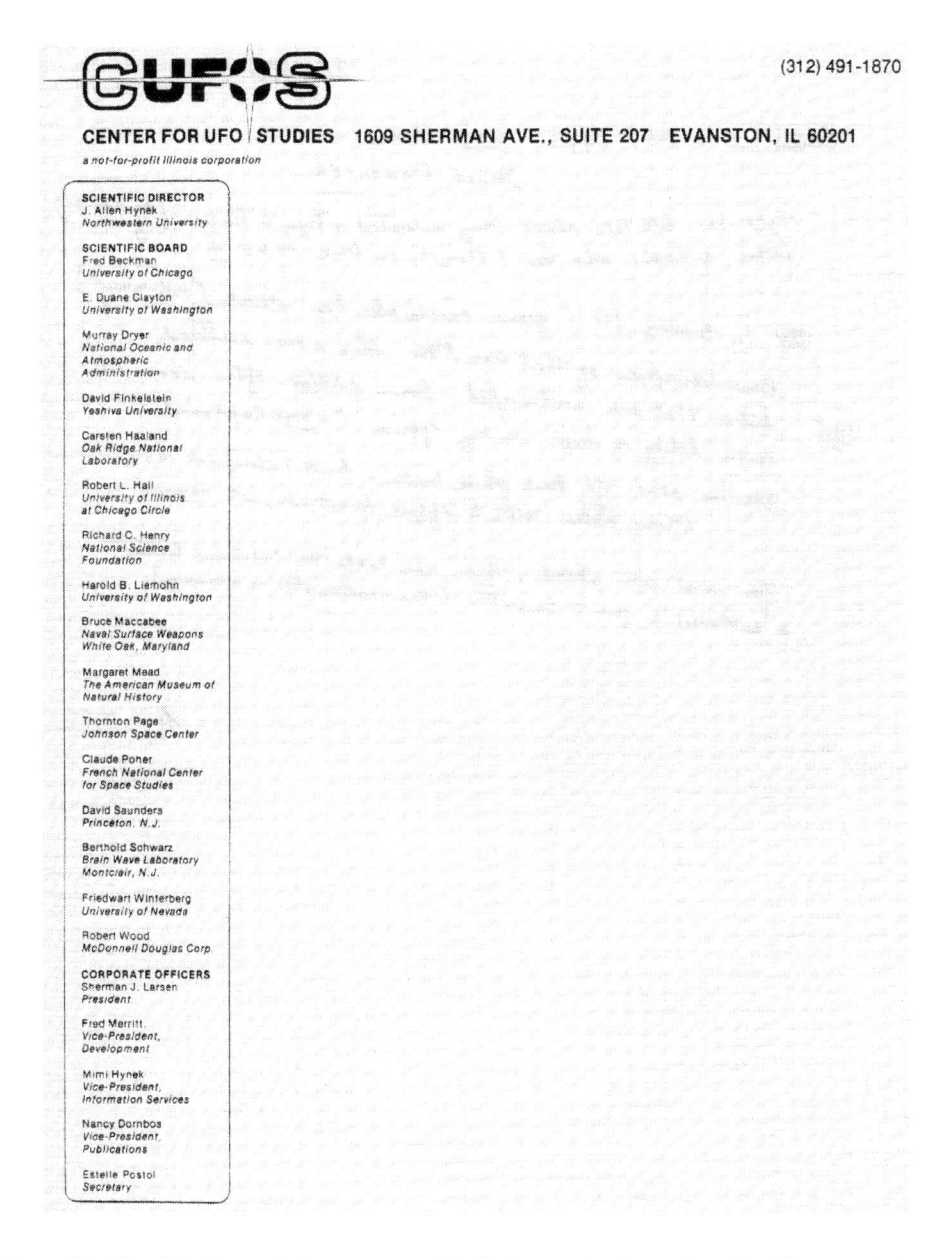

a not-for-profit Illinois corporation

SCIENTIFIC DIRECTOR
J. Allen Hynek
Northwestern University

SCIENTIFIC BOARD
Fred Beckman
University of Chicago

E. Duane Clayton
University of Washington

Murray Dryer
National Oceanic and Atmospheric Administration

David Finkelstein
Yeshiva University

Carsten Haaland
Oak Ridge National Laboratory

Robert L. Hall
University of Illinois at Chicago Circle

Richard C. Henry
National Science Foundation

Harold B. Liemohn
University of Washington

Bruce Maccabee
Naval Surface Weapons White Oak, Maryland

Margaret Mead
The American Museum of Natural History

Thornton Page
Johnson Space Center

Claude Poher
French National Center for Space Studies

David Saunders
Princeton, N.J.

Berthold Schwarz
Brain Wave Laboratory Montclair, N.J.

Friedwart Winterberg
University of Nevada

Robert Wood
McDonnell Douglas Corp.

CORPORATE OFFICERS
Sherman J. Larsen
President

Fred Merritt,
Vice-President, Development

Mimi Hynek
Vice-President, Information Services

Nancy Dornbos
Vice-President, Publications

Estelle Postol
Secretary

Figure 83. Hynek's dream had come true. He had organized a truly scientific association to investigate UFO phenomena, the Center for UFO Studies. He had many foremost scientists and academics, such as Margaret Mead, on his board of Directors and could investigate in a scientific way.

```
                                              Box 1096
                                              Wellfleet, Mass.
                                              02667
                                              August 8, 1984
```

Dear Dr. Scott,

I am very sorry to be so remiss in answering your letters. I am sending Jennie Zeidman copies of your earlier letters, so that she is fully informed of the details of your case - rather, of your various sightings over the years. I am sorry Dr. Hynek was unable to get to Columbus, but since that's his old teaching base, and he knows many people at OSU, perhaps he'll get there this fall. I have discussed your reports with him.

Jenny Zeidman should have your confidence, as she is the investigator most easily equipped to look into the matter. I am very glad you took the initiative and contacted her.

As I'm sure you know, this network of investigators is self-funded and self-generated, and no one has accused us of obvious efficiencey. For this I'm sorry, but I know you understand. There is one thing I want you to do for me, and that is to write me the name and address of your sister in Indianapolis, as I will be there this fall, and want to interview her in person.

                              Thank you for your patience,

Figure 84: In 1984 my sister and I reported some weird UFO events we had experienced since childhood to his CUFOS. Several people discussed them with Hynek. A letter from abduction expert, Budd Hopkins, who interviewed my sister's family and tried to hypnotize me, told me that he had discussed our sightings with Hynek.

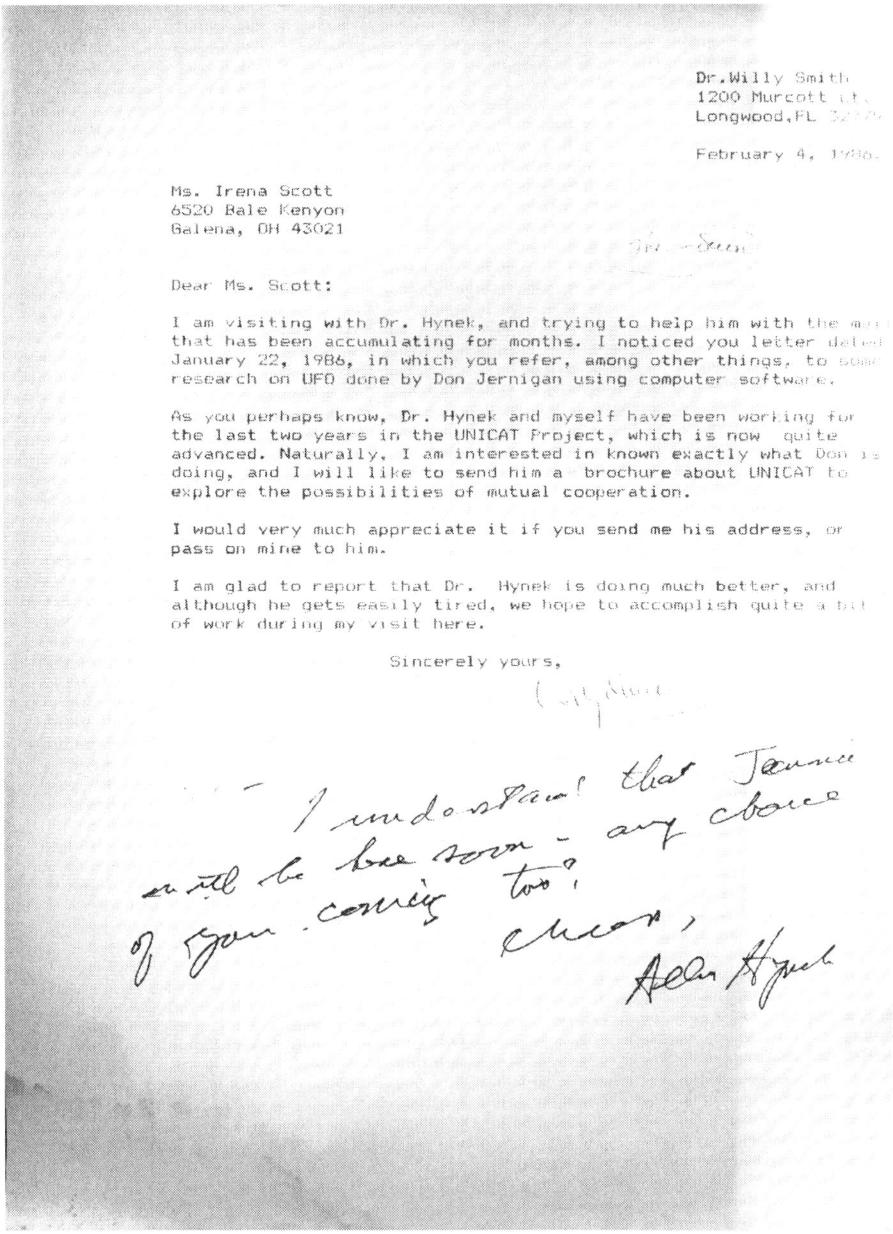

Dr. Willy Smith
1200 Murcott Ct.
Longwood, FL 32779

February 4, 1986

Ms. Irena Scott
6520 Bale Kenyon
Galena, OH 43021

Dear Ms. Scott:

I am visiting with Dr. Hynek, and trying to help him with the mail that has been accumulating for months. I noticed you letter dated January 22, 1986, in which you refer, among other things, to some research on UFO done by Don Jernigan using computer software.

As you perhaps know, Dr. Hynek and myself have been working for the last two years in the UNICAT Project, which is now quite advanced. Naturally, I am interested in known exactly what Don is doing, and I will like to send him a brochure about UNICAT to explore the possibilities of mutual cooperation.

I would very much appreciate it if you send me his address, or pass on mine to him.

I am glad to report that Dr. Hynek is doing much better, and although he gets easily tired, we hope to accomplish quite a bit of work during my visit here.

Sincerely yours,

Figure 85: The last handwritten message I have from Dr. Hynek was to me. He was ill and near death at the time, but continued working in the UFO field instead of taking it easy.

Figure 86: J. Allen Hynek, who was the director, walking toward the Northwestern University's Lindheimer Astrophysical Research Center. The telescope's twin domes and distinctive crisscrossed supporting braces instantly made it a campus landmark. The Chicago Chapter of the American Institute of Architects designated the structure as outstanding in its class (Credit: Jennie Zeidman).

Figure 87: This photograph shows J. Allen Hynek, Jennie Zeidman, and Charles Bowen, the editor of Flying Saucer Review (FSR) (Credit: Jennie Zeidman).

CHAPTER EIGHT

WHO DID THE SR-14 AND WHY DOES NO ONE KNOW?"
THE "OTHERS LIST"

More mysteries

Who did the *SR-14* study?

Although John Center is not listed on the Pentacle Memo, he very well could have worked on it. This is because of yet another mystery associated with *SR-14*. Although it is amazing, no one knows who actually did the work on *SR-14*.

Since the metallurgists at Battelle generally worked together, published together, and appeared to know each other, it is quite astonishing that they seemed to have no idea of who the 12 or so were who did the study, as described previously. No one could recall even one individual.

SR-14 itself did not list the authors or researchers, why? Why does there appear to be no record of who they were? Why does no one remember who they were, including those who worked on the project?

Possibly this was because of the security and perhaps only the workers knew in detail who they were, what they did, and understood the results. Perhaps because of security, the government did not want anyone to know who did it. After all the entire project was highly secure until exposed by the Pentacle Memo.

However a new handwritten document found in Battelle material (Figure 51) gives a list of 12 people.

Perhaps these are the 12 or so people mentioned in "The Pentacle Letter and the Battelle UFO Project," who did the research. Or maybe they would be people knowledgeable about the *SR-14* study, or maybe they were people's guesses about who was involved.

Three were definitely knowledgeable about it because two were on the Pentacle Memo, Rieppal and Jackson, and one left a note showing she knew about it.

And most of the rest had close associations with the scientists listed on the Pentacle Memo, such as publishing with them, and thus would probably know them and what they were doing.

But not only did these researchers have associations with those on the Pentacle Memo, they also had associations with those in the *Second Progress Report*, which had Center's piece. In examining these people in detail, most appear to be involved with metallurgy, as are the scientists listed on the Pentacle Memo.

This Battelle list, I will call the "Others List"

This "Others List" include: Art Schwope, Frank Holden, Walter Boyd, Perry Rieppal, Art Elsea, Connie Voldrich, Paul Frost, Lloyd/Loyd Jackson, Fred Bagby, Nelson Crites, Bob Jaffe, Horace Grover, and Bill Sherenbig? It is unknown what this list represents, but noticeable that two of these people are listed on the Pentacle Memo, Rieppal and Jackson.

And other documents show that Connie Voldrich is especially interesting. Voldrich also had a long-time association with Cross and others. This group began working together even before 1947 and when the group was working on titanium rather than nitinol. She published with many of the head people on the Pentacle Memo such as Howard Cross, and with people associated with him, and some of her handwritten material indicates that she knew something about the classified, hidden nature of the Battelle studies.

These people had worked and published also with those on both the Pentacle Memo and on the *Second Progress Report*. Thus, if any list of people might be the researchers working on the Battelle study, these could be likely because of their many connections to these researchers, for example:

Art Schwope worked with researchers in the Pentacle Memo and those in the Second Progress Report. He published with Loyd Jackson of the Pentacle memo and thus associated with these researchers. He is the senior author of *Creep in Metals* with Shober, F.R. and Jackson, L.R.[122] Schwope has published additional articles in the field of metallurgy. A co-author is H. J. Grover who is also in the others list with Schwope.

The Internet contains a list of Schwope's many publications: "A. D. Schwope's scientific contributions while affiliated with Battelle Memorial Institute (Columbus, United States) and other places." For example, he has published with M. W. Mallett of the *Second Progress Report*: "Hydrogen Embrittlement of Zirconium" by R.W. Dayton, A.D. Schwope, · G.T. Muehlenkamp, H.A. Saller, and M.W. Mallett.[123]

Thus he published with Jackson of the Pentacle Memo and Mallett on the *Second Progress Report*.

Frank Holden At Battelle he worked as a research engineer and manager and from which he retired in 1986 after 35 years. He also worked in phase diagram and alloy development studies, funded by the various government agencies that were getting underway in 1950 and 1951. This was a commercial research project on alloy development supported by Remcru that started at Battelle and would have profound implications in the future of titanium alloys. It was performed by Dr. Robert Jaffee and his staff of research engineers, which included Holden. Robert Jaffe is also included in the others list with Holden.

Walter Boyd Walter Boyd in all likelihood knew John Center, for they had likely worked together. He worked with W. F. Simmons and with R. I. Jaffee. Boyd authored, "High-Strength Materials for Pressurized-Water In-Pile Tubes," with WF Simmons, R. P. Sopher, and F.H. Lyon that was done at Battelle. Simmons was also the first author on the *Second Progress Report*. This paper also included John Center's paper, thus Boyd knew Simmons and also likely John Center. Boyd is an author of *The Effect of Composition on The Mechanism of Stress-Corrosion Cracking of Titanium Alloys in Nzo4, And Aqueous and Hot-Salt' Environments*, by J. D. Boyd, P. J. Moreland, W. K. Boyd, R. A. Wood, D. N. Williams, and R. I. Jaffee (of the Others List). He is listed in the acknowledgments of *Uhlig's Corrosion Handbook*, By Herbert Henry Uhlig.

Perry Rieppal was also on the Pentacle Memo.

Art Elsea He authored papers with A. Westerman of the Pentacle Memo and, thus, knew these scientists. One such report was the *Quarterly Progress Report on Alloys for High-Temperature Service To 800 degrees*, by EE Fletcher, AR Elsea, and AD Westerman. (A V. W. Ellsey is listed on the Pentacle Memo.) He is also an author of *Final Report on Investigation of Boron in Armor Plate (OD-87): Endurance and Other Properties of Some Boron-containing Carbon Steels and NE 9400 Type Steels, by* J. M. Berry, J. S. Jackson (Of Battelle Memorial Institute), A. R. Elsea, and C. H. Lorig 1944.[124] Lorig was on Second Progress Report with Center.

Elsea wrote a number of additional technical repots with C. H. Lorig of the *Second Progress Reports* some as early as 1944.[125]

Paul Frost He was an author of a Battelle technical report, "The Extrusion of Titanium," by AM Sabroff, WM Parris, and PD Frost. This report is given as a related article to the *Second Progress Report,* which included John Center's portion. Its authors were: J. H. Jackson, P. D. Frost, A. C. Loonam, L. W. Eastwood, and C. H. Lorig. It was published in February 1949, (pp. 149-168).[126]

Loyd Jackson was also listed on the Pentacle Memo.

Fred Bagby was a senior program manager for Army programs at Battelle Laboratories, Columbus, Ohio.

Nelson Crites worked at Battelle and with a friend designed and patented a several things, such as improvements on pacemakers as well as a few other designs for NASA. He developed a pressure-sensitive elastomeric transducer.

Horace Grover also worked with the researchers (Jackson) listed on the Pentacle Memo. He was the first author of the book, *Fatigue of Metals and Structures,* with S. A. Gordon and L. R. Jackson.[127] It is described in Amazon.com as a book for those who want to go deep in the engineering related subject of their majors. And his listings include numerous additional papers he authored with Jackson and sometimes also with Schwope. One of his publications is *Fatigue Strength and Related Characteristics of Joints in 24s-T Alclad Sheet*, by H. W. Russell, L. R. Jackson, H. J. Grover, and W. W. Beaver published in 1944.[128]

Bob Jaffee would very likely have known John Center because he worked with Howard Cross for many years and he also would know the principal people in the *Second Progress Report*. He had numerous publications with CM Craighead, such as *Nature of the Line Markings in Titanium and Alpha Titanium Alloys* by CM Craighead, GA Lenning, and RI Jaffee in the *Journal of Metals*. Craighead was an author of the *Second Progress Report*, which included John Center's paper.

Jaffee was associated with Cross and Connie Voldrich of the Others List. He was mentioned prominently in *Titanium: A New Metal for The Aerospace Age*, by Charles R. Simcoe, as an important pioneer in the field and as a research metallurgist who conducted the research on this first titanium project as described in more detail under Connie Voldrich.[129] These Battelle scientists, who were also authors of the *Second Progress Report* that included John Center, held an important place in the development of titanium. Jaffee also worked with W. Hodge and R. I. Mallett of the *Second Progress Report*.[130,131]

Jaffee was a native of Chicago and received his B.S. Degree in Metallurgy at the Armour Institute (now Illinois Institute of Technology). He received graduate degrees from Harvard University and the University of Maryland. He began his career as a research engineer at the University of California and worked at several other laboratories before joining Battelle in 1943.

Connie Voldrich is especially interesting; she was a member of a group of Battelle researchers on the Second Progress Report who worked together before Roswell. Thus she likely knew Center. She began working with Cross and Jaffee around 1946 or earlier. And she wrote a document that mentioned *SR-14*, but said she didn't work on it; hence she knew about it. She said she was interested in UFOs and that the subject came up all the time. Hence, she must have paid attention to the subject. The others interviewed did not seem to show this interest. She admitted that she knew about it, which suggests that others, who weren't cleared, also did. Her comment that *SR-14*, "was kept pretty well under cover. If I did know, I wouldn't tell. Because it was classified" is telling.

She with others including some on the Pentacle Memo were pioneers in this metallurgical field as described in some of excellent general historical information about the development of titanium in "Metals History Titanium: A New Metal for the Aerospace Age," by Charles R. Simcoe.[132] It gives information about this work and the early metallurgical research of Battelle, WP, and similar organizations in general. It also shows that some of the scientists listed on the Pentacle Memo and the "Others List" had worked together on titanium projects before Roswell.

This piece tells about how Battelle and some of its scientists were at the heart of it all in the development of Titanium. Some of these main figures in titanium development are also the main figures in, or are connected with, the Battelle UFO project. These Battelle scientists were also authors of the *Second Progress Report,* which included John Center.[133]

> Battelle Memorial Institute started with a small staff of experienced researchers under Horace Gillett from the Federal Bureau of Standards. [Cross had worked as an assistant metallurgist for the Federal Bureau of Standards]. It grew slowly in the first few years of the great depression. By the late 1930s and into the war years of the 1940s the staff had grown to several hundred personnel.
>
> The research metallurgists who conducted the research on this first titanium project would become pioneers in the field… Robert Jaffee, Howard Cross, and Connie Voldrich would remain at Battelle to work on titanium for the next 10 to 12 years. This latter group would continue at Battelle until retirement.

This first program, funded by the Air Force Air Material Command [of WPAFB], was performed by, Craighead, Simmons, and Eastwood.at Battelle [who were authors of the *Second Progress Report* with John Center].

Eastwood was Supervisor of the Magnesium Foundry.

Craighead and Simmons were research engineers in this group.

Eastwood was from Wisconsin with his undergraduate and graduate studies at the University of Wisconsin. He was an assistant Professor at Michigan College of Mining and Technology and was a research metallurgist at Alcoa before joining Battelle.

Craighead was educated at Penn State and had worked at Alcoa and Reynolds Aluminum.

Simmons was from the University of Michigan with experience at Packard Motor Car Company.

This group conducted a project covering a large number of alloy additions to titanium. Their published papers in the *Transactions of the American Institute of Metallurgical Engineers* in 1950 contained hardness, strength properties and phase diagram results.

Research activities accelerated in 1950 and 1951. The Army Ordnance Corps at Watertown Arsenal began a large program of in-house research under Dr. Leonard D. Jaffe, and a major program of contract research with outside firms.

The Air Force at Wright Patterson Air Force Base, Dayton, Ohio began extensive in-house and contract programs at this same time. This work was placed at Battelle... and other laboratories.

As the phase diagram and alloy development studies funded by the various government agencies were getting underway in 1950 and 1951, a commercial research project on alloy development supported by Remcru was started at Battelle. This research would have profound implications in the future of titanium alloys. It was performed by Dr. Robert Jaffee and his staff of research engineers, which included Russell Ogden, Dan Maykuth, Frank Holden [also on the Others List] and Dean Williams, with the assistance of Dr. Walter Finlay of Remcru. *Robert Jaffee* was a native of Chicago and received his B.S. Degree in Metallurgy at the Armour Institute (now Illinois Institute of Technology). He received graduate degrees from Harvard University and the University of Maryland. He began his career as a research engineer at the University of California and worked at several other laboratories before joining Battelle in 1943.

Their program was an investigation of alloys of titanium and aluminum with the addition of a third element. None of the previous work at Battelle included alloy systems of titanium and aluminum, therefore, Jaffee and his group were free to perform this study without conflict with the government supported research at Battelle. Many alloy compositions were examined and patents applied for in a broad range of alloys. The most important of these alloys were ones containing titanium with aluminum and vanadium. Later an alloy in this group would become the most important one in aerospace applications."

This last section of information is especially interesting because of its mention of a broad range of alloys and those with titanium with aluminum and vanadium. Nitinol, of course, is a Titanium alloy, as will be discussed.

Thus, although it is unknown why these people on the "Others List" are there, they certainly had ties with both those listed on the Pentacle Memo, and with those in the *Second Progress Report*, also. Hence they might be the unidentified people working with those Pentacle members, or suspects.

Moreover these people would have numerous connections with Elroy John Center, further suggesting that his report might be based upon fact. Some individuals were on the Pentacle Memo and some on the Second Progress Report. Some had begun working together before Roswell.

******

CHAPTER NINE

A SMALL OHIO TOWN, ROSWELL, AND ADVANCED METAL ALLOYS

Although at the time I received this report, it seemed strange that a little company in the small town of Cambridge, Ohio, would be one to possibly receive a piece of the Roswell or similar debris.

However as I continued to investigate, I discovered that this account is so loaded with information that it could provide a book in itself. Maybe it could provide a series of smoking cannons instead of a mere gun.

Battelle's receiving it would make sense because of its top professional metallurgists. However, after reading up on the history of titanium, it now is more understandable. There were a number of additional unique aspects of this report that differ from many others, but may make more sense with today's knowledge.

Several additional incidents involving materials study in the late 1940s and early 1950s resembled the account of John Center. The following events happened at a time when no one had heard of Roswell. In addition, alloys containing aluminum, steel, nickel, and vanadium were being considered as an alloy with titanium.

My first experience with Shield Alloy of Cambridge Ohio involved research on it as a Superfund Site. One thing I especially remember is that they sold tailings, which could contain radioactive substances as gravel and construction material. We always joked that the people of Cambridge didn't need headlights at night as they drove into their driveways.

My report contained the information that not long after the Roswell event, some researchers at the Vanadium Corporation of America (now Shield Alloy), were asked to investigate a strange metal material. In 2009, I interviewed Robert Orndoff, PhD, whose father, Robert Orndoff, was a metallurgical supervisor at Vanadium.[134]

The younger Orndoff's uncle, Richard Callender, was a supervisor at US Steel across the Monongahela River from Vanadium.[135]

When the younger Orndoff was a child in the late 1940s or early 1950s, his father told him he was involved in the metallurgical analysis of a special shipment of an unknown metal. The researchers refused to work on the metal unless they knew its history. They were told it came from space and was found after a crash in New Mexico; it was the resulting debris, they were told, after the crash of either a meteor or an alien spacecraft.[136]

Orndoff's father described the material as a shovelful of metal pieces and dirt. The metal was burned and carbonized, and it looked like the burned cinders from a powerful explosion. The researchers initially speculated that the metal was from a meteorite, but they were surprised to find that it did not have the composition expected of a meteorite. Orndoff thinks his father told him the metal contained silicon, magnesium, cobalt, chromium, aluminum, steel, nickel, vanadium, and titanium. The researchers felt the metal had been manufactured, and they thought it was from an alien spacecraft. Orndoff said his father, his uncle, and several others later discussed the material. Orndoff thought that his uncle, who also might have received a sample to analyze, thought the metal was crystalline. Orndoff recalled quite a bit of conversation about the metal among his family and their associates, but eventually the talk died down. Orndoff pointed out to me that because these people hadn't heard of Roswell and weren't aware of any UFO crashes, they lacked today's perspective for interpreting the facts.[137]

The younger Robert Orndoff has been knowledgeable about technology and metallurgy from an early age. I interviewed him several times about the material and had e-mail correspondence with him.[138]"An example is shown in Figure 52.

This report is interesting for several reasons. For one, it is well documented. These reporters are highly credible. The younger Robert Orndoff has been knowledgeable about technology and metallurgy from an early age. His profile in the Muskingum University Biographical Section Alumni Today (2013) shows: a B.A. with majors in Biology and Psychology at Muskingum College, New Concord, Ohio; a PhD in Psychology (Biological Psychology) at the University of California at Berkeley; a Post-Doctoral Clinical Fellow at The Johns Hopkins University School of Medicine and Hospital in the Departments of Psychiatry and Pediatric Endocrinology. He served as a professor at Long Island University in New York and Muskingum College in Ohio and he also was Director (and owner) of a full-service Mental Health Clinic. His father is also well documented.[139]

The United States Steel Corporation facility is the Cambridge Works at Cambridge, Ohio.[140]

The account is very compatible with much of the additional information about possible Roswell material. For one reason, it involved material that the researchers had to first seek information about. They sought the information because they could not identify it. They were then told it came from a crash in New Mexico and might be either a meteorite or an alien craft.

This is similar to what the Battelle researchers were told about the unidentified metal they were to analyze. They were told at first that it might be from Russia, but when they began to analyze it, they thought it was from an alien craft (as I have discussed in *UFOs Today*).

Another interesting observation is that this Shield Alloy material looked like the burned cinders from a powerful explosion. Although the Roswell reports said that something exploded, most of the purported metal that they tell about is shiny, clean, and can change shape. Thus this account is in closer agreement with the initial Roswell reports.

Orndoff described the material as a shovelful of metal pieces and dirt. This also is more closely in line with the original reports than are those of a shiny material.

This is because the Roswell event was initially described as a gouge in the earth. Orndoff's information is compatible with that - a shovelful of metal pieces with dirt that came from an explosion. This agrees with that description better than other descriptions.

Some of the original descriptions of the gouge, debris, and evidence of an explosion are given in Roswell Proof:[4]

>Major Jesse Marcel: Roswell chief of intelligence; long, narrow debris field. 3/4 mile long
>Tommy Tyree: Mack Brazel ranch-hand; sheep detoured a mile around debris field
>Bill Brazel Jr.: Rancher Mack Brazil's son; long/narrow field, ~1/4 mile; gouge at northern end
>Bud Payne: Neighboring rancher; got to southern edge of debris field
>M/Sgt. Louis Rickett: Roswell Army counterintelligence Corp; gouge; large cleanup operation
>Walt Whitmore Jr.: Son of Roswell radio station KGFL owner; gouge; later changed stories
>Brig. Gen. Arthur Exon: Former C/O Wright-Patterson AFB; later overflew debris field area; gouges
>Robin Adair: Associated Press photographer; tried to overfly debris field; gouge on ground
>Jason Kellahin: AP reporter, large balloon crash site at Brazil's place
>Bessie Brazel Schreiber: Daughter of Mack Brazel; football field size area
>Phyllis Wilcox McGuire: Daughter of Sheriff George Wilcox; large burn area; football field size
>Barbara Dugger: Granddaughter of Sheriff Wilcox; large burn area
>Sheriff George Wilcox: United Press account of what Brazel reported; small, singular object
>Sgt. Robert Porter: Accompanied Marcel to Fort Worth; small quantity of wrapped debris
>Lt. Robert Shirkey: Roswell operations officer observed loading of Marcel's plane; boxes of debris
>Sgt. Robert Smith: Air transport unit; involved in loading crates of debris into C-54's; debris cleanup
>Sgt. Robert Slusher: Roswell B-29 flight engineer, unusual July 9 crate shipment; met by mortician
>"Tim": Another crewmember with Slusher; same story
>Cpt. Sheridan Cavitt: Roswell chief of counterintelligence; tiny 20-foot square crash area
>Charles Moore: Former Project Mogul balloon engineer; how balloon crashes spread out
>Press reports (Brazel interview; Ramey 25-foot description), FBI telegram, USAF Roswell report

It appeared from this same source that something had exploded above ground rather than landing in one piece.

>It looked as if the thing had hit and bounced, scattering debris in the field. The gouge wasn't very deep but was about ten feet wide in places. The whole thing was about five hundred feet long.
>Apparently the way it cut into [the ground], whatever hit the ground wasn't wood or something soft. It looked like metal. [Adair didn't think that it had skipped as it hit the ground. It was his impression that it had come down flat.] Right straight down and right straight back

up when it left. It took off the same damned way. It didn't side off or slide off. It went straight up just like it came straight down. [Adair said that he saw two sites] One of them wasn't very distinctive. The other was plainer."

Thus, this report is more compatible with the original descriptions of the gouge and debris field than are many others.

But there are still other reasons why material might have been given to this out-of-the-way branch of a company. They are described in *Summary Technical Report of Division 18,* whose authors, as mentioned, were Vannevar Bush, James B. Conant, and Clyde Williams, as discussed earlier.

The report not only has authors with some linkages to UFOs, but also involves many of the people who later appeared in the WP-Battelle UFO studies. But this was done in 1946 the year before Roswell. It shows that connections had already formed between the scientists taking part in the UFO studies, those in the *Summary Technical Report of Division 18 document,* The Vanadium Corporation, and US Steel.

For example, the preface of this report tells that:

> This summary technical report is based in part on an editorial summary of most of the reports of Division 18 that was written by Dr. H. W. Gilliett, a member of Division IS and of the War Metallurgy Committee. Indeed, much of Dr. Gillett's summary has been incorporated verbatim into this summary technical report by these who prepared the several chapters.
> Chapter 2, "Armor," was prepared by Dr. C. H. Lorig of Battelle Memorial Institute and Supervisor of Atmor Metallurgy Research, War Metallurgy Committee.
> Chapter 5, "Metal for High Temperature Research," was prepared by Mr. Howard C. Cross of Battelle Memorial Institute and Supervisor. of High Temperature Metals Research, War Metallurgy Committee.

Both Loring and Cross were authors of the Second Progress Report that included Center.

Clyde Williams, the President of Battelle, was the Chief of the War Metallurgy Division (Div. 18), NDRC and the Chairman of the War Metallurgy Committee. He was a co-author of this report and as mentioned previously, his co-authors had some connections with UFOs.

This document shows that a connection existed between these Battelle researchers and not only the Vanadium Corporation of America but also US Steel from as early as 1944.

> Under OSRD contracts, laboratories of the following organization were engaged to work cooperatively on the project…Battelle Memorial Institute, …United States Steel Corporation Research Laboratories…Vanadium Corporation of America.

This report also includes papers of many additional authors that were included in the Pentacle Memo, the *Second Progress Report*, and the Others List. These authors co-authored with many others on the three lists.

Examples include:

Development of Improved Electrode Coatings, (C. B. Voldrich, P. J. Rieppal. and others, OSRD 4394, Progress Report M-371, Battelle Memorial Institute, Nov. 12, 1944. Div. 18-601.132-M1). Rieppal is listed on the Pentacle Memo and Voldrich is of the Others List. They authored several papers together.[142]

Additional papers in the same document show that many connections existed between these Battelle researchers and not only the Vanadium Corporation of America but also US Steel. One paper is *Development of Improved Electrode Coatings*, (C. B. Voldrich, P. J. Rieppal. and others, OSRD 4394, Progress Report M-371, Battelle Memorial Institute, Nov. 12, 1944. Div. 18-601.132-M1).

Other evidence also exists of cooperation between the Vanadium Corporation, US Steel, and Battelle. The report mentioned above says.

> Development of New Gun Steels in February 1944, the Research Group, Subcommittee on Gun Forgings, Ferrous Metallurgical Advisory Board, Army Ordnance Department suggested the establishment of Project NRC-81 (OD-S-M), Development of High - Strength Gun Steels. Although the OSRD contract was placed with the Vanadium Corporation of America, the research program was a cooperative effort. The temperature of steel, the compositions for which were selected by the War Metallurgy Committee Project Advisory Committee, were made by the Midvale Company, the specimens were prepared and heat treated by the Vanadium Corporation of America, and the tests were made by the United States Steel Corporation Research Laboratories, by Watertown Arsenal, and by the Vanadium Corporation of America.

Yet another interesting observation in connection with this is the composition of the material.

Orndoff thinks his father told him the metal contained silicon, magnesium, cobalt, chromium, aluminum, steel, nickel, vanadium, and titanium. The researchers felt the metal had been manufactured, and they thought it was from an alien spacecraft. Possibly a reason why the scientists thought this material was unearthly was that at that time people may not have combined that many materials into one alloy.

This alloy contained both titanium and nickel, which are in Nitinol. It is unknown when scientists began making alloys containing both of the substances.

However not too long afterward the discovery that Orndoff mentioned, the Vanadium Corporation of America began to test quite a number of substances into making alloys: This included Nickel, Titanium and Boron. Could the idea for these new tests of a number of substances have come from the composition that Orndoff described?

> It is certainly to be expected that among the possible combinations of precipitation-hardening elements in an austenitic matrix, new elements or combinations, some as yet untried, may be materially superior to those so far evaluated.

The Vanadium Corporation of America, one of the contracting laboratories on Project NRC-8, melted and cast a large number of Cr-Ni-Co and Cr-NiCo-Fe base alloys with considerably higher molybdenum or tungsten additions than the majority of the alloys tested in the balance of the program. Preliminary appraisals of the effects of these additions were made by means of high-temperature hardness determinations. In these alloys, the effects of additions of other elements, including vanadium, boron, beryllium, titanium, and aluminum on the hot hardness were also determined. Some of these alloys possess very high hardness at 1500 F. some as high as 400 Brinell. Stress-rupture properties at 1600 F have been determined on a few of these alloys. Ductilities upon rupture tend to be low. Testing was restricted by lack of facilities, but at least four of the alloys show properties at 1600 F superior to those of the best cast cobalt-base alloy. It is obvious that there is opportunity for still further improvement in this family of alloys, improvements that might be of great portent to the gas turbine. To date, the effects of carbon content, heat treatment, and melting practice (deoxidation and grain size) on strength and ductility are not known.

Tests were made on 96 heat-resisting alloys. These alloys were principally of Cr-Ni-Fe, Co-Cr, Cr-Ni-Co, and Cr-Ni-Co-Ft bates. Some were made available in wrought form while others were supplied in the form of premium cast test pieces, tests were also made on material from large forged disks of four heat-resisting alloys. Alloys for high-temperature service contain a considerable amount of chromium to confer resistance to oxidation, and a considerable amount of nickel or cobalt or both to render the alloy austenitic, since austenitic alloys far surpass ordinary ferritic steels in high-temperature strength.

Thus Shield Alloy was testing Nickle and Titanium in alloys from that early date. Nitinol is made of Nickle and Titanium.

It is also interesting that boron was tested. As mentioned, Bragalia said that Center had told Nicholson that UFO crash debris was stored in a secure safe and that some of the material contained the element boron. The other substances tested were some of the ones that Orndoff's father had described. Could the idea for testing these substances come from the Vanadium company's analysis?

Orndoff thought that his uncle, who also might have received a sample to analyze, thought the metal was crystalline.

The idea that the metal was crystalline might have seemed strange then, but Nitinol, for example, is crystalline and much testing was done to make such crystalline substances.

This is why it shows "memory" properties.

The properties of nitinol depend upon its dynamic heat sensitive crystalline structure. When Nitinol is deformed in the martensite phase, the crystalline structure is not damaged. Instead the crystal structure transforms moving in a singular crystalline direction. When heated the material returns to its "remembered" lest stress austenite structure.[143]

There were numerous additional papers listed in the same document authored by both Voldrich and Rieppal apart and together.

Thus these organizations had been working with some of the principal Battelle titanium experts and those working on its UFO project for several years before Roswell.

This information would suggest that if Battelle had received and studied an unidentified metal, so might have the United States Steel Corporation Research Laboratories, and the Vanadium Corporation of America. This also would agree with Orndoff's account.

In general this information has a number of unique elements that are in common with the initial descriptions of the Roswell event, the development of alloys, and the creation of nitinol. Thus, this could provide additional unique evidence that some kind of alien metal might have been farmed out, tested, and new ideas and progress in alloy composition might have been made.

Timken Furnace
There is still additional evidence that something might have been farmed out from WP for testing. This might be why there are numerous similar accounts of this in Ohio. Because WP is in Ohio, it would have close connections with other Ohio companies.

Ralph A. Multer was an "A class" truck driver for the Timken Roller Bearing Company of Canton, Ohio in the summer of 1947 when on a hot day in August or September he and two other drivers were asked to go to a nearby railroad yard, pick up three trucks and bring the loads back to the plant. He was planning to meet his young wife, they had been married the previous year, for lunch. He was on a four-hour shift and hoped he wouldn't be late. Upon his arrival at the rail yard, Ralph and the other drivers were given three flatbed trucks to drive back to the plant. The trailer on each truck had a load covered with a canvas tarpaulin. The load on Ralph's truck was the largest. It covered the entire width of the trailer and part of its length. The convoy was escorted by officials, but Ralph never said who these escorts were.

When they arrived back at the plant, they were met by several men who identified themselves as FBI. Being curious, Ralph asked what the loads were. The agent replied that they were parts of a "flying saucer" that had been recovered in New Mexico and that the new Timken furnace was going to be used to try to melt down the material. As his wife remembers the story, he was further told not to discuss the matter with anyone. Ralph had a security clearance as part of his job, so this revelation was being made within that context. The agent climbed up and pulled the tarp back to partially expose the load. From what Ralph could see, it was a "brushed aluminum" colored metallic object that appeared to have been blackened in places as if someone had tried to use a torch to cut off pieces of it. He did not see the loads on the other trucks.

When Ralph met his wife for lunch he was late. At first he didn't tell her why he had been late. However, after some prodding on her part and a promise not to talk to anyone about it, Ralph finally told her what had happened. A week or two later he ran into two of the furnace operators during the lunch period and he asked them what had happened with the material. They replied that the furnace "couldn't touch it." They couldn't break it or melt it. He never did learn what happened to the material after that. However, word got around the plant about the "flying saucer" and people were joking about it.

In the years that followed, Ralph's wife noticed that the experience had changed him; she said, without elaboration, that the experience "never left his mind from then on." She always believed his story, noting, "He had no reason to make it up." Ralph passed away a number of years ago.

This event occurred in August or September 1947, only a month or two after the Roswell crash. Jones and I tried to validate Multer's story by contacting retired Timken employees who'd worked at the plant at that time. MORA contacted six retired management and plant-engineering employees, including George L. Deal, a 35-year employee who served for many years as Timken's Vice President of Finance. None of the six admitted having heard anything about Multer's story, but as one noted, "Timken could keep a secret."

In July 2010, Ed Balint of *The Repositor* (a Canton, Ohio, newspaper) contacted me after coming across our information about the Timken connection on the Internet. Balint was investigating the story and had found a Timken retiree, 84-year-old Dominick T. Rex, who recalled hearing about Multer. Rex had worked at Timken from 1946 in the roller bearings plant. He said he'd heard some kind of rumor about a truck driver, and he thought this referred to Multer. But the elderly man didn't remember hearing about a crashed UFO. Balint also interviewed Multer's daughter, who recalled that Multer had repeated his story several times, always in the same form.

Balint's article was published a month after he first contacted me. It elicited several responses from the public, including from a caller who said his uncle had worked for the Air Force and had seen four alien bodies from the Roswell crash. Two were dead, one was injured, and a fourth told the military how to care for the injured alien, the caller said.

An additional account comes from Kevin Meggs, who in 1982 was attending Wright State University and taking a course in statics and dynamics. One night while discussing UFO phenomena, an older classmate said that as a young engineer in the late 1940s or early 1950s, he and fellow WP researchers were asked to test an unusual piece of material, the origin of which was never revealed. The material was foil-like, very thin and about three feet square. It wouldn't crease or bend. In one test, they fired projectiles at the material and it absorbed the projectiles and the energy they carried, dropping the projectiles to the floor of the test chamber. The material wasn't penetrated. The classmate said engineers were told the tests were classified and that they should never discuss them with anyone. During this conversation Meggs asked about Hangar 18. His classmate said he'd heard that a building at WP contained items retrieved from a flying saucer. He added that the building contained a test chamber where the temperature could be varied. The classmate knew little about the building or what went on inside, but he thought it had a three-digit number.

Jones and I investigated additional reports about the examination of possible UFO debris in Ohio, including one involving the North American Aviation Company in Columbus. We interviewed the daughters of North American Aviation employee Roy Beck (who'd been described in *UFOs Today*, in an earlier UFO incident at the Ohio Penitentiary). In 1963, Beck showed his daughters black-and-white photographs of alien bodies that he said were from a crashed flying saucer. He said he borrowed the pictures from another employee there. The alien looked like what we call a "grey" today. Beck said he had photographs and the information about them through his work at North American, where he and others had been asked to determine what the material from the flying saucer was made of and how it worked. Beck told his daughter they couldn't even scratch the material. She believes his work at North American on the flying-saucer parts-many of which were quite large, he said—took place in 1953 or 1954. She remembers her father saying at least one very large truck was used to move the parts out of the plant and back to WP.

Jones and I investigated additional reports about the examination of Roswell debris, included one involving the Monsanto Research Corporation near Dayton, Ohio. The Monsanto report included stories about government contracts with WP for reverse-engineering studies of gravity waves.

It might seem odd that so many stories about crash debris come from Ohio, however as mentioned, Ohio has been one of the nation's leading industrial and technological states and is the home of WP, thus, it's not surprising that if alien debris existed, it might find its way to Ohio. Moreover before Roswell, people were not yet aware of UFO debris stories and had no reason to associate strange substances with UFOs, but many early stories exist.

******

CHAPTER TEN

THE TREND EXPLODES–USAF RESEARCH ON UFOS IS DESTROYED FOREVER, DARK SIDE AND DEATH

SR-14 had astonishing results with P-values that are unheard of in normal scientific research, and much else. However, the serious study then ended almost with an explosion.

Here the written notes of "The Pentacle Letter and the Battelle UFO Project" by Jennie Zeidman, Michael Swords, and Mark Rodeghier (Appendix II), sometimes diverged from the handwritten copy, which gives a better view of what they called this Death and "Dark Side of the Force"

It is unknown if the studies really ended and it would be astonishing if the government with its top scientists and everyone else failed to notice the amazing results of *SR-14*. Vallée questions whether it really did end, or became invisible. *SR-14* started under high security, but people did find out about it. Perhaps after this it became much more secure, as Vallée stated:

> To this day there are UFOlogists who claim the letter [Pentacle Memo] was unimportant. Yet there are indications it may represent the point of major bifurcation when the most serious part of the official study plunged underground while Blue Book continued as a public relations exercise, the visible effort by the military to gather UFO reports from American citizens.[144]

Exploration of UFO phenomena came to a screeching halt, for such mundane reasons as traffic jams and clogged lines of communication as mentioned previously, not because the phenomenon was unworthy of study.

This is where the handwritten documents are of interest because they diverge from and express some events better than the typed one (Appendix 11) as follows:

"UFOs a'flappin'" this was the colorful way these events are recorded in the handwritten Figure 53. Sometimes the UFOs act like they are trickster, humorous animals. Here while a scientific study is underway, the UFOs gave a powerful demonstration over the Nation's capital. They gyrated, appeared and disappeared, flapped, could be picked up by radar, blithely flew over restricted airspace over the most important point of the government, and much else. It was quite amazing that it took a very long time for the Air Force to scramble jets.

Perhaps today's term, Flap, for a UFO wave came from this image of UFOs flapping over the White House.

"The BIG FLAP and the Washington D.C. Merry-go-round created great excitement and confusion around the government and the PENTAGON." The PENTAGON is capitalized here–maybe to emphasize that this display was right over the place where much of the UFO study took place.

The phenomenon was certainly making itself evident and putting on what has often been described as a display, as it has done on other cases. The BIG FLAP is also capitalized perhaps as a sarcastic way to describe the government's reaction of confusion, concern, and stupidity. The term "Merry-go-round" would seem to emphasize this description, the government went through their motions, but had no directed action.

It seems to have been this flap and its consequent clogging of lines of communication that aroused intelligence officials to the security problems inherent in UFOs. It was Wright-Pat's View that publicity spawned more reports. And so the logic was to reduce publicity and emotionalism on UFOs as a requirement for the protection of communication channels.

It is quite amazing that no one seemed to know that the phenomena appeared to be demonstrating its existence right in their face, but instead of this, they worried about whether it would cause a traffic problem.

As mentioned, the typed copy says, "[This seems to be the point at which the CIA really went on the alert about the UFO problem" alongside this is a note saying, "Not clear."

This whole passage feels a bit sarcastic.

The general reaction to this was to cover it up and the public was told that it was due to a slight temperature "inversion." This was soundly disputed by thinking people, such as Ruppelt and Dr. McDonald.

For example, I remember a huge atmospheric inversion over central Ohio where all over this area there was a stench that lasted for days. But people just went outside, coughed, and came back in. No one watched a spectacular UFO display with it.[145]

This should have been a beginning, but it was the death knell.

The government was making many attempts to scientifically examine the subject as described. Dewey Fournet was astonished not only by UFO descriptions, but also by the close-minded resistance that many Pentagon officers had to even contemplate the thought that they might be extraterrestrial technology. He undertook a legendary Top-Secret study to break down what he thought were foolish and potentially unhelpful mental blocks to something that could turn out to be the solution to these incidents.

His study was undertaken in the fall of 1952 and he later said that he knew that it was completed and classified Top Secret, but he never saw the final copy. He took several of the cases that he used to make a presentation to the Robertson Panel. There the mystery of the study resided, there was little hope of retrieval for UFO historians, just like its legendary cousin, the 1948 "Estimate of the Situation," the total disappearance of which was mentioned before. Obviously when such reports disappear, the public is being manipulated. But such a disappearance is evidence that someone is swallowing up the evidence. A chunk later surfaced.[146]

A part of the study basically was a way to examine wether the motion of a UFO as it flew through the air was under intelligent control. Dewey Fournet developed a motion study. These were good ideas and with today's technology, it might be better examined.

Dr. Joseph Kaplan had a suggestion to use spectrum analysis as a method to study the objects. An object that emits light will have a definite spectrum. The initial step in his suggested plan was to gather the spectrum of the object. The spectrum will then be matched with those of known objects such as meteors, stars, etc., so that known objects could be eliminated. These spectra may be used to give an indication about their composition.[147]

As they tried to obtain information of more scientific value Kaplan and the RAND Corporation suggested putting long-focal length double lensed cameras in UFO hotspots.

Then the "Dark Side of the Force" enters. This is the CIA. Although in July 1952, the "UFOs a'flappin," stirred interest, now this agency severely downplayed such ideas as the ETH in favor or mundane causes. In other words their views of UFO phenomena in terms of the dangers of traffic jams prevailed against all the other happenings

Here the importance of UFO phenomena is diminished and instead of thinking about what it means, it is presented somewhat as just a traffic jam problem. Intelligence officials wanted to "reduce publicity" and emotionalism about UFO. And this is where their public announcements and "studies" went from then to now, such as in the following Robertson Panel.

However here the CIA really seemed to pay attention to the UFO problem and, as mentioned, went on the alert.

Such activities could show possible interactive behavior, Figure 54. Some government workers must have perhaps subconsciously noted this as the UFOs flippantly cartwheeled and acrobatically spun over the Pentagon.

These prosaic people never admitted any fear that they might be interactive with us or perhaps even dangerous; they generally attributed the fearful reactions to the public such as that to the movie *War of the Worlds*. They used this as an example of why they should not inform the public about UFOs. Although if UFOs are dangerous, the opposite should have been done and, of course, they also might have contended with some fear themselves.

Indeed right here in this document, some of these fears are voiced and the government was definitely worried.

Here they actually admit that there is something to it, "The contacts at [Air Defense Command] ADC HQ are convinced that they're dealing with devices of some sort." So they admit that UFOs exist and are viewed as material devices. And not only the AF and the Pentagon were concerned, so were additional agencies.

Then they voiced their actual fears: "Because 'devices' seem to have monitored MAINBRACE, it is suggested that we prepare for UFOs at the H-Bomb blast, Project Ivy."

Here the government again admits that not only do UFOs exist; they are under intelligent control. This is because they use the word, monitor. If UFOs were simply prosaic elements, they would not monitor us. Monitor generally means: to observe and check the progress or quality of (something) over a period of time; to keep under systematic review. It implies that the checker has intelligence. This action was a result of UFO behavior and the officials were certainly aware of its military importance. Operation Mainbrace, September 14-25, 1952, was a naval exercise organized by the North Atlantic Treaty Organization (NATO). It involved armed forces from many countries–the United States, the UK, Canada, France, Denmark, Belgium and the Netherlands. It was also large– approximately 80,000 men aboard 1,000 planes and 200 ships participated in this display of force meant to demonstrate NATO's effectiveness in the event of a Soviet Union attack on Western Europe. However associated with this massive exercise were a number of high-quality UFO sightings. The observers included military radar operators, who watched a silver, circular object perform impossible maneuvers and show incredible acceleration.

A press photographer who was aboard the flagship managed to get photographs, but these were never released to the public. Some rumors exist that General Eisenhower was aboard this flagship. These sightings are still unexplained. And the government likely had classified information that made it even more concerned.[148]

WP, BB, the AF, Pentagon, ADC, but also NATO were now privy to this. NATO covers a large area of the world and contains some of the top first-world countries. So at this time a very large number of governments and agencies were on the alert and apprehensive.

They were so concerned (fearful) about this activity that they also thought the H-bomb blast could be monitored, or perhaps even affected by UFOs. They set up an important project in readiness for this, Project IVY.

On November 1, 1952, the U.S. detonated the first hydrogen bomb. This was under Project Ivy. It was the first nuclear bomb to get much of its explosive energy from fusion, or the joining of atoms, instead of only from fission, the splitting of atoms.[149] Some of the people in the Pentagon had the idea that there were beings, earthly or otherwise that could be interested in our activities in the Pacific, as was reported in Operation Mainbrace. Consequently BB had been directed to get ready for this–to get transportation to the test area to set up a reporting net, brief people on how to report, and analyze their reports on the spot. They took this very seriously.[150]

BB already was working on plans for an extensive system to track UFO's by instruments. Brigadier General Garland, who had been General Samford's Deputy Director for Production and who was riding herd on the UFO project for General Samford, was the chief at ATIC, having replaced Colonel Dunn, who went to the Air War College. Garland was in favor of trying to get some concrete information, whether positive or negative, about the UFO's. Their planned tracking system would replace the diffraction grid cameras that were still being developed at ATIC.

As soon as possible, they were planning to gather a group of scientists and let them spend a full week or two studying the UFO problem.[151]

I was unable to find the typed manuscript for the portion after, "a variation on an already known theme."

The handwritten text continues.

> It was, I believe, Dr. Walter Riedel of CSI-LA, who suggested some aerial pyrotechnics over the ocean to test out the accuracy of civilian reporters.

The above was bracketed with an added note on the side, "Yes, this idea is from CIA–FOIA 2-9-55 about CIA operative hearing Riedel speak of this controlled hoax sometime apparently in 1952." The handwritten document then continues;

> Meanwhile the CIA is taking the matter of UFOs right up to the NSC, and considers the subject a matter for the PSYCHOLOGICAL STRATEGY BOARD (both as to security and possible OFFENSE?). The key man pushing this is Dr. H. Marshall Chadwell, CIA Assistant Director for Scientific Intelligence. [VERY HIGH UP] In November and December, the CIA began marshaling its own scientific "consulting group" of high stature to review the matter.

Following this is the page missing from the typed version but shown in our illustrations.

Thus not only WP, BB, the AF, Pentagon, ADC, and NATO but the NSC were involved. This is a very large group to have been aware of and concerned about the UFO activity.

The CIA gave the appearance of concern about the UFO subject.

The whole trend-of-things explodes and USAF research on UFOs is ruined forever

Figure 55 describes in detail the dark side and its participation in demise of serious UFO study.

> December 1952...the whole trend-of-things explodes and USAF research on UFOs is ruined forever.
> At Bluebook, things are going along naively assuming that everything's alright with the Pentagon–CIA. They are completing plans for an Advisory Group overseership of the data–a preliminary look-over has been suggested prior to a main group of highest prestige.
> The technical equipment for spotting UFOs has been either developed or planned and the Northern New Mexico spotting grid concept is also completed. (The Battelle–"Pentacle" plan). [There is a margin note here to [Explain this plan?]. On page 199 of his book, Ruppelt's reports the estimated cost of this grid-plan to be $ 250,000 in instrumentation and $ 25000/year in operating costs. Despite the expenses ATIC (WRPAT intelligence/"T-2") Ok'd the plan and sent it to the Pentagon.
> However at the CIA the whole attitude of the UFO problem is going in a different direction: squelch the subject in the public's (and, apparently, the lower military's) eyes. CIA also is talking to high-powered scientists about reviewing the problem: Julius Stratton, Lincoln Lab, Max Millikan, Cal Tech (Robertson)(Lauritson), Lloyd Berkner, Jerrold Bacharies...Dr. Chadwell is still the key man doing this surveying. A powerhouse USAF–CIA–IAC meeting is held at CIA Director's review of the UFO problem by top scientists, the review to be planned

by the CIA and the scientists selected by the CIA. General Samford agreed to fully cooperate, saying this was a problem of intelligence and defense. (i.e. security is the only issue). Max Millikan of CENIS was given task of recruiting the proper scientists. His budget was $ 5000, (so it was obvious that this was to be a "quickie" with a set agenda). Within a couple of days, Robertson was 'on-line' and ready to meet with Ruppelt preliminarily. Also Fred Durant had entered the story as the go-between for the CIA and WRPAT (actually Durant and E. Tauss had been involved at least since November talking to Colonel Bower).

Although the CIA was now claiming UFOs to be nonexistent, this was reviewed by the CIA director–as high as it could go. And the CIA appeared to be over the AF in this matter.

After this the whole study just drifted away. Death and Destruction: Figure 56, describes in detail the demise of serious UFO study. Below is the typed write-up of this section.

Ruppelt is described in the handwritten version as (naïve boy) because of his belief that he was still a participant in a legitimate study.

> [The "preliminary look" at Blue Book data, which occurred in Dayton in December (or maybe in very late November, Ruppelt doesn't always get the dates exact) was in Ruppelt's naive mind an open-ended study by top scientists. Actually, it seems to have been the "ritualistic" going-through-the-motions of legerdemain endemic to CIA covert actions. That this latter seems obvious results from Ruppelt's report that 4 people reviewed the files (in late November/December) for three days, and recommended that a "High Court" of scientists be approved to look at this subject. The Pentagon approved this recommendation in one hour!
>
> It's obvious that this recommendation was expected and planned for. Also, the recommendation contained the names of the six men recommended to serve! Only the date (late December/early January) was still open. [I (Swords) believe that the whole deal was a "done deal" in the CIA/NSC; that the WPAFB meetings were in early December, that Dr. Chadwell (who writes to Hynek telling him how he enjoyed meeting with him in Dayton earlier in the month) was the leader of the CIA-science team, and that poor 'ol Ed Ruppelt had no idea that the die was already cast.] (Robertson and Durant visited Wright—Pat in the second week of December, also.)
>
> K. In January 1953, these events took place:
> The "Pentacle Letter" was written The Robertson Panel convened William T. Reid, a Technical Director at Battelle, completed the correspondence relative to the statistical analysis/IBM punch—card project.
>
> Ruppelt still didn't clearly hear what was being said. The Blue Book project continued for a little while on momentum. The CIA maintained a lot of interest in probing cases and persons (Ex: Fred Durant wanted Hynek's info on APRO (Feb '53). Hynek seems to have talked to Durant about APRO at the Robertson Panel.
>
> Later, Blue Book personnel dissipate. Ruppelt takes temporary leave. During that leave, the Pentacle Plan (for controlled UFO events) was rejected, but diffraction cameras on bases were ok'd. Investigations were transferred to ADC.

The Aerial Phenomena Research Organization (APRO) was an important UFO research group started by Jim and Coral Lorenzen.

So at this point suddenly there was much high-level proof of the reality the UFO phenomena: the one in a billion statistical chance found in the *SR-14* report, the UFO wave over the restricted air space of the central area of the government, the Mainbrace and the idea that that preparations for UFOs at the H-Bomb blast were made, a recognition of not only the existence of UFOs but of intelligent control, and a concern that drew in many organizations and people, and much else.

So here of all places, suddenly the CIA kills UFO study.

Did they make some kind of discovery here that caused them to stop, or to make any more study very secured? Did the leak of the Pentacle Memo make them even more concerned about security? Did something scare them to the point of stopping or hiding the investigation? Could they have been under some form of influence by UFO phenomena itself (I was told that Dr. Hynek considered that there might be some form of interaction between some governments and UFO phenomena). Or what?

But this activity isn't just history, it is the state of affairs to this day.

******

CHAPTER ELEVEN

THE MOST IMPORTANT QUESTION–WHY KILL THE STUDY

But why kill the study at the point where it was bearing fruit, especially when it almost seemed that the UFOs were putting on a display to show their reality and power in 1952?

In other words, by the standard statistical methodology used in scientific studies, there is a much greater than simply overwhelming probability that some UFO phenomena represent something real. Despite this, the government's representation was that that *SR-14* found nothing. This conclusion is unethical and an unconscionable error. Unconscionable conduct is defined as a statement or action so unreasonable it defies good conscience. It is amazing that these scientists must be totally bereft of conscience or ethics.

Why would these scientists make such a huge, gross, error?

1.   They are stupid. Any scientist who has ever used statistics would realize that a probability of one in a billion is impossible odds.

2.   They didn't understand statistics.

3.   They were brainwashed. They just assumed that what the government said was right.

4.   They were fearful of the government (which was paying them) and went along with anything it claimed.

5.   They began a strong cover-up, but continued the studies.

6.   Could something in the government have come under the control of the phenomenon, or some other agent?

7.   Although this has not been discussed as a reason for a cover-up or stopping the studies, one would wonder if something terrified them. The UFOs over the pentagon and project Mainbrace were very alarming. And the government actually was so alarmed that it was preparing for what UFOs might do when they set off the Hydrogen bomb, Project Ivy. Perhaps they had to change or do something to affect the UFO phenomenon–or perhaps they did–the UFOs didn't show up for the bomb explosion. Later there were reports that UFOs could change the targeting coordinates of nuclear missiles.

Something like that had happened before, for example, to Albert Bender. In 1952, he founded the first worldwide civilian UFO investigatory group, the International Flying Saucer Bureau (IFSB), and its magazine, "Space Review." This group led to important spinoff organizations, including the most important ones, the Aerial Phenomena Research Organization (APRO), Civilian Saucer Investigation (CSI), National Investigations Committee on Aerial Phenomena (NICAP), and MUFON–the world's top UFO groups.

In 1962, Bender collaborated with Gray Barker on the book, *Flying Saucers and the Three Men*. This resulted from his 1953 discoveries that caused him to think that he had finally found the truth about UFO phenomena and its cover-up. He planned to reveal this information in the October issue of the *Space Review*, but he was visited by three MIB. They terrified Bender to the point where he not only did not publish the report, but quit UFO investigation altogether. He left a warning to those engaged in saucer work, to be very cautious.

This warning was so strong that Bender withdrew from UFO investigation. This withdrawal was so complete, that the UFO field did not even notice that this original founder was still alive; he died very recently at age 95 on March 29, 2016.

This experience is similar to the Arnold's many strange events at the beginning of UFO study, which also included involvement with MIB.

Another such explanation is that these people were engineers and therefore would not understand science. "The Pentacle Letter and the Battelle UFO Project," provides a lengthy explanation:

> From our interviews, it is clear that, no matter what was written in the report, Battelle understood its charge to be the determination of whether any reports were caused by structured technological vehicles. That is certainly the question that was on the Air Force's mind in 1952 when the Battelle project began, and it is the natural question to be investigated by engineers, who comprised the bulk of the project staff and were the managers of the endeavor.

And it is certainly how the government and many agencies viewed the situation in 1952.

> Our interviews revealed plainly that Westerman, Reid, and Rieppal think like engineers when it comes to their work, and they carried this attitude with them to the UFO project. Engineers are not just trained in various physical sciences; they also expect in their work to analyze physical specimens, conduct experiments, and make physical measurements (recall the main point of the Cross letter). This was not possible in the UFO project because no physical evidence was available... Instead, they worked with witness reports that were often unreliable.
> In its summary to Special Report No. 14, Battelle states, "it is considered to be highly improbable that reports of unidentified aerial objects examined in this study represent observations of technological developments outside of the range of present—day scientific knowledge." In the conclusions the authors reiterate this point, stating too that "the probability that any of the UNKNOWNS considered in this study are 'flying saucers' is concluded to be extremely small," then adding the telling comment, "since the most complete and reliable reports from the present data, when isolated and studied, conclusively failed to reveal even a rough model." We return to this point below.
> In two articles in the old series of the *Journal of UFO Studies*, "Scientific Investigation of Unidentified Flying Objects," Bruce Maccabee has exhaustively considered the statistical results of the Battelle study. He notes that the authors did not mention these findings in their

concluding remarks, perhaps because they could be seen as contradicting their conclusions. Maccabee points to these intriguing results: (1) that the sightings labeled "Excellent" in quality are more likely to be classified "Unknown"; (2) that the Unknowns were, in general, visible long enough to have been identified but were not; (3) that cases from military observers, who were better witnesses, had a higher percentage of Unknowns; and (4) that the characteristics of the Unknowns did not match the Knowns on such things as color, shape, speed, and duration.

Why would the authors of the report have ignored these incontrovertible findings? The Battelle staff were engineers, and engineers were not accustomed in 1953 (or today) to searching for statistical relationships in data that came from humans, not scientific instruments. As further evidence of this point, the Battelle team took 12 of the most reliable unidentified reports and tried to construct a working model of a UFO. If, as an engineer, you are attempting to determine whether some UFOs are structured craft, then the exercise makes sense. But when the effort, not surprisingly, failed, the conclusion was not that the project might be impossible because of the limitations of human testimony, or that there might be more than one model of UFO involved, or that some natural phenomenon might be the root cause. No, the conclusion was that "there is a low probability that any of the UNKNOWNS represent observations of a class of 'flying saucer.'"

We therefore suggest that since the Battelle team couldn't construct a UFO model and because of the participants' training and scientific mindset, the exclusive use of statistical data to conclude that some structured craft were being reported was essentially inconceivable to them. It was far easier and conservative to ignore the statistical tests when writing the report. This is not scientific dishonesty: it is a real—life instance of how presuppositions may affect the work of scientific projects.

While we didn't discuss the report in these terms with our interviewees, one recalled the impossibility of building a model, and all of them commented on the unreliability of witness testimony. Not one noted that their goals included the search for psychological phenomena or unexplained natural phenomena that might explain some reports. Our interviewees, then and now, thought of the focus of their study in terms of whether it could be demonstrated that UFOs were structured craft.

The extreme secrecy is another factor; the left hand did not know what the right hand was doing:

> By January 1953, Battelle had coded several thousand UFO reports but had not begun any serious statistical analysis. Its personnel were, however, intimately familiar with UFO reports, since they had been engaged in evaluation conferences with Blue Book personnel to decide upon an explanation for every report received. As we have indicated, the Battelle UFO project was only a small part of Project Stork, but the latter project was so secret that, 14 years later, Hynek would still believe that Project Stork dealt only with UFO research. This secrecy, and Battelle's attitudes toward its clients, are crucial for an understanding of the Cross letter, as we explain below.

We conclude this article with what we believe is an important insight into the manner in which Battelle handled the UFO project and wrote its final report (which became Special Report No. 14).

Compared to the infamous Condon Report, Battelle's final report is a model of scientific honesty. Nevertheless, there are parallels between the two in the divergence between the body of each report and the conclusions based on that evidence. In Condon's case, as has been amply documented; Condon blatantly ignored the work of his own team, for reasons that may have been personal, professional, organizational, or a combination thereof. In the case of Battelle, the situation is much less egregious, but the authors of Special Report No. 14 did seemingly disregard the intriguing statistical findings of the study.

Battelle states its primary goal in the UFO project thus: "This study was undertaken primarily to categorize the available reports of sightings and to determine the probability that any of the reports of unidentified aerial objects represented observations of 'flying saucers.'" By "flying saucers" Battelle meant, as defined in the introduction, "a novel, airborne phenomenon, a manifestation that is not a part of or readily explainable by the fund of scientific knowledge known to be possessed by the Free World." (Notice how this leaves open the possibility of Soviet technology, not surprising given the goal of Project Stork.) Though the definition states "airborne phenomenon," it is immediately followed with the statement that this "would include such items as natural phenomena that are not yet completely understood [or] psychological phenomena" (our emphasis). It is hard to imagine an airborne psychological phenomenon, and this confusion of mission is central to an understanding of the Battelle study.

Summary

Our investigation of the Cross letter led us to a reconsideration of the Battelle UFO study. Though somewhat flawed, it remains one of the best scientific studies of the UFO phenomenon. Far from being evidence of government manipulation of the Robertson panel or of the existence of a secret study not part of Blue Book, the Cross letter was, in a very real way, a shining moment for Battelle. The institute attempted to prevent the CIA from proceeding with the Robertson panel because the effort was premature, too brief, and doomed to fail because reliable data were not available.

We can quibble with this last point, but if Cross and colleagues had succeeded, who knows how it would have changed the history of UFO study?

Another theory is that these people and the government scientists lied. Possibly this was due to some form of pressure from somewhere.

A theory of my own is that new methods of UFO study were coming into existence. Around that time, the scientists may have already been thinking about developing "Spy-in-the-sky" satellites that could photograph earth from above. Previously such methods as positioning cameras in hot spots, diffraction grating photography, and photography such as gun camera from jets were used. Such photography would be very difficult to do because UFOs are unpredictable and difficult to photograph by this method. However using satellites above, scientists would have a method to produce much better photography. Perhaps this is a reason that the project was suddenly closed. I worked on this photography at that time, and the photography is still classified (I videotaped an interview from a government employee about this).[152]

Another theory remains as probably the most acceptable theory, that there is a cover-up. This information would be much more classified than *SR-14*.

No threat?–My own Experience
From my own experience, I think cover-up is a more likely explanation. But this takes place very high in the government. The next two government studies the Robertson Panel and the Condon Report were obviously fake.

All the studies merely say that the UFOs present no threat. This is weasel wording to give the impression that UFOs don't exist. But they never said that they don't exist.

The general conclusions of all the previous studies is that "none of the things seen, or thought to have been seen that pass by the name of UFO reports, constituted any hazard or threat to national security." This conclusion is ridiculous for several reasons.

For one it purports to tell us whether UFOs exist, but instead diverts to a statement that they are not a threat to national security. That gives people the opinion that the government had investigated and found that UFOs do not exist. This is deliberately misleading.

For another reason, since they provide no information about whether or not UFOs exist there is no reason to be sure that they present no threat to national security.

For example approximately thirty percent of the cases used in *SR-14* were unsolved. Despite this, the study concluded, that nothing should be done with them in the expectation that they would not contribute to the advancement of science. Even more astonishing was their response to the question of a national defense issue of the reports, they claimed that the history of the past 21 years has repeatedly led Air Force officers to conclude that none of the things seen, or thought to have been seen that pass by the name of UFO reports, constituted any hazard or threat to national security. How would they know that if they couldn't explain nearly one third of their data? They added, that they know of no reason to question the finding of the Air Force that the whole class of UFO reports does not pose any defense problem.

From my own experience I have found them to be a threat to national security, as follows:

In July 1968, I worked for the DIA in a highly classified GS-11 (PhD-level) position in Washington DC. This work was with satellite photography and done under code word security clearances that were above Top Secret, and some of which were the most highly classified in the government. Two of these code words were "Keyhole" and "Talent" (TK). This work was done in a vault in a windowless building, where we had to work a safe combination, pass before a one-way mirror, and through a security check just to enter the workplace. The work involved identifying all flying objects over certain airspaces.

The photography that I used remains highly classified today.

This work was very secure and vital because the 1960s were a time of the Cold War with its intense vigilance by the US in the face of a perceived Soviet threat. The US maintained reconnaissance operations via satellite technology and aircraft over flights of the Soviet Union and elsewhere. Jeffrey Richelson's *America's Secret Eyes in Space: The U.S. Keyhole Satellite Program* (1990) describes the Keyhole Program as one of the most significant military technological developments of the last century and perhaps in all history. The photoreconnaissance satellite played an enormous role in stabilizing superpower relationships because it helped dampen fears of weapons that the other superpowers had available, and because it showed whether military action was imminent. Much information about photoreconnaissance satellites and similar technology is still classified. Photoreconnaissance satellites are crucial to the military, and satellite and aircraft imagery also can provide new and valuable intelligence about UFOs. This work remains some of the most highly secured in the government, and according to Dr. Bruce Ashcroft also takes place in the extremely secure WP area, the NASIC, building 856.

Today it is still exceptionally classified and recently has been in the media because of e-mail news. Its status, "TOP SECRET//SI//TK//NOFORN" level must be handled with great care under penalty of serious consequences for mishandling. Every person who is cleared and "read on" for access to such information signs reams of paperwork and receives detailed training about how it is to be handled, no exceptions—and what the consequences will be if the rules are not followed. In the real world, people with high-level clearances are severely punished for willfully violating such rules."[153] So I did not carry away or mention any of this specific information.

In 1968, I was working in a section called Air Order of Battle in the Soviet/East Europe Division, Eastern USSR Branch (I published my government Standard Form 50 from this position in my book, *Inside the Lightning Ball: Scientific Study of Lifelong UFO Experiencers*, to prove that I held this position). Our duties included identifying and recording all flying objects viewed via this satellite photography in this area, such as aircraft and missiles. I think the CIA was the recipient of our reports.

My supervisors reported a UFO on this film to their superiors.

The object that they had reported was in photographs that were taken over water. I looked at the photographs and I could tell by the water's wave pattern that the object was above the water and not in it. As I recall, the object was over the Black Sea. It was to the west of a mountain range that had a group of buildings; there might have been a Soviet military installation on its other side. The object was photographed on at least two missions (a mission was one 90-minute satellite pass around the earth). It was in a slightly different place during each of the two passes, but it was in the same general area in both.

I made enlargements of the photographs and manipulated the object's size until I had two photos that showed the object from two different viewpoints with the object the same size in each. Thus, I could examine the object's shape stereoscopically. It was saucer-shaped, with a dome. This dome was tall in comparison to the brim—almost like that of a top hat. However, the shape may have been distorted by my method of reproducing and enlarging the photos.

The protocol required us to report the results of our photographic analysis to the CIA, and the supervisors of my area said they'd reported the object as a UFO. I am unaware of any time that our supervisor's professional judgment about the identity of objects in the photos was questioned because they were the government's own top authorities. However, the CIA did not accept this report. The CIA insisted the object was an illusion caused by an imperfection in the film. The DIA analysts protested that because the object had been photographed on two different missions, there could not be such a photographic imperfection.[154] The CIA, however, was adamant.

To determine whether the object might indeed be an illusion caused by an imperfection in the film, the analysts sent the film to sensitometry and densitometry specialists (called sensydensy). These experts analyzed it and reported that there was no imperfection and that a real object had, in fact, been photographed. My supervisors reported these results to the CIA, but the CIA continued to insist the object did not exist and was an illusion caused by flaws in the film. The specialists who analyzed the film thought this was highly unusual behavior on the part of the CIA. As far as I know, the Air Order of Battle section was the DIA's top organization for analyzing overflight information, and I know of no other time that the section's professional opinion was questioned.
In this case, what should have happened is that the CIA should discuss the material with the experts in a courteous professional manner. If the experts were wrong, the reasons why should have been pointed out. This would improve the country's proficiency in photointerpretation.

But what did happen is interesting–instead the CIA gave an explanation that was weirder than the UFO–almost as if it were taunting the professionals. The images were very, very definitely not film flaws. If the CIA experts knew what caused them, they should have given constructive information, rather than ridiculous replies.

Moreover a misidentification in the government's Photographic Interpretation Office could potentially start WWIII. This was highly classified and significant work. Because our work could easily involve UFO phenomena, I think we should have been informed in some way about it. We had a need to know, but we did not. Instead, we experienced something that could be seen as harassment from the government. This suggests that a much higher government agency can interfere with and maybe actively harass even people working in the government in areas that should be concerned about UFO phenomena.

In addition, I later discovered that the DIA has a significant, maybe vital, role in both UFO investigation and its cover-up. For one, many suspect that it might be the agency that collected UFO reports after BB was terminated on December 17, 1969. For example, John Greenewald, of the Black Vault in "The Defense Intelligence Agency's UFO Files" said.

> The Defense Intelligence Agency, their mission is to provide timely, objective and cogent military intelligence to. . . .the decision makers and policymakers of the U.S. Department of Defense and the U.S. Government. Did they take an interest in UFO sightings? They sure did, and The Defense Intelligence Agency has hundreds upon hundreds of blacked out investigations into the UFO phenomenon.[155]

Moreover, some of its released documents show that in 1968, when this occurred, the DIA was actively investigating UFOs; thus, some department likely was aware of our report.

In other documents, he said that the Central Intelligence Agency and Defense Intelligence Agency have conducted UFO investigations that have not been publicly released. This might be the majority of their documents on the subject.

And these agencies have been involved for a long time; the CIA sponsored the 1953 Scientific

Advisory Panel on Unidentified Flying Objects, also known as the "Robertson Panel."

Our experience with this DIA behavior suggests that a department monitors UFOs along with other flying objects. Because their response to our report was ridiculous and insulting to the specialists professional expertise, it may also cover-up and debunk UFO reports. These activities also reminded me of the Kenneth Arnold events, where it appeared that a higher government echelon acted independently of the rest of the government from the very beginning.

Many investigators, such as Timothy Good, have backed up this DIA information. This experience suggests to me that somewhere in the government is or was a group with knowledge of UFO activity. Moreover, it's likely that our Air Order of Battle section would have been monitored because it possessed widespread and the most recent coverage of the earth's surface and air space. And we should have been the agents to find the UFOs.

This inside the DIA experience certainly made me think that the government was involved in cover-up activities. In fact, it even made me slightly wonder if aliens were running the government.

This program is likely vital for UFO study, for as Stanton Friedman has observed, the government probably knows the most about the UFO subject, and its best evidence might be its photoreconnaissance programs. He mentions that the best equipment for monitoring UFOs is satellite or ground-based radar or high-performance cameras, and these are operated by government agencies.

He added that much of the data generated by spy satellites is born classified. Government agencies are always on the lookout for equipment coming in from orbit and recovery teams are instantly alerted when information comes in.

Because of the technical expertise exposed through this photography, it is among the most classified material in the country and this is regardless of whether UFOs are involved.

Moreover, as more information becomes known about DIA overseas investigation, UFOs associated with water, and UFO activity in the Black Sea area of the world, perhaps this information might help to shed light on our DIA experience or our experience might help in the examination of additional little-known UFO events there.

Thus, my conclusion about this is that the DIA lies. No matter what was on the film that the DIA Air Order of Battle sectioned turned in as a UFO, it was definitely something that had been photographed. It was not a flaw on the film. The DIA used a lie that was patently obviously false when they said it was a flaw on the film. It is unknown why they would use such a blatant lie about this, rather than a more sophisticated version. This ridiculous response, of course, made me think that some government organization was aware of UFO phenomenon and we had experienced part of the cover-up.

Indeed the CIA itself was formed very soon after the Kenneth Arnold and Roswell events. It was created under the National Security Act of 1947 that President Truman signed on July 26, 1947.

Truman appointed the Deputy Director of CIG, Roscoe H. Hillenkoetter as its first director. Hillenkoetter is listed on many Internet sites as among notable people that have publicly stated that UFO evidence is being suppressed. After retirement, he became a member of the board of governors of NICAP, a UFO investigatory group, from 1957 to 1962. He wanted public disclosure of the UFO evidence.

Thus such government photographic interpretation offices as I worked in are important in investigating UFO events and photography. But it appears that the government does not even disclose UFO information to those working in pertinent fields.

This alone is a threat to national security

But this debunking strategy seems to work, such as in the 2017 report about Harry Reid's UFO investigations.

However some other events were also associated with this.

My supervisors told me about this, after I had mentioned UFOs in a conversation with my colleagues. As I recall they included Frank Reams, a high-ranking civilian; William Carlisle, an Air Force Major; and Rick Shackelford, a civilian. I think Frank Reams may have had a high position, such as GS-14. To my surprise, no one ridiculed me. This was because in 1968 (before I'd begun working in that section), they had observed a UFO on their TK photography, as mentioned above.

This, however, led to my own smoking gun experience while working for the DIA, as Timothy Good reported in *Need to Know: UFOs, the Military, and Intelligence*.

I did not even think of reporting my sighting or talking about it because I had some top security clearances. The subject of UFOs was looked down upon; people thought you were mentally disturbed if you thought you saw one, and this could lead to losing your security clearances. If you lost your clearance, you lost your job.

But immediately after the experience, I wrote very detailed notes about the whole thing and still have them, because I intended to report it sometime.

The event is described below:[156]

The reason I had mentioned the subject of UFOs was that on the weekend before, my sister and I had had a close, prolonged sighting of objects. This sighting itself may have lasted an hour or two, but its after effects continued for two days until the morning I went to work. This has been described in detail in several articles and books, such as *Inside the Lightning Ball*.

A portion of this event could have involved a threat to national security.

My sister and I were driving around Boston. As we left the area, we had seen two objects. We had just driven by one that had been on the ground, around 50 feet from the car that contained light that went through a spectrum of color. When we passed it, the inside of our car lit up in green. I saw no light beam on the outside of the car.

Then we had parked to watch a large flying object. It had seven large square windows that were blinking in a sequence as it passed very slowly over us.

It was close, I had the camera up and ready, and I could have easily photographed the object's bright inside through the windows, which would have shown up well in the photograph (I have seen and videotaped lots of blimps near freeways including ones with lighted sides at night). Just then, a truck driver pulled over in front of us and the driver walked toward us. I thought this was great because we would have another witness. But no. He walked up, stood beside me and asked us what we were looking at. We would not say UFO around a strange man at night, but pointed at it and acted like it was a type of airplane.

When I did this, he rotated 180 degrees in the opposite direction, looked up to the same azimuth, and said he did not see anything. Then he rotated back and asked the same question. When I pointed the second time, he did the same thing. Then he rotated back and pointed at his head, which I interpreted as the crazy sign. He then returned to his truck, but didn't drive away as someone checking us might do. Instead he stayed in his truck watching us.

Later the object began seemed to go through a patterned sequence of actions and I drove into the Interstate to turn the car around at the next intersection. He took off, drove right behind my car by a few feet, began to tailgate, and beamed his bright headlights into my mirror such that I was blinded. He definitely chased us; he stayed right behind no matter what I did–such as change lanes, speed up, etc. Even though he was in a truck, he kept up with us no matter how fast I accelerated. I thought for sure we would be killed, but was able to get away.

I had always wondered whether this was just some kind of weird coincidence or something deliberate. I even did when I wrote my book. But more recently, I realized that it was not coincidence. This was because I realized that if a person points at something, another person trying to see it will look around in the direction of the point. This is not what he did. He looked in the exact opposite direction. Thus, he knew where it was. And he did it twice. Thus I also think that his trying to kill us was no coincidence.

Hence I think this would constitute a threat to national security because he appeared to attempt to kill us while I was working for the DIA, with security clearances in highly secured work.

I also think this obstruction to the report of our DIA section, apparently came from the CIA. It was obvious that some high-ranking portion of the government was involved.

People constantly talk about disclosure with reports that they know the inside secrets of the government. However if they really did know these things, they could take the information to scientists who could use it. Because no one is flying around in a UFO, the information probably hasn't been disclosed.

Another reason to wonder about disclosure is that if the disclosure involves two parties, both parties have to be a part of the disclosure. For example if someone discloses UFOs, and nothing lands on the capital or that sort of thing, the disclosure doesn't prove anything.

******

CHAPTER TWELVE

THE REAL DR. J. ALLEN HYNEK

Peel off the layers of mild-mannered professor, ace astronomer, inventor, rocket man, pipe-smoking tweedy UFO expert, media hungry peacock …and what is really there?

He was born to be an astronomer. He was born under Halley's Comet, lived an amazing life as it circled the sun, and as he expected – when it came back, he died. This was just like another Halley's Comet man, Mark Twain a generation before, who like Hynek had a very developed sense of humor, curiosity, tendency to not accept the common place, toy with words, and to question everything. Both were highly aware of current events and had commentary-sometimes humorous,

Dr. Hynek's writings in his own handwriting may show more than any of his many other writings, what the real J. Allen Hynek was like. His letters are shown here with commentary about the meaning and history behind what he said.

They show his personal feelings and sincerity about UFO phenomena, but also his humor, mischievous nature, creativity, imagination, and even a tendency to tease.

Through the letters, one gets the feeling of knowing him. They tell of his real nature much better than his more formal typewritten writings, because these are off-the-cuff, spontaneous messages that he did not have to go to a computer, think about, and then type and edit. And by its nature, such longhand writing is much less formal and shows his inside nature much better than his more formal, polished writings. Here he is relaxed and writing to familiar friends.

The letters also show aspects of his life and UFO investigations that have not been mentioned in other publications. Thus, they add much material about him that has not been known. They demonstrate the huge amount of work he put into the UFO field while maintaining his positions as astronomer, professor, family man, inventor, writer, dedicated scientist, advisor to director Stephen Spielberg, movie star, and much else. They particularly show his strong interest in UFO information from scientists and from scientific study, although he was interested in everything. He often went over such scientific work in fine detail studying the methodology and results. In other words, where did he get the time?

These letters show what was probably the most important point of Hynek's life. He made a gigantic transition from being a debunker to starting his own UFO organization–his crowning glory.

There are many new and unexpected things to learn about Dr. Hynek, as will be shown.

These letters are very valuable for other reasons. Anything that Hynek wrote about UFOs is of interest to a student of UFOlogy. His voluminous writing includes books and many, many articles in all types of publications. Like all active researchers, he also wrote private letters, reports, and notes that have been seen by only a few colleagues and friends. And some of these are shown in our illustrations:[157]

Thank you to Jennie Zeidman for allowing me to use these letters from her collection of Hynek's material. Mark O'Connell said that Hynek maintained close ties with his former students and with his BB assistant Jennie Zeidman, who had taken a job at Battelle, which was another unexpected consequence of Project Stork. I am very honored to have been allowed to use her material and some of Hynek's letters.

Based upon their correspondence over the years, it is seen that he shared more with Zeidman than he did with any other friend besides his wife. She was one of the first to know that he was writing a book about UFOs, and he asked her for editing advice, and encouragement. This was *The UFO Experience: A Scientific Inquiry*. Zeidman and Hynek are shown together in Figure 57.

The first thing about Dr. Hynek that people are not aware of, is that, although he might be called "Mister Blue Book," he was not a part of the main BB UFO study. Although he is seen as the Father of UFOlogy, a chief UFO proponent, and worked for BB, the main AF UFO study was taking place in secret at Battelle, while he was working for BB but it was a separate study that he was not a part of.

That is one reason why he was excluded from meetings.

BB was not a serious scientific study; it was a public relations kind of project of which he was aware. The actual serious study was done under Blue Book, but it was then classified as secret and done at Battelle, under Howard Cross and others. Hynek had realized he wasn't receiving the best reports, but kept at it in order to continue to be in contact and find out what was going on.

Dr. Hynek had been my childhood hero long before I knew anything about his UFO work through his astronomy columns in the *Columbus Dispatch*.

J. Allen Hynek, PhD, (1910-1986), was central to the development of UFOlogy. Hynek was involved in all aspects of UFO study and was scientific adviser to UFO studies undertaken by the U.S. Air Force under three consecutive names: Project Sign (1947-1949), Project Grudge (1949-1952), and BB (1952-1969). He worked on these projects at Battelle, WP, and OSU. He is widely considered the founder of the concept of scientific analysis of UFO evidence.

Although best known as an UFOlogist, his credentials as a scientist and author are impeccable. He received his B.S. from the University of Chicago and his PhD in astrophysics from Yerkes Observatory, and he specialized in the study of stellar evolution and in the identification of spectroscopic binaries.

As an astronomer with the Smithsonian Astrophysical Observatory in Cambridge, Massachusetts, he was responsible for tracking the earth's first artificial satellite, Sputnik. At OSU, he was Professor of Astronomy, Director of McMillin Observatory, and Assistant Dean of the Graduate School. During World War II, as a civilian scientist at the Johns Hopkins Applied Physics Laboratory, he helped to develop the United States Navy's radio proximity fuse.

He was Chairman and Professor of the Astronomy Department at Northwestern University, Professor and the Director of the Lindheimer Astronomical Research Center at Northwestern University, and Visiting Lecturer at Harvard University from 1956 to 1960. He oversaw significant expansion of Northwestern's Astronomy Department and made many important contributions to his field, such as his pioneering work on image orthicon astronomy, which combined television technology and telescopes. The image orthicon greatly enhanced the telescope's light gathering abilities, and the National Science Foundation proposed that this could be the most significant astronomical advance since photography.

In addition to being a well-known astronomer, he participated in rocket research for projects including the V-2. He worked at White Sands Proving Ground and at the Redstone Arsenal in Huntsville, Alabama. He has been referred to as one of the nation's leading men in the field of rocket research.

As an author, he wrote an astronomy textbook, and his articles appeared in numerous periodicals, including an astronomy column for *Science Digest* and a column called "Scanning the Skies" for the *Columbus Dispatch*. He wrote five enormously successful books on UFOs and many articles published in popular magazines. Probably because he initially was a skeptic, the Air Force employed him to work for BB, a project created to investigate reports of UFO sightings, through the 1950s and 1960s. Hynek was able to explain away most of the reports, but some eluded him; this led him to become less of a skeptic. In 1973 Hynek went against the establishment and founded the Center for UFO Studies (CUFOS) to conduct research that the government no longer publicly pursued. Hynek eventually stopped thinking that alien spacecraft visited the earth; instead, he became convinced that some sightings were events in an alternate reality or universe.

Chiefly in response to the government study called the Condon Report, Hynek wrote *The UFO Experience* (1998), in which he famously presented three classes of "close encounters." Director Stephen Spielberg used *Close Encounters of the Third Kind* as the title of his blockbuster film about UFOs. Hynek served as technical advisor to the film and made an appearance in it.

Hynek's handwritten letters revel many unexpected aspects of this mild-mannered professor. He had a superb sense of humor, but not only this, he was also a poet. He was endowed with a strong tendency to jest and humorously harass when he saw an opportunity:

An example is in a letter to Jennie Zeidman, who was in the UK (Figure 58):

> Hi!
> Congrat that you are going to solve the problem of Rendlesham Forest! Give my very best to Jenny Randles and Dot. I'll be agog to hear of your adventures? Cheers
> You must come visit! Allen

Hynek had some quick note stationary showing an alien delivering a letter to him. It had good antennae, a mail pouch, and its UFO was behind it.

The Rendlesham Forest incident, that took place over several nights in December 1980, is often called "Britain's Roswell." It is well-known throughout the world and continues to fascinate.

It consisted of a series of sightings of unexplained lights near Rendlesham Forest, Suffolk, England, that have become linked with claims of UFO landings. The events occurred near RAF Woodbridge, which was at the time used by the United States Air Force (USAF). Its personnel, including deputy base commander Lieutenant Colonel Charles I. Halt, claimed to have seen what they viewed as a UFO sighting.

This event is the most famous of reported UFO events to have happened in the United Kingdom, and it also ranks as one of the best-known UFO events worldwide.

Jennie would have her hands full solving this one and Hynek was agog.

Noted British UFOlogist Jenny Randles saw Hynek as both a mentor and a role model. Randles first reported the Rendlesham events in the *London Evening Standard* in 1981 and then co-authored with the local researchers who uncovered the events, the first book on the case in 1984 - *Sky Crash: A Cosmic Conspiracy*.

Randles saw Hynek as a person of integrity; he taught her scientific method and logical thinking. Randles is said to have been a British consultant to the Dr. J Allen Hynek Center for UFO Studies Journal *International UFO Reporter*.

The next letter (Figure 59), must have been written in 1971 or before because he is working on the book. It is from Northwestern University Department of Astronomy. He must have returned from London. His book is coming along, thus the letter must have been sent around 1971.

He says:

> Hi
> Thought you might be interested in a lovely tour – so I stopped in at the UAA office in London just with you in mind!!
> Book coming along –
> Cheers
> Allen

Jennie was not in London, but interested so Hynek decided to take the tour for her.

Figure 60 may have been written July 1971. He was at a Holiday Inn in Santa Fe, New Mexico, and was still working on his book.

> 1, 2, 3, 4, 5 July.
> Hi –
> Have to take in the opening of the Santa Fe opera (and to check a few UFOs –Snippy at Alamosa – a mysterious remnant of San Antonio – – you name it! – all good grist for the book mith?.
> The enclosed matches your enclosure – diplomacy & proof.? skied? my ass! –
> Cheers
> Allen

Hynek liked operas and attended one there.

It has been unknown if he did any research on animal mutilation. Thus, this would provide some new information about his UFO investigations, because the above letter shows that he did investigate the subject.

The Snippy event began in Colorado's San Luis Valley. It was considered the first mysterious animal mutilation. It occurred on September 8, 1967, on the King ranch outside of Alamosa. The victim was an Appaloosa horse named Snippy. When it was found, the head and neck had been defleshed. The exposed bones were clean and white, and no blood was visible. Its cuts were cauterized, which led a local Denver pathologist to speculate that they had been done with a laser scalpel. Laser scalpels were pretty much science fiction in 1967.[158] Some accounts say that Snippy's brain and stomach had been removed.[159]

Also fifteen tapering, circular "marks" were found in the area, with flattened brush. Six indentations two-inches across, four-inches deep, and formed a circle.

> June 23
> SS+2
> What is W?IC? Say – did you see *TIME* (Jan 28). I wonder where they got that picture of me. I hate to be associated with that other guy – even in print – but there you are! –Maybe this will do some good. Amazing what came out of a simple letter to Physics Today.
>
> By now you have the Zeidman version of Chap. 16. The book she is done. I will try to get a whole copy to you – but Xeroxing a whole book is somewhat of a problem

This letter (Figure 61), written in 1971, was sent from the Corralitos Observatory Astronomy Department, Las Cruces, New Mexico.

The photograph to which he refers is in a *Time* magazine, June 28. 1971 issue. It has his photograph beside a photograph of a Zanesville, Ohio, UFO made in November 1966.[160] It is considered to have been a hoax and this is why he hated to be associated with it. The man, Ralph Ditter, made these photographs simply to please his daughter and then hung them in his barbershop. Customers noticed the good photographs of a close UFO and that started the excitement in the media. Photography experts at RAND Corporation said it was a hoax. This photo still shows up in books and magazines.

The overall article was negative and told that BB had closed because there were fewer UFO sightings, and because the Condon Committee report claimed that most UFOs have prosaic explanations (this is certainly questionable).

It mentioned that Dr. Hynek complained of a news blackout about the subject and has established an informal BB of his own. He added that reputable observers often made reports, and the reporters are not necessarily ding-a-lings. The title of the photograph was "Not always sighted by ding-a-lings."

The letter he refers to is likely the two-page letter from Hynek, to the Editors of *Physics Today* dated 15 February 1971.[161] *Physics Today* is a prestigious scientific journal.

Hynek was as active in astronomy as he was in the numerous other facets of his life. For example at the Corralitos Observatory Hynek oversaw a significant expansion of Northwestern's Astronomy Department and made many important contributions to his field, such as his pioneering work on image orthicon astronomy, which combined television technology and telescopes. The image orthicon greatly enhanced the telescopes' light gathering abilities.[162] This was the most significant astronomical advance since photography according to a National Science Foundation proposal.

O'Connell in his book about Hynek adds says that according to Ridpath, "At one of the Baker-Nunn sites (Las Cruces, in the New Mexico desert) Hynek and Whipple had experimented with a television camera attached to a telescope. From this has developed what Hynek calls 'image-orthicon astronomy,' a branch of observing that has grown vastly in popularity since Hynek helped pioneer it."

He with others published in scientific journals about this, for example, Dunlap, J.R., E.J. Weiler, and J.A. Hynek. "Astronomical Photometry and Other Recent Applications of the Image Orthicon." in *Advances in Electronics and Electron Physics*.

A three-page article about Hynek was in the respected scientific journal, *New Scientist* dated 17 May 1973. It was titled "*The man who spoke out on UFOs.*"[163]

This letter (Figure 62) may have been written in 1972, because he mentioned that he would plug the book. He had previously mentioned going to London for this and in this letter, he listed the other places in his schedule.

> Sorry I can't make it to CMH (Columbus International Airport) just now-but in late July I will have to go to Dayton and I'll try my best to come to CMH too.
> (why CMH? –why not CMO at least).
> Scott & Jack are both pilots now. Scott is flying up to B.R. early in July & we will explore some library? To ck month.
> NBC (local Chi) is doing a ½ hr on Hynek – at work and at play – TV shots in office at home – with Mimi and kids – ain't we got fun. Will air this fall. I'll plug the book.
> My schedule: July 1-July 25 B.R.
> July 26 – Aug 9 Chic, Dayton, Cols etc.

Aug 11 – Sept 1 B.R.
Sep 5-23 London
We <u>could</u> meet in London! FSR could provide chaperone.

It is unknown what he was doing in London

In this short page, his sense of humor and irreverence bubbles forth, such as his questioning of the designation of the Columbus Airport as CMH, which stands for "Columbus Municipal Hangar," the original name for the airport, which likely dates back to when the airport was just a hanger. (CMH today is the John Glenn Columbus International Airport (CMH), formerly known as Port Columbus International Airport).

It appears that a local Chicago NBC affiliate is planning to do a show about Hynek at work and at play. He remarks "ain't we got fun."

Besides everything else he keeps a busy travel schedule that includes several stops in Ohio and in London.

His children were Scott, Roxane, and Joel. He mentions that both sons were pilots.

He cannot stop from teasing Jenny, here about using FSR for a chaperone. This probably made her feel very safe. She must have been planning to travel overseas too.

FSR was a UK UFO magazine (*Flying Saucer Review*) that had been highly successful. In the 1950s, FSR was recognized as the leading international organ in the world on the subject.[164] It was well done, printed by quality litho on fine art paper, produced by a team of more than seventy experts and specialists from Britain and twenty other countries. It used numerous PhDs, doctors of medicine, astronomers, physicists and other scientific experts.

Probably no one knew that Hynek was a poet.

His next letter (Figure 63), concerns Zeidman's trip to Israel:

> to be like. Now that you've visited Israel, why not equal time on the air for Egypt? – Go ahead – open the dammed canal for them. Maybe we should have hit? Britannia sub/? the waves – instead of waive the subs.
>
> ---
>
> Both books are now done – How do you like <u>Astronomy One</u> for a title. Zoftich? – or something By the way, How is Glotz' been?
> Cheers, Allen
> A Thunder god went for a ride
> Upon his favorite filly
> I'm Thor, he cried!
> His horse replied –
> You forgot your thaddle, thilly! –
> (-it's the heat!)

211

Apparently the passage about the Thunder god was a poem about a lisping god that was going around at that time. But he has some other word play, although it is unclear, "sub/? the waves – instead of waive the subs." Waive might mean surrender.

It is unknown who or what Glotz' is.

I am unsure of what Zoftich means. One definition says "healthy, young, and vigorous." A variation is used to describe a woman, zaftig. Some definitions say that Zaftig has been juicing up our language since the 1930s (the same decade that gave us Yiddish-derived futz, hoo-ha, and schmaltz, not to mention lox). It comes from the Yiddish zaftik, which means "juicy" or "succulent" and which in turn derives from zaft, meaning "juice" or "sap."

Thus the letter contains not only poetry, but some interesting words and word play.

He tells her that while she is there, she should go ahead and open the canal. This is probably the Suez Canal.

The Suez Canal is very important. When open it carried a sixth of the world's trade and an even greater proportion of its oil. It was the first canal that directly linked the Mediterranean Sea to the Red Sea. It was actually dug and opened in 1869.

The Canal was closed five times; the last time was the most serious one since it lasted for 8 years. The Canal was then reopened for navigation in 1975. When it was closed, trade suddenly had to be rerouted around the Cape of Good Hope at the end of Africa. In 1974, it was a stagnant cesspool. When it had closed it was a massive shock to much of the world. Prices rose and it changed consumption patterns.

So, Jennie would have her hands full.

Hynek in his natural state was playful, curious, mischievous, liked wordplay, had a huge vocabulary of some odd words, and much interest in the world news and what was happening. He seemed to want to change things.

Dr. Hynek's interest in and sincerity about UFO phenomena is demonstrated in the following letter (Figure 64). He takes time out from his busy schedule to do much traveling and interviewing of UFO witnesses. He gets to the bottom of things by difficult research including interviews and collecting the actual prints and negatives involved. He does not just read something and then make a snap judgment, as many others did and do.

> June 28
> Accutron Time
> Hi Jennie –
> Nu – so what else is nu? Maybe Gov?
> Much happening in the UFO field though nothing is getting into the papers.

> Just got back from California where I interviewed two continental Air Lines pilots – made a typical sighting.
> Interviewed Pfeiffer, whose UFO picture was in *LIFE* (October 28, 1966) – genuine – saw original negs & will get prints. Color.
> Got original negative from Kandili Obs. In Istanbul of "satellite" going across sun's

Possibly his comment about the date and Accutron Time is a joking reference to his having a time and date, but he left out the year. The Accutron time was kept by the vibrations of a tuning fork running on an electronic circuit. This was before electronic watches.

As usual, he has some word play. Nu looks as if he is using it as a question to ask What's new? Maybe that is the fashionable statement for then.

About the UFO field, he has his usual comments about news suppression and that much is happening but it is not being reported in the newspapers. This censorship always bothered him because it gave the public a false image of UFO activity.

Hynek was very sincere in his interest in UFOs. He didn't just read articles about UFOs, he made investigations himself. While working for BB he spent his own money and time making these hands-on investigations, when he heard of a sighting that BB didn't give him. Because he did this himself, he sometimes asked the observers to send a report to BB, so that he could officially look at it. He was always disturbed when he found out about sightings that BB didn't tell him about.

In this letter, he had just returned from California where he interviewed two Continental Airline pilots in California. He drew a disc and remarked that it was a typical sighting.
A piece about the Pfeiffer sighting began.

> 1966 was a good year for UFO sightings and reports of alleged humanoid encounters. In October 1966, *LIFE* magazine published a photo and claimed a sighting of a UFO by 'respected aviation industry executive, 'James Pfeiffer.' It was probably a fluff piece to fill column inches and hasn't left any legacy at all… Nevertheless, it's a photograph of something and I wonder if anyone can identify it? [165]"

The Pfieffer photograph looks somewhat like a top or a hot air balloon but it did not act like one. Hynek thought Pfeiffer and the photograph were genuine (there had been some question about who Pfeiffer was). The object was spheroid-shaped, roughly 70 feet in diameter, with a smooth construction. It first hovered at about 1,500 feet above the lagoon-side restaurant where it was seen, sped away at around 200 mph, and then abruptly changed direction at a flat 90-degree right turn. It then settled down in the woods across the water while emitting a high- then low-pitched whining sound. This was loud enough to bring the restaurant workers out to watch. The Air Force agreed that he had seen something.

Hynek got the original negatives and planned to make prints in color.

What Hynek described as a report from the Kandili Observatory in Istanbul of two satellites going across the sun is likely a mystery sighting discussed in several scientific journals. It definitely was not a satellite.

The Kandili Observatory is a very old observatory first founded in 1868 by the Ottoman government. Beginning in 1965 it started operating an H-α (hydrogealpha) filter that was used to capture the electromagnetic spectrum centered on the H-α wavelength (around 656.3 nm). Its staff consisted of two astronomers, two technical assistants, and one observer.

One astronomer, Dr. Dizer, published what they observed on August 23, 1966, in the February 1967 issue of *Sky & Telescope* (p. 123). Dizer wrote that while observing solar flares he and other astronomers saw "two artificial satellites" crossing the solar disc appearing to the naked eye as dark spots. The second one was observed seventeen minutes after the first one. They photographed it at 9:27 GMT.

Soon other astronomers reacted to the article: in the March *Sky & Telescope,* an astronomer at the Case Institute of Technology in Cleveland (p 135) made calculations showing that the observed image did not result from any publicly known artificial satellite or aircraft.

They had checked the times, positions, and apparent size of the visible satellites and rockets.

This debate then moved to a different astronomical journal *Planetary and Space Science*, where other astronomers continued the debate. The object remains unidentified.[166]

The photographs provided good data; they had an exact time and a record of the exact telescope settings.

Dr. Hynek had carefully watched both the UFO and scientific literature and investigated good cases himself. This work was not part of BB.

With the Kandili Observatory sighting, he obtained the original negative and analyzed it.
I was unable to find a report of this sighting in the BB files.

Here he analyzed the original negative under a microscope and concluded that it was not a satellite. The object in the photograph appeared to be spherical.

" Dr. Hynek's letter continued (Figure 65):

> Disc. Mathematically impossible to be a satellite – under microscope: = [the drawing of a somewhat spherical object with three horizontal lines through it].
> = Titled "UFO!
> Wait until I publish that enlargement:
> Your letter:
> But first, a ?message from – – – –
> Our newly automated telescope is working fine – computerized. Press a button – it crosses a galaxy on the TV screen. Press again – 30 seconds later – the next galaxy on the program. All

in shirtsleeves – arm chair environment! You must come visit. No place in the world (except maybe Rooshia) being observed this way. Now to your letter: a

In that day, an automated telescope probably seemed like a miracle.

This letter (Figure 66) was from the Corralitos observatory.

> Kite flying by strange men should be prohibited!
> Your observation of the pollution balloons have been transmitted to Col. Quintanilla.
> Good work! Questions
> 1.   There is a definite flow of UFO reports now – but they don't hit the papers.
> 2.   The Scorpion sank or if you prefer didn't come up.
> 3.   I fear the January 24 case moved into the well known ambiguity dead end. Maybe yes, Maybe no. Not really usable in a "court of law." There is so little time. That one must concentrate on cases of close

It appears that a UFO case might have been designated a kite. And it appears that another sighting might have been identified as pollution balloons. These were balloons sent aloft to monitor various forms of air pollution.[167]

Dr. Hynek then asks questions, or makes some comments.

The first one is about suppression of UFO information, which he has mentioned numerous times. He is irritated when he finds good cases, but nothing in the papers. In this case it appears that there are many UFO reports, but that the media is not reporting these.

The second case about the Scorpion might be about the Kinross Incident, a famous aviation accident which many still believe shows proof of an extraterrestrial encounter.

On November 23, 1953, radio operators at Sault Ste. Marie, Michigan saw something unexpected at St Mary's River. St Mary's River marks the border between Michigan, US, and Ontario, Canada. The radar operators identified the target in restricted airspace. An F-89C Scorpion jet was scrambled from Kinross Air Force Base to investigate it.

The ground radar operator could see two blips on his radar screen, one was the Scorpion and the other was the unknown target. The operator directed the pilot towards the object. Then the operator watched as the two blips appeared to merge into one. But instead of a crash, one blip continued along its previous course. A huge search then took place, but it appeared that the scorpion was not found. If this were the case, Hynek's notes said the Scorpion sank. However this appears to not be entirely certain even today.[168][169]

This incident is listed in BB, but I was unable to find additional information there.

Zeidman's mention of pollution balloons and Hynek's comment to transmit the information to Quintanilla, might refer to the Portage County UFO sighting in which Quintanilla, then the head of BB, explained one of the world's best sightings first as a balloon and then as Venus/Echo satellite.

This was very heavily investigated by Dr. Hynek, who using scientific principles completely disagreed with Quintanilla.

This was the Portage County UFO chase. I had the original documents for this.[170][171][172]

Its BB investigator was Col. Hector Quintanilla, who was the head of BB from 1963 until its official closure December 17, 1969. This case shows much about both Quintanilla and BB. Quintanilla did not care anything about the actual observations or the facts in the case. He ascribed the sighting to prosaic objects that in no way resembled the observations by a variety of witnesses, who were also government officials.

BB supported his stance, even though Dr. Hynek and other very credible scientists disputed it. This case also shows what BB had become after the events mentioned above and after *SR-14* had finished.

It illustrates why Hynek was so irritated with the "investigations." He did his in a scientific way, by actually investigating, collecting and analyzing the evidence, deciding how credible the witness was, and that sort of thing. BB just presented any wild idea it could think of, rather than investigate.

This Portage County UFO chase was one of the world's most dramatic and best-verified UFO encounters, and one of the world's most important UFO events. It involving a police chase and multi-state sighting, and is thought to have inspired the UFO pursuit sequence in Stephen Spielberg's *Close Encounters of the Third Kind*. In addition, it helped spur the creation of the Condon Committee, a group that undertook a government-supported investigation of UFOs. Our investigation showed that even today information about it is evolving. I have remained in contact with one of its original investigators, Rick Hilberg, as described in *UFOs Today*:

And because the facts indicate that authorities knew about the UFO before it reached Ohio and there appeared to also be a cover-up at is termination (possibly around Sharon Massachusetts), a cover-up may have been in place at the beginning and throughout the events, as will be described.

On April 17, 1966, police chased a rapidly moving UFO across multiple state jurisdictions. The event was very credible because it involved police officers. Law enforcement personnel are highly accurate and believable witnesses because they're trained to observe incidents in detail, to avoid responding emotionally to situations, and to focus on "just the facts" when describing an occurrence. In addition, because police departments keep careful records, UFO cases involving law enforcement are well documented. Moreover, local police tend to resent or disdain their federal counterparts, and so they are less likely to engage in the kinds of cover-ups associated with the US military, the FBI, and the CIA.

The UFO may have first been seen in Michigan. The police chase ended south of Pittsburg, Pennsylvania, but the object may have been sighted later in the Massachusetts area. However, the event has come to be named after the Ohio County where its pursuers spotted the object. It is also known as the Spaur/Neff case after the two officers who led the chase.

In the early morning of April 17 when three Benton Harbor trash collectors in southwest Michigan were startled by a flying object of such dazzling brightness that they couldn't look straight at it. Ohio police were notified to be on the lookout for this object, according to an article published in the *New Castle News* in Pennsylvania on April 18. Thus, the authorities already knew something about the object

The chase itself began just before 5:00 a.m. Deputy Sheriff Dale Spaur and Mounted Deputy Wilbur "Barney" Neff, both of the Portage County Sheriff's Department, were chatting with a utility pole repairman when, to their amusement, they overheard a police radio report about an Akron woman who'd seen in the sky a bright object as big as a house. As the dispatcher and police personnel on the radio laughed at the report, Spaur, Neff, and the technician joined in.

Minutes later the deputies responded to a call to investigate an abandoned automobile by the side of the road between the towns of Randolph and Atwater, on Route 224 south of Ravenna, Ohio. When they arrived, the officers noticed the car was filled with radio equipment. Painted on its side was the emblem of a triangle and a bolt of lightning. Above this were the words "Seven Steps to Hell."

The deputies left their scout car to investigate. That's when they first saw the bright object in the sky. As it rose from the horizon, it approached them, hovered 75 feet overhead, and bathed them in light.

Spaur later gave this account during an interview with Air Force Major Hector Quintanilla, head of Project Blue Book:

> I always look behind me so no one can come up behind me. And when I looked in this wooded area behind us, I saw this thing. At this time it was coming up . . . went up to about treetop level, I'd say about one hundred feet. It started moving toward us. . . . It was so low that you couldn't see it until it was right on top of you. As it came over the trees, I looked at Barney and he was still watching the car . . . and he didn't say nothing and the thing kept getting brighter and the area started to get light. . . . I told him to look over his shoulder, and he did.
> He just stood there with his mouth open for a minute, as bright as it was, and he looked down. And I started looking down and I looked at my hands and my clothes weren't burning or anything, when it stopped, right over on top of us. The only thing, the only sound in the whole area was a hum . . . like a transformer being loaded or an overloaded transformer when it changes.
> I was petrified, and, uh, so I moved my right foot, and everything seemed to work all right. And evidently he made the same decision I did, to get something between me and it, or us. . . . So we both went for the car, we got in the car and we sat there.

The UFO moved east and paused again. By now the object was about 250 feet away and still shining brilliantly. Spaur later described it as an oval, about 40 feet in diameter and about 21 feet thick, with a rounded bottom from which a conical spotlight shined onto the ground below. It returned, and Spaur and Neff, now in their cruiser, punched the microphone button and told Sergeant Henry Shoenfelt at the Ravenna police station that the object was there. "He comes back with . . . 'Shoot it!'"

Spaur said:

> After we got to thinking it over, it wasn't such a good idea to shoot it. . . . It was low, and it was big, and great God Almighty . . . it just moved right up and stopped; . . . it wasn't two hundred fifty feet in front of the car. And everything was lit up . . . it was big as a house! . . . like looking down the middle of hell. . . . It was very bright; it'd make your eyes water.

Sergeant Shoenfelt asked if they had a camera, and he asked if they could follow it or stay with it until the police could get a camera there.

The two followed the light along Route 183 and then on Route 224, where they paced beside it at 86 miles an hour. By now it was 300 to 500 feet in the air, and it lit the ground under it. They again were able to clock its speed, and reported that it was traveling 103 miles per hour.

After that they crossed the Berlin reservoir and traveled into Mahoning county; Spaur said it came back toward them:

> And when it did, it angled, you could see it silhouetted against the sky and the beam of it was . . . going straight behind it. . . . And you could see the whole back third of a metallic object . . . you could see it just as plain as . . . and I thought then we could identify it. . . . I could see only one projection. And all this I kept radioing back. Everything that I seen, I gave it to the other cars, and Bob at the radio; I gave it to the other counties as I was going. . . . It changed direction probably two or three times. . . . I never seen anything like it. It was a monster.

At one point the object stopped and waited for them to catch up:

> It lost probably half its altitude, so help me God, it went down over [Route] 51, waited as we came up to it, it went right up to the left, it went right straight up about five, six, seven hundred feet and took off again, right at the same pace.

The chase was witnessed by both civilian and government personnel. On April 18, several local newspapers, including the *Albany Times Union* and the *New Castle News,* reported that hundreds of area people watched the object and that jets had been scrambled. Many accounts said six or seven police departments reported the object. In an article titled "No Reports UFO Seen in County," the *Albany Times Union* stated that reports also came from Air Force Reserve pilots, based at Youngstown, who said they attempted to follow the object but that its speed was too slow for their jet trainers That same day the *New Castle News* in Pennsylvania noted that as soon as the reports started coming in, jet pilots at Youngstown Airport were up in the skies, but the jets were too fast for the UFO.

Law enforcement personnel throughout the area were aware of the UFO because calls from civilians flooded the switchboards of sheriffs' offices and police stations along the route. Gerald Buchert, a police chief in Mantua, Ohio, reported that he photographed the object.

One person who monitored the police broadcasts was Patrolman H. Wayne Huston of East

Palestine, Ohio, and he radioed to the deputies that he would join the chase. Soon he saw the bright light streak through the sky with Spaur and Neff in pursuit. Huston joined the chase, and the three officers crossed the Pennsylvania state line near Rochester. The UFO was now headed southeast, but Spaur and Neff, who'd been chasing it at a high speed for nearly 80 miles, were out of their jurisdiction and low on gas. Their superiors radioed to them to abandon the chase at 5:30 a.m.

Meanwhile in Salem, Ohio, eight miles south of the UFO's path along Route 224, policemen Lonny Johnson and Ray Esterly were listening to police radio reports and watching for the object. At about 5:30 a.m., they spotted it. They reported that it was two miles away and hovering at an altitude of 10,000 feet—the same altitude as a commercial jet that was passing at the time. As they watched, two smaller jets approached it. When the jets and the object disappeared, these two officers drove back to headquarters.

At about 5:20 a.m. in Conway, Pennsylvania, 30 miles south of New Castle, another police officer, Patrolman Frank Panzanella of the Conway Pennsylvania Police Department, was on patrol when he saw a stationary object shining brightly in the sky. Unsure of what he was seeing, Panzanella stopped his car and got out to watch it as Spaur and Neff pulled up.

Spaur, Neff, Huston, and Panzanella stood and watched the UFO, which was hovering at 3,500 feet. They could see the moon in the sky above it, and a bright star near the moon (later determined to be Venus). Panzanella saw an airplane pass below it and radioed his police dispatcher, John Beighey of Rochester, to ask him to contact the Greater Pittsburg Airport. The air traffic controller there confirmed that the object was being monitored on airport radar. Within minutes, the officers heard police radio chatter about jets being scrambled to intercept the object. In a statement to the Air Force, Panzanella later wrote:

> I saw 2 other patrol cars pull up and the officers [Neff, Spaur, and Huston] got out . . . and asked me if I saw it. I replied SAW WHAT! Then pointed at the object and I told them that I had been watching it for the last 10 minutes. The object then moved out towards Harmony Township approximately 1,000 feet high, then it stopped then went straight up real fast to about 3,500 feet. I then called the base station told the radio operator to notify the Pittsburgh Airport. . . . The operator got the airport on the line and told them what happened, . . . we kept watching the object and at that time a passenger plane passed to the left.

Panzanella gave the following account to investigator William Weitzel of the National Investigations Committee on Aerial Phenomena (NICAP):

> John Beighey, the Rochester Base Radio Operator, or a voice going into his microphone, said, "They're sending two [jets] up." Also heard a voice saying the object was on radar. . . . The radar report was heard before we saw the plane fly under the object. I also saw two streaks of smoke or something in the sky, like jet contrails, apparently coming in such a way that, if continued, the streaks would have circled the object. The front of the growing streaks was to the object's left, above the object.

Spaur mentioned the same incident in his report to BB's Hector Quintanilla:

We could see these planes coming in. When they started talking [on the radio] about fighter planes, it was just as if that thing heard every word that was said; it went PSSSSHHEW, straight up, and I mean, when it went up, friend, it didn't play no games, it went straight up.

As Spaur, Neff, and Huston prepared to drive back to Ohio, Panzanella said he intended to wait around to see if the object would return. However, the dispatcher from Rochester radioed to Panzanella with a request that the Ohioans come to the Rochester station for a police interview. Panzanella sped off to catch them. Just before he did, Panzanella spoke via police radio with Patrolman Henry Kwaianowski of Economy Borough (just east of Conway); Kwaianowski reported seeing a metallic, football-shaped object flying at the same altitude as two jets.

Spaur, Neff, Huston, and Panzanella went to the Rochester station, where Spaur spoke briefly by phone to an unidentified man he later identified as "some colonel." This colonel tried unsuccessfully to persuade Spaur that he had simply misidentified some normal phenomenon. The colonel eventually agreed to report the event to WP, headquarters of BB.

The Portage County incident received considerable media attention. Scientists contacted Spaur the same day as the chase. And of course, the US government became involved. As an article published six months later in *The Plain Dealer* put it after this chase, Spaur's daily routine was washed away immediately through public ridicule.

Spaur, Neff, and others had described many interesting, unique, and specific aspects of the object. For example, Spaur and Neff observed that if their police cruiser had to slow for traffic or road conditions, the UFO would slow, too, as if it were waiting for them to catch up with it. They had related this observation to others via radio. However they were not the only ones to observe this interactive behavior. As reported in the *New Castle News*, two local married couples surnamed Matteo and Roth, who were driving when they first sighted the same UFO, thought at first that it was a reflection. But when they stopped and rolled down the window, they still could see it. When they stopped, the object stopped. When they moved the car, the object began moving. They repeated this and observed the same results. As they followed it for several miles, they watched it move from one side of the car to the other. Mrs. Roth described it as very frightening.

In his interview with Quintanilla, Spaur gave many specific answers further describing technical details about the object. About changes in object's light intensity, he said:

> It would maneuver, this part [the part shining the light] would be a real bright, blue light, or a white-blue light, like a mercury vapor or something; a white light. The only thing that would change is, it would get brighter when it would go up and then it would seem like it would lose part of its intenseness, of the light as it would come back down to us.

He also described the appearance of the object's upper portion: "You could see it very plain, and it was like an aluminum top that's been used for a while; it was definitely a silver, or light color, but it wasn't like chrome." This account is similar to Kenneth Arnold's 1947 description of the objects he saw. Spaur also said that when the object maneuvered, "The nose part of this thing when it was going forward . . . would be down. . . . If it wanted to go straight up, it would level out. It was all, beautiful maneuvers; they were clean." It also appeared to gain altitude as it passed over cities: "When we got to Canfield, it went up, to about, I'd say pretty close to two thousand feet. After it cleared the area of Canfield it came back down."

The government investigation begun by "some colonel" continued the next day, April 18. Major Hector Quintanilla interviewed Spaur and his fellow witnesses several times. He at first made the ridiculous conclusion that the men had seen a balloon. Then on April 22, he made the even more ridiculous conclusion that the officers had experienced an optical illusion, had become confused, and had chased an Echo communications satellite and the planet Venus. The Air Force denied that jets were scrambled to pursue a UFO that morning.

Spaur and Neff's superior, Sheriff Ross Dustman of Portage County, defended his deputies, saying the object was not a satellite and not Venus; Venus would not be 50 feet above a road and moving from side to side. Portage County Judge Robert Cook (an acquaintance of Spaur's and Neff's) also supported the deputies' judgment; he contacted the US Congressional Representative from Ohio, William Stanton, and characterized the Air Force investigation as grossly unfair to the two deputies. Stanton wrote a letter of complaint about the Blue Book investigation to Defense Secretary Robert S. McNamara and demanded that the Air Force Commanding General reopen the investigation. When the Air Force refused, Stanton went to the Pentagon and spoke to Air Force Lieutenant Colonel John Spaulding, who agreed to send an investigator to the scene.

To everyone's dismay, that investigator was Quintanilla. The official conclusion, called the "Echo/Venus Explanation," remained unchanged. This explanation was highly questionable, however, because several witnesses saw both Venus and the object at the same time. Numerous officials contested the "Echo/Venus Explanation," including Hynek, University of Arizona atmospheric physicist James E. McDonald, PhD, Portage County Sheriff Ross Dustman, and NICAP investigator William Weitzel.

However having such highly credible authorities disagree with Quintanilla, did not faze him at all. He was as mean spirited and illogical as ever. And even though his conclusions were contradictory to logic, he went ahead and destroyed the lives of the observers.

Meanwhile, although Spaur, Neff, Huston, and Panzanella asserted they'd heard radio confirmation that the UFO was tracked by radar at the Greater Pittsburgh Airport, officials at the airport denied that such tracking had occurred and that such a statement had been made via radio. After the BB investigation of the Portage County case, the officers found their lives had changed forever.

Immediately after the UFO event, deputies Spaur and Neff had been tired and shaken. Neff's wife Jackelyne said that she hoped she would never see her husband like he was after the chase. He was real white, almost in a state of shock. He had been through the wringer. Spaur's wife Daneise reported that she'd never seen her husband more frightened. He acted strange, and listless, she said. He just sat around, and was very pale. Later, he got real nervous. He would disappear for days and days, when she wouldn't see him.

Patrolman Wayne Huston, who'd been with the East Palestine police department for seven years,

quit his job within six months of the chase, changed his name, and moved to Seattle where he became a bus driver. He admitted he quit because of the incident. People, including the local authorities, had laughed at him. City officials don't like police officers chasing flying saucers.
During the months after the event, the wife of Portage County Deputy Wilbur Neff said that people ridiculed him. He doesn't talk about it now. Once he said that if the thing landed in his back yard, he wouldn't tell a soul.

Deputy Sheriff Dale Spaur, the primary figure in the incident and the only one named in the Blue Book report, suffered the most. In addition to experiencing persistent nightmares, he was ridiculed mercilessly for months and hounded by the media. One night two months after the encounter, he was driving alone at night in his cruiser when he thought he saw the UFO again. A month later, during a flash of tension and confusion, he shook his wife violently, leaving bruises. She filed assault charges; he was jailed and lost his job.

In October 1966, six months after the UFO chase, *The Plain Dealer* reported that Spaur's wife had filed for divorce. Spaur had taken a job as a house painter. Strapped by child-support payments, he was living alone in a dingy motel room, eating cereal and a single daily sandwich. He had lost 40 pounds. He was broke.

In utter desperation Spaur turned to God for help. On the first Sunday that Spaur attended services at a local church, the minister, eager to help him feel welcome, introduced him to the congregation as that man who chased flying saucers. Spaur felt he had become a freak.

Huston, Neff, and Spaur clearly felt mentally strained from the incident and its aftermath. Like many disaster survivors and combat soldiers, they seem to have suffered what today would be called post-traumatic stress disorder (PTSD). They may even have experienced a mental anguish similar to that reported by alien abduction victims. But instead of receiving the help they needed, they were ridiculed.

Over the two days following the Spaur sighting, numerous UFO sightings occurred in Massachusetts, including the Sharon Saucer case, named after the town of Sharon, Massachusetts. UFOlogist, Diana DeSimone of Newton, Massachusetts, has suggested to me that this case might have been included the same object that Spaur and Neff chased.[173] The Sharon Saucer, reported in Raymond Fowler's 2001, *UFOs: Interplanetary Visitors*, was seen in the city of Sharon, just south of Boston.

As in the Spaur case, officials denied the object existed.

A friend of Fowler's, who was employed at a Boston radio station, told him that during that hectic period, his supervisor would not allow him to include UFO reports arriving by Teletype on the newscasts.

Fowler added that several days after the Sharon sighting, Air Force personnel from Hanscom Field in Bedford, Massachusetts, made an official inquiry into this event. He also found that the Air Force had instructed the Sharon police not to comment on the incident; thus, the sighting received little publicity.

Police were told to maintain a separate, nonpublic log for further UFO reports in the area. The use of a separate police log is, by itself, evidence of a cover-up; in conjunction with reported government actions during the Spaur case, the Sharon account suggests that a cover-up plot had been in place from the beginning of the Spaur sighting.[174]

Early in 1997, Bill Jones and I began a re-investigation of the Portage County UFO Case. We learned that Portage County deputies Dale Spaur and Wilbur Neff had both died. One of the two other police officers, who joined in the chase—either Patrolman Wayne Huston, or Patrolman Frank Panzanella—had also died, but we did not learn which one.

Mantua, Ohio, Police Chief Gerald Buchert, who had photographed an object, had also passed away. Jones telephoned Buchert's son and asked if anyone in his family would be willing to discuss the events of that night in 1966. The son was pleasant, but he insisted no one wanted to talk. He did, however, point out that once when his children were playing the game *Trivial Pursuit*, they saw their grandfather's name as an answer to one of the game's questions. The children asked to know more and the parents told them the story, but it had not been discussed in the family since. When asked why the family refused to talk about this part of its history, the son replied it was too upsetting and painful. Yes, the family still had the photographs, but he insisted that the photos would stay with the family.

We tried to reach witnesses, as well as the spouses of the deceased officers, to learn what has occurred in their lives since the event, but we were unable to make contact with any of them. Jones and I had ended the article we wrote with the statement that, beyond yielding a question for the board game of *Trivial Pursuit*, perhaps this painful and life-changing affair should just pass into history.

However, this case has had such important ramifications that it did not pass into history, and it may remain active. For example, on April 5, 2008, I received an email from a Washington state investigator about another re-investigation of the Spaur case. He made the following remark about why the event was important:

I have never failed to make the Dale Spaur case a premiere case because it so aptly illustrates the Actual Reality as faced by pilots, military personnel, average citizens, and cops. Then there is the Official Reality that is created in the media, this time via a villain called Major Quintanilla of Blue Book.

Figure 67 which shows a continuation of the previous letter, could in a way tell the history of UFO exploration from the beginning until it was written. It covers the massive effort of those who actually followed the scientific method in their struggle vs. the debunkers. The history behind these comments is explained and it played out on a very national scene.

> Encounters – e. g. Dr. de Vaucouleus told me over the phone of a case reported to him by a physicist in Arkansas – triangulated on a glow in the woods as effective power output of craft to be 400 megawatts!!!. Even I couldn't call that swamp gas – I wonder what Menzel would call it.

4. Condon did not sue *Look*. Science called me Thursday morning. They want to do a story on Condon – it so happens that their man will be in Boulder the week that I am there – we have agreed to meet. Should be fun! I'll let you know.

So – when something comes up, go after it. I'll make sure any out of pocket expenses are taken care of! Allen

As mentioned before, Hynek was not the limelight seeker as he had been described. He was sincere and sacrificed greatly to explore UFO phenomenon. Here he tells Zeidman that he will cover her expenses if she finds something to investigate.

In the years after his life as a debunker, Hynek doggedly pursued his research against terrific obstacles. One example, involved his work with Dr. Gérard Henri de Vaucouleus as described in the following.

When Hynek began to wake up to the fact that he wasn't seeing the best cases–maybe the Air Force wasn't even getting them or it was shunting some cases away from WP and into some other intelligence pathway at Air Defense Command. He reached out to certain civilians to try to get better reports and this also included professionals such as astronomers. He traveled to France with the famous astronomer Gerard de Vaucouleurs to visit Aime Michel and look at Michel's files from the 1954 wave.

He also reached out to the little-known-today powerhouse triad of NYC researchers,...Isabel Davis, Lex Mebane, Ted Bloecher...He actually would show up at their place almost in disguise --- another testament to his timidity. Hynek would share USAF information [doubtless against his security oath] and they would share case information back.[175]

Maybe this was a testament to his bravery, rather than his timidity, for he was going against the general set-up to explore the UFO subject any way he could, even in disguise, and still be able to continue.

Aimé Michel in 1958, published his book about the 1954 wave of UFOs in France. He had devised a theory called orthoténie and had posited so-called "alignments." These were straight lines that corresponded to large circles traced and centered on the earth. Michel claimed that UFO sightings could be concentrated along such grid lines. He theorized, for example, that there was a line known as "Bavic" where, six out of nine UFO observations cited in the press on 24 September 1954, aligned. He also wrote numerous articles on UFOs, mysticism, the animal kingdom and many others

Dr. Gérard Henri de Vaucouleurs (1918 –1995), like Hynek, had a lot to lose during these ventures. de Vaucouleurs was a very well qualified and respected French astronomer. He had an early interest in amateur astronomy and received his undergraduate degree in 1939 at the Sorbonne.

He was also fluent in English, he spent 1949–51 in England, 1951–57 in Australia, the latter at Mount Stromlo Observatory, 1957–58 at Lowell Observatory in Arizona, and 1958–60 at Harvard.

He was appointed in 1960 to the University of Texas at Austin, and spent the rest of his career there.

His initial work concerned Mars and while he was at Harvard, he used telescope observations from 1909 to 1958 to study the areographic coordinates of features on the surface of Mars. His later work was chiefly the study of galaxies. He co-authored the *Third Reference Catalogue of Bright Galaxies* with his wife Antoinette (1921-1987), a fellow UT Austin astronomer. His specialty included reanalyzing Hubble and Sandage's galaxy atlas and re-computing the distance measurements using a method of averaging many types of metrics such as luminosity, the diameters of ring galaxies, brightest star clusters, etc., in a method he called "spreading the risks." During the 1950s he promoted the idea that galactic clusters are grouped into superclusters.

The de Vaucouleurs' modified Hubble sequence is now a widely used variant of the standard Hubble sequence.

De Vaucouleurs has been awarded the Henry Norris Russell Lectureship by the American Astronomical Society in 1988. He was also awarded the Prix Jules Janssen of the Société astronomique de France (Astronomical Society of France) in the same year. He and his wife and longtime collaborator, Antoinette de Vaucouleurs, produced 400 research and technical papers, 20 books and 100 articles for nonprofessionals.

Dr. Vaucouleurs provides strong evidence himself that the UFO subject should be taken seriously by scientists.[176] The bravery of both Hynek and de Vaucouleurs, who had their scientific reputation at stake but explored the UFO territory anyway was shown in this 1958 venture. Michel had just published seminal research about the European UFO wave of 1954. The astronomers were curious, and skeptical, about the claims of landings and the presence of humanoids described in innumerous reports. Hynek told Michel that he had been astonished to find so many such cases in *Flying Saucers and the Straight Line Mystery* and that he doubted that the original data existed. But if it did, they would like to make photocopies of it. Hynek, de Vaucouleurs, and their assistants spent several days photographing the documents. This was additional information they considered while trying to understand UFO phenomena.[177]

It appeared in Hynek's letter that de Vaucouleurs had taken a report by an Arkansas physicist who examined an object in a woods. They had calculated that the object's power output was 400 megawatts.

Hynek's next comment included a humorous comment about his famous swamp gas episode. At the time it began, Michigan was a hotbed of UFO activity and Hynek was the official AF UFO debunker. It was his job to explain away UFO events as prosaic phenomena. This also provided an epiphany in Hynek's life and involvement with UFO phenomena.

The swamp gas episode had been turning point in Hynek's life and relationship with UFOs. This relationship began in 1948, soon after Kenneth Arnold's sighting. Hynek was teaching astronomy at OSU, when three men came to see him from WP. The visited and then asked him what he thought about UFOs. He told them it was a lot of nonsense, and junk, which made them happy. They needed an astronomy consultant and he matched their idea. He would also get a top-secret clearance. This was during Project Sign (a BB precursor). Some of the personnel were taking UFOs seriously and prepared an estimation of the situation for General Vandenburg. But the negative side came out ahead and the serious ones were removed to different positions.

Hynek stretched himself far to give negative explanations and responded to implied pressure by the AF. And as a scientist, he felt that everything had to have natural explanations. Eventually he changed his mind. One reason was the unyielding attitude of the AF, and another was the good caliber of many witnesses.

But what really pushed him over the edge was the swamp gas episode.

This was a slow change however. After the Robertson Panel of 1953, everything needed to be debunked under Pentagon instructions. Scientists such as Dr. Donald Menzel (mentioned in this letter) from Harvard stuck to the negative viewpoint.

But after the swamp gas episode, a congressional hearing was called for and the recommendations were to take the UFO problem from the AF and give it to university to study. This is how the Condon Committee (also mentioned in this letter) began.[178]

These swamp gas events were spectacular. The case made the front pages of newspapers across the nation and even involved a future President.

It began in the spring of 1966 in Michigan. At that time Hynek was the chief scientific consultant to BB. For several weeks UFOs had been reported by both the public and authorities in Michigan. The ruckus was approaching a state of panic. On March 20, observers reported a strange object close to a swamp. Police officers and others watched a football-shaped object with multi-colored lights. Later the object's light intensified and it passed over the observers making a whistling sound.

On March 21, lights were seen by numerous coeds in a swampy area near Hillsdale College. The local Civil Defense Director was also witnessed the sighting. The lights would move around, but when the Police were called, they would vanish.

Dr. Hynek arrived with instructions to investigate and give a statement. Hynek sloshed around in the swamp some and then said that he had no idea what was going on. Later either he decided to or others instructed him to say that the sightings could have been caused by swamp gas. Later a press conference was held in Detroit. Hynek suggested to a group of unruly reporters that the cause might be swamp gas. Soon news stories across the country and many political cartoons reported that the culprit had been swamp gas.

Gerald Ford, who became a US president, with others demanded a Congressional hearing. Shortly thereafter, *Life* magazine published an article, which generally poked fun at the swamp gas events.

This episode made nearly every newspaper in the country. Hynek spent a week interviewing witnesses, and wading through the swamp. He said he provided what he thought at the time was the only explanation possible–swamp gas. He added in his book that he went on to emphasize, "I couldn't prove it in a court of law, that that was the full explanation."[179]

The mild-mannered professor became a national laughingstock.

Hynek's viewpoint began to change afterward and he eventually became perhaps the most vocal of people wanting UFO phenomena to be studied.

But some effects from the episode linger. Meanings of the term "swamp gas" include "nothing to worry about," a big deal over nothing, or the idea of concealing something. His, "prove it in a court of law," (mentioned in one of his earlier letters) was from then on associated with this episode.[180]

Hynek's next comment about Menzel also touches on quite a history of the UFO story.

This person mentioned in Hynek's letter, Dr. Donald Menzel, received his PhD from Princeton. Lick Observatory employed him until 1932 when he took a position at Harvard. He was President of the American Astronomical Society from 1954-56.

Menzel's later work was on gaseous nebulae. This work with several others defined many of the fundamental principles of the study of planetary nebulae. He authored *A Field Guide to the Stars and Planets*, which was a part of the Peterson Field Guides.

He was among the first American astronomers to place modern physics at the center of his astrophysical practice. He employed quantum physics in the study of the nature of gaseous nebulae; the solar atmosphere, chromosphere, and corona; and in exploration the structure of the atom itself. He also founded two solar observatories and was of major importance in international astronomy at midcentury.

He worked in many fields. As the war ended, he was engaged in communications and code breaking, and began to sense the importance of control of wave propagation responsibilities. With Dr. Edward Condon (of the Condon Report), then director of the Bureau of Standards, he described the need for an agency to provide such services after the war. This included a worldwide network of ionospheric and weather data gathering and a centralized facility for processing the information. This multimillion-dollar activity was approved and resulted in the establishment of the civilian Central Radio Propagation Laboratory (CRPL) of the National Bureau of Standards.

He established many organizations, such as a radio astronomy facility in Fort Davis, Texas. He interacted with many prominent people, such as John Kennedy and J. Robert Oppenheimer.

But in addition to many other such contributions in a number of fields, Menzel took the time to become an almost compulsive UFO skeptic, authoring or co-authoring popular books that debunked UFOs. In 1968, he testified before the U.S. House Committee on Science and Astronautics - Symposium on UFOs, that he considered all UFO sightings to have natural explanations.

Menzel may have been the first prominent scientist to give his opinion in this matter. Although Menzel's astronomical research was said to have sound, his UFO research was described by many as shoddy and his theories even laughable – a story is that one Condon Committee member laughed so hard that she fell off her chair. But because he was a prominent astronomer, he was believed. He sometimes worked as a consultant for the Condon Committee.

He once reported a sighting of his own, but later changed his description to make it more prosaic.

Some believed he led a double life. He was shown to have been a consultant to the National Security Agency (NSA), and had a rarefied "Top Secret Ultra" clearance. Thus he belonged to both the academic community and the black world of military projects.

Some claimed that he belonged to the MJ-12 group, which is reported to have been a secret group of highly placed people formed in 1947 who took UFOs seriously, as mentioned. It is questionable however whether such a group existed. But if it did, such an action would be two-faced. Stanton Friedman, saw Menzel's debunking as a cover for his actual work with MJ-12.[181]

Although both Hynek and Menzel began as debunkers and Menzel may have been the first prominently known scientific debunker, their relationship changed. Antagonism built up between the two in many instances. In *Close Encounters of the Third Kind*, Hynek described Menzel, "the self-styled arch enemy of UFOs," "Dr. Donald Menzel, of Harvard, has taken a characteristic opposite view. In his *Analysis of the Papua-father Gill Case*…he dismisses the entire case as a sighting of Venus under the hypothesis that Reverend Gill was not wearing his glasses…" which was incorrect in respect to Venus and his glasses.

In another instance in the same book, Hynek said:

> The Pentagon's official attitude was largely dictated by the scientific fraternity. After all, not even a major general wishes to be laughed at by highly placed members in the scientific hierarchy. One example was, of course, Harvard astronomy professor Dr. Menzel who took a seemingly compulsive interest in the flying saucer question even though this subject was far removed from his scientific field. He loudly proclaimed that UFOs were nonsense and particularly championed the "mirage theory" of flying saucers. He ascribed properties to mirages, and mirage properties to UFOs, which have since been shown to be completely untenable, even by the air force itself.

It remains unknown what the cause of Menzel's compulsive interest in debunking UFO phenomena was, because he certainly went off the beam as a scientist in doing this.

Hynek's opinion of both Menzel and Condon and their "scientific" approach to UFOlogy is given several times in *Close Encounters of the Third Kind:*

> Much later in the year Condon spoke at the National Bureau of Standards in Washington. "According to the reports that came from members of that audience…Condon concentrated almost the entire talk on three of the crackpot cases with which he had been involved."

I think the National Academy would also agree in its appraisal of the application of the scientific method that *no scientist should willfully allow ridicule to be an accepted part of his scientific method.* When, however, a subject seems to be beyond the pale of science…raillery and banter at the expense of the other fellow does not bother the scientist's conscience. Thus Dr. Menzel's written reply on a serious questionnaire that asked "what should be done about UFO reports that can't be explained," was, "Throw them in the wastebasket!"

Dr. Condon apparently felt UFOs beyond the pale of science (even though his report is entitled *Scientific study of Unidentified Flying Saucers*), for he too resorted to banter and jokes at the expense of the other fellow.[182]

In his letter, Hynek then adds that "Condon did not sue *Look*." I have found nothing in the literature about this, but the story behind this comment would suggest the idea might have crossed Condon' mind and perhaps Dr. Hynek was privy to some of his thinking.

The Condon study's shortcomings came to light when John Fuller's exposé was published in the May 1968 issue of *LOOK* magazine and titled, "Flying Saucer Fiasco." Fuller laid bare the numerous questionable actions and attitudes exhibited by some of the Condon Committee's foremost members. This caused a predictable widespread public indignation and even some scientists started questioning the UFO project's objectivity and purpose.

Dr. David Jacobs mentioned that when the American Association for the Advancement of Science (AAAS) covered the ongoing Committee controversy in an issue of its official journal *Science*, Condon at first promised to give an interview probably in hopes of offering his side of the conflict. Soon thereafter, however, the *Science* editor reported that Condon announced that it would be "'inappropriate for *Science* to touch the matter, withdrew his offer of cooperation, and proceeded to enunciate high-sounding principles in support of his new-found belief that *Science* should not [review] the subject until after the publication of his report.'"

The Condon committee's last report was released in fall 1968. Condon wrote in the introduction, titled, 'Conclusions and Recommendations' that their general conclusion was that nothing has come from the study of UFOs in the last 21 years that has added to scientific knowledge. This led them to conclude that further study of UFOs likely cannot be justified in the expectation that science will be advanced.

Hence, despite the evidence that was amassed—nearly 30% of the cases investigated by the committee were judged to involve "unknown" craft or other unexplained phenomena—the study's final report, that Condon himself wrote, stated that no basis existed for the continuation of Air Force investigation of the UFO phenomenon. Thus if one had read only Condon's remarks, but not the actual report, one could conclude that the view of UFOs, as an objective reality, had been irrefutably disproved. However, an actual examination of the report yields an entirely different impression.

Hynek then mentions that the journal, *Science*, wanted him to help them with a story about Condon and, maybe with a lot of control (maybe glee), and after all this history he remarks, "Should be fun!

This UFO story and debate was among the top news stories of that day.

Science is a highly prestigious journal. It is considered "the world's leading journal of original scientific research, global news, and commentary."[183] *Nature, Science*, and *Cell* are the world's most prestigious scientific journals. They are extraordinarily competitive and a scientist can make a career with just a single paper in one of these journals.[184]

Life and *Look* were top magazines of that time. Some say *Life* was "The greatest magazine ever published."

> No contemporary magazine could duplicate *Life's* success, and not just because 1945 was such a monumental year. No modern magazine has remotely close to its influence. The most popular magazine in America, *Life* circulated 4 million copies a week, and was read by 13.5 million people—10 percent of the population. The largest weekly magazine now, *People*, has a smaller circulation than Life even though the U.S. population is 2.5 times as large as it was then. And in an age before TV, *Life's* photographs were a dominant way that Americans saw the world.[185]

Hynek had had a number of publications in *Science* magazine.[186]

Hynek finishes this with the awesomely restrained remark after all this history with, "Should be fun!

He then adds to Jennie that if anything comes up, to go ahead and investigate. He will reimburse her.

It was during the Swamp Gas years that I first saw Dr. Hynek. At this stage in my life, I had tried hard to get into the field of astronomy. I at first majored in it at OSU. Then when I began applying for work, I discovered that every position in this field was male-only, whether they advertised it or not. I had to change my major, my minor, and do many extra hours of courses and work, while I worked my way through college–which was very expensive.

When I graduated, there was still no chance of entering the field of my choice. However, they did hire females for mapping (cartography). Indeed the AF Aeronautical and Information Center (ACIC), was even mapping the moon. I quickly applied for this and began working there as a cartographer.

This was when I first saw Dr. Hynek. He spoke at ACIC. This was remarkable, because it was a hard-core scientific organization (making maps for airplane pilots and astronauts) and Hynek spoke about UFOs. I thought this was hard to believe.

The talk was very well attended and I was able to see my childhood hero.

ACIC would not appear to be a place where Hynek would be expected. It was formed in August 1952. This U.S. Air Force Center was created by merging the Aeronautical Chart and Information

Service, established in Washington, D.C., with the Aeronautical Chart Plant, located in St. Louis, Missouri. The ACIC – an organization of the National Geospatial-Intelligence Agency had consolidated all the services and facilities in St. Louis.

During the 20 years of its existence, the ACIC was critical in supporting U.S. efforts in many places, such as in Vietnam–deploying the Point Positioning Database targeting system, which gave U.S. aviators better targeting accuracy. It also was important in space including: providing charts and graphics to assist the planning and execution of the Apollo 11 mission to the moon, which included determining lunar orbits and finding landing sites. In 1972, ACIC was folded into the Defense Mapping Agency that consolidated multiple mapping agencies and assumed responsibility for producing and distributing maps, charts, and geodetic products and services – and was renamed the DMA Aerospace Center.[187]

Because of his credentials, Hynek was able to speak at many such highly scientific organizations.

The next letter (Figure 68) was sent from Dearborn Observatory at Northwestern University on what may have been August 26, 1972 (it appears that Jennie thought maybe that was the date).

> Aug. 26, 1972?
> Dear Jennie –
> How do you like these apples! Now I know how Copernicus must have felt when he got the Inquisition/improvisation/Imprivition? of the Pope!
> The British edition will be published on Oct. 26 and I may go to London to help plug it (does Lazarus have a London outlet!!!).
> All goes well here – how's with you?
> Cheers,
> Allen

This was likely sent in 1972 because it appears that his book has been published and the British edition would be published on October 26.

His remarks about how do you like those apples and his remark about Copernicus may have referred to a review of his book that had come out in *Science* magazine on the day before he wrote the letter.[188]

In general this was a quite favorable review as the first and last paragraphs show:

> If there is one thing more difficult than writing a responsible book on Unidentified Flying Objects, it is to write a significant critique of such a book without falling into controversy. I have a difficult feeling that Hynek has been more successful in this task than I will be in mine. Hynek's book is more than just an attempt to justify the scientific interest in UFO phenomena. It is, in fact, Hynek's version of what the Condon Report should have been, intertwined with a pungent critique of the study on which he reported. This study was supported by the Air Force and formally reviewed and approved by the National Academy of Sciences. Thus Hynek not only defends UFOs but necessarily attacks the scientific establishment that has set them aside. Could our modern scientific institutions be as limited as their predecessors were when the

scientific authority refused to accept the reality of meteorites, hypnosis, continental drift, germs, troy, Atlantis and the Pleistocene Man? Or do UFOs really belong to the realm of non-reality to which science affects ghosts, religious miracles, astrology, dragons, ESP, the abominable snowman, and the monsters of Loch Ness?...

In defense, Hynek's defense of UFOs as a valid, if speculative, scientific subject is more credible than Condon's attempt to act as if they did not exist. The fact that Hynek received absolutely no support from NASA or the NSF for the study of UFOs may be considered a rather dismal symptom of the authoritative structure of established science. It is also disappointing that *Science*, which has earned the respect of American scientists and occasionally the foolishness of American bureaucrats by providing an independent forum for controversial views, has failed to publish a responsible refutation of the Condon Report, treating it at the same time. place as a news item. As a result, the substantial criticisms raised by Hynek now have not been adequately addressed. So, from that juror's point of view at least, Hynek has won a reprieve for UFOs with his numerous pages of provocative reports of unexplained reports and his articulate challenge to his colleagues to tolerate the study of something they can not understand.

This review covered the many problems Hynek had with the Condon report and the government attitude about UFOs in general. Hynek was very critical of both and presented good scientific reasons why. Maybe this is why he felt like Copernicus, who was right in the long-term but could have been burned at the stake in the short-term, "Copernicus is burned at the stake for heliocentric theory."[189] The heliocentric theory is that the earth goes around the sun, rather than the common idea of that time, that the sun circles the earth.

The government obviously chose Condon over Hynek, because Hynek understood the subject and would have presented a scientific analysis. Condon did not care about science and just followed the government line to debunk the subject–a disservice that will live long into the future. This hurt Hynek as had been described.

Many of the actual researchers who worked on the study disagreed with Condon's conclusions and with good reason.

Others who read Hynek's review also upheld Hynek's view:

> Nevertheless a number of dedicated scientists have continued to investigate UFO reports under the sponsorship of various civilian organizations. Dr. J. Allen Hynek, chairman of the department of astronomy at Northwestern University, and for twenty years a consultant to the Air Force Study, has recently published a book, *The UFO Experience,* which takes issue with the Condon report. Dr. Hynek's book was favorably reviewed in *Science*, the weekly journal published by the American Academy for the Advancement of Science. While there has been no great clamor for another government investigation, it was quite clear the case against UFOs is no longer closed.[190]

His next comment was that he might go to London to help plug the book. He asks if Lazarus has a London outlet!!!

It appears that he is referring to Lazarus, which was then the chief department store in Columbus, Ohio. At that time there were few bookstores in the area, the chains such as Borders did not yet exist, and Lazarus was not only Columbus' main department store, but also the area's chief bookstore.

Figure 69 shows Hynek and Zeidman in what may have been a book signing.

Figure 70 is my first collected handwriting from Hynek. This was from a book signing, *The UFO Experience,* he did in the Lazarus department store in Columbus, Ohio, in 1972. It went well and he may have made the remark about Lazarus in relation to his London trip in the letter above, hoping he could have the same smooth experience there.

This letter (Figure 71) was also sent from Northwestern University on Jan. 29, 1973.

> January
> Hi!
> My man in Berkeley says metal not sintered – has coniodal [conchoidal?] fracture and appears vitreous – and is not brittle like turyt carbiate [tungsten carbide?],
> Meteorite marks in thermal impacts are not abrasion impacts – vast difference under microscope he says.
> Tune in next week.
> W and Si are each soft – so are W and C (except in combination – wc [the little room on the left]) so we must await detailed quantification results
> (over).

Because of the analysis and his mention of his man in Berkeley, Hynek's comments in this letter likely relate to a beginning, preliminary analysis of a metal found in the Väddö (Swedish island in the Baltic Sea) UFO incident, which occurred on 9 November 1958. Also Hynek's comment in a later letter were that he has no more news on the Swedish incident also suggests that he is writing about this event.

This sighting and a metal object found afterwards are unique and interesting as described below:
> Some six miles later the car engine started to cough and then stopped. Even the headlights went out. Despite several attempts to start, the engine remained lifeless. Stig, who was seated behind the wheel, had nothing else to do but accept what had happened when Harry burst out: "Take a look, Stig, a star that's moving." Amazed they saw a huge shining object descend towards them. "I looked at the sky, which was all clear, when Harry called out," Stig relates. "When I looked up I saw a shining object and told Harry: 'Damn strong searchlights the AA Command has got nowadays. Different to when I did my service.' Harry thought it was a thunderball, but I doubted that. I had read somewhere that the largest thunderballs ever seen were the size of a football and this object was much larger." While they were discussing different explanations for their sighting, the silent and odd object came closer. It made a turn over the Väddö bay to the left of the road. Then it returned, and to the great surprise of Stig and Harry, it landed across the road in front of the car some 300 feet away. Puzzled, they stared at the glowing object and its neon-like glow that lit up the surroundings. Harry saw, for instance, a barn-like building on a hill, a quarter of a mile from the object, clearly lit by the light.

Although the light was intensive, it wasn't directly dazzling. In the strong glow Stig and Harry could see blurred details of an object that looked like a flattened-out ball. Since it reached to both sides of the road, the length was estimated to be 53 feet and the height to be twenty or 23 feet. The object did not seem to be standing directly on the ground, but with some space between, although no struts or landing gear could be seen. No creatures could be seen either. On the other hand it looked like fire underneath the object, like a delimited light beneath. Furthermore the object seemed to be surrounded by glowing veils of mist dazzling around the object. It could be compared with what can be seen above the road surface on a hot summer day.

"We then began talking about getting out of the car to take a closer look. But it never became more than an idea, because at the same moment the strange object rose from the road. It made a turn to the left, returned across the road and then disappeared with a high speed up in the sky to the right. When the object had disappeared like a small dot in the distance, we left the car to check the engine. It was then that we noticed that the air was stifling and sultry and it felt heavy to breathe. We opened the hood and Stig looked at spark plugs and cables with a flashlight without finding anything wrong. He then asked me to turn the ignition key and the engine started up at once. Relieved that nothing was wrong, we jumped into the car again to get going."

Harry was interested in what they had seen and he therefore asked Stig to stop at the place where the object had been seen. At the "landing spot" Harry got out and looked around. The first thing he saw was that the grass on both sides of the road was pressed down in a semicircle. Amazed by the finding, Harry called: "Come here and have a look, Stig – something's been here". Stig took his flashlight and stepped out of the car and took a look. The two friends wandered about looking with wonder. "I spotted something on the ground that gleamed when I let the light hit it," Harry says. "To my surprise it was a smooth hot piece of metal. It was so hot that I could hardly hold it. He came to me and he could see it too. What surprised us besides the heat was that it was so heavy considering its small size. It was triangular and had the size of a matchbox," Stig continues. "It must have been because of its smoothness and heaviness that I brought it along, otherwise I probably would have thrown it away."

After Stig and Harry had looked around the place, they returned to the car and drove on to where they were going.

Rumour now began to spread about their pieces of metal and their experience. Stig came in contact with engineer Schalin in Linkoping, to whom he sent one of the pieces. The result from the examinations amazed Schalin completely. The piece of metal has the hardness of sapphire and the specific weight of 15.2. Sharp diamond discs just slides [rotary disc saw] over its surface and it can take several thousand degrees heat without getting the slightest red-hot.

After many attempts to get the metal analyzed, they found someone who would do the analysis:

One of the three pieces is lost to the US air force. The two remaining pieces kept on puzzling its neighborhood for several years. In the early 70's one of the remaining pieces finally arrived at Berkeley University in California, insured for 50,000 sw. crowns. All this due to the American magazine the *National Enquirer*, which had set a reward for anyone who could present a real evidence for the existence of 'flying saucers.' At the Berkeley University, the examinations were made under guidance of Prof. James Harder. It took the scientists more than three years and thousands of dollars were spent on the examinations. One could now establish the fact that the piece of metal consisted of tungsten carbide, cobalt and few traces of titanium. But the hardness and composition puzzles the investigators.

Furthermore they could establish the fact that it was manufactured, it was sintered under enormous pressure. But by whom and in what way, couldn't be explained. 'We doubted if machines for such pressure existed except within diamond manufacturing,' prof. Harder said in his statement. As time went on the piece of metal returned to Sweden through among others the State Department... Anyway, the enigma of the Väddö case and its pieces of metal is still not solved. This most interesting UFO event that took place more than 20 years ago still puzzles and activates UFOlogists both nationally and worldwide. The final word has not been added to Stig's and Harry's widely discussed experience and there is all reason in the world to get back to the unique Väddö case." [191]

Sintering is the process of compacting and forming material into a solid mass by heat or pressure without melting it to the point of liquefaction. It can happen naturally in mineral deposits or as a manufacturing process that can be used with metals, ceramics, plastics, and other materials. The atoms of the materials diffuse across the boundaries of the particles, which fuses the particles together and creates a solid piece.

W is the chemical abbreviation for Tungsten, Si for Silicon, and C for Carbon. Hynek jokes that WC can also stand for Water Closet.

Would you believe indentation pressure of 1800 kg/sq. mm & so hard that SiC saw won't cut? Well ------

This must have been a remarkable material (Figure 72). SiC is also known as Carborundum, which is the trade name for silicon carbide, an artificial crystal. It is widely used today as a material in abrasive cutting blades (such as a rotary disc saw). It is used for cutting metal or steel. Hence the substance is harder than steel.

The indentation pressure is a measure of hardness in certain metals. In material's behavior, indentation pressure is equivalent to hardness; it is the material's resistance to inelastic deformation by indentation. The sample is certainly impressive.

Dr. James Albert Harder, (1926 – 2006), Hynek's probable man at Berkeley, was a professor of civil and hydraulic engineering at the University of California, Berkeley.

Harder had also applied his physical sciences background to the study of UFOs. In his 1968 Congressional testimony, Harder mentioned physical analysis of magnesium fragments found in 1957 near Ubatuba, Brazil, and that said to have come from an exploded flying saucer. This magnesium was of very high purity. Harder suggested that the lightweight metal, which is normally very brittle, might become exceptionally hard and strong if it were purified and made free from crystalline defects. If so, it would be an excellent metal for the construction of a flying device. Today construction of such high-strength metals is thought possible using the emerging field of nanotechnology.

Another of Harder's theories came from a sighting of an oval UFO by a chemist who lived near Phoenix. Webb had been wearing Polaroid glasses and noticed three concentric dark rings around the object. He thought this might be explained by a very powerful magnetic field surrounding the object that would cause polarized light from the sun to be rotated, or the Faraday effect. But how this magnetic field could explain the object's propulsion was unclear. He thought it might be related to gravitomagnetism, which is an analog of electromagnetism, predicted from general relativity. Theoretically a gravity-like field can be generated by a moving mass, but such an effect is normally minuscule. Harder did not know how a practical gravitomagnetic force might be produced.[192]

His next letter (Figure 73) was sent from the Lindheimer Astronomical Research Center on Valentine's Day probably in 1973.

> Valentine's Day–
> Hi!
> The Dutch have the good sense to recognize me as an authority on the subject – (note
> The big print on the dust jacket. I wonder if my publishers will ever learn!
> Cute letter from there too, Isn't it!
> Carry on!
> No late news on the Swedish incident
> –Allen
> (over)

Hynek takes life with much humor.

This must have been after his book was published because he jokes that the Dutch recognize him as an authority–because they put big print on the dust jacket.

Then he adds that he wonders if his publisher will ever learn this. He remarks that he received a cute letter from them also.

His remark about having no news on the Swedish incident likely refers to the Väddö incident described above. Apparently it may have taken around three years for an analysis of the material to be done.

The next letter (Figure 74) was from the Northwestern University astronomy department, dated June 15, 1973, and told about a cruise:

> Dear Jennie –
> OK – I won't worry – glad to know you as a H? suave? away from an operation – in two directions, of course!
> A week from today we sail - & a funny? T h o m u t t f. I got called up by the cruise director asking if the Hyneks would mind sharing a table with the Armstrongs! So – tell Barry I should be able to get the autograph for him!
>
> Did I tell you I'm going

This letter could be somewhat historic because it might actually confirm that Armstrong did have an interest in UFOs. This is because they asked Hynek if he would be interested in sharing a table with Armstrong. It might be that Armstrong requested this seating. Information on cruise ship seating is, "You can request your own table or to be seated with other people. Select your dining preferences at the time you book your cruise."[193] And Armstrong had a choice of some real celebrities to be seated with too, as will be shown.

Many people have wondered about whether Armstrong had an interest in UFO phenomena and this might provide a smoking gun that he did.

As an investigator for MORA, I discovered additional information suggesting that Neil Armstrong had an interest in UFOs. Dr. Hynek had met Armstrong several times and perhaps the following came about because Hynek and Armstrong knew each other.

UFOlogists Pete Hartinger, Bill Jones, and some other investigators told me of the possibility that Armstrong's was interested in UFOs. UFOlogist and writer, Leonard Stringfield was involved in a key report on government-connected UFO informants.

Astronaut Neil Armstrong, the first person to walk on the moon, and astronomy professor J. Allen Hynek knew each other and may have worked together on this. Stringfield knew of more than 50 government-connected informants who'd divulged information about UFO events. However, he refused to release their names, and his critics insisted that without the identities of the sources, the stories lacked credibility. Stringfield recognized this problem, but he had promised to protect the identities of his informants, and felt that if he didn't he'd get no further information from them or anyone else. Stringfield said that a number of years ago when retired astronaut Neil Armstrong was on the board of directors of a Cincinnati bank, Armstrong and Hynek approached Stringfield with a proposal to protect the names of the government-connected informants. Armstrong said Stringfield could put his list of names in a safety deposit box at Armstrong's bank, to which it was assumed Armstrong would also have access. The intention was that in the event of Stringfield's death, the names wouldn't be lost, but Stringfield rejected the idea.

There is no proof that this happened; however, Armstrong and Hynek did communicate, as shown by a letter from Armstrong to Hynek now in the possession of CUFOS. In addition, investigator Jenny Zeidman has reported that Hynek and Stringfield met and discussed UFOs. These accounts also support rumors of Armstrong's interest in UFOs.

I have also visited and interviewed Leonard Stringfield, but do not recall whether I asked him about Armstrong and UFOs.

Leonard Stringfield (1920-1994) was an Ohio UFO researcher who spent much time examining WP. From 1953 to 1957, he investigated UFO activity in cooperation with the Air Force. His books include *Inside Saucer Post, 3-O Blue*, and *Situation Red. The UFO Siege*! He published a series of six "Status Reports" to update information on this subject. He served as the Director of Civilian Research, Interplanetary Flying Objects (CRIFO—one of the world's largest research groups during the mid-1950s) and published a monthly newsletter, ORBIT. In 1957 he became the public relations adviser for the civilian UFO group, National Investigations Committee On Aerial Phenomena (NICAP), under the direction of Donald Keyhoe, his friend since 1953. From 1967 to 1969, Stringfield also served as an "Early Warning Coordinator" for the Condon Committee. During the 1970s, he authored a number of books about alleged UFO "crash-retrievals," recoveries of alien spaceships, and alien bodies. He worked as the Director of Public Relations and Marketing Services for DuBois Chemicals, a division of Chemed Corporation, Cincinnati.

Hynek tells Zeidman to tell Barry that he should be able to get Armstrong's autograph. Barry was Zeidman's husband, who worked in Battelle's Advanced Mechanical Systems Section.

It appears that Zeidman had some health concerns and told him not to worry but he did anyway. Hynek said that they would sail a week from then and seemed quite excited about this.

Hynek's next letter (Figure 75) is a continuation:

> Around the world in 80/2 days? London, Bangkok, Perth, Sydney, Melbourne, Aulaied?, Austland, New Guinea, Samoa (governor's mansion I expect) and then have to start classes again. Aug 8 – Sep 16 (I. A. U. & UFO tour)
> See you in October,
> Allen
> P.S. – who's Polish? – The beagle?

The trip Hynek was talking about was the African Eclipse Cruise July 1973.

Hynek seemed very thrilled about this excursion and listed some of the countries and cities he would be visiting. He even expects to visit the governor's mansion of Samoa.

He may have been referencing French writer Jules Verne's book, *Around the World in Eighty Days*, when he said, "around the world in 80/2 days."

The I. A. U. likely is the International Astronomical Union.

And he has two PSs:

> PS_
> I don't have Jane Ganu's address. Will you help out and tell her that October 27 is fine. A gala Meeting!
> PPS _ Tell her also that the cruise will have a special evening panel [Asimov, Armstrong, Sullivan and me] on "Life in the Universe." [Worth the price of admission!].

This trip (Figure 76) was the July 1973 Canberra's African Eclipse Cruise. The panel he would be a part of was called, "Life in the Universe." Although Hynek was well known, he was a member a of panel having Superstar status. Neil Armstrong of course was world famous, as the first human on the moon and for additional exploits as a pilot.

Isaac Asimov was a world-famous writer and a biochemistry professor at Boston University. He was well-known for his works of popular science and science fiction. He was such a prolific writer that he wrote or edited more than 500 books and about 90,000 letters and postcards.

With Robert A. Heinlein and Arthur C. Clarke, he was considered one of the "Big Three" of science fiction writers. His best-known work is the "Foundation" series; his other major series are the "Galactic Empire" series, the Robot series, and the *Galactic Empire* novels. He wrote hundreds of short stories, including the novelette "*Nightfall*," that in 1964 was voted by the Science Fiction Writers of America group as the best short science fiction story of all time.

Asimov was also noted for his nonfiction, such as *Guide to Science*, the three-volume set *Understanding Physics*, and works on much else–including astronomy, mathematics, history, William Shakespeare's writing, and chemistry. He has an asteroid (5020), a Mars crater, a school, and an award named for him.[194]

This once-in-a-lifetime cruise made the news all over the world and is described in detail in several places:

> On June 30, 1973, the P&O luxury liner Canberra rendezvoused off the coast of West Africa with one of the longest solar eclipses of our lifetime. Among the many features of the June 22 through July 8, cruise were the numerous courses in scientific and cultural fields.
> Dr. Phil S. Sigler and Ted Pedas's distinguished teaching staff for the "Voyage to Darkness — African Eclipse Cruise" included the following:
> ASTRONOMY
> Dr. Franklyn M. Branley—Chairman on Leave of the American Museum, Hayden Planetarium, New York.
> Dr. Mark R. Chartrand III—Education Director and Assistant Astronomer of the American Museum—Hayden Planetarium, New York
> Dr. Allen J. Hynek— Director of the Dearborn Observatory and Chairman of the Astronomy Dept. at Northwestern University.
> Dr. Charles H. Smiley— Retired Chairman of the Department of Astronomy at Brown University and Leader of an unprecedented 14 Solar Eclipse Scientific expeditions.
> Mr. Walter Sullivan—Science Editor for the *New York Times*.
> Dr. Gerrit Verschuur—Associate scientist for the National Radio Astronomy Observatory.[195]

The Armstrong and Hynek family spent two weeks together as they shared the table.

Because the Armstrongs and Hyneks spent this much time together, one might wonder if they discussed UFOs. It was said that they did. They had things in common, Armstrong was from Ohio, and Hynek spent many years working in Ohio.

Hynek lists New Guinea as one of the countries he visited during this journey. Although he was busy and tired, with his usual energy he set about studying the UFO situation. This was the famous 1959 Papua, New Guinea sighting where Father William Gill and others waved to UFO occupants and they waved back. This was definitely a Close Encounter of the Third Kind.

Hynek interviewed both the Reverend that originally had documented the Gill case and Father Gill himself. He interviewed six of the original witnesses who recalled the event quite well.

Father Gill began as a UFO skeptic. On April 5, Gill and 38 other people watched a light in the sky that had the apparent diameter of five full moons. It was disc-shaped, had a smaller structure on top, silent, and had four legs. Four beings were moving around on top of it. A blue light would shine up from the object at regular intervals and the object was associated with a number of smaller objects. The entire sighting lasted for more than four hours.

The object came back the next day. When people waved at the beings, they waved back. One waved a torch and the craft made a pendulum-like movement. People waved for them to land. Most of the village watched.

This was a case where Dr. Hynek and Dr. Menzel had disagreed, as mentioned before. For example Menzel claimed that Father Gill was not wearing his glasses and that the people mistook Venus as the object. This was not true.[196]

Figure 77 shows Hynek as he likely looked at this time.

But this letter contains much else good news. The October 27, 1973, date Hynek refers to the meeting where he would accept a 1973 Ohioana Book Award from the Ohioana Library Association for his book *The UFO Experience*.

Much was going on in Hynek's life and in the UFO field at that time. Hynek appeared to be looking forward to this when he wrote the letter and called it a gala meeting.

Although from these letters one would expect Hynek to be elated, something had changed, by the time he attended as Jennie described later:[197]

> I have written previously of my time with Hynek on October 26, 1973, and of his obvious unhappiness and agitation over events that had occurred at Wright Field during the previous few hours. These present notes provide some background details of an historic nature, and more personal memories of the following day, October 27, 1973, which I have not previously published.

Below are excerpts from this piece:

> Five months after the closing of BB and the termination of his twenty-one year "scientific consultancy to the Air Force", Allen Hynek was once again under contract to the Foreign Technology Division at WP. He was listed as a "Special Government Employee" (the quotation marks exist on the contract sheets). This work, under Civil Service status, continued through four consecutive annual contracts, with the stipulation that his service was not to exceed 20 days per year…He actually worked only a few days each contract period. Although his contract was renewed effective May 4, 1974, he was paid only for one day during the pay period and there is a notation on the sheet which indicates Termination – "no other work available." Soon after October 26, 1973, which was probably his next-to-last, and almost

certainly a most significant and traumatic working day, Allen Hynek announced the formation of his Center for UFO Studies…

In the fall of 1969, when Blue Book folded, Hynek expressed his mixed emotions (some would say sour grapes) by saying, "Good! Now I can write my book." (We consulted regularly about the manuscript, and *The UFO Experience* was published in 1972.) He seemed to have removed himself from official government UFO work forever. Then, in a letter to me dated May 1, 1970 (his 60th birthday) he says "…the AF has asked me to be a consultant again – starting this summer – but on what I don't know! All I know is that I had to go through the whole clearance process again. It may be Rooshian (sic) devices or it may be UFOs." In a letter to me of June 19th, he says "My new WPAFB assignment is official, but as yet I haven't been called in for anything!"

Wait a minute, here! Russian devices? Allen Hynek? Hynek was an astronomer, for heaven's sake, a mild-mannered professor…What was he doing with Russian devices? For that matter, what was he doing with UFOs? Even more germane, if, as the government insisted, UFOs were of no consequence and of no relevance to national security, why would an astronomy professor need a security clearance in the first place?

Hynek was often asked, "how he got into the UFO business," and his answer was by rote:…According to Hynek, his UFO consultancy was by pure happenstance.

Well, not exactly. In fact, not exactly at all.

The Air Force, it turns out, did not just pick Hynek's name out of a hat; he wasn't chosen by coincidence…He was actually a logical and obvious choice. For Hynek was a rocket man.

If asked, "What did you do during the war? Hynek's answer was open and ingenuous. "I was at Johns Hopkins, working on the radio proximity fuse." Indeed, in 1942 he was granted leave from his Assistant Professorship at OSU to work at the Applied Physics Laboratory. On a basic "Who's Who" sheet from his early years at OSU he wrote, "Supervisor of technical reports at Applied Physics Laboratory during the war," and on another sheet dated May, 1944, "of (sic) the staff of John-Hopkins (sic) University, 1942-."

After the war, Hynek's academic stars rose quickly. He…advanced to full professor…served as director of OSU's McMillan Observatory…was appointed an assistant dean of the Graduate School, and he managed to pursue his own specialty, a long-term program on stars with composite spectra and on the infra-red spectra of double stars.

But there was even more on his plate. In addition to his many other activities, and undoubtedly as an offshoot of his wartime work, Hynek had an ongoing position with the V-2 rocket program at White Sands Proving Ground, New Mexico. He did not mention this to his students. Even Jacques Vallée's ego-biographical *Forbidden Science* (1992), which places great emphasis on the two men's intellectual intimacy, mentions Hynek's proximity fuse work but nothing of the V-2 connection. Yet, though mention of his current or previous government aerospace work failed to reach the "outside world," the May 1948 issue of The *OSU Alumni Monthly* (p. 9) refers to Hynek as "one of the nation's 'name' men in rocket research." It is also noted that he "has been summoned several times by the government to serve as observer at rocket launchings in New Mexico." A year later, presumably after he became UFO connected, the May 1949 issue of the *Monthly* refers to Hynek as "nationally known in the field of rocket research," (but does not mention any UFO connection).

It was not until the publication in 1992 of David DeVorkin's book *Science with a Vengeance: How the Military Created the US Space Sciences after World War II*, that many of Hynek's UFO associates became aware of the full extent of his involvement in post-war V-2 research. I do remember him making a trip to Huntsville, Alabama during 1953, and me picking him up right away and asking, "Redstone Arsenal?" He said yes, and upon my further inquiry acknowledged that he had met Werner Von Braun, or perhaps knew Von Braun, but that was the extent of it.

The DeVorkin book contains no less than 14 references to Hynek's involvement and contributions to the development of upper atmospheric research. And once I started looking, I found other references as well. Buried in his extensive bibliography is a hand-written reference to Chapters 10-19 Inc. of *New Weapons for Aerial Warfare*, Little Brown & Company edited by Joe C. Boyce. No date is given, and I have been unable to track it down, but its location in his list of publications places it between 1946 and 1950.

Why was it okay for Hynek to say, "I worked on the proximity fuse during the war," but not to advertise that "after the war I worked on the utilization of captured V-2 rockets as vehicles for instruments for upper atmospheric research?" I have considered the possibility he was sensitive that he had some degree of working relationship with the Project Paperclip gang – the captured German scientists brought to work in the United States (away from the sure clutches of the Soviets). A simpler answer is that Hynek's UFO image needed to be divorced from any previous government connection.

But Hynek was derelict in his duties to the Air Force. As time progressed his adherence to "the party line" became more and more difficult. The "sport" of the job was long past, replaced by a growing frustration and anxiety over his difficult position. He was supposed to be pacifying the public, downplaying UFO reports, yet he was becoming increasingly aware of the importance of the phenomenon, and of the gross inadequacies of the Air Force "investigation." Conversely, the Air Force was becoming unhappy with Hynek. He wasn't exactly a loose cannon rolling on the deck, but neither was he the perfect "yes man" they required. He found himself in a precarious double balancing act, not only with the Air Force, but also with his public position. When I was a student in his "Astronomy 500" class the fall of 1952, he told us of his consultancy, and that as far as he could tell, UFO reports were primarily the result of misinterpretations of normal events or aircraft. Years later it was revealed that as early as the summer of 1952 – months earlier – at the time of the great Washington National over flights, he had already written the first of several letters to the Air Force pointing out the need for an in-depth scientific study. Invariably he was ignored. In effect, the Air Force was saying, "Just supply us with meteors, or Venus, or lenticular clouds, and mind your own business."

Despite his considerable background in aerospace work, and a track record of scrupulous security checks, it had been decided he was to be left out of the inner circle. In January 1953, when he returned from the Robertson Panel, he expressed to me (in retrospect, very naively) his bewilderment at having to "sit in the hall" during some of the sessions. The final insult, of course, was the failure of Northwestern University to be granted the "scientific study" which ultimately became the fiasco of the University of Colorado's Condon Report. Hynek said it was analogous to appointing a non-cook as chef-maître of Maxim's.

Hynek was used. He was abused. He was trapped. Increasingly frustrated and bitter, he wanted no more of the Air Force's game. But if he resigned, he would lose the little access he did have to the data. He began to photocopy for his own future use all of the Air Force material which he was allowed to see. And he bided his time.

After his initial mention of a new contract in his letters of May and June 1970, I find nothing in my correspondence file for the next three years on the subject of working at WF.

In January 1973 Hynek was informed that *The UFO Experience* had won the Ohioana Library Book Award as the best book by an Ohio or Ohio-connected author in the field of general non-fiction in 1972. The award (a soggy chicken salad lunch and a medallion) would take place in Columbus the following October 27th. I knew early on about this, and received a letter from him dated September 28 announcing that he would be at WF during the day of October 26. Could I pick him up and drive him back to Columbus? Of course.

Meanwhile, the eastern United States had exploded into the great fall UFO flap of 1973. Not a day went by without newspaper and television coverage of UFO sightings....The two outstanding cases in the news were Pascagoula and Coyne and they vied for attention – even front-page attention – with bulletins from the Middle East. By the end of October the Yom Kippur War took prominence, and it was announced that WF was on high security status as a staging and departure base for supplies headed for Israel. It was in this environment that I picked up Hynek and drove him to Columbus. I had never seen him in such mental distress.

The following day we met at noon at the awards luncheon (he had stayed at a hotel, not with my family) and he still seemed preoccupied.

We exchanged pleasantries with our tablemates, including astronaut (later Senator) John Glenn, also an award recipient. A few minutes remained before the speakers would be called to the microphone. Hynek and I discussed the UFO flap then in progress.

Someone at our table asked him the usual "what about the bodies at WF?" and of course Hynek said he had no information on the subject. Then he turned to me, and in a quiet aside said that he had heard of – or did he say "knew" of? – a crash and retrieval at or near Holloman AFB, near Alamogordo, New Mexico. I believe he said bodies had been taken to Holloman.

I was stunned. Never before had he made such bold statements to me. Activities at the speakers' table precluded further conversation. I took out a 3x5 card and wrote, "When did the Holloman incident take place?" Allen wrote "1962?" on the side (note question mark). I wrote, "Who leaked it to you?" Allen wrote. "The AF." (Note the underline.) I sputtered some further question, and at that moment he was called to receive his award. At the first available moment I pursued the topic, but he would only protest that he had already said too much. The subject was closed. Mindful of the protocols and responsibilities associated with classified information, but much to my later regret, we never discussed it again.

Fifteen years later I learned that Allen had spent that morning with Leonard Stringfield – very possibly their first meeting. Stringfield was a persuasive fellow, and as his special interest was crash-retrievals (almost always, alas, from anonymous sources) it was a natural assumption that it was he who had told Allen about the Holloman incident. So why would Allen have said (with underline) "The AF?" All he needed to say was, "I can't tell you."

But Allen was angry at the Air Force. The previous day there had been a showdown at FTD. One of the most intense UFO flaps was in full swing, and the Air Force was doing nothing. He had challenged them. "Why aren't you doing something?" he later told me he had said. And he had received only stony faces in reply. It wasn't a question of a Mid-East-War-going-on-and-we-can't-be-bothered-with-UFOs. It was a question of, regardless, the Air Force "would do nothing about" UFOs.

The total picture of Hynek's 1970 – 1973 few-days-a-year work at Wright Field leads me to believe that the subject was indeed UFOs, not "Rooshian devices," and that the time was spent essentially on de-briefing sessions. Apparently through those years, although Blue Book was dead and gone, the Air Force still had Allen on the hook, and he could be reeled in on

command. I imagine that they were keeping track of what knowledge he had acquired between meetings, and the progress of his thinking on the subject. In other words, was he a threat, or not? The October 26th meeting had been scheduled at least a month in advance, so although propitious, it was not a case of, "There's a UFO flap on, call Hynek."
  No doubt Hynek was hoping he would pick up some useful information in the bargain.
  Undoubtedly, the Air Force profited more than Allen did from these meetings.

It is unclear what Hynek was doing for the AF at that time. Zeidman carefully calculated how much he worked for FTD from 1970-1974, although he was supposedly not working. Figure 78 shows Zeidman's handwritten preliminary notes for this piece, which give more information.

In these notes, she also mentions the date of October 26, and that it had been scheduled in advance. She figured that he had scheduled this himself so that he would be available for the Ohioana award, rather than having the AF schedule it. Thus he would conveniently be in Dayton at the time of the award ceremony in Columbus. In addition, it appeared that while he was in Dayton, he would also meet Leonard Springfield.

As mentioned above Hynek may have had some kind of contract with McGraw-Hill that appeared to be similar to his WP contract. After that, it appears that he began working for WP again (Figure 78).

> On Oct 26, 1973, JAH dissociated himself irrevocably from the AF UFO Investigation? The discovery was a long time coming. For 21 years he had been the gov [Xed out] AF's scientific consultant on UFOs" When BB folded in Dec 69 would not be advanced by the further study of UFOs (Insert The NSF declared that " ? Hynek ostensibly faded from the official UFO scene. However unbeknownst to the public, He had managed to maintain a toe in the door – docs returned from ___ indicate he worked as a consultant "for ___ days in 70, __days in 71, __-___ ___

  Hynek always told people he was the innocent bystander who got into this that he happened to be appointed for the job simply because he was a professional astronomer, and he was close by (OSU is 60 miles from WP). But this was not exactly true. In fact it wasn't the truth at all. When I first met Hynek, as the start in the fall of 52, he said (when asked, "what did you do in the war?" that he had been exempt from active service because he was "at John Hopkins working on the proximity fuse." O.K. But what did he do after the war. He was an active staff member of the Paper Clip Project."

The next examination explores this further (Figures 79 and 80):
  2/13/92
  Re: Allen & FTD 70-73
  Regardless of what he was doing at FTD, the fact that he worked so little – (at the most 10 days per year, at the least 1 day-) suggests that this was in no way an "important or high-priority activity. Indeed, it could suggest a kind of "courtesy" appointment – an insider friend of his sympathetic to A and "the work," got him the appointment. Yet – that theory is contradicted by the fact that he had to get re-cleared - quite an involved bit if the job was merely "busy work." I assume that the work at WP, as reflected on the Form 50's was the only work. i.e. it was counted as work if he were at WP (on the premises). The term "no other work available" is interesting. Is this a standard category when a contract is not research?"

Re the last day (October 26, 73) it was scheduled a month or more in advance and, it figures, by Allen himself – (because he was gonna be in CMH the following day for the book award). And that was the only day he worked all year.

One wonders if they were "trying to get rid of him" earlier on, & he had to request the Oct date himself, rather than them calling him in.

I cannot let go of the idea that his uneasiness, antsy – somewhat bad humor on the ride to CMH had to do with what he learned that day. H goes beyond his very? "let go" (we don't need you….) and certainly it wasn't a question of money- a few hundred bucks a year.

When, next day, he wrote the card, then clammed up, what was left unsaid?

Another theory: WP wanted to be able to "interview him"/etc in depth, at intervals, to see what he was up to. Naw, that doesn't work either. They could do it with moles better. Or most simply, they would just send someone out to Chicago to spend ½ a day with him – the only expense would be taking him to lunch – and no written record of his employment.

Side note Maybe getting re-cleared was a technical necessity because of time lapse between jobs

Zeidman studied the time he put in carefully (Figure 81).

It is known that he worked for McGraw Hill shortly after he dissociated with BB, but his exact positions at that time are unclear.

There is not much information about the contract with McGraw-Hill. It was mentioned by Vallée as discussed earlier. This Battelle document supports this, but it is extremely confusing. Hynek is on record as working with McGraw-Hill on a textbook named *Astrophysics*, in 1951 and this seems logical. However it is difficult to find any information about Golden Eagle, except in the Vallée book and the Battelle document above.

McGraw-Hill is best known as a book publisher. McGraw-Hill Education is a learning science company and it is one of the big three educational publishers. It provides customized educational content, software, and services for all levels of education. It also provides reference and trade publications for many professions such as medical, business, and engineering.

The Battelle document says that Hynek went to work for the McGraw-Hill Information Division. He began working for McGraw-Hill after BB closed. The only mentions I can find about this are the Stanton Friedman documents and the Battelle document, which adds information to the Vallée book. This Battelle document reports that at first he was not a government employee, but he became one in four months. The author may have been looking for a Civil Service Document that might show this. It also mentions NASA with a word that looks like Calstpan. This is confusing also because his position under BB was with the government, thus, one would think that if this had been a continuation of that general organization, he would still have been working for the government.

It then reports that Box 27 is blanked out and asks why. "3DL" and AFSC are also mentioned.
From Vallée, it appears that Hynek's contract with McGraw-Hill was with something like BB, but called Golden Eagle. From this one could ask if this related to another UFO study, a project to

study foreign materials, or both. This is further suggested when he says that it was previously called White Stork. This was the Battelle contract under which Battelle studied UFOs.

Could a contract that included UFO study have been made with McGraw-Hill after BB closed?

Figure 82 shows a high point in his life; he had just founded the Center for UFO Studies, and this letter was written from there. Hynek had established it as a way to continue the scientific study of UFOs. This letter was likely written in the fall of 1973 after the Coyne helicopter event.

> Hi Jen –
> This is the letter to Coyne (vs!).
> Since you won't buy Klass' book (don't blame you) –I'm enclosing a Xerox of the pages relevant to the Coyne case. Please ask Coyne specifically about Klass' charges – that he pushed the [collective lever] to go up instead of to go down.
> Make the bastard (Klass) eat his words!
> Cheers
> Allen

This letter is about the Ohio Coyne helicopter case. Hynek and Zeidman both investigated the Coyne UFO incident, one of best-documented and best-investigated UFO sightings. Hynek was writing about Philip Klass who used to be the ace UFO debunker and arch enemy of the scientific study of UFOs. Zeidman could not stand him and had run-ins with him. That is why she would not buy any of his books.

I think I heard part of a debate between Jennie and Klass because I once was in a radio station (I think it was a PBS station (WOSU) near the Olentangy River Road in Columbus) where Jennie debated Klass about the Coyne case. As I recall he claimed the object was a meteor because he claimed that it did not hover over the helicopter.

Hynek was mentioning that in the presence of the UFO, the helicopter rose into the air. No one had been aware of this and Coyne had set the collective lever into a dive to avoid a collision with the object. Then they discovered the helicopter had risen.

This is an excellent argument against Klass's stance. And Hynek told her that this should make Klass eat is own words.

Below is a description of the event from Zeidman's write up ("A Helicopter-UFO Encounter Over Ohio," by Jennie Zeidman, 1979, Center for UFO Studies)

The event took place near Mansfield, Ohio, when an Army Reserve helicopter crew of four men encountered a metallic-looking, grey, cigar-shaped object. During the incident, a light beam lit up the cockpit, the helicopter made a quick ascent, and witnesses both in the aircraft and on the ground described the object. Jennie Zeidman, Bill Jones, and Warren Nicholson intensively investigated and gave me additional information. The government involvement in this was strange and intriguing. [198]

On a clear, calm, starry night, when the moon was in its last quarter and just rising, a UH-1H helicopter left Port Columbus International Airport flying northeast toward its home base of Cleveland Hopkins International Airport. In command in the right front seat was Captain Lawrence J. Coyne, a 36-year-old pilot with 19 years of flying experience. The other crewmembers were John Healey, a Cleveland police officer who was the flight medic; Robert Yanacsek, a computer technician; and Arrigo Jezzi, a chemical engineer.

The helicopter was cruising at 2,500 feet above sea level at an airspeed of 90 knots when, 10 miles south of Mansfield, Healey saw a single red light to the west, flying south. Two minutes later at 11:02 p.m., Yanacsek noticed a red light on the southern horizon. He watched it for about a minute and called it to Coyne's attention. Coyne assumed it was distant air traffic and told Yanacsek to keep an eye on it. After another half minute, Yanacsek announced the light had turned toward the helicopter and seemed to be on a converging path.

Coyne verified Yanacsek's assessment. Thinking the light was an Air National Guard F-100 from Mansfield, he put the UH-1H into a powered descent of 500 feet per minute. He established radio contact with Mansfield control tower, 10 miles northwest, but the radio contact failed. Jezzi attempted UHF and VHF transmissions without success. Coyne later learned that the Mansfield airport had no tape of their transmissions and that the last F-100 in the vicinity had landed at 10:47 p.m.

Meanwhile the mysterious red light continued its bearing and increased in intensity, so Coyne boosted his rate of descent to 2,000 feet per minute and his airspeed to 100 knots. The last altitude he noted was 1,700 feet. Just as a collision appeared imminent, the object abruptly halted in its course and hovered above and in front of the helicopter for 10 seconds.

The object was a featureless gray metallic structure, cigar-shaped and domed, with windows along the dome. To the witnesses it covered a space nearly equal to the width of the front windshield. The red light observed by the four men was coming from its bow, and a white light became visible at its slightly indented stern. As the men watched, a green pyramid-shaped beam, like a directional spotlight, became visible from the lower rear section. This green beam of light passed over the helicopter's nose, swung up through the windshield, and bathed the cockpit in green light.

The object then flew off to the west. Only its white taillight was visible, and this light maintained its intensity even as its distance increased. Finally the UFO made a sharp turn to the right, heading toward Lake Erie. The men watched it move away, and Jezzi later said it traveled faster than the 250-knot limit for aircraft below 10,000 feet. There had been neither noise, nor any turbulence from the object, except for a bump as it moved west.

When the object had stopped hovering, the men noticed their magnetic compass disc was making four rotations per minute and their altimeter read 3,500 feet: a 1,000 foot-per-minute climb was in progress. Coyne insists the collective lever (one of three flight control inputs) was still bottomed from his evasive dive. Because it could not be lowered, he had no alternative but to lift it. After gingerly maneuvering the controls as the helicopter reached nearly 3,800 feet, he regained control of the helicopter.

All four men had been aware of the dive, but only Coyne was aware of the climb. The helicopter was brought back to the flight-plan altitude of 2,500 feet, radio contact was achieved with Akron-Canton Regional Airport, and the flight proceeded uneventfully. The duration of the sighting was longer than that for a typical meteor. In addition, the object hovered, changed course, and emitted light strong enough to illuminate the ground.

UFOlogists Bill Jones and Warren Nicholson later investigated and found there were ground witnesses for this event.

These witnesses were a woman and four teenagers. Driving south from Mansfield at 11:00 p.m., they saw a single, steady, bright red light flying south through the sky. They watched for half a minute until it disappeared. Five minutes later, as they drove east on Route 430 approaching the Charles Mill Reservoir, they became aware of two bright lights—one green and one red—descending toward them from the southeast. The red light appeared to be in front. As Conley pulled onto the shoulder of the road, the lights slowed and moved to the right of the car. The family noticed another group of lights, some flashing, and they heard a beating sound—the helicopter—approaching from the southwest. Two of the teens jumped from the car and watched both the helicopter and the object, which they described as like a blimp, as large as a school bus, and pear-shaped. The object covered an area (subtended an angle) equal to a cigarette box held at arm's length, and it hovered over the helicopter, now around 500 feet above the road and the trees.

The object's green light flared, and the witnesses saw what looked like rays coming toward both the earth and the helicopter. Everything around them turned green: the helicopter, the trees, the road, the car, and the ground. The two witnesses outside the car ran back to it, and the driver accelerated to move the car. No one was sure when the object stopped hovering, but they agreed it crossed to the north side of the road, moved east briefly, then reversed direction and climbed northwest toward Mansfield, taking the same flight path reported by the helicopter crew.

Some Ohio UFO investigators reported that Mansfield residents thought there had been a power failure that night in the area of the helicopter encounter. One witness looked out a window and saw the UFO, the helicopter, and the green light at the same time. This person also said the power went out in the area at that time.

Unlike many UFO witnesses, Coyne was never harassed. On the contrary, he was promoted several times. However, government personnel later made inquiries about the dreams of the helicopter crew.

A strange government interest in this is shown by the fact that three weeks after the event Coyne received a call from a man who identified himself as being from the Office of the Surgeon General of the US Army Medical Department. This caller asked if Coyne or other crewmembers had had any unusual dreams since the UFO experience. Coyne had had two.

In one, he was outside his body. In the second, he was holding a bluish white sphere in his hand and he heard a voice say, "The answer is in the circle."

Coyne said that every two months he was telephoned and asked a series of questions about whether certain things had happened to him or if he had dreamed of them since his UFO experience. He was told to question the rest of the crew as well, and to mail their answers to the Pentagon.

Crewmember Healey said the Pentagon contacted him with similar questions; in particular, he was asked if he ever dreamed of body separation. He had. He was also asked if he had dreamed of anything with a spherical shape. He hadn't.

In his 1991 book, *The Watchers: The Secret Design behind UFO Abduction*, author Ray Fowler says the CIA has an interest in extra-sensory perception (ESP). He thinks the agency is investigating whether a link exists between UFOs and ESP and whether UFO witnesses might have ESP abilities. Fowler thinks the questions asked of the helicopter crew were based on investigations of abductions within the ranks of the military and NASA. He asserts that this crack in government secrecy lends credibility to abduction cases. The Coyne event was not thought to involve abduction, but perhaps the government felt that because a green light was shined on the witnesses the incident was abduction-like. Or perhaps the helicopter's inexplicable climb suggested abduction.

Either way it is evidence that some government component is studying the mind control/telepathic/psychic aspects of UFO phenomena.

The green light has been a matter of interest in this case. Both the helicopter crew and the ground witnesses saw the light, and the crew associated it with magnetic anomalies in the helicopter. However, debunker Phil Klass, a member of the Committee for the Scientific Investigation of Claims of the Paranormal (CSICOP—now called the Committee for Skeptical Inquiry), believed the green light the crew saw was actually the effect of a green-tinted windshield in the helicopter. On the other hand, it is known that the green windshield tint is very subtle and not even as dark as the tinted windows of many cars. In bright sunlight, there was a faint and barely noticeable tint of green in the cockpit, but this was not strong enough to cause a light shining through the windshield to appear green or to give the effect of the cockpit turning green.

However such green lights are very interesting, because they have been reported numerous times in association with UFO phenomena, and because they can have strange effects. For example in the Schirmer abduction, a green light seemed to be a sort of tractor beam. And in the case of the Soviet Aeroflot airliner flying over Minsk, in an effect somewhat like the Coyne case, it shot out a blob-like object that cast a greenish tint over the landscape. When one of the beams projected into the cabin, it caused weird effects including multiple lights of different colors and fiery zigzags. The beams outside changed shape to mimic the plane. Walter Webb once said that beams of light focused on UFO witnesses often precede impressions of missing time and abduction scenarios and perhaps there is an association to this also.

I discussed Klass's comments with Zeidman and she recalled her debate and that Klass said the UFO had been in sight for only a second or less and had been a meteor. Zeidman, however, affirmed that the object was in sight for longer than this and thus, it could not have been a meteor.

I was very familiar with the Coyne case because I had investigated these times and published several papers (including in scientific journals) about a mysterious blast that heralded an abrupt series of UFO events that began around 9:00 pm on October 11, 1973.

These events included a strange booming sound, UFO sightings, and entity encounters, and it may have been the most widely experienced event ever to have been associated with UFO phenomena. With the exception of the Krakatoa volcanic eruption of 1883, the 1973 boom could be the most widespread audible sound on record. Not only were there reports of a thunderous boom, but beginning around 9:00 p.m. on October 11, police switchboards were swamped with reports of UFOs, close encounters, alien abductions, mutilations, and similar events. Central Ohio law enforcement agencies received 150 UFO reports on October 17, six days after the initial activity, and this is the largest number of UFO sightings ever recorded in a 24-hour period. This wave and the nature of the sightings were so extensive that some referred to it as an invasion. The precipitous increase of multi-state sightings has come to be known as the UFO Wave of 1973, and unlike most UFO events that leave behind little proof; the 1973 events included an unprecedented abundance of evidence. This included Dr. Harley Rutledge's study, which may be the best UFO research ever done. Additional smoking gun evidence includes seismograms of the boom.

Two seminal events during this time included the Coyne helicopter event and a happening in Pascagoula, Mississippi.

Right at time of the sound, the Pascagoula Abduction, considered one of the world's most credible abduction cases, took place in Mississippi on October 11, 1973, at about 9:00 p.m. The two witnesses, Charles Hickson and Calvin Parker, began their report to the sheriff's office by saying they had seen a strange object land while they were fishing.

They sensed something behind them and turned to see an oval-shaped aircraft that was illuminated by a blue light and making a buzzing noise. Its hatchway opened, and three naked beings floated out. These beings were ghostlike and pale, with wrinkled skin, wide blinking eyes, and conical projections where their noses and ears should have been. Instead of hands, they had claws—crab-like pincers—and instead of two legs, each had a round pedestal.

The beings somehow caused Hickson to float into the aircraft, and they did the same to Parker, who fainted. Hickson could not move his body while he was in the craft. For 30 minutes, a large, eye-like device physically examined the men.

After the abduction, fearing they wouldn't be believed, neither wanted to report what had happened. Finally, however, they did report the event. At first they telephoned the Keesler Air Force Base, but a sergeant told them that the Air Force no longer investigated UFO reports. Next they called the Jackson County sheriff's office. The abduction occurred on Thursday, and by the following Monday, Charles Hickson and Calvin Parker were famous throughout the country. Authorities believed them for several reasons, including the fact that even when they thought they were alone together, Hickson and Parker discussed the encounter as a real event and continued to show fear as they spoke of it.

The Center for UFO Studies was Dr. Hynek's crowning glory (Figure 83). Through the years as his opinion about the UFO phenomenon changed, he wanted more and more to investigate the subject in a scientific manner and had been disgusted with the way the government was doing things. At this time he set up his own organization the way that it should have been done.

Hynek set it up with a stellar group of scientists having positions at a variety of top universities and in in many relevant fields of expertise. Such nationally known researchers as Margaret Mead joined his staff.

Several years after this letter was written, I reported some UFO experiences that my sister and I had. Several people investigated and discussed the events with Dr. Hynek, such as Budd Hopkins in the letter above (Figure 84).

Hynek had also called me and we spoke on the phone.

Dr. Hynek's next message was to me (Figure 85).

> Hi –
> I understand that Jennie will be here soon – any chance of your coming too?
> Cheers
> Allen Hynek

Perhaps this is the last handwritten message he sent.

It shows his dedication to UFO phenomena. Even though he was gravely ill and about to die, he was willing to sacrifice his time to continuing his UFO work by inviting me to his home in Arizona to talk to him.

Figure 86 shows Hynek, who was the director, walking toward the Northwestern University's Lindheimer Astrophysical Research Center, and Figure 87 shows J. Allen Hynek, Jennie Zeidman, and Charles Bowen, the editor of *Flying Saucer Review* (*FSR*).

At this time he was ill and near the end of his life. He died two months later on April 27, 1986. Jennie's trip to see him was made just before he died.

But even through his illness and knowledge that he did not have long to live, he continued work on the UFO topic. He worked with Dr. Willy Smith on the development of a computerized database. Smith's PhD in 1964 was from the University of Michigan. He worked at an Atomic Energy Commission Facility in Puerto Rico, and then devoted the rest of his professional career to education, teaching physics at the University of Michigan and other places. He became interested in UFOs in the fifties. He decided, in 1980, to devote himself full time to the study of the UFO phenomena. By the end of 1983 with Dr. Hynek, he initiated the UNICAT Project, first conceived as a database of high-quality UFO cases. Later, the project expanded into a full-fledged research activity and it presently has many collaborators and associates all over the world.[199]

As Mark O'Connell in *The Close Encounters Man*, described his illness and death. Hynek was to give a talk about his recent trip to France to lobby for GEPAN. Willy Smith was also there to make a presentation of the ways UNICAT would catalog UFO data so that the scientific community would pay attention-in other words to make a scientific bases for UFO study using computers.

But when Hynek took the stage, he faltered and David Jacobs asked to deliver the paper for him. During the ensuing Q&A session, Hynek had trouble answering the questions.

The next day Hynek came to the table with Willy Smith but did not want to eat.

Several weeks later he was diagnosed with prostate cancer and had surgery for this. But while he was in the hospital, a brain scan revealed a brain tumor.

I talked to him on the phone around this time and he was trying to find out more about brain cancer and what to do.

When Hynek showed up for his brain surgery, he appeared frail and walked slowly. He began radiation treatments.

I have some of Zeidman's photographs from this time and he actually looked fairly good for his age and condition, but not as vigorous as in the many days of his good health.

Zeidman, who had always ribbed him about his prediction that he would die when the comet returned, had a long-standing date with him and Mimi to go comet watching when Halley's Comet returned, which was the trip mentioned in my letter.

In March as they traveled through southern Arizona, they turned their Honda off the main highway onto a gravel road where other sky-watchers had taken up positions.[200] She said there was a silence of the moment and compared to that felt in an art museum or a religious site.

Hynek had brought along the last issue of *Sky & Telescope* and they began to identify the stars. Then in a moment the spaceman who was born under the comet seventy-six years earlier was having his last encounter with it. [201]

> Hynek told friends he wanted to go out the way he came in– 'with the comet.' Some of his first astronomy students recalled Hynek telling them the comet would be back, in 1985-1986. Look for it, he said. The man whose phrase Steven Spielberg borrowed for his film *Close Encounters of the Third Kind* had a proverbial last wish: he wanted to see the comet again before he died, like Mark Twain, who saw it at the beginning and the end of his life.
> So at 4 A.M. on March 26, 1986, Allen Hynek climbed into the Honda's reclining right-hand seat, a pillow beneath his head, the March issue of *Sky & Telescope* and a pair of binoculars in his lap, his wife Mimi at the steering wheel, his longtime friend and fellow researcher Jennie Zeidman in the back. All were filled with Allen's great expectancy as they passed observer-filled cars parked off to the side and continued into the desert where they found a quiet place to park on a dirt road.
> 'The three of us got out of the car. Gravel crunched underfoot, traffic hummed in the distance and there were the low whisperings of other observers nearby,' Zeidman remembers. 'We could have been in an art museum or at some religious place, where there is great respect for the privacy and emotion of others.'
> They spotted Saturn and Mars easily enough. Then they thought they saw the comet, but were mistaken. They turned their flashlights to the charts so they could try again. Hynek leaned

against the car. Suddenly, there it was! 'No wonder we hadn't seen it before,' Zeidman says. 'It was just now rising, the tail streaming like a feather in its cap.' Hynek stood in silence as his mythic comet rose and the Earth turned. Soon they knew it was time to leave, and they did. It was all over so quickly. Hynek had gotten his wish.

He died a month and a day later, on April 27, 1986.

The world lost an extraordinary soul.

******

CHAPTER THIRTEEN

CONCLUSIONS

We found many, many smoking guns in this research. Some have the potential to confirm the many legends about UFOs and others differ.

Perhaps the most important discovery was J. Allen Hynek, himself. Through his letters, we can know him as a person, rather than simply a UFO expert or astronomer. He was very human with a great sense of humor, and tendency to joke. There has always been much controversy about whether he was truly interested in UFO phenomena, or was just getting attention. The reality is that he was very dedicated to exploring the subject, went about it in a scientific manner, and often with personal sacrifice.

His letters discussed many episodes and events in his life. They provide almost a diary of the most important points in his life, such as when he dissociated from the government and set up his own agency. They also tell about his investigation of some interesting UFO cases.

We also were able to directly explore the secrets of WP and there are many. Collins, Doty, Schmitt, Carey, Carl Day, Len Stringfield, and Stan Friedman have interviewed many people about WP. They have heard stories about a vast portion of the base being underground with bunkers, tunnels large enough for trucks, manmade hills in Area B, and large hangars with no windows. They had observed clusters of ventilation pipes coming out of the ground with no buildings around them, and large open areas with heavy metal doors going into the side of a hill. They were told that the Propulsion Research and Development building had a walkway/ramp that lead to an underground door, and also heard about underground-refrigerated rooms. Others have told about these highly secured areas, such as the Blue Room. And there are many stories about Hanger 18.

We have not only been inside WP's sacred corridors, including the most hidden of it all, but have photographed some. Thus, unlike others, we have not only been there and seen the actual areas, but we also have something with which to actually document this information.

For example, there are many stories about Hanger 18. Most people have identified this with WP Building 18. But with our informants and on-base investigation, we have found a more likely place for this building. This is one of a group of actual Hangers. Our source told us which one. This is a more probable place because it is a real hanger, it was built before 1947, and it was on the old WF runway. We have photographed it from on base and seen its surroundings.

The Roswell debris is said to have been unloaded to Hanger 18 from a B-29 that carried it from Roswell. We have photographed a B-29 in front of this group of hangers. We even wondered if the B-29 might still be at WP. Perhaps it is the one we photographed.

However although Buildings 18 and 23 are called Hangers 28 and 23, by other authors who think they are the Hanger 18, they look nothing like hangers and are not near any of the former runways. There is no history that they ever were hangers.

We investigated and photographed Building 18 and Building 23, where UFO debris and aliens are said to have been stored. We did find some possible evidence that a sub-basement area exists in Building 18 and this might connect to a passageway into Building 23.

Other accounts tell about a vast portion of the base being underground with bunkers, tunnels large enough for trucks, manmade hills in Area B, and large hangars with no windows. There are tales of clusters of ventilation pipes coming out of the ground with no buildings around them, and large open areas with heavy metal doors going into the side of a hill.

We have driven through Area B and what we saw in some ways supports and in other ways conflicts with this description.

For example, there are tales that Building 620, the Avionics Laboratory, is the location of large important vaults at WP. Our photography may provide smoking gun evidence of this.

Collins and Doty told that one entrance to the underground vault system, according to their sources, was down a set of stairs under the avionics tower. He writes that there were two freight-sized elevators under the tower. One of these went to a second basement area.

Our photography could certainly be used to confirm this, because a large, heavy-duty ramp goes into Building 620. We photographed huge doors through which trucks could easily enter. We have not seen photographs of this previously.

But unlike the other stories of the large open areas with heavy metal doors going into the side of a hill, we did not see this.

However it certainly appears possible that trucks could enter through Building 620, travel down the reported elevators, and then through the series of tunnels. We also saw digging in long narrow strips that might have gone into the tunnel areas.

Collins and Doty said that double vaulted doors in 620 led to a long hallway with a second set of double vaulted doors to an elevator and stairs and then a tunnel that led to one of the chief vaults under the north parking lot of 620. This is where debris and possibly even aliens are said to have been stored.

We also saw and photographed this parking lot at a time when much digging was in progress in that area. The machines we photographed here were used for the digging. They were the excavator type with long bucket arms used to dig holes and move dirt. They were not the type used to resurface a parking lot, such as scrapers and graders. In addition, large piles of dirt were in various areas here that were not road debris.

This photography could confirm that this vault exists.

Another legendary area is that where the Project BB headquarters and the Blue Room are located. Although these buildings have been torn down, the NASIC building has taken their place. This building is so secure that it has been identified as the office of record for the Blue Room. We have photographed and been inside this building and even attended a meeting about UFOs here that gave us a suspicion that secure work on UFOs might still be going on. It is the building where work on satellite photography takes place and this might be a logical successor to the gun camera and posted cameras whose planning was described in the Pentacle Memo.

Thus the photography and our memories might confirm some of these legends and reports.
We were also the first to interview the Holt sisters about the Cordell Hull account of aliens and craft stored in a Capital basement.

The documents from Battelle are unpublished and tell much secret information about the BB investigation. They contain new material about a number of UFOlogists and government workers and tell of many little-known connections. They also show inside information about many at the top of the hierarchy of UFOlogists, celebrities, and scientific investigators.

For example, we have information about the views of three presidents of Battelle.

They cover the inside story of BB and detail its turning point, demise, and examine how this occurred. It delves deeply into the many mysteries associated with it. For example, it explores who the people that did the actual research on *SR-14* were. It tells about the Screwball OSU professor and much else about the interaction associated with these people.

We also probed Roswell and Memory Metal. We were the first to report the smoking gun that a Battelle scientist, Elroy John Center, told that he had examined alien artifacts. Because there has been much suspicion that Battelle examined Roswell, or other, UFO debris, and because of the extreme interest in Memory Metal, this has been covered millions of times in the media already. We have continued this investigation with new findings.

I found additional examples suggesting that material that may have come from an extraterrestrial source was examined by other organizations. One was Shield Alloy of Cambridge, Ohio. Although I wondered why such a small nondescript company would be the one to receive this debris, I found many connections to WP and Battelle. The description of the material they received differed from many others, but it was more in line with the actual description of the debris. I found many hidden connections among corporations in this investigation.

Interesting points include his interactions with Neil Armstrong and the possibility that we have some confirming evidence of Armstrong's interest in UFOs.

This also goes into a psychosocial study of why the highly significant statistical findings of the massive *SR-14* were ignored and even lied about. It also details the lying behind the Robertson Panel and gives an inside view of the interactions associated with this and the Pentacle Memo.

One reason such ideas as those behind Roswell are not accepted is because they are not prosaic. This is the same reason perfectly logical results such as the less than one billion to one chance found by good statistics in *SR-14* are unacceptable. The ideas are weird; they consist of aliens flying space ships around earth, landing and crashing. And they show things that are not under human control, which our controlling government and religious structures do not seem to tolerate–the entire universe should be entirely under human control.

However you do not have to reach into the supernatural to consider the possibility that something from space crashed at Roswell, or elsewhere.

Altogether, we not only found many such smoking guns, but unlike many, we can document these findings. We have also found much chicanery, fudging, lying, and other ways to misrepresent UFO phenomenon. The initial UFO studies were done in a scientific organized manner. But at the very time, headway in understanding the phenomenon occurred; the government changed the entire field into buffoonery. Our present view of UFOs is from a government media campaign, rather than actual study.

This book can help to answer some questions, such as how did today's state of affairs come about? And what in the early history of UFOs caused the subject to arise out of very serious concern from both scientists and government authorities into the view of ridicule seen today? It looks at the motives of some of the researchers and examines the mechanism of the cover-up. But BB is still filled with many mysteries. And we still know nothing about major questions, Why does the cover-up exist? And What are UFOs?

******

REFERENCES

"15 Sightings of UFOs Reported Near Dayton," *Columbus Dispatch* October 11, 1973: 13A.
Alberta UFO Study Group. "Summaries of Some Recent Opinion Polls on UFOs." *Extraterrestrial Contact*. 2011. <http://www.ufoevidence.org/documents/doc999.htm>.
Aldrich, Jan. Project 1947: A Preliminary Report. *UFO Research Coalition*. 1997.
Allen, William. "The Branch Office." *Reader's Digest* January, 1985: 157-162.
Andrus, Walter, and Irena Scott, eds. *The Fiftieth Anniversary of UFOlogy*. MUFON 1997 International UFO Symposium Proceedings: Mutual UFO Network Inc., 1997.
___. *UFOs in the New Millennium*. MUFON 2000 International UFO Symposium Proceedings: Mutual UFO Network Inc., 2000.
Arnold, Kenneth, and Ray Palmer. *The Coming of the Saucers*. Boise, ID, and Amherst, WI: Kenneth Arnold and Ray Palmer, 1952.
Balint, Ed. "Canton's Close Encounter," *The Repository* August 22, 2010: A1, A6.
Barker, Gray. *MIB: The Secret Terror among Us*. Jane Lew, WV: New Age Books, 1983.
___. *The Silver Bridge*. Clarksburg, WV: Saucerian Books, 1970.
___. *They Knew Too Much about Flying Saucers*. New York: University Books, 1956.
Beckley, Timothy Green. *MJ-12 and the Riddle of Hangar 18: The New Evidence*. New Brunswick, NJ: Inner Light—Global Communications, 2003.
Bender, Albert K. *Flying Saucers and the Three Men*. New York: Paperback Library, 1968.
Berlitz, Charles, and William L. Moore. *The Roswell Incident*. New York: Grosset & Dunlap, 1980.
Bragalia, Anthony. "The Final Secrets of Roswell's Memory Metal Revealed." *The UFO Iconoclast(s)*. June 7, 2009. <http://ufocon.blogspot.com/2009/06/final-secrets-of-roswells-memory-metal.html>.
___. "Roswell Alcoholics: The Alien Anguish." *The UFO Iconoclast(s)*. March 14, 2010. <http://ufocon.blogspot.com/2010/03/roswell-alcoholics-alien-anguish-by.html>.
___. "Roswell, Battelle & Memory Metal: The New Revelations." Posted by Maria Luisa de Vasconcellos. *Light Eye: Tribute to an UFO Watcher*. August 8, 2010. <http://fgportugal.blogspot.com/2010_08_01_archive.html>.
___. "Roswell Debris Confirmed as Extraterrestrial: Lab Located, Scientists Named." *The UFO Iconoclast(s)*. May 26, 2009. <http://ufocon.blogspot.com/2009/05/roswell-debris-confirmed-as.html>.
___. "Roswell Debris Inspired Memory Metal Nitinol; Lab Located. Scientists Named." *MUFON UFO Journal* (July, 2009): 3-10.
___. "Roswell Metal Scientist: The Curious Dr. Cross." *The UFO Iconoclast(s)*. May 21, 2009. <http://ufocon.blogspot.com/2009/05/roswell-metal-scientist-curious-dr.html>.
___. "Scientist Admits to Study of Roswell Crash Debris." *The UFO Iconoclast(s)*. August 16, 2009. <http://ufocon.blogspot.com/2009/08/scientist-admits-to-study-of-roswell.html>.
"Brilliant Fireball Flashes across Midwest," *Columbus Dispatch* December 10, 1965: 1A.
Brown, Dan. *The Lost Symbol*. New York: Doubleday Books, 2009.
Burrafato, Kim. "Redfern Sheds Light on the Real 'Men in Black.'" *MUFON UFO Journal* (August, 2011): 3 and 19.
Burrell, Paul, and Paul Althouse. "Ross and Pike Counties, Ohio April/May 1996." *Ohio UFO Notebook* 12 (1996): 8-10.
Burrell, Paul, Delbert Anderson, William E. Jones, and Irena Scott. "Dancing Red Lights, Logan,

Ohio, October/November, 1995." *MUFON of Ohio Newsletter* (November, 2009): 4-5.
Carey, Thomas J., and Donald R. Schmitt. *Witness to Roswell: Unmasking the Government's Biggest Cover-Up*. Franklin Lakes, NJ: New Page Books, 2009.
___. "*Inside the Real Area 51: The Secret History of Wright Patterson*," Franklin Lakes, NJ: New Page Books, 2013.
Chamberlain, Von Del, and David Krause. "The Fireball of December 9, 1965, Part I: Calculation of the Trajectory and Orbit by Photographic Triangulation of the Train." *Journal of the Royal Astronomical Society of Canada* (August, 1967): 184-90.
"City Couples, Ohio Police Chase UFO," *New Castle News* April 18, 1966: 1.
Clark, Jerome. *The UFO Book*. Detroit: Visible Ink Press, 1998.
___. *Unexplained! 347 Strange Sightings, Incredible Occurrences, and Puzzling Physical Phenomena*. Detroit: Visible Ink Press, 1993.
Coleman, Ted. *Jack Northrop and the Flying Wing*. New York: Paragon House, 1988.
Collins, Robert M., Richard C. Doty, and Timothy S. Cooper. *Exempt from Disclosure*. Vandalia, OH: Peregrine Communications, 2005.
Condon, Edward U. *Scientific Study of Unidentified Flying Objects*. Boston: E.P. Dutton, 1969.
Denzler, Brenda. *The Lure of the Edge: Scientific Passions, Religious Beliefs, and the Pursuit of UFOs*. Berkeley: University of California Press, 2003.
___. "Who Are We?" *MUFON UFO Journal* (May, 1977): 9-14.
Desguin, Lillian Crowner. *UFOs: Fact or Fiction?* Laguna Hills, CA: Aegean Park Press, 1992.
Dolan, Richard. *UFOs and the National Security State: An Unclassified History, Volume 1: 1941-1973*. New York: Keyhole Publishing, 2000.
Dunlap, J.R., E.J.Weiler, and J.A.Hynek. "Astronomical Photometry and Other Recent Applications of the Image Orthicon." *Advances in Electronics and Electron Physics* Vol. 40, Part B, 1976, Pages 901-911.
Fawcett, Lawrence, and Barry J. Greenwood. *Clear Intent: The Government Cover-Up of the UFO Experience*. Englewood Cliffs, NJ: Prentice-Hall, 1984.
___. *The UFO Cover-Up: What the Government Won't Say*. Old Tappan, NJ: Fireside, 1990.
"Fireballs Are Blamed in Elyria Grass Blazes," *The Plain Dealer* December 10, 1965: A1.
"'Fireball' Slams into County from Lake Erie to Eaton," *The Chronicle-Telegram* December 10, 1965: 1, 3.
Fowler, Raymond E. *UFOs: Interplanetary Visitors*. Bloomington, IN: iUniverse, 2001.
___. *The Watchers: The Secret Design behind UFO Abduction*. New York: Bantam, 1991.
Friedman, Stanton. "Arsenic and (the Same) Old Story: Media Fascination with Aliens Is Misguided." *MUFON UFO Journal* (January, 2011): 8-9.
___. "More 'why'questions." *MUFON UFO Journal* (October, 2016): 6-7.
___. "A Scientific Approach to Flying Saucer Behavior." In *Thesis Antithesis: Proceedings of a Symposium Sponsored by A IAA and World Future Society* (Los Angeles, CA, September, 1975): 22-36.
___. "*Top Secret/Majic*. New York, Marlowe & Company, 1996
"From Albert Rosales' 'World of Strangeness,' 2008—# 83." *Truth Seeker Forum*. March 18, 2009. <http://truthseekerforum.com/?s=elk+county+pa>.
Fuller, John. *Interrupted Journey: Two Lost Hours aboard a Flying Saucer*. New York: Dial Press, 1966.
Good, Timothy. *Above Top Secret: The Worldwide UFO Cover-Up*. New York: Quill Publishing, 1989.

___. *Need to Know: UFOs, the Military, and Intelligence*. New York: Pegasus Books, 2007.
Hall, Richard. *The UFO Evidence*. New York: Barnes & Noble, 1997.
___. *Uninvited Guests: A Documented History of UFO Sightings, Alien Encounters, and Cover-Ups*. Santa Fe, NM: Aurora Press, 1988.
"Have We Ever Had a Piece of a Flying Disk?" *The Big Study*. December 18, 2009. <http://thebiggeststudy.blogspot.com/2009/12/have-we-ever-had-piece-of-flying-disk.html>.
Hesemann, Michael, and Philip Mantle. *Beyond Roswell: The Alien Autopsy Film, Area 51, & the U.S. Government Cover-Up of UFOs*. New York: Marlowe & Company, 1998.
Hilkevitch, Jon. "In the Sky! A Bird? A Plane? A . . . UFO?," *Chicago Tribune* January 1, 2007: 1.1.
Holt, Turner Hamilton. *Life's Convictions*. New York: Vantage Press, 1956.
Hopkins, Budd. *Intruders: The Incredible Visitations at Copley Woods*. New York: Random House, 1987.
___. *Missing Time*. New York: Berkley, 1983.
Hynek, J. Allen and Necia H. Apfel. *Astronomy One*, W.A. Benjamin, Menlo Park, California, 1972.
___. *The UFO Controversy in America*. Bloomington, IN: Indiana University Press, 1975.
___. *The UFO Experience: A Scientific Inquiry*. Chicago: Henry Regnery Company, 1972.
Jacobs, David. *UFOs and Abductions: Challenging the Borders of Knowledge*. Lawrence, KS: University Press of Kansas, 2000.
Jacobsen, Annie. *Area 51: An Uncensored History of America's Top Secret Military Base*. New York: Little, Brown and Company, 2011.
Jones, William E. "Another MJ-12 Document." *Ohio UFO Notebook* 11 (1996): 11-14.
___. "Books and Articles of Note." *Ohio UFO Notebook* 10 (1995): 14-18.
___. "Confirmation of UFOlogy's Darker Side." *Ohio UFO Notebook* (July, 1993): 4-7.
___. "Confirmation That J. Allen Hynek Communicated with Neil Armstrong." *MUFON of Ohio Newsletter* (Spring, 2008): 7-8.
___. "Darlington, Ohio, October, 1953: A Case That Can't Be Documented." *Ohio UFO Notebook* 1 (August, 1991): 15-17.
___. "Historical Notes: Thomas Mantell." *MUFON UFO Journal* (April, 1990): 18-19.
___. "Human Mutilations Again." *Ohio UFO Notebook* 6 and 7 (July, 1993): 13-14.
___. "Information, Disinformation, Hints, or Lies ?" *Ohio UFO Notebook* 11 (1996): 24-25.
___. "Neil Armstrong and Len Stringfield." *Ohio UFO Notebook* 9 (1995): 20-21.
___. "Point Pleasant, West Virginia Moth Man Follow Up." *Ohio UFO Notebook* 1 (August, 1991): 12.
___. "Project Grudge/Bluebook Special Report 13." *Ohio UFO Notebook* 15 (1997): 1-2.
Jones, William E., and Irena Scott. "June 20-23, 1985, Columbus." *Ohio UFO Notebook* 12 (1996): 19-22.
___. "Laurie, Missouri." *Ohio UFO Notebook* 12 (1996): 26-27.
___. "North American Aviation, Columbus, Ohio, Test Site for UFO Materials?" *Ohio UFO Notebook* 12 (1996): 35-37.
___. "The Spaur Case—Reporting a UFO Can Be Hazardous to Your Health." *Ohio UFO Notebook* 14 (1997): 36-40.
___. "U.S. Navy Support of UFO Research." *Ohio UFO Notebook* 11 (1996): 5-6.
Jones, William E., and Eloise G. Watson. "Pre-World War II 'Creature' Retrieval?" *International UFO Reporter* (Winter, 2001-2002): 6-30.

Keel, John. *The Mothman Prophecies*. New York: Saturday Review Press, 1975.
Kelleher, Colm A., and George Knapp. *Hunt for the Skinwalker: Science Confronts the Unexplained at a Remote Ranch in Utah*. New York: Paraview Pocket Books, 2005.
Keyhoe, Donald. *The Flying Saucers Are Real* (reprint). New York: Cosimo Classics, 2004.
Klass, Philip J. "CIA Mission." *MUFON UFO Journal* (February, 1993): 20.
Lang, Richard. "The SIP Project—Star Team Report." *MUFON UFO Journal* (July, 2009): 7.
___. "Woman and Dog Observe Multiple Lights, Orbs." *MUFON UFO Journal* (August, 2009): 9-10.
LIFE_Magazine_Trent_Photoshoot_1950 - Roswell Proof. "1950 LIFE Magazine Trent UFO photoshoot." http://www.roswellproof.com/LIFE_Magazine_Trent_Photoshoot_1950.html
Maccabee, Bruce S. *Historical Introduction to* Project Blue Book Special Report No. 14. Evanston, IL: Center for UFO Studies, 1979.
___. *The FBI CIA UFO Connection*. New York: Richard Dolan Press, 2014.
___. "Scientific Investigation of Unidentified Flying Objects," parts 1-2, *JUFOS*, vols. 1 (1979) and 3 (1983).
McAndrew, James. *The Roswell Report: Case Closed*. Washington, DC: Headquarters, United States Air Force, 1997.
Morrell, David. *The Shimmer*. New York: Vanguard Press, 2009.
Moseley, James. *UFO Crash Secrets at Wright-Patterson Air Force Base*. Wilmington, DE: Abelard Productions, 1991.
"No Reports UFO Seen in County," *Albany Times Union* April 18, 1966: n.p. Newspaper clipping. Irena Scott Private Collection, Lewis Center, OH.
O'Connell, Mark. *The Close Encounters Man*, New York: HarperCollins, 2017.
Oberg, James. "French 'Flap' a Flop?" *MUFON UFO Journal* (September, 1992): 21.
"Photos Taken of 4 UFOs," *Columbus Dispatch* October 18, 1973: 1A.
Project Blue Book Special Report No. 14 (Analysis of Reports of Unidentified Flying Objects). Wright-Patterson Air Force Base, OH: Air Technical Intelligence Center, 1955.
Project-1947 – Air Intelligence Report 100-203-79, "Analysis of Flying Object Incidents in the U.S." Headquarters United States Air Force Directorate of Intelligence, Washington, D.C., 1949.
"RAAF Captures Flying Saucer on Ranch in Roswell Region," *Roswell Daily Record* July 8, 1947: 1.
Randle, Kevin D. *A History of UFO Crashes*. New York: Avon Books, 1995.
___. *The UFO Casebook*. New York: Warner Books, 1989.
Randle, Kevin D., and Donald R. Schmitt. "Roswell and the Flying Wing." *International UFO Reporter* (July/August, 1995): 10-12.
___. *The Truth about the UFO Crash at Roswell*. New York: M. Evans and Company, Inc., 1994.
___. *The UFO Dossier: 100 Years of Government Secrets, Conspiracies, and Cover-Ups.* Detroit: Visible Ink Press, 2015.
___. *UFO Crash at Roswell*. New York: Avon, 1991.
Randles, Jenny. *The Truth Behind Men in Black: Government Agents -- or Visitors from Beyond*. New York: St. Martin's Paperbacks; St. Martin's, 1997.
___. *The UFO Conspiracy: The First Forty Years*. New York: Barnes & Noble, 1987.
___. *UFO Retrievals: The Recovery of Alien Spacecraft*. London: Blandford Press, 1995.
Reams, Frank B. "Troy, Ohio, July 1, 1991." *Ohio UFO Notebook* (December, 1991): 44-45.
___. "TV Show Encourages UFO Reports." *Ohio UFO Notebook* 9 (1995): 22-23.
Reams, Frank B., and Barbara Spellerberg. "Columbus, Ohio, Late Fall 1966 Ohio Penitentiary

Sighting—Preliminary Report." *Ohio UFO Notebook* 1 (August, 1991): 7-9.

Reddit UFOs/CaerBannog. "Kevin Randle Distances Himself from Schmitt, Carey, Bragalia & Dew's "Roswell Slides." https://www.reddit.com/r/UFOs/comments/2xntee/kevin_randle_distances_himself_from_schmitt_carey/

Richelson, Jeffrey T. *America's Secret Eyes in Space: The U.S. Keyhole Satellite Program*. New York: HarperCollins, 1990.

Ridge, Francis. *Regional Encounters*. Mt.Vernon, IN: UFO Filter Center, 1994.

Ring, Kenneth. *The Omega Project: Near-Death Experiences, UFO Encounters, and Mind at Large*. New York: William Morrow & Co., 1992.

Rondinone, Peter. "Antimatter." *OMNI Magazine* May, 1982: 114.

Rosales, Albert. "1935-1939 Humanoid Reports." *UFOInfo*. 2011. <http://www.ufoinfo.com/humanoid/humanoid1935.shtml>.

Ruppelt, Edward J. *The Report on Unidentified Flying Objects*. New York: Doubleday, 1956.

Rutledge, Harley D. *Project Identification: The First Scientific Field Study of UFO Phenomena*. Englewood Cliffs, NJ: Prentice-Hall, 1981.

The (St Mary's) Evening Leader, "Big Blast, UFO's Shake People Over Wide Area," October 12, 1973.

Schuessler, John F. *The Cash-Landrum UFO Incident*. La Porte, TX: Geo Graphics, 1998.

Scott, Irena. "A Photograph and its aftermath" *International UFO Reporter* (September/October, 1990): 12-14.

___. "Bedroom Light" *International UFO Reporter* (March/April, 1988): 14-15.

___."Additional Information Wright-Patterson AFB (WPAFB)." *Ohio UFO Notebook* (January, 1994): 23-24.

___. "CIA, UFO Photography, and Tunnels." *Ohio UFO Notebook* (July, 1993): 34-40.

___. "Crisman, Military Intelligence, and Roswell." *Ohio UFO Notebook* (May, 1992): 27-32.

___. "DCSC Update." *Ohio UFO Notebook* (January, 1994): 34.

___. "Description of an Aerial Anomaly Viewed over Columbus, Ohio." *Ohio Journal of Science* 88.2 (1988): 23.

___. "Examination of Social and Environmental Factors in Relation to Unidentified Aerial Phenomena." In *American Association for the Advancement of Science Abstracts of Papers 153rd National Meeting* (Chicago, IL, February 14-18, 1987): 93.

___. "Fear and ambiguity in Massachusetts" *International UFO Reporter* (July/August, 1988): 14-17.

___. "Informants." *Ohio UFO Notebook* (January, 1994): 24.

___. "Inside the Lightning Ball: Scientific Study of Lifelong UFO Experiencers, UK: Flying Disk Press, 2018.

___. "Interview with Budd Hopkins." *Ohio UFO Notebook* (January, 1994): 23.

___. "Interview with an Informant." *Ohio UFO Notebook* (July, 1993): 19-23.

___. "Investigation of a Sound Heard over a Wide Area." *Ohio Journal of Science* 87.2 (1987): 11.

___. "Is MORA under Surveillance?" *Ohio UFO Notebook* (July, 1993): 32-34.

___. "More Cattle Mutilation Information." *Ohio UFO Notebook* (January, 1994): 35.

___. "Observation of an Alien Figure." *International UFO Reporter* (January/February, 1987): 20-25.

___. "Ohio UFOlogists." *Ohio UFO Notebook (*January, 1994): 27.

___. *Ohio UFOs (and Many Others)*. Columbus, OH: Greyden Press, 1997.

___. "Ohioans in Aerospace Exploration." *Ohio UFO Notebook* (January, 1994): 31.
___. "Photogrammetric Analysis of a Photograph of an Aerial Anomaly." In *American Association for the Advancement of Science Abstracts of Papers 154th National Meeting* (Boston, MA, February 11-15, 1988): 86.
___. "A Power Failure." *Ohio UFO Notebook* (January, 1994): 34.
___. "Rectangular UFOs." *Ohio UFO Notebook* 12 (1996): 14-18.
___. "Scientists should look closely at the Big Bang, 1973's great wave of UFOs," *MUFON UFO Journal* (March, 2011): 6-7.
___. "SR-71 explanation for the Big Bang of 1973 poses some thorny problems," *MUFON UFO Journal* (May, 2011): 8-9.
___. "Survey of Unidentified Aerial Phenomenon Reports in Delaware County, Ohio." *Ohio Journal of Science* 87.1 (1987): 24-26.
___. "The Ohio UFO Crash Connection and Other Stories." *Ohio UFO Notebook* (Summer, 1994): 19-20.
___. "Tracking Traces." *MUFON UFO Journal* (September, 1991): 8-9.
___. "UFO Activity over Ohio." *MUFON UFO Journal* (May, 1986): 4-5.
___. "UFO Reports from the North Columbus Area, Report 1." *Ohio UFO Notebook* (July, 1993): 24.
___. "UFO Reports from the North Columbus Area, Report 2." *Ohio UFO Notebook* (July, 1993): 24-25.
___. *UFOs and the Millennium*. Columbus, OH: Greyden Press, 1999.
___. *UFOs Today: 70 Years of Lies, Misinformation and Government Cover-up*, UK: Flying Disk Press, 2017.
___. "Wright Patterson Air Force Base." *Ohio UFO Notebook* 6 and 7 (July, 1993): 35-40.
Scott, Irena, and Pete Hartinger. "Defense Construction and Supply Center (DCSC)." *Ohio UFO Notebook* (July, 1993): 27-29.
Scott, Irena, and William Jones. "Aircraft Missing, South Dakota, Summer 1957." *Ohio UFO Notebook* 13 (1997): 10-11.
___. "Bruce Ashcroft." *Ohio UFO Notebook* 10 (1995): 2-4.
___. "The Little Green Men of Wright-Patt." *Ohio UFO Notebook* 10 (1995): 1-2.
___. "The Ohio UFO Crash Connection and Other Stories." *Ohio UFO Notebook* (Summer, 1994): 19-20.
___. "An Original Crash Story Remembered." *Ohio UFO Notebook* 9 (1995): 1-6.
___. "Roswell, the B-29, and the FUGO Balloons." *Ohio UFO Notebook* 6 and 7 (July, 1993): 30.
___. "Telephone Conversation with Len Stringfield." *Ohio UFO Notebook* (Summer, 1994): 31.
___. "UFO Sighted over Missile Base in Southern Indiana." *MUFON UFO Journal* (December, 1999): 10-11
___. "Wright-Patterson Air Force Base Historian Investigates the Roswell, New Mexico Flying Saucer Crash Story." *Ohio UFO Notebook* 9 (1995): 1-3.
Shawcross, Tim. *The Roswell Files*. Osceola, FL: Motorbooks International, 1997.
Sider, Jean. "Results and Reasons for the Roswell Crash." *Ohio UFO Notebook* (1995): 7-11.
Sider, Jean, and Irena Scott. "French Flap Goes Largely Unnoticed." *MUFON UFO Journal* (May, 1992): 6-7.
___. "Roswell and Its Possible Consequences on American Policy." *MUFON UFO Journal* (December, 1992): 10-11.
Simmons, C. W., C.T. Greenidge, C.M. Craighead, and others. "Second Progress Report Covering

the Period September 1 to October 21, 1949 on Research and Development on Titanium Alloys Contract No. 33 (038)-3736." Columbus, OH: Battelle Memorial Institute, 1949.

Spearing, Robert. "New witness surfaces in Pantex Plant case." *MUFON UFO Journal* (December 2016): 12-15.

Story, Ronald D. *The Encyclopedia of UFOs*. Garden City, NY: Doubleday, 1980.

Stringfield, Leonard H. *Situation Red. The UFO Siege!* Garden City, NY: Doubleday, 1977.

Sunlite. "Confessions of a sinister, stalking, lying Skeptic!" http://home.comcast.net/~tprinty/UFO/SUNlite1_4.pdf

Swords, Michael D. "The Portage County (Ravenna), Ohio, Police Car Chase, April 17, 1966." Historical Document Series No. 4. Chicago: The J. Allen Hynek Center for UFO Studies, October, 1992.

___. Swords, Michael D. "Project Sign and the Estimate of the Situation," *Journal of UFO Studies, New Series*, Vol. 7, (2000): 27-64.

Tester, Joseph. "Evidence shows SR-71 Blackbird may have caused the Big Bang of 1973." *MUFON UFO Journal* (April, 2011): 4-5.

"Technical Report No. F-TR-2274-IA Unidentified Aerial Objects Project 'Sign' AMC Wright-Patterson Air Force Base. (B1 UFO 1947)." Wright-Patterson Air Force Base, OH: Air Mobility Command, 1947.

Thompson, Richard. *Alien Identities: Ancient Insights into Modern UFO Phenomena*. Alachua, FL: Govardhan Hill Publishing, 1995.

"Tritium Consolidation Comparison Study: Risk Analysis, DOE/DP/00248-H1." Wright-Patterson Air Force Base, OH: December 1992.

UFO Cover-Up? Live! By Barry Taff and Tracy Tormé. Dir. Martin Pasetta. Host Mick Farrell. LBS and Seligman Productions. KTLA, Los Angeles. October 14, 1988.

"UFOs A to Z: Cooke, Charles, Lt. Col." *UFOS at Close Sight*. November 17, 2010. <http://wiki.razing.net/ufologie.net/htm/c.htm#cooke>.

Vallée, Jacques. *Forbidden Science*. Berkeley, CA: North Atlantic Books, 1992.

Von Keviczky, Colman. "The 1973 UFO Invasion, Parts I-IV." *Official UFO* (Collector's Edition) Fall, 1976: 10-20.

Webb, Walter, *Encounter at Buff Ledge*, Chicago, Il: CUFOS, 1994.

___."Inside Building 263: A visit to Blue Book," 1956." *International UFO Reporter* (September/October, 1992): 3-5.

Weitzel, William B. "The Portage County Sighting." *National Investigations Committee on Aerial Phenomena (NICAP) Report*. Washington, DC: NICAP, April 8, 1967.

Wilkins, Harold. *Flying Saucers on the Attack*. New York: Ace, 1954.

Young, Kenny. "The Lebanon Correctional Institute, April 8, 1993." *Ohio UFO Notebook* 12 (1996): 27-28.

___. "The Monsanto Research Complex and the 'Seeding' of America." *Ohio UFO Notebook* 15 (1997): 9-12.

___. "The Wrong Liberty, Ohio—How Ohio Police React to UFO Incidents." *Ohio UFO Notebook* 13 (1997): 1-8.

Zeidman, Jennie. *Helicopter-UFO Encounter over Ohio*. Evanston, IL: Center for UFO Studies, 1979.

WPAFB. "National Air and Space Intelligence Center History." http://www.wpafb.af.mil/library/factsheets/factsheet.asp?id=21928

___. "I Remember Blue Book." *International UFO Reporter* (March/April, 1991): 7-23.

___. "Internal Lighting." *International UFO Reporter* (July/August, 1988): 21.
___. "Investigating UFOs—Lessons from a Teacher and Mentor." *Ohio UFO Notebook* 21 (Summer, 2000): 1-7.
___. "J. Allen Hynek—A 'Rocket Man.'" *Ohio UFO Notebook* (Summer, 1999): 2-5.
___. and Mark Rodeghier. 'The Pentacle Letter and The Battelle UFO Project." *International UFO Reporter* (May/June, 1993): 4-22.

******

APPENDIX I THE PENTACLE MEMO

It said:
SECRET
SECURITY INFORMATION

G-1579-4

cc: B. D. Thomas
     H. C. Cross/A. D. Westerman
     L. R. Jackson
     W. T. Reid
     P. J. Rieppal
     V. W. Ellsey/R. J. Lund   January 9, 1953
     Files
     Extra [handwritten]

Mr. Miles E. Goll
Box 9575
Wright-Patterson Air Force Base, Ohio

Attention Capt. Edward J. Ruppelt

Dear Mr. Goll:

This letter concerns a preliminary recommendation to ATIC on future methods of handling the problem of unidentified aerial objects. This recommendation is based on our experience to date in analyzing several thousands of reports on this subject. We regard the recommendation as preliminary because our analysis is not yet complete, and we are not able to document it where we feel it should be supported by facts from the analysis.

We are making this recommendation prematurely because of a CIA-sponsored meeting of a scientific panel, meeting in Washington, D.C., January 14, 15, and 16, 1953, to consider the problem of "flying saucers". The CIA-sponsored meeting is being held subsequent to a meeting of CIA, ATIC, and our representatives held at ATIC on December 12, 1952. At the December 12 meeting our representatives strongly recommended that a scientific panel not be set up until the results of our analysis of the sighting-reports collected by ATIC were available. Since a meeting of the panel is now definitely scheduled we feel that agreement between Project Stork and ATIC should be reached as to what can and what cannot be discussed at the meeting in Washington on January 14-16 concerning our preliminary recommendation to ATIC.

Experience to date on our study of unidentified flying objects shows that there is a distinct lack of reliable data with which to work. Even the best-documented reports are frequently lacking in critical information that makes it impossible to arrive at a possible identification, i.e. even in a well-documented report there is always an element of doubt about the data, either because the observer had no means of getting the required data, or was not prepared to utilize the means at his disposal. Therefore, we recommend that a controlled experiment be set up by which reliable physical data can be obtained. A tentative preliminary plan by which the experiment could be designed and carried out is discussed in the following paragraphs.

Based on our experience so far, it is expected that certain conclusions will be reached as a result of our analysis which will make obvious the need for an effort to obtain reliable data from competent observers using the [... unreadable...] necessary equipment. Until more reliable data are available, no positive answers to the problem will be possible.

Mr. Miles E. Goll -2- January 9, 1953

We expect that our analysis will show that certain areas in the United States have had an abnormally high number of reported incidents of unidentified flying objects. Assuming that, from our analysis, several definite areas productive of reports can be selected, we recommend that one or two of these areas be set up as experimental areas. This area, or areas, should have observation posts with complete visual skywatch, with radar and photographic coverage, plus all other instruments necessary or helpful in obtaining positive and reliable data on everything in the air over the area. A very complete record of the weather should also be kept during the time of the experiment. Coverage should be so complete that any object in the air could be tracked, and information as to its altitude, velocity, size, shape, color, time of day, etc. could be recorded. All balloon releases or known balloon paths, aircraft flights, and flights of rockets in the test area should be known to those in charge of the experiment. Many different types of aerial activity should be secretly and purposefully scheduled within the area.

We recognize that this proposed experiment would amount to a large-scale military maneuver, or operation, and that it would require extensive preparation and fine coordination, plus maximum security. Although it would be a major operation, and expensive, there are many extra benefits to be derived besides the data on unidentified aerial objects.

The question of just what would be accomplished by the proposed experiment occurs. Just how could the problem of these unidentified objects be solved? From this test area, during the time of the experiment, it can be assumed that there would be a steady flow of reports from ordinary civilian observers, in addition to those by military or other official observers. It should be possible by such a controlled experiment to prove the identity of all objects reported, or to determine positively that there were objects present of unknown identity. Any hoaxes under a set-up such as this could almost certainly be exposed, perhaps not publicly, but at least to the military.

In addition, by having resulting data from the controlled experiment, reports for the last five years could be re-evaluated, in the light of similar but positive information. This should make possible reasonably certain conclusions concerning the importance of the problem of "flying saucers".

Results of an experiment such as described could assist the Air Force to determine how much attention to pay to future situations when, as in the past summer, there were thousands of sightings reported. In the future, then, the Air Force should be able to make positive statements, reassuring to the public, and to the effect that everything is well under control.

Very truly yours,

[unsigned]

H. C. Cross

******

APPENDIX II THE PENTACLE LETTER (UNPUBLISHED DRAFT) by JENNIE ZEIDMAN, MICHAEL SWORDS, AND MARK RODEGHIER

In his 1992 book *Forbidden Science*, Jacques Vallée devotes a third of the volume, and a great deal of emotion, to "Pentacle."

The letter, dated January 9, 1953, classified Secret, and sans letterhead, is addressed to Mr. Miles E. Goll at Wright-Patterson AFB, for the attention of Capt. Edward J. Ruppelt. Goll...and an acting chief of the Analysis Division of T—2 (technical intelligence) at Wright—Pat. Major elements of the letter are (1) a recommendation that the already-scheduled scientific panel meeting in: Washington in mid—January (the Robertson Panel) be postponed; (2) that the organization the letter writer represents has examined thousands of UFO reports (and found them lacking in data quality); and (3) a recommendation that controlled, manufactured (i.e. hoax) UFO events be set up in various locations of the United States as a test of public response and observational acuity. Buried within the second paragraph of the letter is the statement that "we feel that agreement between Project Stork and ATIC should be reached as to "what can and cannot be discussed at the meeting in Washington."

Vallée thinks the letter is a major UFO document, the smoking gun which proves at last (what we've really known all along); that a secret project did indeed exist above and beyond Project Blue Book, and that the Robertson Panel of scientists, convened by the CIA in 1953, were unscrupulously fed material selected to lead them astray. So devastated was Vallée by the discovery of this document that major decisions of his life have been based upon his interpretation of it.

When *Forbidden Science* was published in June 1992, Jennie Zeidman proposed that the mysterious Pentacle was Howard C. Cross, in 1953 an Associate Coordination Director at Battelle (Columbus, Ohio.) Within a few days...her theory confirmed....
This article will present the historical context in which the letter was written (Swords), background material on Battelle and interviews with the surviving "cc:"s, (Zeidman) and an analysis and statement of the position of CUFOS with respect to these findings (Rodeghier).

Key Elements in a Pre—Pentacle USAF History

The following chronology/scenario was constructed by Michael Swords. Each element can be substantiated from documents in the CUFOS files. Comments of interpretation or analysis are shown in brackets.

In September 1951, Lt. Jerry Cummings, a Project Grudge officer, went to the Pentagon by request of Major General Cabell, head of USAF Intelligence. Cummings blasted Wright—Patterson's project disorganization and impotence at collecting proper data to solve the UFO problem. Cabell, [seemingly always sympathetic to research on this topic], was shocked (as were other generals) and ordered an overhaul and upgrade of the investigation unit.

In October and November 1951, Captain Edward Ruppelt began to take the project lead. Visiting scientists had said that the most crucial missing elements in the investigations were better estimates on size, velocity, and altitude of the objects. The project people began to think about better ways to get this sort of information.

In December 1951, Colonel Frank Dunn (MCI) and Ruppelt were called to the Pentagon to report on renovation of the project. They reported to General Samford (replacing Cabell) and General W.M. Garland, assigned to keep tabs on UFO assessment. The Project's upgrade was still "hot".

Ruppelt got the go—ahead to go to "Project Bear" (Battelle) and contract with them for help. Battelle was to help in 3 ways:

1. Employ a psychologist to assess what one might legitimately be able to expect from an observer's observational abilities and memory accuracy, and design a form to maximize the accuracy and data~richness desired in this research.

2. Do a statistical study of all available UFO reports; break them down according to about 100 variables which would be extractable from the new questionnaires, and place these on IBM punch cards for rapid sorting and pattern analysis.

3. Be on call for standing advice, ex.: better ideas about cases or data gathering, plus employment of an astronomer for continuous assessment of astronomical alternatives [**They already had Hynek??**]

From January through March, 1952, Ruppelt was trying to find better ways to collect UFO data. He established good relations with ADC (Air Defense Command), who were concerned about an increase in the number of radar cases. ADC agreed to help in 3 ways:

1. Use radarscope cameras to take pictures of scope activities whenever there was a UFO target manifesting.

2. Scramble fighters to make close approaches to UFOs if possible.

3. Organize the Ground Observer Corps to act like a UFO-spotting network, something which might also create coincident sightings allowing triangulation.

Meanwhile, Ruppelt was being called to Washington every two weeks. Dewey Fournet was appointed to relieve some of this. In the Project Grudge Status Report #3 (Jan 31, 1952) Ruppelt reported that UFOs tended to concentrate in certain geographical areas: White Sands and Albuquerque, New Mexico were two of the six noted. In Status Report #4 (Feb. 29, 1952) the continuance of Green Fireball reports was mentioned. In Report #5 (March 31, 1952) an "organized" watch for UFOs (with cameras) at Holloman AFB (NM) was reported. Dr. Joseph Kaplan, USAF Scientific Advisory Board (and Green Fireball researcher) came to Wright-Pat to suggest better data-gathering. He suggested cameras equipped with diffraction gratings for spectral analysis.

In Boston, the Air Force Technical Advisory Group (the "Beacon Hill Group") suggested the deployment of various detection devices in locations of concentrated UFO sightings. Devices could include sound detectors, and possibly cameras.

In April and May, 1952, interest in UFO phenomena and obtaining better information and advice was still "hot." Ruppelt visited RAND and UCLA (Kaplan) to talk about cameras and data gathering. Some talk was going on, at least within WP Intelligence, if not between AMC and the Pentagon, about the need to increase Blue Book's abilities to operate.*** [Need mention of name change—Grudge to BB].**

This lead to a letter by Colonel Dunn (MCI) to General Samford (5—23—52) requesting an increase in scope which would include a council of name scientists and government officials to continually advise Blue Book, and stand behind pronouncements to ensure public confidence.
Meanwhile, Ruppelt was still visiting the Pentagon, Samford et al, about every two weeks. Many Pentagon intelligence people believed the ETH. One Colonel suggested that stripped-down highest speed pursuit jets with cameras be made available.

In June, 1952, Colonel Edward N. Porter, Deputy Director for Estimates, handled the reply to Dunn for General Samford. In his letter (6-2-52), he stated that Pentagon thinking saw the Council idea as a very good one, and further recommended an outside contractor to intensively look into "the UFO problem" in hopes of an early resolution. RAND Corp. was suggested. RAND had already been contacted about the possibility.

Blue Book was elevated to Section status at T-2. (The Intelligence division at Wright—Patterson AFB). Ruppelt was now directly under MCIA Colonel Donald Bower. Bower went to the West Coast (RAND and Kaplan) to get their ideas about data gathering. The recommendation was to place extreme long focal-length cameras, double—lensed (one with a diffraction grating) around the United States in UFO hot spots. This project was considered a red-hot A-1 priority.
Ruppelt and Dunn were called to the Pentagon in mid—June due to an increase in east coast sightings. One Colonel on Samford's staff [It could have been Porter] took the lead in broaching the ETH as a serious but neglected theory. A Directive which resulted from this meeting was to take further steps to obtain positive identification of UFOs. (Ruppelt's own low—expense, low—tech hope of getting triangulation data spontaneously from multiple observers—say in cities or by GOC net——wasn't panning out.

The Pentagon, ADC, R & D Board et al were wild about saucers then. All were talking about a Top-Secret project, a Big Push, to solve the problem and reveal it to the public.

It was at this point that General Samford shut the lid down on all this enthusiasm by telling WPAFB to continue the directions they were going in.

[An aside: One wonders if the "excess" enthusiasm about ETH, solving all, revealing all, wasn't getting too uncomfortable for Black Box security—leak watchers].

Back at AMC—T—2. Colonel Jack O'Meara (Dunn's assistant) was preparing some thoughts about an Advisory Council for the project. This was a letter to Colonel Porter at the Pentagon, pursuing the concept of an Advisory Council and also a separate contractor to resolve the problem. The note indicates that Kaplan was actually actively involved, and even Von Karman. A Who's Who of science and technology giants (Including Teller, Doolittle, Whipple. van Allen, Langmuir, Zwicky, etc., etc.,) are mentioned.

The tone of the draft letter was to get going in the next couple of weeks.

Battelle was being consulted about questions to ask during the Advisory Council meeting at Wright—Pat.

By July, 1952, A giant UFO flap was underway, with UFO flybys over Washington airspace. The big flap and the Washington Merry-

—Go—Round created great excitement and confusion around the government and the Pentagon. [It seems to have been this flap and its consequent clogging of lines of communication which aroused intelligence officials to the security problems inherent in UFOs.] It was Wright-Pat's View that publicity spawned more reports. And so the logic was to reduce publicity and emotionalism on UFOs as a requirement for the protection of communication channels.)

[This seems to be the point at which the CIA really went on the alert about the UFO problem, recommending that it deserved attention right up to the National Security Council.]

In August 1952, Wright—Pat and the Pentagon were still trying to obtain better data and better advice. Cameras were still a high priority idea, as was the formation of an Advisory Council. But now that seemed less formal: perhaps the Council would only give ideas and comment upon reports. Allen Hynek travelled around polling astronomers.... [The fact that Kaplan was still involved with the diffraction cameras means that the idea of mounting them in hot spots must have still been part of the discussions.]

Meanwhile, the "Dark Side of the Force", the CIA, was beginning to issue forth. with assessments and recommendations involving UFOs. A new project was set up in "P & E" Division [Plans and Estimates??] On August 22, the USAF briefing for the CIA severely downplayed all three technological hypotheses (USA, USSR, ETH) in favor of mundane and atmospheric causes, and pointed out the public hysteria dangers if we were under genuine Soviet attack. The CIA was now operating under a totally different view of UFOs than is WPAFB and much of the Pentagon.

In September, October, and November 1952, Blue Book continued to travel [Ruppelt??], meet with scientists, and actively discuss data—gathering. The contacts at ADC HQ were convinced that they're dealing with devices of some sort. Because such "devices" have monitored Operation Mainbrace, it is suggested that we prepare for UFOs at the H—Bomb test blast, Project Ivy. The diffraction cameras, however, still were not ready. Frank Dunn left WPAFB and is replaced by Samford's UFO~man, General Garland, as MCI. The idea about a Scientific Council Advisory Group has dwindled to a lower key project to get some top men to study data for 1 or two weeks.

Sometime during this period, the idea that had been bouncing around, that of setting up spotting stations with special equipment gridded out all over northern New Mexico, was crystallized. [Battelle's "Pentacle Letter" suggestions are only a specific statement of ideas that had been around for a long time.] Battelle's seemingly "original" addition of a series of "normal" military targets as "controls" to determine accuracy and functioning of the observers (and equipment) was also only a...Tauss had been involved at least since November, talking to Colonel Bower.)

[The "preliminary look" at Blue Book data, which occurred in Dayton in December (or maybe in very late November, Ruppelt doesn't always get the dates exact) was in Ruppelt's naive mind an open-ended study by top scientists. Actually, it seems to have been the "ritualistic" going—through—the—motions of legerdemain endemic to CIA covert actions.] That this latter seems obvious results from Ruppelt's report that 4 people reviewed the files (in late November/December) for three days, and recommended that a "High Court" of scientists be approved to look at this subject. This recommendation was approved by the Pentagon in one hour!

[It is obvious that this recommendation was expected and planned for.] Also, the recommendation contained the names of the six men recommended to serve! Only the date (late December/early January) was still open. [I (Swords) believe that the whole deal was a "done deal" in the CIA/NSC; that the WPAFB meetings were in early December, that Dr. Chadwell (who writes to Hynek telling him how he enjoyed meeting with him in Dayton earlier in the month) was the leader of the CIA—science team, and that poor '01 Ed Ruppelt had no idea that the die was already cast.] (Robertson and Durant visited Wright—Pat in the second week of December, also.)

K. In January 1953, these events took place:
The "Pentacle Letter" was written
The Robertson Panel convened
William T. Reid, a Technical Director at Battelle, completed the correspondence relative to the statistical analysis/IBM punch—card project.

Ruppelt still didn't clearly hear what was being said. The Blue Book project continued for a little while on momentum. The CIA maintained a lot of interest in probing cases and persons (Ex: Fred Durant wanted Hynek's info on APRO (Feb '53). Hynek seems to have talked to Durant about APRO at the Robertson Panel.

L. Later, Blue Book personnel dissipate. Ruppelt takes temporary leave. During that leave, the Pentacle Plan (for controlled UFO events) was rejected, but diffraction cameras on bases were ok'd. Investigations were transferred to ADC.

The Battelle Connection…

"Battelle is an international technology organization that serves industry and government in developing, managing, and commercializing technology. With a wide range of scientific and technical capabilities, it helps put technology to work for clients in 30 countries….

The point is, that Battelle is not now, nor was it ever, a "government think tank."

At the time of the Pentacle letter, I (Zeidman) worked §t_ McMillin Observatory on the OSU campus, but I worked for Battelle. In *IUR* Vol. 16, Number 2, March/April 1991, I discussed those times at length in an article called "I Remember Blue Book." I knew Howard Cross and some of the other "cc:s" of the Pentacle letter, and during the summer and autumn of 1992 I interviewed those who survive. As a token gesture to their privacy, I will relate what each said as a separate "info—bit", but I will not identify who said what. First a word about each man:

Howard Clinton Cross, a native of Washington, D.C., came to Battelle in 1929. During a long and distinguished career (primarily in metallurgy) he rose through the ranks and was at various times advisor to such agencies as the Office of Scientific Research and Development, The National Defense Research Committee, the Atomic Energy Commission, The USAF, USN, and the National Advisory Committee on Aeronautics. Cross died at age 88 on March 30, 1992 (probably when Forbidden Science was already in galley.)

I remember Cross as a white—haired, square—faced, no—nonsense old salt whom I feared and respected 40 years ago. I can easily believe Vallée's description of Howard's flare of temper and his confiscation of Allen's notes.

David Bertram Thomas was in 1953 an Associate Director and Acting of Battelle. He retired in 1968 as President. He had a PhD in chemistry.

Arthur B. Westerman, a metallurgist, came to Battelle in 1942 as a research engineer.

Lloyd R. Jackson, a Battelle Coordination Director, was degreed in metallurgical engineering.
William T. Reid was a Battelle Technical Director in 1953. His specialty was fuel engineering.
Perry J. Rieppal was a Battelle Division Chief in 1953. His specialty was welding engineering.
Vernon W. Ellzey was a geologist and mineral economist. (And obviously the "V.E." I referred to in my *IUR* paper).
Richard J. Lund, a geologist, was Manager of Information and Analysis at Battelle in 1953.
* 9|! * * * * * >1! *
None of the men I interviewed remembered the specific letter (which I showed them). But I learned the following:

One of the men claimed to be the person who actually came up with the "controlled test" idea. The test was never implemented.

One man recognized the generalities of the letter, and claimed that he probably had contributed to it; he recognized phrases he had used to protect Battelle (the 'ol "CYA" strategy)

One of the men said he had never been interested or kept up to date with the subject of UFOs, and thought the subject was "a lot of hooey."

One of the men was the same person I referred to in my *IUR* paper——the man who had said (referring to Battelle's interpretation of the data) "we were concerned, we were concerned."

Howard Cross and one of the men were against Battelle taking any UFO—related work. Clyde Williams, then Battelle President, brought the project in with the rationale that there might be "pay dirt" in the data.

One of the men said that Battelle received no additional funds for this work: the project was hidden within Project Stork. About $150,000 was spent from the Stork allocation to fund the UFO work. (Not the $600,000 quoted by Vallée.) Needless to say, there was general resentment within the ranks about extra work with no extra pay.

[This is as good a place as any to attempt to explain (once again) Project Stork: The mission of Project Stork was to assess the capabilities of the Soviet Union to conduct technological warfare. Battelle's UFO work was hidden (and funded) within Project Stork. There were contractors and locations other than Battelle where Stork work was done. The quotation from Allen Hynek in Vallée's book (page 294) that the Robertson Panel put an end to Project Stork is blatantly incorrect. Stork continued at Battelle for many years thereafter. It is my belief that Allen Hynek heard the name Stork in conjunction with the Battelle work, was not told (had no "need to know") of its Soviet intelligence connections, and assumed it referred only to the Battelle UFO work.]

******

FOOTNOTES

[1] http://www.policestateusa.com/2014/hill-family-museum-outing/
[2] Anonymous, interview with the author, June 4, 1993.
[3] Julia Shuster, interview with the author, March 9, 2012.
[4] International UFO Museum and Research Center, Roswell, New Mexico, archives.
[5] Walter Andrus and Irena Scott, eds, *The Fiftieth Anniversary of UFOlogy*.
[6] Hynek was involved in all aspects of UFO study, and was scientific adviser to UFO studies undertaken by the U.S. Air Force under three consecutive names: Project Sign (1947-1949), Project Grudge (1949-1952), and Project Blue Book (1952-1969). He worked on these projects at Battelle, WPAFB, and OSU. He founded the concept of scientific analysis of UFO evidence.
[7] Anonymous, interview with the author, June 4, 1993.
[8] *Inside the Real Area 51: The Secret History of Wright Patterson,* pg. 50
[9] https://www.messer.com/news-and-insight/wpafb-building-23-set-to-open-in-june-after-restoration-and-renovation
[10] https://digital.library.unt.edu/ark:/67531/metadc717094/m2/1/high_res_d/769475.pdf
[11] Irena Scott and William Jones "Bruce Ashcroft." Ohio UFO Notebook 10 (1995): 2-4
[12] https://www.accesscorp.com/offsite-storage/underground-vaults/
[13] https://www.accesscorp.com/offsite-storage/underground-vaults/
[14] https://www.mydaytondailynews.com/news/how-this-secretive-wright-patt-unit-grew-into-one-the-country-most-important-watchdogs/PK4CS4uOSri9vrBXMrfG0H/
[15] http://roswellproof.homestead.com/exon.html
[16] At the July 1, 1989, annual MUFON Symposium in Las Vegas, Nevada, William Moore, in his talk "The Status of the UFO Situation in 1989," described the campaign to discredit Bennewitz.
[17] A verified document is one that either has been issued by a known and acknowledged source or has been authenticated by such a source.
[18] In 1978 some Canadian documents from 1950 and 1951 appeared; these mentioned a secret US government UFO study group operating via the Pentagon's Research and Development Board and headed by Vannevar Bush, PhD
[19] https://blog.fold3.com/august-1963-ufo-reports-in-project-blue-book/
[20] https://www.cia.gov/library/center-for-the-study-of-intelligence/csi-publications/csi-studies/studies/97unclass/ufo.html
[21] This information comes from a list of Project Blue Book UFOs that have never been identified. Don Berliner of the Fund for UFO Research posted this list on the Internet for UFO research.
[22] I also searched for evidence that Cross had published research about nitinol, and I found none. Cross's co-authors in work on titanium (other than Simmons, Greenidge, Craighead) included L. C. Page, J. W. Freemen, L. W. Hodge, J. A. VanEcho, and C. H. Lorig. I also looked for information about the authors of the *Second Progress Report*: Simmons, Greenidge, Craighead, and the others. I found no articles by Greenidge or Simmons. Some of VanEcho's research included work with "superalloys," also called high-performance alloys. Cross, Craighead, Eastwood, Hodge, and Lorig had worked with boron.
[23] Jennie Zeidman, interview with the author, September 29, 2009.
[24] In addition, there is no proof Cross knew that physical evidence of UFO debris existed. But

even if he did not, the fact that he was a metallurgist studying UFO phenomena under a government contract suggests that someone at Battelle or WPAFB may have had knowledge of UFO debris. If the individual who was assigning scientists to the UFO project was aware that UFO debris was involved, this individual would probably have appointed researchers with credentials appropriate to the study.

[25] https://www.esd.whs.mil/Portals/54/Documents/FOID/Reading%20Room/UFO/proj_b1.pdf?ver=2017-05-22-113513-837

[26] http://www.legacy.com/obituaries/seattletimes/obituary.aspx?n=bertram-david-thomas&pid=1941309

[27] https://www.legacy.com/obituaries/star-gazette/obituary.aspx?n=perry-Rieppal&pid=87901417

[28] According to archived records of the former UFO study group National Investigations Committee on Aerial Phenomena (NICAP), on December 12, 1952, Cross and Project Blue Book were visited by H. Marshall Chadwell, PhD (head of the CIA's Office of Special Investigations), Howard Percy Robertson (of the Robertson Panel), and Frederick C. Durant, PhD (a missile expert and Robertson Panel member).

[29] https://nepis.epa.gov/Exe/mf.cgi?Dockey=650274099

[30] https://apps.dtic.mil/dtic/tr/fulltext/u2/633037.pdf

[31] They likely included investigations of Soviet inventions, Soviet metallurgy, and Soviet aerospace development. Some Stork projects in the 1950s focused on Soviet and Chinese technology. One Battelle employee told me that Stork had originally been housed at the National Electric Coil Company across the Olentangy River from Battelle. It was highly secured then, and its relocation to Battelle included flashing patrol cars and secured containers. Later it was housed on the fourth floor of Battelle Building 10. An important early project was to design a system using 5" x 8" cards to index technical information (prior to computers). Only later was Stork identified with the UFO projects.

[32] Jennie Zeidman, interview with the author, September 29, 2009, and September 30, 2016; and October 6, 2016, e-mail message.

[33] Bill Jones, interview with the author, June 9, 2011.

[34] https://archive.org/details/ProjectBlueBookSpecialReport14/page/n45

[35] https://blog.fold3.com/august-1963-ufo-reports-in-project-blue-book/

[36] https://blog.fold3.com/august-1963-ufo-reports-in-project-blue-book/https://www.wlwv.k12.or.us/cms/lib/OR01001812/Centricity/Domain/1334/baseball%20physics.pdf

[37] https://www.golfchannel.com/article/jason-sobel/iron-byron-repeat-after-me

[38] https://sgbonline.com/sgmas-baseball-and-softball-council-names-new-chairman/

[39] https://www.wlwv.k12.or.us/cms/lib/OR01001812/Centricity/Domain/1334/baseball%20physics.pdf

[40] https://archive.org/details/ProjectBlueBookSpecialReport14

[41] http://www.cufon.org/cufon/pentacle.htm

[42] https://epdf.tips/forbidden-science-journals-1957-1969.html

[43] https://www.fringepop321.com/the-majestic-documents.htm

[44] https://www.fringepop321.com/the-majestic-documents.htm

277

[45] https://www.fringepop321.com/the-majestic-documents.htm
[46] https://epdf.tips/forbidden-science-journals-1957-1969.html
[47] April 2018 MUFON JOURNAL
[48] https://wikivisually.com/wiki/Stanton_T._Friedman
[49] (https://doi.org/10.1152/ajpregu.1987.253.1.R71), and (https://www.physiology.org/toc/ajpregu/253/1)
[50] (https://link.springer.com/article/10.1007/BF02186300).
[51] The Pentacle Letter and The Battelle UFO Project, May/June 993 International UFO Reporter Volume 18, Number 3 —1 I
[52] https://www.socscistatistics.com/tests/chisquare/Default2.aspx.
[53] http://www.physics.csbsju.edu/stats/contingency_NROW_NCOLUMN_form.html
[54] https://www.students4bestevidence.net/p-value-in-plain-english-2/
[55] https://stattrek.com/online-calculator/chi-square.aspx
[56] https://archive.org/details/ProjectBlueBookSpecialReport14/page/n45
[57] http://www.physics.csbsju.edu/cgi-bin/stats/contingency (https://www.ncbi.nlm.nih.gov/books/NBK126161/) number chart (If it's $1/10^9$ (one in a billion), or $1/10^{12}$ one in a https://archive.org/details/ProjectBlueBookSpecialReport14
[58] *The Secret History of Extraterrestrials: Advanced Technology and the Coming* https://books.google.com/books?id=Z1ooDwAAQBAJ&pg=PT172&lpg=PT172&dq=it+is+extremely+unlikely+that+it+would+be+left+to+a+lowly+Air+Force+captain+to+make+this+selection+ufo&source=bl&ots=nTYHLzYSNI&sig=PvapJQQbEKc47ObA-fXYSkb_pbM&hl=en&sa=X&ved=2ahUKEwju-M_M9IjfAhXD64MKHSyWCB8Q6AEwAHoECAkQAQ#v=onepage&q=it%20is%20extremely%20unlikely%20that%20it%20would%20be%20left%20to%20a%20lowly%20Air%20Force%20captain%20to%20make%20this%20selection%20ufo&f=false
[59] http://aimehq.org/programs/award/bio/clyde-williams-deceased-1988
[60] http://www.astronomyufo.com/UFO/SUNlite1_4.pdf
[61] http://scarc.library.oregonstate.edu/coll/pauling/catalogue/pauling04.html
[62] https://en.wikipedia.org/wiki/Linus_Pauling
[63] http://www.dtic.mil/dtic/tr/fulltext/u2/200806.pdf
[64] https://www.atlasobscura.com/articles/the-fbi-debunked-these-ufo-documents-in-the-most-childish-way-possible
[65] http://www.dtic.mil/dtic/tr/fulltext/u2/200806.pdf
[66] https://en.wikipedia.org/wiki/Vannevar_Bush
[67] https://www.geni.com/people/Vannevar-Bush/6000000013039967781
[68] https://www.geni.com/people/Vannevar-Bush/6000000013039967781
[69] http://roswellproof.homestead.com/smith_papers.html
[70] https://www.rand.org/about/history/a-brief-history-of-rand.html
[71] https://www.rand.org/about/history/a-brief-history-of-rand.html
[72] http://www.ufoupdateslist.com/1998/may/m08-017.shtml
[73] https://en.wikipedia.org/wiki/Curtis_LeMay
[74] https://www.atomicheritage.org/profile/james-b-conant
[75] http://www.cufos.org/UFO_History_Gross/1953_01_02_History.pdf
[76] https://atlantisrisingmagazine.com/article/the-roswell-miracle-metal/
[77] http://www.dtic.mil/dtic/tr/fulltext/u2/b232051.pdf

[78] http://www.dtic.mil/dtic/tr/fulltext/u2/200806.pdf and (https://archive.org/stream/warmetallurgy01unit/warmetallurgy01unit_djvu.txt
[79] https://archive.org/stream/organizingscient00stew/organizingscient00stew_djvu.txt
[80] https://en.wikipedia.org/wiki/National_Defense_Research_Committee
[81] https://www.quora.com/What-is-the-most-impressive-weapon-of-World-War-II-apart-from-the-atomic-bomb
[82] http://www.dtic.mil/dtic/tr/fulltext/u2/616728.pdf
[83] https://www.rand.org/about/history/a-brief-history-of-rand.html
[84] http://www.majesticdocuments.com/pdf/sarbacher-steinman-29nov83.pdf
[85] https://lisaleaks.wordpress.com/page/63/?cat=-1
[86] http://www.v-j-enterprises.com/nexusavi.html
[87] https://en.wikipedia.org/wiki/Douglas_Aircraft_Company
[88] WIKI NASIC in 1953
[89] Anthony Bragalia, email to the author, July 5, 2010.
[90] Anthony Bragalia, "Roswell Alcoholics: The Alien Anguish."
[91] This government-funded scientific research occurred under ventures such as Project Sign, Project Grudge, and Project Blue Book. (The American government had been studying UFOs even before the Roswell crash, and it is known that authorities initially called UFOs "unidentified aerial objects." The names of these pre-Roswell research undertakings are unknown, however.) A fourth endeavor was called Project Stork. Subsequently the government used two-word names for these projects, such as White Stork and Have Stork. An informant told me that yet another UFO project was called something like Gold Eagle. Some information from Stork, White Stork, Have Stork, et al., supported the findings of Projects Sign, Grudge, and Blue Book, and some contradicted these findings.
[92] Anonymous interview with a Battelle worker the author, September 24, 2009.
[93] https://en.wikipedia.org/wiki/Clyde_Tombaugh
[94] https://en.wikipedia.org/wiki/Lincoln_LaPaz
[95] Information about Simpson was provided to me by a Battelle employee who knew him.
[96] Co-authorship by Simpson with Cross, Center, Craighead, or Eastwood would link Simpson to government UFO studies, but I found no such co-authored papers.
[97] Anthony Bragalia, email to the author, July 5, 2010.
[98] Have Any Materials Been Recovered from ETs/UFOs? (http://rigorousintuition.ca/board2/viewtopic.php?t=28942&p=352146)
[99] WPAFB. "National Air and Space Intelligence Center History." http://www.wpafb.af.mil/library/factsheets/factsheet.asp?id=21928
[100] Because some people interviewed are currently employed by Battelle or have only recently retired, I haven't divulged information herein that might identify some informants.
[101] During my communications with Jennie Zeidman, she noted that the original mission of Stork was to ascertain the capability of the Soviet Union to engage in technological warfare. Thus, the Stork projects were not necessarily tied to Battelle UFO work.
[102] In the 1950s and 1960s Battelle was under a long-term Air Force contract to evaluate Soviet and Chinese aerospace technologies in conjunction with the ATIC.
[103] This information suggests that in addition to nitinol and titanium, boron was an element of interest in Battelle's metal studies during the period of the studies.
[104] *The Uranium-Carbon System* by M. W. Mallett, A. F. Gerds, And H. R. Nelson

[105] Center, E. J., *Topical report on the direct micro determination of uranium using a modified fluorophotometer* Oak Ridge, Tenn: U.S. Atomic Energy Commission, Technical Information Service, [1951]), by E. J. Center and U.S. Atomic Energy Commission (page images at HathiTrust

[106] Center, E. J., *Topical Report on the Direct Micro Determination of Uranium Using a Modified Fluorophotometer*, by E. J. Center (Volume 3006 of AECD, U. S. Atomic Energy Commission, Technical Information Service, 1951, and sold by Google Books.

[107] Center, E. J., *Topical Report on the Direct Micro Determination of Uranium Using a Modified Fluorophotometer*, by E. J. Center (Volume 3006 of AECD, U. S. Atomic Energy Commission, Technical Information Service, 1951, and sold by Google Books.

[108] *Topical report on spectrophotometric determination of small amounts of uranium in phosphate rock, shales and similar materials* (Author: E J Center; U.S. Atomic Energy Commission; Battelle Memorial Institute. Publisher: Columbus, Ohio. : Battelle Memorial Institute, 1947. Series: BMI (Series), 97. Edition/Format: eBook**:** Document : National government publication : English.

[109] *The Chemical Analysis of Zirconium and Zircaloy Metals.* (Oak Ridge, Tennessee : United States Atomic Energy Commission, Office of Technical Information, 1957.

[110] Center, E. J., *Research on A Method for Determining Boron in Boron Steels*, (Report Number: WADC TR 56-517, Author(s): C. T. Litsey, D. L. Chase, E. J. Center, Corporate Author: Battelle Memorial Institute, Date of Publication: 1957-06.

[111] *A modified HC1 volatilization method for determining oxygen in zirconium* (Oak Ridge, Tenn. : United States Atomic Energy Commission, 1952), by Manley William Mallett, E. J. Center, A. F. Gerds, J. J. Tighe, and U.S. Atomic Energy Commission (page images at HathiTrust).

[112] *Preparation and Examination of Beryllium Carbide* by M. W. Mallett1, E. A. Durbin1, M. C. Udy1, D. A. Vaughan1 and E. J. Center. 1954 ECS - The Electrochemical Society. It is unknown why but in some references to this paper Center is left out as an author) (http://jes.ecsdl.org/content/101/6/298.short and https://www.researchgate.net/publication/241997577_Preparation_and_Examination_of_Beryllium_Carbide

[113] *Progress report for the month of April, 1947 : contract no. W-38-094-eng-27*, (Author:
E J Center; H R Nelson; H A Pray; A C Richardson; U.S. Atomic Energy Commission.; All authors, Publisher: [Oak Ridge, Tennessee] : [U.S. Atomic Energy Commission, Technical Information Service], 1947. Series: U.S. Atomic Energy Commission.; AECD, Edition/Format: eBook : Document : National government publication : English).

[114] *A modified HC1 volatilization method for determining oxygen in zirconium* ((Oak Ridge, Tenn. : United States Atomic Energy Commission, 1952), by Mallett, Manley William, E. J. Center, A. F. Gerds, J. J. Tighe, Battelle Memorial Institute, and U.S. Atomic Energy Commission.

[115] *Topical Report on the Direct Micro Determination of Uranium Using a Modified Fluorophotometer"*, AECP-3006 (1951).

[116] Investigation of The Effects of Magnetic Flux on Dislocation Movement and Alignment. A. C. Eckert, Jr. and H. Newman, General Motors, Corporation, Indianapolis, Indiana. USAF, A5SD, TR 61-217, June, 1961, Contract No. AF 33(616)-7116.

[117] *The Encyclopedia of X-Rays and Gamma Rays (Contributing Authors include* A. C. Eckert, Jr. General Motors Corp., Allison Div.)

[118] *Dislocation Movement and Alignment as Affected by Magnetic Flux: Observations by X-ray Diffraction Topography*, by A. C. Eckert, Jr 258.

[119] *Commercial and experimental carbon blacks* (by Clark, G. L., A. C. Eckert, Jr., and R. L. Burton:Industr. Engng. Chem. 41 (1949) 201)

[120] *Quantitative analysis of UO• -U• O• mixtures by x-ray diffraction* (Oak Ridge, Tenn. : U.S. Atomic Energy Commission, Technical Information Branch, 1949), by F. N. Bensey, A. C. Eckert, U.S. Atomic Energy Commission, and Carbide and Carbon Chemicals Corporation)

[121] Additional people who worked with Center found in Summary Technical Report of The National
Improvement of IMW Alloy Aenwr Steels. Part XVI—Study of the Effect of Boron on Steals Suitable for Use in Armorfrom 3 to 6 Inches in Thickness, M. C. **Udy**, Philip C. Roscnthal, and other», OSRD 6294, Final Report M-619, Battelle Mc moritil Institute, Nov. 6, 1945. Div. 18-202-M6. Improvement of Low Alloy Armor Steels. Part XI—Causes of Quench Cracking in Cast Armor Steel, M. C. Udy, M. K. Barnctt, and others, OSRD 4667, Final Report M-465, Battelle Memorial Institute, Feb. 6, 1945. Div. 18-201.1-M3. Improvement of Low Alloy Armor Steels. Part XV—Determination of Martensite Transformation Points, M. C. **Udy**, G. K. Manning, and others, OSRD 5028, Final Report M-511, Battelle Memorial Institute, Apr. 30, 1945. Div. 18-201.2-M6 117. Improvement of Low Alloy Armor Steels. Part XVIII—Continuation. Development and Evaluation of an Economical Corrosion Resisting Alloy for Quarltrmaster Items, H. A. Pray and F, W. Fink, OSRD 4673, Final Report M-469, Battelle Memorial Institute, Feb. 5, 1945. Div, 18-901.2-M2.

Altogether these researchers made little sense in relation to the purpose of the study. However if an analysis of some type of substance were embedded into this work, it would make a lot of sense. Read https://www.hjkc.de/_blog/2014/02/09/2413-ufo-forschung---/.

[122] https://ntrs.nasa.gov/search.jsp?R=19930083435.

[123] https://www.researchgate.net/scientific-contributions/2005714631_A_D_Schwope.

[124] https://books.google.com/books/about/Final_Report_on_Investigation_of_Boron i.html?id=snOAswEACAAJ

[125] https://books.google.com/books?id=TvdGAQAAIAAJ&pg=RA1-PR31&lpg=RA1-PR31&dq=%22C.+H.+Lorig%22+%22Battelle%22&source=bl&ots=ZQ8tmt7jwt&sig=fxE1L5xfcsMpGF3wgutEAC0Y-DA&hl=en&sa=X&ved=2ahUKEwiB4a3b_4neAhWEhpAKHbMNCeQQ6AEwB3oECDAQAQ#v=onepage&q=%22C.%20H.%20Lorig%22%20%22Battelle%22&f=false,
https://books.google.com/books?id=yl8rAAAAYAAJ&pg=PP39&lpg=PP39&dq=%22C.+H.Lorig%22+%22Battelle%22&source=bl&ots=fl0RS9RCw6&sig=SaPQYhc05r8anf2j27E89eixJA0&hl=en&sa=X&ved=2ahUKEwiB4a3b_4neAhWEhpAKHbMNCeQQ6AEwDHoECB0QAQ#v=onepage&q=%22C.%20H.%20Lorig%22%20%22Battelle%22&f=false…. Keyhole

[126] https://lib.dr.iastate.edu/cgi/viewcontent.cgi?article=13212&context=rtd

[127] https://www.amazon.com/Fatigue-Metals-Structures-H-Grover/dp/B002H3BEEO.

[128] https://digital.library.unt.edu/ark:/67531/metadc54922/

[129] http://metals-history.blogspot.com/

[130] https://www.google.com/search?num=100&safe=active&ei=F1jFW8H5GYSNwgSzm6SgDg&q=%22W+Hodge%22+%22Battelle%22&oq=%22W+Hodge%22+%22Battelle%22&gs_l=psy-ab.3...40915.40915..42775...0.0..0.76.76.1......0....1j2..gws-wiz.rbrGAvJwJFY

[131] http://contrails.iit.edu/reports/2817

[132] http://metals-history.blogspot.com/2010/04/titanium-new-metal-for-aerospace-age.html

[133] http://metals-history.blogspot.com/2010/04/titanium-new-metal-for-aerospace-age.html)

[134] http://fortvance.org/FV_Docs/Obituaries_OP.pdf

[135] http://delibra.bg.polsl.pl/Content/35568/BCPS_38899_1945_Steel---production--.pdf

[136] A meteorite was reported in New Mexico circa November 1947. Lincoln LaPaz, PhD, and *Life* photographer Allen Grant, who had just photographed the flight of the Spruce Goose, were among the searchers, but this meteorite was never found.

[137] At Battelle, however, a different situation might have existed: some people likely knew through the grapevine that work on UFOs was going on there, and employees would thus have been more attuned to the significance of the studies.

[138] Robert Orndoff, email to the author, September 26, 2009, and additional interviews.

[139] http://fortvance.org/FV_Docs/Obituaries_OP.pdf

[140] https://digital.case.edu/downloads/833707163

[141] https://roswellproof.homestead.com/files/ROSDEBRI.DOC

[142] http://www.dtic.mil/dtic/tr/fulltext/u2/200806.pdf

[143] https://www.imagesco.com/articles/nitinol/03.html)

[144] http://www.unknowncountry.com/insight/ufos-and-national-security-state-jacques-Vallée

[145] https://www.dispatch.com/article/20161220/LIFESTYLE/312209961

[146] http://www.project1947.com/articles/swordsfournet.htm

[147] http://www.cufos.org/UFO_History_Gross/1952_01_05_History.pdf

[148] http://www.thinkaboutit-ufos.com/operation-mainbrace/

[149] http://time.com/4096424/ivy-mike-history/

[150] https://www.nicap.org/mock.htm

[151] http://www.sacred-texts.com/ufo/rufo/rufo16.htm

[152] (DIAPhotosStillClassified)

[153] http://www.thedailybeast.com/articles/2015/08/12/the-spy-satellite-secrets-in-hillary-s-emails.html

[154] I recall seeing at least three pictures—probably two pictures from one mission and one from another.

[155] http://rense.com/general16/eef.htm

[156] Scott, Irena, UFOs Today: 70 Years of Lies, Misinformation and Government Cover-up (UK: Flying Disc Press

[157] http://www.cufos.org/hynek_prefix.html

[158] http://www.openminds.tv/new-mysterious-mutilations-in-colorados-san-luis-valley/742

[159] https://archive.org/stream/Fbi-CattleMutilationInvestigationfoia/FBImuteFiles_djvu.txt

[160] https://ufologie.patrickgross.org/htm/zanesville66.htm

[161] http://ufos-scientificresearch.blogspot.com/2017/06/

[162] https://findingaids.library.northwestern.edu/agents/people/1473

[163] https://books.google.com/books?id=A1iqVQgvZnAC&pg=PA422&lpg=PA422&dq=%22Hynek

%22+%22Ridpath%22+%22new+scientist%22&source=bl&ots=C8giEWphxH&sig=hj0D3JnSc6KArBq9UZbxF4vw56s&hl=en&sa=X&ved=2ahUKEwiCtrmRr_feAhUIW60KHeycCigQ6AEwA3oECGEQAQ#v=onepage&q=%22Hynek%22%20%22Ridpath%22%20%22new%20scientist%22&f=false

[164] http://www.fsr.org.uk/
[165] http://www.abovetopsecret.com/forum/thread826460/pg1
[166] http://www.wikiufo.org/cieloinsolito3.pdf)
[167] http://www.mde.state.md.us/programs/Air/AirQualityMonitoring/Pages/Balloon.aspx
[168] https://fearoflanding.com/history/another-unsolved-mystery-the-kinross-incident/
[169] https://www.earthfiles.com/2006/10/07/updated-1953-kinross-afb-mystery-f-89-found-in-lake-superior/
[170] Information in this chapter about this incident comes from the following sources: Michael D. Swords, "The Portage County (Ravenna), Ohio, Police Car Chase, April 17, 1966," in Historical Document Series No. 4, which contains the original case reports, notes, documentation, and newspaper clippings; William B. Weitzel, "The Portage County Sighting," in *National Investigations Committee on Aerial Phenomena (NICAP) Report*; William E. Jones and Irena Scott, "The Spaur Case—Reporting a UFO Can be Hazardous to Your Health," in *Ohio UFO Notebook*; Ronald Story, *The Encyclopedia Of UFOs*; and Jerome Clark, *The UFO Book*.
[171] The material in this section is from Diana DeSimone's and Raymond Fowler's material, which DeSimone sent to me.
[172] http://www.cufos.org/Portage-County/1966_04_17_US_OH_Portage-County_NICAP_Weitzel_P-13_UFO_Reportr.pdf
[173] DeSimone sent me additional material about sightings in that area.
[174] The material in this section is from Diana DeSimone's and Raymond Fowler's material, which DeSimone sent to me.
[175] http://thebiggeststudy.blogspot.com/2013/01/idle-ufo-musings-two-j-allen-hynek.html
[176] https://en.wikipedia.org/wiki/G%C3%A9rard_de_Vaucouleurs
[177] http://www.bluerosereport.com/anomalycomm/forum/viewtopic.php?f=20&t=418s
[178] http://www.cufon.org/cufon/hynekint.htm
[179] (*Close Encounters of The Fourth Kind: Alien Abduction, UFOs,* and the Conference at M.I.T. Penguin Books, 1996. By C.D.B. Bryan)
[180] https://www.phantomsandmonsters.com/2016_03_13_archive.html
[181] https://www.encyclopedia.com/people/science-and-technology/astronomy-biographies/donald-howard-menzel and http://wiki.ufohqs.com/index.php?title=Donald_Howard_Menzel
[182] http://wiki.ufohqs.com/index.php?title=Donald_Howard_Menzel
[183] http://www.sciencemag.org/site/about/index.xhtml
[184] https://www.quora.com/What-are-the-most-prestigious-scientific-journals-of-biology
[185] http://www.slate.com/articles/life/history/2013/12/life_magazine_1945_why_it_was_the_greatest_magazine_ever_published.html
[186] http://www.ufoevidence.org/documents/doc597.htm; Hynek, Allen J., "UFO's Merit Scientific Study", Science, October 21, 1966; and Hynek, J. Allen, "Twenty-one Years of UFO Reports", American Association for the Advancement of Science, 134th Meeting, December 27, 1969.
[187] https://www.nga.mil/About/History/NGAinHistory/Pages/ACIC.aspx

[188] Bruce Murray, "Reopening the Question" review of "J. Allen Hynek's *The UFO Experience*, *Science*, August 25, 1972
[189] https://www.reddit.com/r/badhistory/comments/1ylr9w/in_which_copernicus_is_burned_at_the_stake_for/
[190] http://www.williamjames.com/Folklore/WORLDS.htm
[191] http://luforu.org/vaddo-stockholm-sweden-europe/, https://verytopsecret.info/2015/07/05/ufo-newsletter-article-the-vaddo-case/, and http://www.ufo.no/archive/Nordic%20UFO%20Newsletter/1981-1%20-%20Nordic%20UFO%20Newsletter.pdf
[192] https://en.wikipedia.org/wiki/James_Harder
[193] https://tipsforfamilytrips.com/cruises/cruise-dining/
[194] https://en.wikipedia.org/wiki/Isaac_Asimov
[195] http://pedasfamily.com/jun22canbLecturers.html
[196] https://www.ufoweeklynews.com/ufo-sightings/father-william-gill-sighting
[197] http://www.mufonohio.com/mufono/hynek.html J. Allen Hynek – A "Rocket Man" by Jennie Zeidman, © 1999 by author
[198] See Jennie Zeidman, *Helicopter-UFO Encounter over Ohio*; and Irena Scott, "A Power Failure," in *Ohio UFO Notebook*.
[199] http://www.oocities.org/ufomiami.geo/Obituary.html
[200] Jennie Zeidman, "The Comet and the Circle," International UFO Reporter, May /June 1986
[201] https://www.davidhalperin.net/j-allen-hynek-and-halleys-comet/

******

FURTHER READING FROM FLYING DISK PRESS

http://flyingdiskpress.blogspot.com/

Irena McCammon Scott, PhD.
UFOs Today
70 Years of Lies, Misinformation and Government Cover-Up
DECLASSIFIED
TIC 12
AA

Irena McCammon Scott, PhD
Inside the Lightning Ball
Scientific Study of Lifelong UFO Experiencers

FOREWORD BY DAVID CAYTON
DIRECTOR, ANIMAL PATHOLOGY FIELD UNIT

CIRCLE OF DECEIT

A TERRIFYING ALIEN AGENDA
IN IRELAND AND BEYOND

DERMOT BUTLER   CARL NALLY

PORTAL

A Lifetime of Paranormal Experiences

Adele Casales Rocha

PHOTO UFO

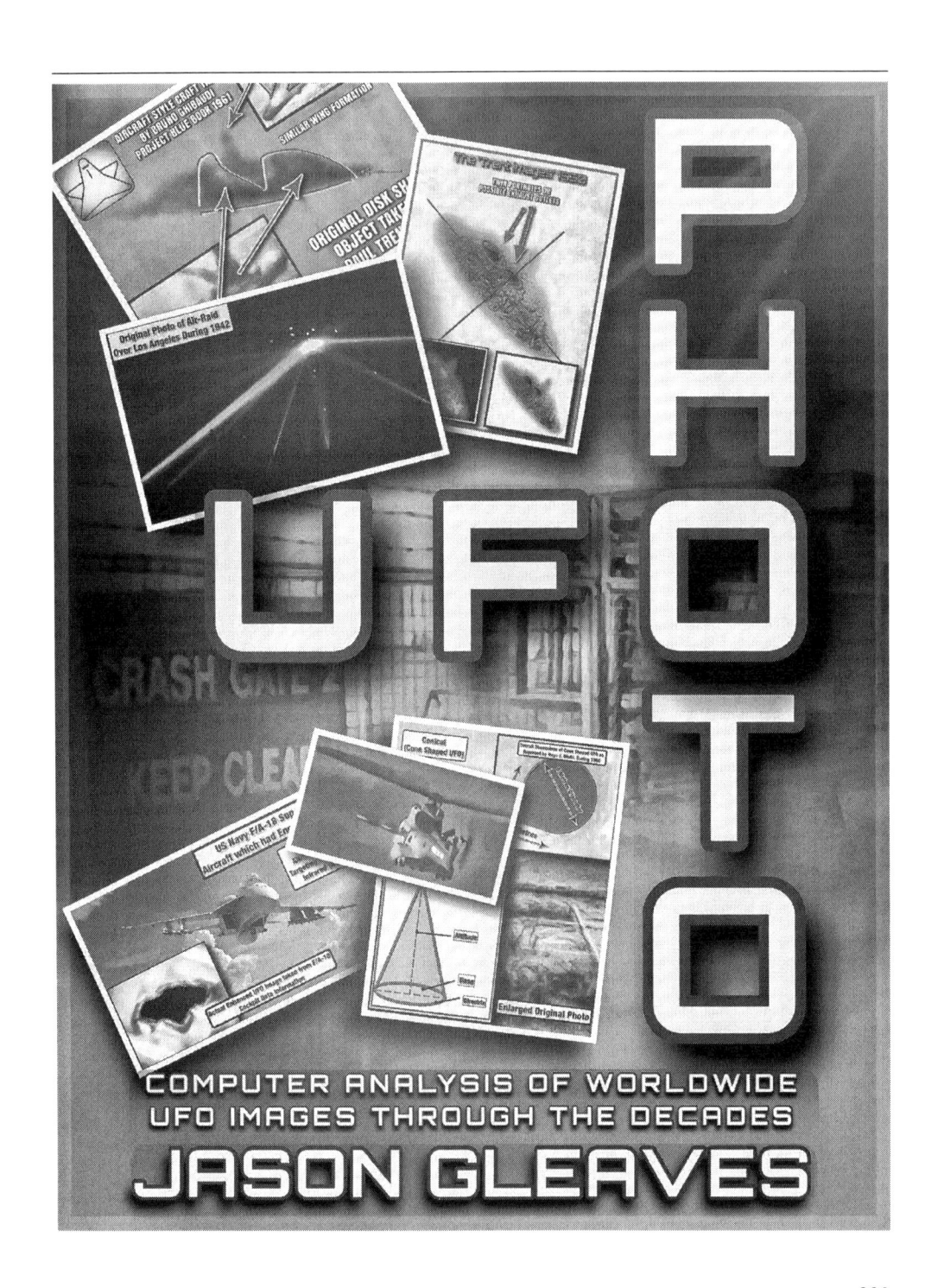

COMPUTER ANALYSIS OF WORLDWIDE UFO IMAGES THROUGH THE DECADES

JASON GLEAVES

Center for UFO Studies

CLOSE ENCOUNTERS at KELLY
and others of 1955

Isabel Davis and Ted Bloecher

PHILIP MANTLE

ONCE UPON A MISSING TIME

a novel of alien abduction

UFO CONTACT AT PASCAGOULA

CHARLES HICKSON and WILLIAM MENDEZ

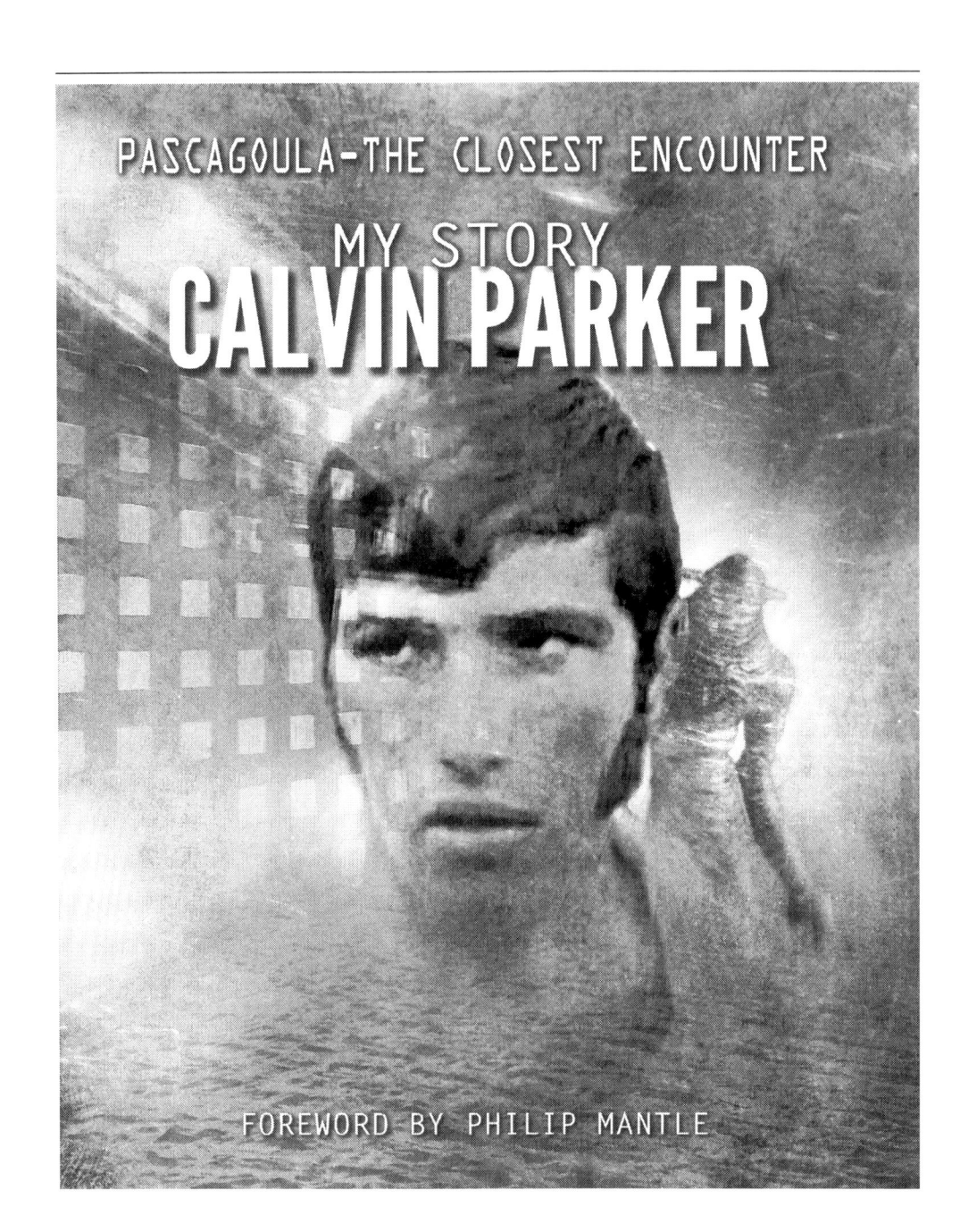

PASCAGOULA—THE CLOSEST ENCOUNTER
MY STORY
CALVIN PARKER

FOREWORD BY PHILIP MANTLE

The Road to PASCAGOULA
(A Research Trip - 1981)

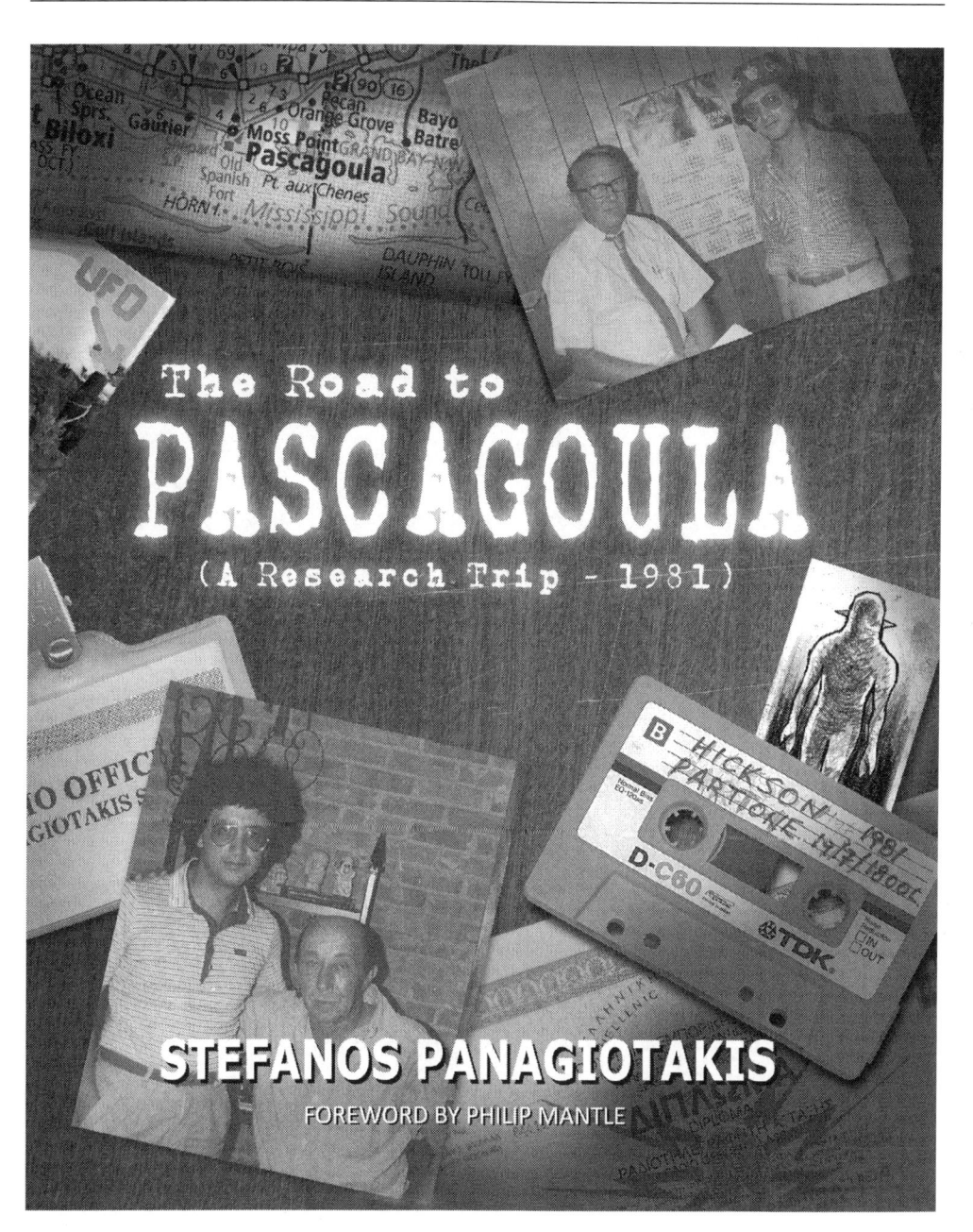

STEFANOS PANAGIOTAKIS

FOREWORD BY PHILIP MANTLE

THE REVEREND FATHER GILL FILES

RUSSIA'S ROSWELL INCIDENT

And Other Amazing UFO Cases From The Former Soviet Union

By Paul Stonehill & Philip Mantle

UFOs OVER ROMANIA

DAN D. FARCAS PH.D.

http://flyingdiskpress.blogspot.com/

Made in the USA
Middletown, DE
04 March 2019